Politics
and
Class Formation
in Uganda

Politics
and
Class Formation
in Uganda

by Mahmood Mamdani

Monthly Review Press
New York and London

Library of Congress Cataloging in Publication Data
Mamdani, Mahmood, 1946–
   Politics and class formation in Uganda.
   Bibliography: p.
   Includes index.
   1. Social classes—Uganda. 2. Uganda—Politics
and government. I. Title.
HN800.U354S615   301.44′09676′1   75-15348
ISBN 0-85345-378-0

First Printing

Monthly Review Press
62 West 14th Street, New York, N.Y. 10011
21 Theobalds Road, London WC1X 8SL, England

Manufactured in the United States of America

Contents

Acknowledgments   vii

Introduction   1

1. Precolonial Uganda   17

2. The Establishment of a Peasant Economy   40

3. Indian Capital: The Formation of a
   Dependent Commercial Bourgeoisie   65

4. Landlords, Tenants, and the Colonial State   120

5. On the Colonial State and
   the Articulation of Modes of Production   138

6. The Formation of the Petty Bourgeoisie   147

7. Petty Bourgeois Politics:
   The Period of Consolidation   189

8. From Independence to the Coup:
   A Fragmented Petty Bourgeoisie   228

9. After the Coup   302

Bibliography   319

Index   329

4049 26

Acknowledgments

The problem of Uganda has today gained worldwide attention. But it has been personalized as the problem of Idi Amin, who is presented as some sort of anthropological oddity. On the other hand, it is Amin's own objective collaboration with the media of monopoly capital that has made this possible.

In this book, I set forth the problem of Uganda as one of class oppression and attempt to analyze it in a historical and social perspective. The principal forces shaping the destiny of Uganda have been the struggles of its working people, not the antics of its so-called leaders, even though these struggles have yet to assume an organizational expression independent of the petty bourgeoisie through whom imperialist exploitation has been mediated. To these real authors of Uganda's history, I dedicate this work.

This book was initially written as a doctoral dissertation for Harvard University. To my supervisor, Professor Karl Deutsch, I am thankful for his consistent liberalism which allowed me to pursue my work unhindered. Although I do not share his faith in empiricism as a method of analysis, I have learned from him the use of tools for empirical investigation.

The research for this book was done in Kampala at Makerere University and in London at the Colonial Archives. The writing was completed at the University of Dar es Salaam. A number of comrades—particularly Issa Shivji, Henry Mapolu, and Harku Bhagat—have helped me to clarify my thinking at various points. To them, my deepest thanks.

—Dar es Salaam
January 1976

Introduction

> The truth is concrete.
>
> —Lenin

> Just as one does not judge an individual by what he thinks about himself, so one cannot judge [such] a period of transformation by its consciousness, but on the contrary, this consciousness must be explained from the contradictions of material life. . . .
>
> —Marx

It used to be that the analysis of the politics of underdeveloped countries was informed solely by the *dualism* of the traditional and the modern. The problems of underdeveloped politics were those of its traditional sector; the solutions were to be found in the modern. The traditional was retrogressive, the modern progressive. It was not as much the presence of conflict in the traditional, but the nature of its articulation and organization that was defined as the problem. Traditional politics—tribal or communal, as the case may be—was desperately in need of a *rational* and *coherent* articulation. The solution was the "modernization" of traditional society. Though seldom articulated, the modern, an "ideal-type," was identified with the best of all

1

possible politics: the Anglo-Saxon, rational, pluralist consensus of laissez-faire, of live and let live—the politics of advanced capitalism.

The optimism of the "modernization theorists" notwithstanding, there was little discernible march toward an Anglo-Saxon politics in the underdeveloped countries. It was necessary that the theory come to terms with this. At the least, it was in need of elaboration. The response of the "modernization theorists" was to borrow from related fields. From Parsonian structural-functionalism came "pattern variables" which enriched the *description* of the dual society. The modern-traditional dichotomy became synonymous with universalism-particularism, achievement-ascription, and specificity-diffuseness. From élite theory came an emphasis on distinguishing modernizing élites from traditional élites and surveying the attitudes of each. From David Easton came the input-output model, with its emphasis on describing the functioning of society as a machine. And finally, from behavioral social science came an emphasis on a rigorous empiricism that sought to comprehend the process of modernization by capturing it in a series of measurable *indicators* (school enrollment, urbanization, voting figures, etc.), thus making possible an "objective" understanding of the process. The limits of this political science were the limits of empiricism. Like the journalist, the political scientist assumed that to *explain* was to *describe* with the utmost detail and the greatest accuracy, with the precision of mathematical figures rather than the ambivalent flow of words. But the point was that, regardless of its methodological rigor, empiricist political science had reduced explanation to the level of description.

Nor did these changes alter the core of the theory, the assumed dichotomy of the traditional and the modern. What was never explained was the dualism itself. The traditional became the repository of all that could not be explained; instead, these problems were explained away. The traditional was simply the not-modern, humankind's original condition, the innocence of its childhood, perhaps burdened with original sin. *It was denied history.*

In Africa, the political scientist identified the traditional with the tribal: tribal society was traditional and primordial, timeless and unchanging.* Conflict was then explained as tribalism. The *form* of the conflict was presented, tautologically, as its own *explanation:* two tribes fight because they are different tribes!

But tribalism is not an explanation but an ideology, one which itself needs to be explained. An ideology is *produced* under concrete historical circumstances and by a particular social group. It is neither timeless, nor does it permeate all classes equally. Quite the contrary, it possesses both historical and class specificity. As a more or less coherent consciousness of a particular social group, it explains social reality from its *particular* point of view. To understand any ideology—be it tribalism, nationalism, or socialism—we must understand its historical origin and development and identify its social base. In other words, whose interests does the ideology articulate? From whose point of view does it explain social reality? To ask these questions is to go beyond the form and grasp the historical content.

At the same time, this is not to ignore the form, which remains important because it is reflected at the level of consciousness. Ideology is not the mechanical production of a class; it is neither deception nor falsehood. It is not *necessarily* a *conscious* articulation of interests. (In fact, when *internalized* as a consciousness, it is usually not.) While it is true that a class produces an ideology, it is also possible that the ideology may in turn capture the class. In our analysis of the politics of tribalism in Buganda from the 1930s to the 1960s we shall have occasion to illustrate this dual aspect of ideology.

Formalism in political science extends beyond the sphere of ideology to other levels where politics manifests itself empiri-

---

* One might further ask what a tribe is. There was a time when the word possessed scientific content, when it characterized those social formations that did not possess a state structure—the communal, classless societies, as, for example, the Germanic tribes. Today, however, every single ethnic group in Africa is referred to as a tribe regardless of the nature of its social development. What is it that makes 2 million Norwegians a people and just as many Baganda a tribe? A few hundred thousand Icelanders a people and 14 million Hausa-Fulanis a tribe? There is only one explanation: racism.

cally: organization and leadership. As with ideology, it is necessary that we go beyond the formal understanding of an organization, beyond its rules and bylaws, its self-description. A school is not necessarily an "institution for educating people" because that is its definition. Similarly, a (farmers') cooperative is not necessarily an organization characterized by popular participation and control; neither is a (workers') union necessarily controlled by those it is supposed to represent. When making an analysis of an organization such as a political party, it is necessary that we make a distinction between participation and control, membership and leadership. A party may have a popular mass base (such as the Kabaka Yekka in Buganda), but its direction may come from one particular class. The object of analysis must be to identify the particular interests that are *materialized* in the functioning of an organization.

In an underdeveloped country a halo surrounds not an ideology or a party but an individual who personifies the state. This leader is supposed to represent "all the people." In Africa, he is sometimes the "redeemer," sometimes the "lion." While bourgeois social science attempts a psychological explanation of his "qualities of leadership," his "charisma," we must ask what historical and social conditions permit the exaggerated importance of an individual. We de-emphasize the psychological, for we seek to understand the social formation and not the individual personality, to write history and not biography. This is not to reduce the "charismatic" leader to his class interests alone, for that would be akin to explaining a social phenomenon by wishing it away; it is, though, to *situate* him. However mighty and lofty a personality, however high and freely a kite may fly, it is of earthly importance precisely because it is tied to the earth.

The dualism of modernization theorists is based on certain assumptions about the structure of society which remain unarticulated; these assumptions have nonetheless found room in the works of their economic counterparts, those who write on economic growth. The theoretical underpinning of growth economics is a *dualism*, but this time between the subsistence sector and the modern sector. Just like his political counterpart, the growth economist analyzes the two sectors *in isolation* from one another.* He has never understood the relation between the two: that the "modern" plantation is productive precisely because it appropriates labor from the "traditional" village, that the "stagnation" of the village is a condition for the "dynamism" of the plantation. Once this relationship is grasped, the "subsistence" sector emerges as the exploited sector and the dynamic "modern" sector as exploiting.

For the growth economist, however, the relations of appropriation do not exist. Underdevelopment to them is a *natural* condition, synonymous with poverty and a low level of development of productive forces. As we shall see, this is equivalent to denying the very problem of underdevelopment. Furthermore, in their analyses, as in their prescriptions, the growth economists assume the autonomy of the economy, of the technical process of production. And so their solutions for "development" are all economic, that is, technical. Their most advanced formulations are about the rate of savings and investment necessary for "takeoff." But determining these is not a technical issue. If savings are to come out of national income, as they must, and if national income comprises rent plus profit, wages, salaries, interest, and taxes, then it is clear that each economic category is the income of a class (the rent of the landlords, the profit of the capitalists, the wages of the workers, etc.). Both the rate and the nature of investment are thus *political* issues. Economics gives way to politics. But the economist refuses to enter the fray, to become "ideological." In the case of the more naive among them—such as W. W. Rostow—the prescriptions appear, to use the words of Hobsbawm, as "those of the cookery book": "Take the following quantities of ingredients *a* through *n*, mix and cook, and the result will be the take-off into self-sustained growth." [1]

The Marxist Critique

The Marxist critique of underdevelopment theory emerged in the field of economics. It denied that underdevelopment was synonymous with poverty, that it was a natural condition that

---

* For a detailed analysis, see Chapter 5.

had characterized all societies at their early stage of development. Nor did it agree that the problem was merely formal, one of classification that could be dissolved by simply redefining the underdeveloped countries as the "new," "emerging," or "less developed" nations.* Underdevelopment, it maintained, was a *historical* condition. It had been created. In Andre Gunder Frank's well-known polemical phrase, what needed to be understood was the "development of underdevelopment."

Even a cursory examination of production in the underdeveloped countries will show that in the last few centuries there has been a radical transformation in the productive activity of the mass of people, not as much in how production is carried out as in what is produced: single cash crops (cotton, coffee, cocoa, sisal, etc.) for export to the metropolitan market. In most economies, this transformation was completed during the phase of colonialism, the period of *underdevelopment*. In terms of the economy, underdevelopment is a process that subordinates production in the territorial economy to the accumulation needs of metropolitan capital. In our analysis of the economic structures in Uganda, we shall attempt to trace this process in detail, and at the same time delineate the various characteristics of the underdeveloped economy.

It is not enough, however, to understand the specificity of underdevelopment at the level of economic structures, as does Andre Gunder Frank. It is necessary that we go beyond the economist's conception of production as simply that of material objects and understand it as also the production of relations and ideas. Thus the necessity of grasping the process of underdevelopment at the level of class formation and politics.

Class as a Relation

The first major critic of Marx's political theory, of the usefulness of class as a concept for political analysis, was Max Weber. Weber made a clear-cut distinction between wealth and power—wealth being a relation between person and thing and

---

* With the United States as "The First New Nation," the title of Seymour Martin Lipset's book.

power being that between person and person. An analysis of social production was an analysis of wealth, not of power. Classes were income groups, with differentiated access to wealth; they did not explain the distribution of power in society. Class was an economic relation, power a political relation.

But the rigid separation between power and wealth becomes ambiguous if we consider not wealth, but *productive* wealth— that is, the means of production. Control over the means of production gives one *dual* control: over both the social product (thing) and the producer (person).

The emphasis on classes as income groups is prevalent today among the neo-Weberians, particularly in the "radical" wing of economics and political science. The welfare economist examines the manner of distribution of the economic surplus, focusing on circulation, not production. At the level of circulation, society does indeed appear as a collection of individual consumers or income groups, and so the "radical" economist proposes an alteration in the manner of distribution through progressive taxation, welfare programs, or a guaranteed income. Our contention is that this leaves the class structure intact; it is merely "re-form." The solution follows from the definition.

If we redirect our attention from circulation to production, from the distribution of the economic surplus to its production,* the central question then becomes who produces and who appropriates (not who gets how much, which leads us to "income groups"). The focus on production becomes a focus on relations of production. And it is at the level of production that individuals and groups coalesce into classes, defined in terms of their relations to a historically determined social process of

---

* The concept of the "economic surplus" was introduced by the late Paul Baran.[2] It can be defined here as the surplus product, the difference between a society's total production and its necessary consumption. The economic surplus is the region of freedom; its use depends upon how a particular society is organized. It is the use a society makes of its economic surplus that determines the character of its future development. Thus the importance of understanding the *mode of utilization* of the ecnomic surplus. The "economic" question of the mode of utilization of the economic surplus, however, cannot be answered without posing a "political" question: Who controls the economic surplus and what are their interests?

production,* and in terms of the manner and form in which they appropriate a share of the economic surplus.†

Two characteristics of the concept of class become clear at this point: first, classes are posed in their opposition.[4] There is no such thing as one class. As Marx began in *The Communist Manifesto*: "Freeman and slave, patrician and plebeian, lord and serf, guildmaster and journeyman, in a word, oppressor and oppressed . . ." Class relations are *contradictory* relations. Secondly, class relations are relations of *appropriation*: central to a class relation is the appropriation by one social group of the labor (or the fruits of the labor) of another social group. Thus, class relations are relations of *power*. They are *political* relations.

It has become fashionable among certain academic circles, particularly the sociological, to equate classes with occupational groups; a class division is taken to be the same as a division of labor,‡ which leads to the conclusion that as long as a division of labor exists class divisions will persist. But a class division is *not* a division of labor. Ten people may assemble a bicycle, each concentrating on making a different part, and control their product collectively. This is a division of labor. A class division would only arise if an eleventh person (or for that matter, one of the ten) in whatever form appropriated a part of the labor of the ten workers.

A confusion arises from the fact that, in practice, *empirically*,

---

* As is well known, there is no formal definition of social class in Marx. According to Lenin, however, social classes are "large groups of people differing from each other by the place they occupy in the historically determined system of production, by their relation (in some cases fixed and formulated in law) to the means of production; by their role in the social organization of labor, and, consequently by the dimensions and mode of acquiring the share of social wealth which they dispose." [3]

† We shall see in our analysis of Uganda how, with qualitative social changes, the *form* of the economic surplus changed from one historical period to another, from the *gift* of the communal household to the feudal lord's *tribute* in precolonial formations to the landlord's *rent*, the merchant's *profit*, and the colonial state's *taxes*.

‡ The following discussion on class division and division of labor relies heavily on informal conversations with Robert Miester, now teaching at the University of California, Santa Cruz.

a class division and a division of labor often intersect. Thus one appears as the other. For example, the petty bourgeois trader both works and appropriates. Any sensible trader, however, when compiling the account sheet, would separate his or her wage (the opportunity cost given the current market) from his or her profit. The dual functions of the individual, as worker and as owner, are reflected in the two forms in which this person appropriates a share of the social economic surplus, as wage and as profit. Empirically, however, the division between the trader and the peasant buyer may appear as only a division of labor. There are also historical reasons that lead to the confusion. Historically, the beginning of class society is closely associated with the existing division of labor. Often, a social group that performs an essential social function (for example, in West Africa, the blacksmith clan that made the hoe, the principal means of production) may use its *objective* position to appropriate for itself an increasing share of the social product.

The point is that a class division is between classes, one social group appropriating the labor (or the fruits of the labor) of another, while a division of labor is *within* a class, *among those who labor*. A division of labor is positive; it is the result of interdependence in the process of production, which makes it a *social process*. A class division, on the other hand, is an *antagonistic* division; it creates *contradictory* interests. And, finally, the division of labor is a technical division, while the class division is a political division.

Class Formation

We see that relations of production are not always class relations. The two coincide only when social production is also social appropriation. In a class society, appropriation has a dual aspect: it is both the appropriation of nature and of the producers; it is natural as well as social appropriation. The beginning of social appropriation is at the same time the beginning of class formation.

In the analysis of class differentiation, two factors emerge as decisive: the appropriation of labor and the participation in the labor process. A rich peasant, one who works his own farm but at the same time employs labor regularly, is thus to be distinguished from an agricultural capitalist who plays no direct part in the labor process but carries out production solely through wage labor. On the other hand, a rich peasant is also to be distinguished from a middle peasant who does not regularly employ labor but relies on family labor for production.[5] In the commercial sector, a trader with retail operations must be distinguished from a businessman whose activities are wholesale. The former are members of the petty bourgeoisie; the latter comprise the commercial bourgeoisie. As a class, the petty bourgeoisie has traditionally included small property owners: traders (as opposed to businessmen) and rich peasants (as opposed to agricultural capitalists). To these two I have added a third social group: those bureaucrats who, although they do not *own* property, are assured privileged access to the social economic surplus. After independence, the state bureaucracy is able to use its education, technical skills, and, most important, its structural base within the state itself to integrate into the small property-owning petty bourgeoisie by acquiring private property individually. The petty bourgeoisie in Uganda, *in its formation*, thus comprised three sections: the bureaucratic stratum, the traders, and the rich peasants (whom I refer to as "kulaks" because that is the popular usage in East Africa).

My purpose is not to be overly schematic. It is necessary to bear in mind that class formation is a *process*, and one should not expect to find *pure* forms in reality. *Transitional* forms must be analyzed as a moment in a historical process. In the Buganda countryside in the 1940s, one could find many individuals who lived in mud-built houses with corrugated iron roofing, the fronts of the houses being shops while the backyards stretched into acres of cash crops cultivated by both family and employed labor. This was the kulak-trader, a member of the emerging petty bourgeoisie. On the other hand, in the north the proletarianization of the peasantry had created a system of migrant labor. Here one could find individual peasants who spent part of the year as plantation workers and the rest as peasants cultivating the land (along with their families) for their subsistence needs. Both peasants and workers, these were the migrant laborers.

At the same time, it is necessary to grasp the specificity of class formation in underdeveloped capitalism. As we shall see, forms that are transitional in early European capitalism, such as petty commodity production on the land, become frozen in underdeveloped capitalism. Unlike in the metropole, the capitalist mode of production is confined to small pockets of the underdeveloped economy. The proletarianization of the peasantry is a process limited in its scope; the vast majority of the population remains as producers on the land, regardless of the differentiation among them.

The Class Struggle

While classes form at the level of production, in their relation to the process of production, they *act* at the level of politics. Class organization is political organization, class consciousness is political consciousness, and class conflict is political conflict. To quote Marx: ". . . the struggle of class against class is a political struggle." [6] An analysis of relations between classes is thus necessarily a political analysis that *incorporates* a historical analysis of economic structures, that is, of class formation.

In our study of politics in Uganda we shall attempt to trace, at the level of production, the process of the formation of some classes and the decline of others. Such an analysis must be historically and socially specific. The formation of the Ugandan petty bourgeoisie was different from that of the petty bourgeoisie in Kenya or Tanzania, in terms of the sections of the economy in which it evolved, the nature of its organization, and the content of its ideology. This difference cannot be grasped in theory alone; it needs a concrete historical analysis—as Lenin put it, "a concrete analysis of concrete conditions." It is history which gives each social formation its uniqueness and specificity.

But if class relations are contradictory relations and the class struggle a political struggle, what explains the cohesion of a social formation, the fact that the class struggle does not tear it apart at the seams? To understand the relative stability of a social formation, we must direct our attention to the role and the nature of the state.

The state* does not simply perform a directly coercive function through its repressive apparatus (courts, police, army, etc.); it also carries out *necessary* political, technical, and ideological functions.[7] At the level of the economy, the state gives stability to, and ensures the continued functioning of the productive process by regulating the economy (by regulating demand, prices, wages, interest, etc.) and by performing the function of accounting (national accounting surveys, etc.). Although it might be argued that here the state functions in the general interest, not on behalf of any particular interest, the fact is that the process of production is at the same time a process of social appropriation. Production relations are at the same time class relations. The process of production the state helps maintain is thus in the *objective* interest of those who appropriate surplus labor and against the objective interest of those whose labor is appropriated. The state is thus a class category.

Let us take an example—the colonial state in its most "neutral" moment. The colonial economy was an agricultural economy. One of the most important positions within the state bureaucracy was that of director of agriculture. In 1917, the director of agriculture in Uganda wrote the secretary of state in England:

> For over four-and-a-half years, I have been steadily working towards five things, viz.:
> (a) To increase cotton production;
> (b) To reduce the percentage of stained cotton exported;
> (c) To bring the cotton grower and ginner into direct contact;
> (d) To improve the quality of the cotton produced;
> (e) In parts of the country where other crops like wheat, coffee, cocoa, and rubber can be successfully produced, to encourage them so as to increase the basis of production.[8]

As our analysis will show, these seemingly technical functions, apparently nonpolitical, were central to the underdevelopment of the Ugandan economy, to subordinating production within Uganda to the accumulation needs of British capital. The

---

* Here I refer to the bourgeois state. Later I shall underline the specificity of both the colonial and the neocolonial states.

function of the director of agriculture was informed by the long-term interests of the metropolitan bourgeoisie. Neither technology nor technocracy are neutral. Both serve those who are in power. Ideology informs technology, while technology is one way of implementing ideology.

At the level of politics, the state unites the ruling class(es) and divides the appropriated class(es). In fact, the ruling class is precisely the class that controls the state; the state is an expression of its unity. The political apparatus of the state provides institutions for the peaceful regulation of conflict between sections of the ruling class (parliament, congress). The state *institutionalizes* politics, not just uniting the ruling class but seeking to contain the contradictions of class society and thereby maintain its unity.* Thus this state of appropriators represents itself ideologically as either a state of all classes or a state above all classes, a guardian of the general interest which is against any particular interest. The ruling class presents its own sectional interests in the guise of the general interest. At the same time, the appropriated class remains confined to the level of production. Since class unity and the expression of class interests can exist only at the level of politics, the appropriated remain divided, a class in-itself but not yet for-itself.

The object of this book is to explain the politics of Uganda in the period between independence (1962) and the Asian expulsion of 1972. To do so we have found it necessary to trace the formation of all those social forces—classes or fractions of classes—which achieved a measure of independent political

---

* This is the aspect of truth which lies at the core of the claim by structural-functionalists that the function of the political structure is "system maintenance." While it was capable of understanding the relative cohesion of the system, the "harmony" within it, structural-functionalism was widely criticized for its one-sidedness, its inability to provide an analysis of contradiction and change. In response, the structural-functionalists gave the political structure another function, "system transformation." Yet this merely begged the question. What was the source of the contradiction whose resolution resulted in this "system transformation," even if under the direction of the state? Where in the system were these contradictory interests situated? To answer the question, structural-functionalism would have had to undergo a theoretical transformation and explain the system in terms of the formation of classes and the struggle between them.

organization during that decade. What follows is thus not a comprehensive study of class formation in Uganda, but only concerns those classes (or fractions thereof) that acted on the national stage up until 1972.

Chapter 1 is a rough sketch of class formation in precolonial Uganda. Chapter 2 explains the structure of the colonial economy that evolved. Chapters 3 to 7 explain the formation of classes within that historically determined process of production. (I have analyzed the Indian petty bourgeoisie as a class distinct from the African petty bourgeoisie and this requires a word of explanation.* As I will show, in their historical formation as in their ideological consciousness, in their political organization as in their relations with the state, the Indian and the African petty bourgeoisies were two *separate* classes, not two sections of one class: while the African petty bourgeoisie emerged as a ruling class, the Indian petty bourgeoisie was very much in the fashion of the nineteenth-century classical European petty bourgeoisie, a "middle" class. At the same time, I do not treat the Asians as one class, but as two distinct classes, the petty bourgeoisie and the commercial bourgeoisie, with their own objective interests and distinctive relations to the state.)

Finally, Chapters 7 and 8 deal directly with political events in the decade between 1962 and 1972 (particularly the Buganda crisis of 1966–1967, the "move to the left" of 1969–1970, the Amin coup of 1971, and the Asian expulsion of 1972) and attempt to explain them in terms of the historically created contradiction and struggle between classes.

Notes†

1. E. J. Hobsbawm, "From Social History to the History of Society," pp. 23–24.
2. In *The Political Economy of Growth*, particularly Chapter 2, "The Concept of the Economic Surplus."

* In East Africa, the words "Indian" and "Asian" are used interchangeably to refer to immigrants from the Indian subcontinent.

† Complete citations of secondary sources are given in the Bibliography.

3. *Selected Works*, vol. 3, p. 248.
4. See Mao Tse-tung, "On Contradiction," *Selected Works*, vol. 3.
5. See Mao Tse-tung, "On the Investigation of the Peasant Movement in Hunan Province," *Selected Works*, vol. 1.
6. *The Poverty of Philosophy*, p. 150.
7. See Nicos Poulantzas, *Political Power and Social Classes*.
8. Director of Agriculture, *Report for the Cotton Industry, 1917*, submitted to the Secretary of State, February 27, 1917, CO 536/84, p. 12 (File No. 8860).

Map of Uganda

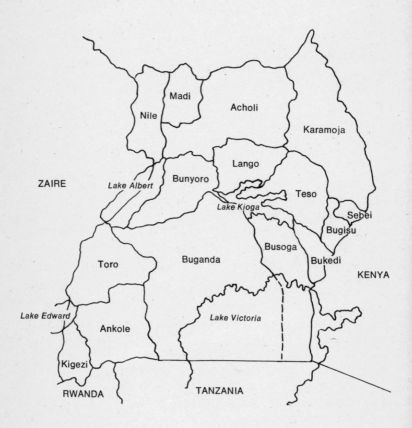

1
Precolonial Uganda

Colonial historians used to "explain" the highly centralized states of sub-Saharan Africa as the result of "Hamitic" or "Nilo-Hamitic" influences in "Negro Africa." [1] Not coincidentally, the Hamites were first and foremost identified as tall, light-skinned Caucasoids with aquiline features. To the imperialist scholars they were the Anglo-Saxons of Africa. Precolonial African history used to begin and end with them.

With the decline of the imperial powers, the Hamitic hypothesis has by and large been discarded. Today, however, we are confronted with revisionist scholars who at the most find virtue inherent in the "Bantu tribes" (in Uganda, the Baganda)*, or at the least characterize the peoples of Africa as Nilotic, Hamitic, and Bantu. [2] Both of these approaches share an "inarticulate major premise": that the history of a people can best be explained by their racial origins. [3] When it comes to the explanation of precolonial African history, ethnology still reigns supreme, whether in the service of imperialism or nationalism.

Human history, however, is a product of human labor, which is in turn the medium of interaction between humans and their environment. [4] Through labor, people appropriate and humanize nature, in the process transforming themselves, making their

---

* Buganda refers to the land, Baganda to the people, Muganda to an individual, Luganda to the language, and Kiganda to the culture.

17

own nature. As people labor, they make history. To understand history, then, we need to look at humans not as racial beings, but as productive beings who find themselves in a particular environment. The development of a people begins with their appropriation of nature and with the social relations they forge in the process of sustaining and reproducing themselves.

An analysis of the historical development of precolonial social formations in Uganda is, however, beyond the scope of this book. Our purpose is limited to delineating the essential features at the dawn of colonialism in the latter half of the nineteenth century. Social development in precolonial Uganda was essentially uneven. Were it possible to turn our eyes to that period, we would find some social formations characterized by the feudal mode of production, some embodying the communal mode, and others in transition. Neither the level nor the character of social development was simply or even primarily the result of the *internal* development of these formations: both were conditioned most severely by external factors, particularly the slave trade.

The Slave Trade

Although it had existed from the earliest times, the overseas slave trade from the East African coast never formed a significant part of the Indian Ocean trade until the French established sugar and tobacco plantations on the islands of Mauritius and Bourbon in the 1770s. Prior to that, but for the solitary and historically insignificant example of southern Iraq in the ninth century,* nowhere in the East were there the enormous labor-absorbing plantations or mines such as those established in the Americas after the crossing of the Atlantic.[5] In the Arabias, India, and China, so far as existing records tell, slaves were items of conspicuous consumption by the royalty and an allied feudal ruling class; rarely did they participate in the *social* process of production.

---

* These ninth-century date plantations in southern Iraq, based on slave labor, were devastated in the aftermath of the Zanj rebellion. I am indebted to Abdul Sheriff of the University of Dar es Salaam for this information.

On the East African coast, the slave trade reached its height in 1840, the year the Sultan of Oman transferred his capital from Muscat to the dependency of Zanzibar. He proceeded to establish clove plantations, and thereby to reorganize the island's economy in order to recapture the Indian Ocean trade by recasting it as a trade in cloves. By 1870, it has been estimated that anywhere from 40,000 to 60,000 slaves were being exported annually from the East African mainland.* Furthermore, for every slave who reached the coast, at least two others died on the way.

The acceleration of the slave trade not only led to the decline of all other kinds of trade; it meant that the very foundation of social production was threatened. In an economy with a low level of technology and plentiful land, the slave trade meant the export of the most *critical* force of production: living labor. The corresponding decline in production was particularly marked among the productive strata. The slave trade concentrated on the export of able bodies, ignoring the very young, the very old, and the disabled. While total production diminished, the proportion of productive members declined even further, while the proportion of dependents *increased* in relation to total population. And where the slave trade undermined both social and productive organization, periodic climatic adversity—serious in any society with a low level of productive forces—brought certain catastrophe: famine, followed by epidemics, which only intensified the process of depopulation. Social production became further subservient to the constraints of the environment.

---

* The upper figure of 60,000 comes from Harris (p. 48) and has hitherto been the most widely accepted. The lower estimate of 40,000 comes from Abdul Sheriff and is probably more accurate. Reasoning that slave trade figures were grossly exaggerated by Livingstone and the British navy as part of the ideology of colonialism, and that these have formed the basis for the estimates used in such recent works as Ogot and Kieran, eds., *Zamani* and Alpers, *The East African Slave Trade*, Sheriff estimates the annual export of slaves at 40,000 on the basis of an examination of customs records. See A. M. H. Sheriff, "The Rise of a Commercial Empire."

The Communal Mode of Production and the Formations in Transition: The North

The part of Uganda to suffer most from the slave trade was the north. Not only was this area the plundering ground for the slave-capturing parties that descended from the centralized kingdoms of the south, exporting their human captives to the East African coast, but slave raiders also entered it from the southern Sudan, even as late as the second half of the nineteenth century.[6] Here population was scarce, productive technology extremely low, and the environment harsh. The water supply was irregular and long droughts were common. In response to historical and ecological factors, two systems of production evolved: simple herding and shifting agriculture. Both practiced regular movement as a necessary aspect of production.

Among the pastoral peoples, such as the Karamojong of the northeast,* herds had to be moved great distances in search of grass and water, putting a definite limit on the possibility of settled life. Agriculturalists, such as the Acholi and the Langi, adapted to the rapid deterioration of the soil by adopting shifting cultivation.† The search for land, water, or grass had important effects on social organization. The constant movement led to the dispersal of families, resulting in a decentralized, "segmental" social unit. Among the pastoral peoples, who moved seasonally, the family assumed *primary* importance over the clan.‡ The comparatively settled life of the agricultural

---

* By "pastoral" peoples we mean those who practiced, first, pastoralism, and second, shifting cultivation. This is in contradistinction to "agricultural" peoples, whose production was based primarily on shifting cultivation, with pastoralism an adjunct.

† Under shifting cultivation, when the productivity of a field is exhausted every few years, it is left to the slow and regenerative effect of grass and bush while cultivation shifts to new lands. For shifting cultivating to be feasible over the long run, it is necessary that the population be small and land relatively plentiful. With a rise in population beyond a certain point, and in the absence of a higher productive technology, production will inevitably fall below subsistence needs.[7]

‡ We are referring to the family as it was organized then: not the nuclear family but to the large extended family. The clan refers to a collection of families who trace their origin to a common ancestor.

peoples led to the formation of larger social units, but even here, given that a household must move once every few years, social solidarity could extend only to a small group, and "tribes" were generally small. In the continual movement in search of water and land customs became specialized and dialects proliferated; in time each group became differentiated.

The relations of production under the communal mode of production were cooperative, not antagonistic. Appropriation did not yet have a dual character, but was confined to the appropriation of nature in the course of production. There was no social appropriation. Given the low level of development of the productive forces, the social surplus was small. Its use was controlled by the individual productive unit, the household. This was a poor and fundamentally egalitarian society. Material distinctions between families were of little importance. Surplus produce took the form of gifts, the giving and receiving of which was emphasized and specified by tradition.

Minimal social cohesion was assured by rites, rituals, and rules of social obligation, and materially cemented by the institution of gift-giving. The production unit—the household—and the social unit—the clan—were the focus of religious practice. Religious reverence was directed at the family and clan as social institutions, and at clan ancestors. Mutual help, obligation to the group, the importance of the family and the clan—all these were emphasized. The most complex regulations developed with regard to land, for though land was not a commodity, it had a use value. For shifting cultivation to survive over the long run, it was necessary that proper use be made of the land. The regulations thus focused on social responsibility in the use of the land rather than on land as private property.

The little division of labor that existed took place within the unit of production, the household. Among the pastoralists, whatever cultivation was possible became the responsibility of the women and the old men, the only permanent occupants of the main settlements, while the able-bodied men took care of the grazing and protection of the herds. Among the agriculturalists, it was the duty of the men to do the heavy work of clearing the new lands, to care for the herds, and to make cloth from bark or leaves. The young men defended the tribe, and the women were responsible for growing the crops.

The most important political and social distinctions were along generational lines. Power was exercised by a council of elders and each generation came to power as it became older. The relation between elders and nonelders was a status relation, not a class relation. The elders as a social group did not *appropriate* the labor of nonelders: membership in the council of elders did not give one privileged access to the social surplus, only privileged status in the society. Similarly, where a chief existed, he was democratically elected and removed. His position, an expression of the solidarity of the tribe, was never hereditary.

Societies such as these, characterized by the communal mode of production, were not static. Contrary to popular belief, their destruction and transformation into class societies did not necessarily await the external impact of colonialism. The germ of this transformation could be found in the relations between these social formations, and the critical factor that led to this process was increased contact with neighboring peoples, which led to either regular trade or systematic raids for cattle, treasure, or slaves, or both. In fact, at the time of colonialism only those formations located in isolated areas, forcibly cut off from the general stream of life by historical factors—such as invasions from more powerful neighbors that compelled them to seek the refuge of isolation—could be said to conform strictly to our description of the communal mode of production. These included the Wamba on the western slopes of the Ruwenzori mountains and the Bagisu on the eastern slopes of Mount Elgon. The other groups were formations in transition to class societies. Radhakrishna Mukherjee has described this process in its historical detail for the many peoples of northern Uganda.[8] The characteristics of these transitional formations were:

1. A growth of centralized authority, a harbinger of state power. Among some groups, the election of chiefs gave way to hereditary succession, and the establishing of "royal" lineages, which undermined the authority of the clans. At the same time, tribute was granted the chief in return for leading the people in war.

2. A regularization of war and preparations for war leading to the supersession of the authority of the clan by that of age classes.

3. An emphasis on territorial organization at the expense of localized clan organization.

The most advanced examples of these transitional formations were Acholi and Lango, which Mukherjee has characterized as "military democracies":

> Military, because war and defense were now one of the prime concerns of the people; and democracy, for the structure of tribal democracy still persisted, although it was now perverted in order to justify the forcible robbery of wealth.[9]

The Feudal Mode of Production: The South

The south was a different ecological zone. Fertile soil, a regular water supply, and the resulting security of agriculture made possible an ordered and settled life, with important consequences for cultural development. A higher level of development of the productive forces made possible a relatively large surplus with the same amount of labor, and this in turn gave rise to a more complex division of labor and to a class division between those who produced the surplus and those who appropriated a large part of it.

In sharp contrast to the north, the peoples of the south developed feudal kingdoms.* These were the southern kingdoms

---

* There has been a long debate on what constitutes feudalism and whether a number of African kingdoms—particularly Bunyoro and Buganda in Uganda—can be characterized as feudal. Marc Bloch, in the conclusion to his study on European feudalism, specified five fundamental characteristics: (1) The fief, usually but not essentially land; (2) the personal nature of the bond of dependence; (3) the dispersal of authority; (4) a specified military class; and (5) the survival, in some form, of the idea of the state.[10]

Both Beattie and Goodie[11] base their discussions on Bloch, whose five characteristics they quote. They retain the term "feudalism" and "its associated vocabulary for the more complex European politics to which they were first applied (and perhaps to other such systems, like the Japanese one, which can be shown to resemble it in all or most of its essential features) and to describe the political institutions of traditional Bunyoro and of other African kingdoms as far as possible in their own terms."

of Buganda, Bunyoro-Kitare, Nkore, Toro, and the kingdoms of Busoga. Here the peasants, the cultivating masses, were subject to the rule of individual lords (chiefs or heads of clans) who could extract as tribute produce and services in return for guarantees of security.* Here, the surplus took the *form* of

---

Beattie and Goodie, like Bloch, fail to distinguish between the feudal *mode of production* and the feudal *social formation*. In fact, those who deny the existence of a feudal mode of production outside Europe have principally argued that the state form in precapitalist Asia or Africa did not correspond to that in Europe. Such an argument ignores the fact that a *variety* of state forms can arise on the basis of a given mode of production. In other words, their argument has tended to confuse the feudal mode of production with the feudal social formation. The mode of production may be present across time and space; the social formation is historically specific.

What, then, is the feudal relation? Here, we agree with Dobb, who defines it as "the performance of obligatory services and exploitation of producer by direct politico-legal compulsion." [12]

Now, let us consider the specific characteristics of Bunyoro as Beattie has stated them:

1. Chiefs where individually appointed by the *mukama* (king), though "the greatest territorial chiefs, of whom in historical times there were a dozen or more, enjoyed a good deal of autonomy, governing their areas rather like private estates."

2. The importance of the allocation of authority, and its origin in the person of the *mukama*, were emphasized by ritual.

3. Ennoblement. Traditionally the king awarded titles and decorations to those he wished particularly to distinguish.

4. The major chiefs were required to maintain houses at or near the capital, as well as in the territories allotted to them, and they had to attend the king's court constantly.

5. The king himself did not reside permanently at his capital, which was frequently changed.[13]

While in Bunyoro there was no specialized military class, in Buganda there certainly was one.

It is incredible, but Beattie's characterization of Bunyoro concentrates *solely* on the relations between the king and the feudal lords: he has *nothing* to say about the social relations of production, the relations between the producers and the appropriators, the serfs and the lords. The point is that Beattie has no conception of feudalism as a mode of production.

* Karugira,[14] in writing of the kingdom of Nkore, maintains that the surplus produce the peasants gave the chiefs and the chiefs shared with the king should be called "presents," not "tribute." Only a paragraph later, however, he states that "the chief needed the protection of the *mugabe* (king) and he too had to keep this link alive by giving occasional presents. . . ." And further: "If the

feudal tribute.* The bulk of the surplus was appropriated not because the immediate producer was owned (as under slavery), nor because the means of production were owned (as under capitalism), but because of a political relation between peasant and appropriator that necessitated extraeconomic coercion.

Despite the existence of a relatively large surplus, the main object of production was still consumption. The need for articles for use, not the search for profit, remained the motivation behind productive work. Tribute was in kind, as use values, and its primary object was consumption not accumulation. To be sure, some form of accumulation did exist: food was converted into cattle and cattle into wives. In Toro, for example, the king gave cattle or women as a gift to those in need.[16] The social position of women, in comparison to the communal formations, had deteriorated: women were a means of production, to be owned, exchanged, and distributed.† The most advanced forms of accumulation were cattle and women, in that order. This was still, however, accumulation in the short run—the lifespan of the cattle and the women.

Peasant producers controlled their own production plans and the productive process. To paraphrase Takahashi, whereas under capitalism the means of production are separated from the producer and productivity develops as if it were the productivity of capital, under feudalism the means of production are combined with the producer and productivity develops as the productivity of the producer.[17] Since, as we have seen, the

---

chief stopped giving these gifts or attending at court for a lengthy period, it was usually assumed that he had 'rebelled' and, in such a case, he lost his position and often his property at the orders of the *mugabe*." Would it not be more accurate and less misleading to term a "gift"—the giving of which is regular, mandatory, and certainly not mutual—"tribute"?

* "The specific economic form in which unpaid surplus labor is pumped out of the direct producer determines the relation of the rulers and the ruled, as it grows immediately out of production itself and reacts upon it as a determining element."—Karl Marx.[15]

† In order to concretely understand the role of women, we would have to distinguish between those instances where they were objects of luxury consumption and those where they played a direct role in the social process of production. In the latter case, they possessed a comparatively higher social status. I am thankful to G. T. Mishambi for this observation.

purpose of production was the immediate consumption of the producer, and the purpose of the lord's appropriation was his own consumption, there was a limit on appropriation. To quote Marx: "Where use-value predominates, no boundless thirst for surplus labour arises from the nature of production." [18] Economic relations were not yet dominant. The relation between producers was *social*, a blood relation, one of kinship; between lord and peasant it was a political *and* a social relation. The political power of the ruling class was *circumscribed* by traditional (social) constraints. Since in a class society the development of the productive forces is necessarily a consequence of the development of the ruling class and the further appropriation of the producing class, such a limit on the exploitation of the producer is a limit on the development of the productive forces and therefore a limit on the overall development of the economy. Thus, social relations put a constraint on the advancement of the productive forces.

The division of labor within the southern kingdoms went beyond sexual and generational lines. Growing crops was the duty of peasant women and of slaves.* The agricultural tasks of peasant men were confined to clearing the land (usually once in a lifetime); they also made cloth from bark and leaves, pounded grain, and built rather substantial homes. The lord laid claim not only to their produce (cloth, food, and beer), but also to their services (recruitment of labor for building or repairing the king's residences, constructing roads, and staffing the army and the navy).[20]

The existence of an agricultural surplus and the expansion of trade in the eighteenth and nineteenth centuries led to the formation of a group of specialized artisans patronized by the lord or the king. By the nineteenth century a degree of regional specialization had begun to develop. Toro had a good supply of

---

* The slaves (both male and female) formed part of the tribute from a vassal to a dominant state. The freedom of peasant women was also heavily circumscribed. Except for princesses, women "were not free to move about without the consent of their husbands or masters, and in the capital every women and girl had some guardian from whom she had to obtain an escort when she wished to visit a friend or relation." [19] In fact, the social position of slaves and peasant women tended to be similar.

copper and the Batoro specialized in copperworking.[21] The Basoga built and supplied the canoes for transport on Lake Victoria.[22] The Kayonza (in Kigezi) and the Banyoro, who made use of their own and northern Acholi iron deposits, had developed a group of smiths and manufactured and exported spear and hoe blades.[23] The Banyoro were also the major suppliers of salt and their pottery was in constant demand throughout the region.[24] In Buganda, the great chiefs had in their service carpenters who could make doors and bedsteads on the Arab pattern, potters who could make cups and waterjugs like those in Zanzibar, and smiths capable of repairing the increasing number of firearms the *kabaka* (king) of Buganda imported.[25]

Although the basic unit of consumption and production in these kingdoms was still the household, and although most social production still took place on peasant farms and for use, the economy was not of a subsistence type. Trade had existed for centuries, and it had two basic characteristics: First, whether between town and country in the same region, between states in different ecological zones, or between the interior and the city-states on the East African coast, this trade had always been *complementary*, not *competitive*. *Intra*regional trade was limited by the division of labor: thus, direct exchange took place between artisans and agriculturalists in Buganda, and between the pastoral Hima (producing milk, meat, butter, hides, and skins) and the agricultural Iru (who were also semispecialized artisans, producing spears, arrows, hoes, milk pots, etc.[26]); on the other hand, *inter*regional trade was primarily between different ecological zones, which specialized in the production of specific use values—for example, dried fish from the main lakes and rivers,[27] salt from the shores of Lake Albert and Lake Katwe,[28] spear and hoe blades from Bunyoro, and bark cloth from Buganda.[29] The trade with the coastal cities grew to substantial proportions in the first half of the nineteenth century due to the increased demand for ivory. Whereas until 1820 the main demand had come from India, after that period there was a rapid growth in demand from Europe and the United States.[30] As a result, the price of ivory increased threefold within sixty years.

Second, this was a trade in surpluses. Unlike what was to be the case in the colonial period, trade did not dominate and dictate production, whose object was still the satisfaction of internal consumption needs.

While the short-distance trade between town and country and between ecological zones involved an exchange of agricultural, pastoral, and manufactured products, the long-distance trade— because the only means of transport available was the human head—was confined to nonagricultural, nonbulky, valuable commodities such as ivory, which could survive the heavy cost of transportation to the coast, and slaves, which transported themselves. In return, the African traders received such articles of luxury consumption as porcelain products, cloth, and metal washbasins[31] from the Arab traders on the coast.[32]

Two Feudal Social Formations: Buganda and Bunyoro

At different periods two dominant kingdoms developed in the southern region of Uganda: Buganda and Bunyoro-Kitare. The earlier of these was Bunyoro-Kitare, which was at the height of its power in the seventeenth and eighteenth centuries. Bunyoro society was divided into a cattle-keeping pastoral aristocracy (the Hima) and a grain-cultivating class of agricultural serfs (the Iru). This was not simply a division, and thus a specialization, of pastoral and agricultural labor, with status distinctions between the two; it was a class division, in which the pastoral aristocracy appropriated a large share of the surplus produced by the agricultural serfs in the form of tribute. The fact that the pastoral aristocracy was ethnically distinct meant that there was no possibility of assimilating individual members from among the conquered into the ranks of the rulers. Conquest *necessarily* meant the domination of the conquered as a group. With each new expansion, the Hima pastoralists became a shrinking minority in relation to the ever expanding number of their subjects, and the problem of controlling the conquered became increasingly acute.

In addition to this social rigidity there were technological limitations on Bunyoro expansion. The primary weapons were the spear and the shield, simple for anyone to use and manufacture. Unable to monopolize the means of force, a ruler's longevity depended on maintaining a sufficient retinue of followers. The relatively small size of the surplus made it difficult to do this, however. The result was that any serious misrule—for instance, an attempt to expand the surplus at the disposal of the royalty through intensified appropriation of the agricultural producers—was likely to lead to a revolt under the aegis of a rival claimant to the throne. Further, as the kingdom expanded the effective control of the ruler was likely to be weakened, making his domain susceptible to revolts, particularly at the periphery.

Such was the fate of Bunyoro-Kitare. In the early nineteenth century the eldest son of Mukama Kyebambe III, "tiring of his father's longevity, carved out for himself the independent kingdom of Toro to the east of the Ruwenzori mountains." [33] At the same time, Bunyoro-Kitare became the target of border attacks from neighboring Buganda, which entered its own expansionist phase at this point.

The secret of Buganda's success and Bunyoro's downfall lay in the former's less rigid social structure. While the majority of the common people in Bunyoro were serfs, distinguishable from the ruling class by occupation and ethnicity, the common people of Buganda were as Baganda as the chiefs, and the Baganda lords did not claim to be an aristocracy of blood. Roscoe called the common people of Buganda "freemen." [34*] The social distinction in Bunyoro was between those born high and those born low; in Buganda it was between the rich and the poor. Bunyoro was a caste society; Buganda a class society.

The implications for the social development of Buganda were enormous. Since the existing hierarchy of lords was not an aristocracy of birth, it was possible for the king to check their pretensions by recruiting individuals of peasant origin and create a separate but parallel political hierarchy as an alternate base of power. Beginning in the eighteenth century, three distinguishable processes emerged. First, the *kabaka*, in order to

---

* Roscoe, of course, called the peasants "freemen" because of the existence of class mobility. This does not deny the existence of a class society, with lords and serfs as the primary classes.

counter the power of regional and hereditary *bataka* (clan) chiefs, began creating a hierarchy of territorial but appointed *bakungu* chiefs. Then, since the *bataka* chiefs also exercised a monopoly over religious authority, the *kabaka* invited propounders of other religious systems (in the mid-nineteenth century, Islam; at the end of the nineteenth century, Christianity) to preach their faith in the Buganda capital. By the end of the nineteenth century the *kabaka* had become *Ssabataka*—head of all *bataka*.[35] Although the existence of *bakungu* chiefs successfully reduced the power of the *bataka*, the *kabaka* soon found it necessary to deal with the pretensions of the overpowerful *bakungu*. He did this by creating a standing army under his personal command. Between 1854 and 1884, Mutesa I—who owed his selection as *kabaka* to the most powerful *bakungu* chief in the land, the *katikiro*[36]—instituted a standing army with a permanent general *(muyasi)* and with subchiefs (*mutongole;* pl. *batongole*) as captains.[37] Mutesa I was also responsible for the creation of a navy, considerable by the standards of any premercantile society.[38]

Thus the absence of a rigid, caste-defined social structure and the presence of individual mobility made possible a degree of concentration of political power around the throne that was far ahead of anything in Bunyoro. The central authority was further enhanced by a change in the technology of warfare with the importation of guns.* Since the *kabaka* monopolized the ivory trade, he effectively controlled the importation and ownership of the guns the Arabs brought to exchange for the ivory. His army was the only one equiped with firearms.

By the end of the nineteenth century, the Buganda state had successfully created an infrastructural basis for a national and mercantile economy. A network of roads constructed and maintained by corvée labor, linked the countryside with the royal capital.[39] Such labor formed part of the annual tax on the

---

* It is important to realize that under different social circumstances the arrival of the gun could have assisted in the disintegration of the kingdom rather than in its centralization. Had Buganda not been a centralized entity to begin with, had the chiefs had the measure of independence from the throne that the Bunyoro chiefs enjoyed, then it is quite possible that they would have effectively used the gun to counter the centralizing policies of the throne.

peasantry, and the chiefs were expected to provide supervision. Early European travelers remarked on the roads that radiated from the capital to all corners of the kingdom. Speke, when he entered Buganda in 1862, remarked that the roads were "as broad as coach-roads, cut through the long grasses, straight over the hills and down the woods into the dells—a strange contrast to the wretched tracts in all the adjacent countries." [40] In contrast, such centralized means of communication were nowhere in evidence in Bunyoro. According to Roscoe, "there were not roads in Bunyoro, but only tracks leading from one part of the country to another." [41]

Centralization—political and infrastructural—made possible a more efficient collection of the social surplus from within and without. Within, the throne collected four different kinds of taxes.[42] First, an obligatory tax was imposed on each married man, both the amount and the timing being regularized from the middle of the eighteenth century: each married man paid, twice a year, twenty-one pieces of bark cloth and one hundred cowry shells.[43] Second, an excise tax was imposed on all food products, cattle, goat, venison, intoxicating drinks, and manufactures such as baskets and carpets. This tax was a specific proportion of the volume produced. Third, customs duty was imposed on the regional trade between kingdoms, such as the exchange of salt and iron tools between Bunyoro and Buganda. And finally, any peasant wishing to be exempt from the national obligation to participate in war paid a tax to the Crown.

Military service had been a legal compulsion for every Muganda since the middle of the seventeenth century. War, and the subjection of neighboring states, became the basis of surplus collection from without. By the end of the nineteenth century, Buganda was receiving a regular annual tribute from the rulers of Nkore and Busoga, and from Karagwe in northwest Tanganyika. The tribute came in the form of cattle, slaves, trade products (such as ivory), and, increasingly, cowry shells.

The amount of tribute the state collected depended in part on the form it took. By the nineteenth century, collection in kind was giving way to currency. As long as the collection of surplus was primarily in kind, there was a limit as to how much could be extracted from each peasant family. Agricultural produce could be stored only over the short run; manufactured articles, such as baskets and hoes, diminished in usefulness for the collecting authority as the numbers collected increased. The collection of a currency surplus, on the other hand, both made possible and increased the incentive for accumulation. Portable currency changed first from ivory disks to glass beads, and, as the volume of trade and circulation of currency expanded, glass beads were discarded because of their limited supply and replaced by cowry shells.[44] The shells were tied together, one hundred on a string. Ten strings formed a unit and ten such units a load. By the nineteenth century the Baganda could count up to a million, although the numbers above ten thousand were only useful in counting the treasures of the *kabaka*.[45]

The process of social development in precolonial Buganda was thus total; it was not at the level of either the economy or the polity alone, but involved both in a dialectical relation. The absence of rigid caste distinctions and the presence of class mobility had made possible political centralization, which became the basis for building an infrastructure and collecting a larger surplus. This in turn provided the material basis for strengthening the very process of centralization. The introduction of the gun and the throne's *political* monopoly over this new technology of destruction further enhanced the process. To understand the consequences for the people of Buganda, however, one must ask what class interests the state of Buganda represented. What were the rising classes and social groups, and what changes were taking place in the mode of utilization of the surplus they controlled?

The new forms of consumption, and the new technology of firearms gave rise to a new social group, the skilled artisans. By the 1880s there existed in Buganda a class of highly skilled professional craftsmen.[46] This group worked in the service of those who had cultivated the new forms of consumption and who controlled the new technology: the *kabaka* and his *bakungu* chiefs. At the same time, the *kabaka* and his chiefs were undergoing a major qualitative transformation. The trade with the Arabs, the monopoly of the king and his chiefs, had assumed major proportions. A feudal ruling class, in response to changed objective circumstances, was becoming transformed into a mercantile ruling class. Simultaneously, the surplus was beginning to assume a dual form, that of feudal tribute and merchant's profit.*

Further, and important, political and economic changes were to come. On the basis of a steadily expanding surplus, there was growing a nonagricultural urban culture. The rising social groups in such urban centers—the chiefs and the traders—had much earlier, in the seventeenth century, adopted such new items of consumption as leather sandals, plates, cups and saucers, glass, and cloth. Initially imported and confined to a tiny group of privileged, these tastes gradually spread across larger segments of the population. Gradually new forms of production were introduced to satisfy these tastes. By the nineteenth century, Baganda artisans were manufacturing sandals, bark cloth, soap, and pottery.[50] Even a colonist such as Lugard, when he first came to Uganda, could not help remarking on the "great progress of civilization" [51] among the people.†
In Buganda a mercantile era appeared to be dawning.‡

---

* This same trend could be observed in other kingdoms of the south. In Nkore, where the long-distance salt trade was known as the "king's trade," [47] the artisan class did ironworking, carpentry, basketry, and pottery, and socially remained a part of the depressed Bairu.[48] However, as Karugira has convincingly shown,[49] even before the arrival of the British new social and economic distinctions were emerging. Among the Banyoro, the pastoral Hima aristocracy was gradually becoming divided into the poor and the rich, while from the ranks of the agricultural Iru commoners a number of individuals who had rendered special services to the king were emerging as "free" men. The Hima were being introduced to a vegetable diet and the Bairu allowed to own productive cows. These tendencies were undermining the caste society and ushering in a class society.

† Similarly, Harry Johnston, his vocabulary liberally sprinkled with colonialist paternalism, wrote the Colonial Office in 1901: ". . . there is no race like them [the Baganda] amongst the Negro tribes of Africa. They are the Japanese of the Dark Continent, the most naturally civilized, charming, kindly, tactful and courteous of black peoples. I can well understand and sympathise with the enthusiasm their missionary friends display when they describe them in Roman Catholic and Anglican publications dealing with missionary work." [52]

‡ It is important that this statement be properly understood. What we are underlining here is the growth of merchant capital *as a tendency* in precolonial Buganda. Certainly, the dominant form of surplus was feudal tribute, not merchant's profit. Although the tendency toward the growth of merchant capital has been slightly exaggerated, this is both permissible and necessary for

But such a society was not to be. Instead, the late nineteenth century saw the colonization of the region, a process that brought about a qualitative transformation. While in 1890 the expanding commerce of Buganda was controlled by a class of trading feudal lords, this same class under colonial rule reverted to being a totally parasitical semifeudal landed class, living off rent and chiefly salaries. In Nkore, where the society had been undergoing a transformation from a caste to a class structure, colonial rule served to rigidify the "traditional" caste distinction between the "aristocratic" Hima and the "common" Iru by appointing only Hima individuals to public office.[53]

While the ruling class of colonial Uganda lived in the metropole, its dominant classes resided in the urban areas. In 1890, Mengo, the capital of Buganda, had 77,000 people; a half century later, before the first major crisis of colonialism in 1940, the capital of Uganda was Kampala, with a population of 40,000. Both Mengo and Kampala were trading towns, but with a difference: in the half century of colonial rule the very *nature* of trade in the region had changed.

The change in the nature of trade could also be seen in the nature of production and the productive classes. While in 1900 Lugard praised the "superior" skill of Baganda artisanal work,[54] and while artisans were an *ascending* group, in 1940 artisanal skills were said to be "scarce"; in fact, from the beginning of the colonial period, artisans were imported from abroad. By 1930, as British social scientist Lucy Mair noted, the inland peoples of Uganda "still export their pots, but native woodwork is now quite obsolete." [55] But it was not just a question of woodwork. Take, for example, the hoe, the most important tool for productive labor in an agricultural economy. Previously manufactured internally, it was now *imported*—from Britain! What had happened to those who worked in copper, the smiths who

---

the purpose of analysis. Scientific analysis must analyze a social formation not as a static empirical reality but as a dynamic process; not only in its being, but also in its becoming.

Second, we are not speaking of the possibility of independent capitalist development in Buganda. Given the level of social development in the late nineteenth century and the subsequent course of history in the region, the discussion of such a possibility would be both speculative and academic.

made hoes from iron, the makers of bark cloth, pots, and baskets? Except for those few who catered to the expanding tourist "industry," the vast majority had reverted to the land, to produce cotton (and later coffee). The fact was that the colonially integrated economy had reduced all labor to the lowest common denominator, that of unskilled labor. In fifty years of colonial rule, the people of Buganda, the leading region in Uganda, had become de-urbanized, their productive activity de-manufacturized. Boldly imprinted on the productive activity of the people were two words: EXPORT-IMPORT. Export for the metropole and import from the metropole!

Furthermore, the *ascending* social groups in the colony, as we shall see, were not those who would challenge the existing state of affairs; they were in fact those who would consolidate it. Whether in agriculture, commerce, or within the state bureaucracy itself, they were as conveyor belts in this colonially integrated export-import economy—they were its overseers and managers. The history of colonialism was a history of underdevelopment.

For the colonial academicians, however, this underdevelopment was either a "natural" trait, the way of being of a "traditional" society, or the burden of a "new" state, a condition of adolescence. For them, underdevelopment did not need to be explained; it was their point of departure, their uncritical assumption. The most prominent of them, C. C. Wrigley, the "historian of Buganda," maintained that "the main reason for the poor success of African enterprise appears to be a general absence of the basic commercial attributes—integrity, assiduity, acumen and thrift." [56] Visiting economists deplored "the East African's lack of economic sense." [57] But this lack of commercial "attributes" and economic "sense" was modern and historical, not traditional and natural; it was the product of human actions and human interests, not a curse of the demons. Further, both the "sense" and the "attribute"—in their absence or presence— were rooted in specific social structures. Underdevelopment, in other words, is a structural, not an attitudinal, condition. The task of colonial history today must be to provide a concrete answer to the question: How did this structural underdevelopment come about and what relations underlay it?

Notes

1. For a recent example of such research, see Kenneth Ingham, *A History of East Africa*, pp. 36–45.
2. See, for example, David Apter, *Political Kingdom in Uganda*.
3. For an interesting discussion on the Hamitic hypothesis, see Basil Davidson, *Lost Cities of Africa*, pp. 9–12.
4. See Karl Marx, *The German Ideology*, pp. 6–30.
5. See Basil Davidson, *Black Mother, Africa: The Years of Trial*, pp. 166–174.
6. John Beattie, *The Nyoro State*, p. 67.
7. The possibility of obtaining a dry-season crop (that is, optimum crop requirements) in the north (at Gulu) is only 4 percent, whereas it is as high as 74 percent in the south (at Entebbe). See UP, *Report of the Agricultural Productivity Committee*, 1965, quoted in C. C. Wrigley, *Crops and Wealth in Uganda*, p. 2. For a short and excellent discussion on shifting cultivation as a system of production, see Clifford Geertz, *Agricultural Involution*.
8. In *The Problem of Uganda: A Study in Acculturation*, pp. 72–87.
9. Ibid., p. 73.
10. In *Feudal Society*, p. 466.
11. Beattie, *The Nyoro State*, p. 26; Jack Goodie, "Feudalism in Africa?", p. 8.
12. Maurice Dobb, "A Reply," in Science and Society, *Transition from Feudalism to Capitalism: A Debate*.
13. Beattie, *The Nyoro State*, pp. 32–34.
14. In *A History of the Kingdom of Nkore in Western Uganda to 1896*, p. 64.
15. *Capital*, vol. 3, p. 919.
16. See Peter Idowu Akingbade, "The History of the Kingdom of Toro from Its Foundation to 1928."
17. H. K. Takahashi, "A Contribution to the Discussion," in Science and Society, *Transition from Feudalism to Capitalism: A Debate*.
18. *Capital*, vol. 1, p. 260.
19. John Roscoe, *The Baganda*, pp. 7–8.
20. See Roscoe, *The Baganda* and other works.
21. Akingbade, p. 87.
22. Roscoe, *The Bagesu and Other Tribes of the Uganda Protectorate*, p. 114.
23. Ingham, pp. 37–38.
24. Roscoe, *The Northern Bantu*, pp. 76, 78.
25. C. C. Wrigley in Fallers, ed., *The King's Men*, pp. 24–26; see also

S. R. Karugira, *A History of the Kingdom of Nkore*, pp. 38–39, and Charles M. Good, *Rural Markets and Trade in East Africa*, pp. 149–167.

26. K. Olberg, "The Kingdom of Ankole in Uganda," in Fortes and Evans-Pritchard, eds., *African Political Systems*, p. 126.

27. Ingham, pp. 37–38.

28. Good maintains that the salt trade dates back to the mid-seventeenth century and covered a region reaching as far as southern Congo, southern Ruanda, eastern Buganda, southern Burundi, and the Wanyamwezi country in central Tanzania. He writes (p. 154):

> Control over sources of salt and its distribution was of major importance in shaping the economics and political relations of a great many African societies. In West Africa, e.g., it is quite certain that the prosperity of the early Sudanic kingdoms such as Ghana (*circa* A.D. 400–1076) and Mali (*circa* A.D. 1240–1475) was based largely on their capacity to control the south-to-north flow of gold and to regulate the importation and distribution of rock salt (exchanged for gold) from the major source areas such as Idjil, Taodemi, and Bilma in the Central and Western Sahara (R. Oliver and J. D. Page, *A Short History of East Africa* [Baltimore: Penguin, 1962], p. 61; and M. R. Black, "The Social Influence of Salt," *Scientific American* [July 1963], pp. 88–98). On the Rhodesian plateau, the Vakaranga peoples of the Monomotapa dynasty attributed their northward migration (nearly 200 miles away from the main gold sources) during the fifteenth century to the exhaustion of their salt supplies (Oliver and Page, ibid., p. 131).

Good continues:

> A regular demand for salt is common in areas where human subsistence depends on livestock. . . . Among the Hima of Ankole, cattle are the foci of economic and social life. Feeding of salt to cattle is a long-established practice and certain types of salt are believed to have definite medicinal properties.

29. Wrigley, *Crops and Wealth in Uganda*.

30. Roger Zwainenberg, "An Economic History of East Africa," p. 14.

31. See John Milner Gray, "Ahmed Bin Ibrahim—The First Arab to Reach Buganda."

32. Good, p. 167.

33. Ingham, p. 45.

34. In *The Baganda*, pp. 12–13; see also Radhakrishna Mukherjee, *The Problem of Uganda*. While he understands well this social difference between the Baganda and other peoples of the south, Mukherjee, in his otherwise excellent study of state formation in precolonial Uganda, fails to draw the important economic, political, and historical implications of this difference in social structure.

35. In two of the counties—particularly the central and highly populated county of Busiro—political authority still remained in the grip
of the *bataka*. See Fallers, "Social Stratification," in Fallers, ed.,
The King's Men, pp. 95–96.
36. A. J. Manners, "Social Stratification and Political Change in Two
East African Kingdoms," p. 134.
37. See Mukherjee, pp. 96–97.
38. Take, for example, the description Stanley gave of the *kabaka's*
navy in 1875:

> The largest canoe seen by me in this fleet measured 72 feet in length, 7
> feet 3 inches in breadth, and was 4 feet deep from keel to gunwale. The
> thwarts were 32 in number, to seat 64 paddlers besides the pilot. There
> were probably over 100 canoes between 50 and 70 feet in length; the
> remaining 80 fighting boats were of all sizes from 18 to 30 feet long.
> . . . The largest class—100 in number—would require on an average 50
> men each to man them, which would be equal in the aggregate to 5,000.
> . . . The canoes for assault would therefore be crammed with fighting
> men, the largest class carrying from 60 to 100 men, exclusive of their
> crews; so that the actual fact is that Mutesa (the king) can float a force
> of from 16,000 to 20,000 on Lake Victoria for purposes of war.

—From Stanley's *Through the Dark Continent*, excerpted in R.
Oliver and C. Oliver, *Africa in the Days of Exploration*, pp. 92–93.
39. Roscoe, *Twenty-Five Years in East Africa*, p. 193.
40. Speke, *Journal of the Discovery of the Source of the Nile*, p. 274.
41. Roscoe, *Twenty-Five Years in East Africa*, p. 260.
42. The analytical distinction of these four taxes is taken from John
Crysostom Ssekamwa, "The Development of the Buganda Treasury
and Its Relationship with the British Protectorate Government,
1900–1955," pp. 7–25.
43. Roscoe, *The Baganda*, p. 252.
44. Roscoe, *Twenty-Five Years in East Africa*, pp. 97, 193.
45. Ssekamwa, "The Development of the Buganda Treasury," p. 13.
46. Wrigley, in Fallers, ed., *The King's Men*, pp. 24–26.
47. Good, p. 151.
48. Ibid., pp. 149–150.
49. Karugira, *A History of the Kingdom of Nkore*, pp. 49–56; see also
Mukherjee, pp. 58–59, 62–65.
50. Apollo Kaggwa, *The Customs of the Baganda*; quoted in Mukherjee,
pp. 96–97.
51. Frederick D. Lugard, *The Rise of Our East African Empire*, p. 433.
52. Harry Johnston, *Africa*, No. 7 Cd. 671 of 1901, p. 16.
53. See Karugira, p. 70.
54. In *The Rise of Our East African Empire*, p. 433.

55. In *An African People in the Twentieth Century*, p. 129.
56. In "The Development of a Middle Class in British East Africa," INCIDI Record of the 29th Session (INCIDI, Brussels, 1956), pp. 216–218; quoted in E. Goldthorpe, *An African Elite*, p. 21.
57. Quoted in Goldthorpe, p. 21.

2

The Establishment of a Peasant Economy

When the period of slavery ended, it was the metropolitan-based export-import companies that were the first to enter Africa. But existing conditions made it difficult for these companies to operate profitably: the productive activity of the vastly diminished population was directed toward meeting their own consumption needs, not those of international trade; also, there did not exist the political (state) power to compel the producers to work in the interest of these trading companies. In a short span, one after another, the merchant companies faced ruin, each turning to its own state for assistance. The competition between trading companies was soon translated into that between *their* states. The entry of metropolitan capitalist states in the "scramble for Africa" began the colonial period in Africa.

The logic of intraimperialist rivalry and not the lure of existing products led to the proclamation of an imperial protectorate over Uganda in 1894.* The fundamental problem of the colonial state, in the long run, was production: what should the colony produce and what were the relations of production to be?

In the short run, however, there was a more immediate and

---

* The word Uganda was taken from the word Buganda, the latter being the first British possession in the region. Colonial usage at the time referred to Buganda as the Uganda Kingdom and to the larger protectorate territory as Uganda.

urgent political problem. The first six years of British involvement in Uganda, from 1887 to 1894, had produced three bloody civil wars and four new kings. Under conditions of no law and considerable disorder, trade was the first casualty. From 1890 to 1899, the trade in ivory, Buganda's principal export, declined sharply. The turmoil was testimony to the fact that in any colony outside control by a few thousand colonists over millions of the colonized was impossible. The immediate problem of the colonial state was the problem of control.

It thus became necessary for the metropolitan power to seek allies in its colonial venture. Colonialism—the implantation of the metropolitan state apparatus in a conquered territory—was not possible without *mediating* this rule through classes physically situated in the colony. In the language of British colonialism, "indirect rule" became a necessity. A class of collaborators —those who would receive partial treatment in return for helping to maintain law and order—had either to be found among the "natives" or brought in from other dependencies. In Uganda, Britain resorted to both measures.

This policy was embodied in the Buganda Agreement of 1900, which created a class of notables, a "landed gentry" that was to exist by the grace of the colonial masters and was thus to find it in its own interest to maintain the colonial status quo—in other words, to be loyal. As stated by Sir Harry Johnston, the framer of the agreement:

> The Land Settlement [was] a practical attempt to establish on a sound basis a ruling oligarchy which, under British guidance, might do for Buganda what the landed aristocracy had done . . . to give stability to the government of England.[1]

The agreement thus parceled out pieces of land to the entire hierarchy—from the king down to the lowest parish chief. Plots were substantial and reckoned in terms of square miles.* Johnston wrote the prime minister, Salisbury, underlining the political significance of the agreement: "I sincerely trust that my recently concluded agreement may cause the interests of the

---

* This is why freehold land in Buganda is today known as *mailo* land, that is, land measured in miles.

Baganda people to become thoroughly identified with the support of the British Protectorate. . . ." [2] There was, however, another side to the agreement. The land allotted amounted to over 9,000 square miles. The remainder—including forest, swamp, bush, and *unused* land—was declared Crown Land. As Johnston explained in a memorandum to the Colonial Office: "One result of this Land settlement has been to make the British Government the owner of more than half the soil of the kingdom of Uganda." [3] The purpose, as we shall see, was to save it for the European planters.

The implementation of the agreement had important consequences for the evolving class structure in the colony. At one stroke the colonial state created a class of powerful but parasitic landlords—parasitic because although they were to consume large amounts of the economic surplus, they played no part in production. Their income was to be derived neither from their own labor nor from supervising the labor of others but from the rent they were to extract from a tenant peasantry. The Baganda landlords were to be a rentier class par excellence. What had been a potentially dynamic precolonial ruling class, increasingly deriving its surplus from trade, was at one stroke converted into a parasitic collaborating class, divorced from both trade and production, central only to the process of consumption.

But Britain's problem in Buganda was not just to create a collaborating class; there was also a need to come to terms with a ruling class and a monarchy that were both politically organized and militarily powerful. As Johnston saw it:

> If there is any country forming part of the Uganda Protectorate which could do us any real harm it is Uganda itself—the kingdom of Uganda. Here we have something like a million fairly intelligent, slightly civilized negroes of warlike tendencies, and possessing about 10,000 to 12,000 guns. These are the only people for a long time to come who can deal a serious blow to British rule in this direction. . . . [4]

Nothing short of undermining the organization and unity of the Baganda feudal lords would do. To achieve this the British successfully exploited and furthered existing divisions within this class. Lord Lugard, leading the troops of the Imperial

British East Africa Company, had joined forces with the Baganda Protestants to defeat the Baganda Catholics at the Battle of Mengo in 1892. When the time came to convert the feudal lords into landlords, it was the leaders of the Protestant faction who received the bulk of the land grants.* At the same time, the *kabaka* was treated as just another lord and given only a slightly larger grant. Thus the landlord class created by the 1900 Agreement was predominantly Protestant. Religion became a political factor in Uganda, particularly in the consciousness of the emerging class of landlords and chiefs.

Once British rule over Buganda was secured, it was this very class that acted as the vanguard in consolidating the rule of the colonial state over the rest of the colony. Baganda armies, under the "loyal" General Kakunguru, were instrumental in conquering the kingdoms of Bunyoro-Kitare and Busoga. In return, the landed class received a minority share of the spoils, signifying the real terms of its partnership with the colonial state. Large areas of east and northeast Bunyoro were incorporated into the Buganda kingdom as a gift from the colonial state. These areas, subsequently known as the "Lost Countries," and to become one of the most explosive political issues in independent Uganda, included 40 percent of Bunyoro's population and both its capital and the burial sites of many of its rulers.[6] The tillers of the soil in these countries became tenants of the *kabaka* and his leading landlord-chiefs. Baganda chiefs were appointed in many of the conquered areas to establish the colonial administrative apparatus.†

---

* The redistribution of chiefly positions (which were tied to the land grants) by Lugard after the Battle of Mengo had already put the Protestants firmly in the seat of power. The Catholics got a few nominal chiefly positions in the west and the Muslims in the midwest, but the Protestants obtained control of *ssazas* (counties) to the east and retained control of those immediately west of center.[5]

† This was another instance of indirect rule. In fact, indirect rule was just another side of the coin that read divide-and-rule, the creation of internal divisions to make the task of colonial rule easier. Thus, Baganda chiefs were appointed in Ankole[7] and Toro,[8] whereas men from Toro were appointed as chiefs among the Wamba.[9] Among the northern Lugbara, the British appointed as chiefs the remnants of Emin Pasha's "Nubi" troops from the southern Sudan.[10] The British also merged the kingdom of Nkore with surrounding areas to make the district of Ankole.

While the Baganda landlords helped maintain social peace, the creation of an underdeveloped economy required the services of another social group, one brought from outside. These were the Asians,* who came for reasons we shall analyze in the next chapter. Here it need only be said that although active as financiers and bankers in Zanzibar and along the East African coast for centuries, Asians did not settle inland in East Africa until the colonization of this area had ushered in an entirely new historical era.† The objective role of the Asian trader was to extend the hold of the market, and thus of the class that controlled the terms of exchange in the market, the metropolitan bourgeoisie. Before this could happen, however, it was necessary to subordinate *production* in the colony to the *accumulation* needs of this bourgeoisie.

Commodity Production for Export

Although the structure of the Ugandan economy was not clear even as late as the 1920s, the forces that provided the impetus to its formation were discernible at the beginning of the twentieth century. In 1902, two events took place that were to prove of great importance to the future of Uganda. The first was the completion of the Uganda Railway, which signified the forging of infrastructural ties with the international capitalist economy and meant that commodities could now be exported in bulk to the coast at prices sufficient to cover the cost of transportation. The rates of carriage from Uganda to England, even after the building of the cartroad from Mombasa to Lake Victoria in 1898, were estimated at 3 shillings a pound, but with the building of the railway they dropped dramatically to between 4 and 6 pence a pound.[11] The technological precondition for subordinating the colonial economy to that of the metropole was satisfied.

---

* Popular usage in East Africa refers to immigrants from the Indian subcontinent as "Asians."

† A number of writers have failed to emphasize the qualitative difference between the precolonial and colonial epochs, treating both under the single ahistorical subject heading: "Asians in East Africa." See, for example, Mangat, *A History of the Asians in East Africa*, and Delf, *Asians in East Africa*.

The specific content of this subordination, however, was not yet evident. Thus the significance of the second major event in 1902, the formation of the British Cotton Growing Association (BCGA), the result of Lancashire's anxiety at being dependent on the United States market for its supplies of raw cotton.[12] In the period following the Civil War, U.S. cotton production rose, but so did its consumption, leading to a considerable shortage in the supply of the raw product available for the rest of the world. By 1900, many of the mills in Lancashire were slowing down. In 1901, at the annual dinner of the Oldham Chamber of Commerce, Benjamin Cooper, chairman of the East Africa Committee, emphasized the danger of Lancashire's reliance on the United States and the need to grow cotton elsewhere within the Empire.[13] As a result, the BCGA was formed. By 1904, the question had become sufficiently important to be included in the King's Speech:

> The insufficiency of the supply of raw material upon which the great cotton industry of this country depends has inspired me with deep concern. I trust that the efforts which are being made in various parts of the Empire to increase the area under cultivation may be attended with a large measure of success! [14]

The first cotton flower was sent to Uganda by the BCGA through a Church Missionary Society missionary, K. Borup, in 1903.[15] Borup formed the Uganda Company and imported 2.5 tons of five different kinds of seeds, which were distributed to twenty-seven chiefs in eight districts of Buganda.[16] The results were so promising that the government took the lead and, through the BCGA, began to import and distribute American Black Rattler seeds to growers in Buganda, Busoga, and Ankole in 1905.[17]

The production of cotton in these early years was the result of compulsion exercised through the *mailo* landlord-cum-chief, rather than directly by the colonial state. As state officials explained,

> The average peasant of the Protectorate [is] so indolent that it [is] unlikely that he would have embarked on it [cotton production] on any considerable scale if he had not been more or less driven to making experiments by the chief or the headman on whose land he happened to be a tenant.[18]

In time, however, state officials became more circumspect. In 1925, when charges of "forced cultivation of cotton" were laid before the Ormsby-Gore Commission, the government maintained that the peasant chose to grow cotton "of his own free will," and released a copy of an instructional telegram from the chief secretary to the provincial commissioner, Western Province:

> I am directed by the Governor to state that the line to be adopted is not to be one of definite pressure towards cotton production. Natives to be informed that three courses are open, cotton, labour for Government, labour for planters, but no attempt is to be made to induce them to choose any one in preference to the others. Only one thing to be made clear that they cannot be permitted to do nothing, and can be of no use to themselves or the country. Inform D. C. Mbarara accordingly.[19]

Such were the parameters of "free will" in the colony! *

Coercion by the chiefs, however, was only part of the explanation for the remarkable success of cotton production in southern Uganda. For one thing, having former feudal lords introduce changes in the commodities produced did not constitute a radical departure from the past: the colonial state merely adapted feudal corvée labor to ensure the production of commodities for export to the metropole. Furthermore, in precolonial Buganda the consumption of such commodities as textiles had already spread beyond the ruling class and there was no need to create a desire for consumer products and cash income. The successful spread of cotton production in the south demonstrated this, as did the fact that in a very short time the peasants began growing cotton on their own plots, not just on the chiefs' lands. The northern regions, however, presented a sharp contrast. Here the production of cash crops was limited, as colonial officers noted, to earning only enough to pay the poll

---

* The 1914 Report of the Commercial and Industrial Policy Committee entitled "What Industries Are Essential to the Future of the Nation: And What Steps Should Be Taken to Maintain or Establish Them" (enclosed in a dispatch from the deputy governor to the secretary of state for colonies) stated: "I would emphasize the need of safeguarding raw material, more particularly cotton, an adequate supply of which is an imperial necessity." [20]

tax.[21] In 1920–1921, 81,000 pounds of lint were produced in Uganda, and 69,000 pounds (or 85 percent) originated in the southern regions.[22]

While cotton was the principal export crop in the first three decades of colonial rule, it was subsequently eclipsed by coffee (also grown predominantly on peasant farms), which became the principal export crop by 1938. Peasant coffee production was first seriously encouraged by the state in 1923 when central nurseries were set up in districts suitable for coffee growing. It became an important crop in Masaka District (Buganda), Bugisu, and Bwemba county in Toro (Western Province).

Acreage Planted to Coffee

	1922	1925	1928	1931	1934	1936	1938
Non-African planters	20,820	18,884	18,408	17,559	13,391	13,472	13,314
African planters							
In Buganda	600	959	4,673	16,970	21,050	27,570	32,255
In Bugisu	400	475	1,134	2,114	4,023	6,080	7,375
In Western Province	—	353	2,924	1,816	5,276	9,853	12,238
Total African planters	1,000	1,787	8,731	20,900	30,349	43,503	51,868

Source: Uganda Government, *Report of the Committee of Inquiry into the Coffee Industry,* 1967, pp. 1–2.

In the early years, the European coffee growers in Uganda vigorously opposed, through their planters' associations, state encouragement of African coffee production. Their principal argument was that the "time [had] come in view of the enormous overproduction of coffee in Brazil to discourage further production of coffee in Uganda." [23] The director of agriculture, however, disagreed:

The argument that we should restrict coffee production because Brazil produces too much has been advanced recently by our local planters' associations. In 1928, a typical year, exports of coffee were as follows (19th Report—Imperial Economic Committee):

	Bags of 132 lbs.	Percent of world production
Brazil	13,881,000	57.8
British Empire	683,000	2.8
Costa Rica	315,000	1.3
Colombia	2,665,000	11.1
Dutch East Indies	1,938,000	8.0
Other countries	4,532,000	19.0

The dominating point is that the British Empire is producing only 2.8 percent of the world's coffee and should be producing a much larger share.[24]

The production of coffee in Uganda was not a response to the needs of the domestic economy, nor a response to a demand from the world capitalist market, but a response to demand from a *section* of that market: the British Empire. It was not in the least "natural" that Uganda be a cotton- or a coffee-growing area. So far as "comparative advantage" was concerned, early British travelers to Uganda had emphasized the excellent opportunities for expanding already existing industries: dairy farming, basketweaving, making bark cloth, fishing, etc.[25] None of these, however, was encouraged by the Protectorate government. A neocolony may respond to demand from the world capitalist market; a colony, however, acts in response to demand from the metropolitan market, *its* metropolitan market. The fact was that the production of coffee, like that of cotton, was in response to the *political* need of the metropolitan power and was undertaken only as a result of the colonial relation; it signified the subservience of production in Uganda to the *accumulation* needs of the British economy. It should thus be no surprise that after independence, when the Ugandan economy was no longer subject to the direct political control of the British state, overproduction of coffee in the world market suddenly became a relevant consideration, determining state policy toward the growers. Thus the 1967 committee of inquiry into the coffee industry recommended that the state pay a bonus to Robusta coffee growers for either uprooting trees or replacing them "by any of the approved agricultural activities," and that the further planting of Robusta coffee be outlawed.[26]

Uganda remained a raw material reservoir for British industry as long as this was beneficial for Britain. When, in 1908, Indian capitalists proposed to set up textile mills in Uganda, the governor wrote in his report that

> projects are being considered by certain Indian capitalists for the establishment of cotton mills in Kampala and Jinja, where the kind of cloth which finds favor with the natives may be produced on the spot. Such projects open up prospects which may not be to the advantage of Lancashire spinners, and are worthy of attention.

Given that possibility, he continued,

> It is a satisfaction to be able to report that the industry is so far mainly in the hands of British firms and that most of the cotton produced in the Protectorate goes to the looms of Lancashire.[27]

Peasants and Planters

Despite the fact that cotton came to be produced on small and scattered peasant farms, at the outset it was not at all clear that this would happen. In fact, so far as the British authorities were concerned, the Uganda economy was to be either a settler or a plantation economy, and not a peasant economy.* In the absence of such staples as West African palm oil, His Majesty's Government hoped "that the results of the administration and the building of the Railway may attract capital and settlers" and instructed the governor to "be always ready to encourage *bona fide* applicants."[29] In 1903, the East Africa Syndicate, a London-based firm, was given exclusive prospecting rights for precious stones and minerals over large areas of Bunyoro and

---

* The same decision was also made for Kenya (the East Africa Protectorate), which was initially no more than a place on the way to Uganda. From the colonial point of view, Kenya's main asset was a cool climate that was sure to attract settlers. Accordingly, the eastern part of Uganda—highland country adjacent to similar areas of Kenya and later to constitute the problematic "white highlands"—was transferred to the East African Protectorate in 1902.[28]

Ankole.[30] The search for the golden egg proved fruitless, however, and the seven or eight settlers who attempted residence in Uganda all "came to grief." Noting this universal failure, the governor advised the Colonial Office in 1909:

Uganda is in every way unsuited for "settlers," if we mean by such a term men possessing more labouring capacity than capital. Persons of that class should be strongly dissuaded from trying their fortunes in this protectorate; the climate would quickly prove to them their mistake and disaster would surely overtake them. On the other hand, and judging by the experience I have gained during twenty-six years in tropical countries, I see no reason why the class of men who does so well in Ceylon, the Straits Settlements, the West Indies and elsewhere as a "planter" should not do equally well in Uganda.[31]

The 1907–1908 Blue Book, an annual report by the colonial administration, repeated that "there are but few parts of the Protectorate which appear to be fitted for European settlement on a colonial scale." On the other hand, it saw "no reason why 'planters,' possessed of adequate capital should not succeed as well in Uganda as they do in the West Indies, Burma, Assam, and other tropical dependencies." [32]

Before a plantation economy could be established, however, a source of cheap labor had to be found. There existed neither a rural nor an urban work force in Uganda, and the creation of a working class was possible only through the direct participation of the state and its entire coercive apparatus. As the British Foreign Office saw the problem:

The uncivilized native desires a life of indolence, complete and undisturbed; the missionaries, who have done much to educate him for agricultural and industrial work, would prefer to see him farm his own small property; while the settlers and plantation-owners depend on him for the labour which will give them a reasonable profit and in the aggregate secure the country's prosperity. There are abundant opportunities for both skilled and unskilled labour; the one attitude that cannot command sympathy is the refusal to work.[33]

The rod that would make certain that the "natives" utilized these "abundant opportunities" for labor was the tax system.

The Buganda Agreement of 1900 imposed a "hut tax" of 3 shillings a year on the African population, the logic being that the tax, payable only in cash, would compel the peasant to seek wage employment. As the Annual Report for 1901 put it, "Habits of exertion were first inculcated by the hut tax." [34] Johnston's successor, Lt. Col. J. H. Sadler, told a meeting of the Royal Institute in 1904: "I have no hesitation in saying that this tax will prove to be the making of the country, not only because of the revenue it brings in but because of the habits of work it inculcates." [35] Bishop Hattersley, writing only a few years later, maintained that "it was the imposition of the hut tax . . . and the new Treaty, that gave the first impetus to paid labour." [36]

As the market economy and production for the market expanded, landlords, planters, and government all vied for the available labor supply. As the problem became increasingly acute, the government in 1905 added a poll tax of 2 shillings to the hut tax. This only temporarily alleviated the problem. The fact that cash-crop cultivation and wage labor were *alternate* forms of earning cash gave a further impetus to the spread of cotton cultivation, particularly in Buganda. An irreconcilable contradiction began to emerge between the plantation and peasant sectors. The peasant sector, at least during this early period, was self-sufficient in terms of labor. The plantation sector, on the other hand, was parasitic, needing to extract labor from the peasantry in order to survive. The state's actions demonstrated that it understood this dilemma very well and was equally clear about the course to be followed.

In the southern areas, it was decided to let the peasants continue to grow cotton provided they donated a part of their time—one month per year—toward laboring for the planters or the government. In 1902, therefore, the Village Headman Ordinance had been instituted. Besides collecting the hut tax, the headman had to "supply" labor to the government and planters. The governor believed he could "reasonably expect the native chiefs, who are supposed to have such authority in the country, to show that they possess sufficient moral influence over their people to induce each man to work for one month at a reasonable wage." [37] In simple terms, the peasant was "legally" compelled to be a wage laborer for one month a year at a "reasonable wage" that would be decided unilaterally by his employer. As the labor problem increased, the duration of this compulsory wage labor was increased from one to two months.[38] After all the pious proclamations about the desire to suppress the slave trade being the prime motive behind colonization, the colonial state ended up substituting forced labor for slavery. Such was the nature of "progress" in the colonies.

In the northern and western parts of the country the consequences of the government's labor policy were even more far-reaching. The core of this area, the West Nile District and the subsidiary areas, including Acholi, Lango, Kigezi, Ankole, and Bugisu,[39] were gradually developed into a labor reservoir for the cash-crop economy of the south, itself a raw material reservoir for the manufacturing economy of metropolitan England. In 1925, for example, when an agricultural officer in the West Nile District succeeded in encouraging cotton production and thereby hindered the recruitment of laborers for the plantations, the director of agriculture informed him that it was official policy "to refrain from actively stimulating the production of cotton or other economic crops in outlying districts on which [it] is dependent for a supply of labour for the carrying out of essential services in the central or producing districts." *[40]

As the structure of production was altered to serve the accumulation needs of the metropole, the entire colonial economy was being underdeveloped. In addition, development within the colonial economy itself was uneven, the result of a qualitative difference in the form of subordination of the north and the south. At the same time, what further distinguished the south from the north was the role of the south in extracting surplus labor from the north to produce raw materials for the metropolitan economy. The impoverishment of the north was thus a condition for the relative prosperity of the south. There was no dual economy here—one traditional, the other modern, one static, the other dynamic. Neither north nor south can be

---

* The policy of "not encouraging" cash-crop production in the north began to change in the late 1920s as the cotton economy found another source of labor, the immigrants streaming into the south from Ruanda. By independence the north was a source of both cash crops and labor. See Chapter 5.

understood unless their relation is grasped both in terms of historical development and contemporary functioning, and unless both are analyzed in relation to the metropolitan economy.

With the weight of the entire state apparatus directed toward solving the labor problem, it is not surprising that there was a rise in plantation activity. The first plantations were established in 1907 by the Uganda Company, then known as the Industrial Mission of the Church Missionary Society evangelists. The Blue Book for 1911–1912 enthusiastically remarked that "the year [has] been remarkable for the great increase in the number of European plantations." Rather optimistically, it maintained that "although plantation crops at present do not figure very largely in the exports, they will probably do so in the near future." [41]

From a total of 2,000 acres under permanent crops in 1911,[42] cultivation expanded to 20,000 acres in 1913–1914,[43] and 25,184 acres in 1915–1916.[44] A planters' association was formed in 1910 and in 1912 the *Uganda Herald*, mouthpiece for settler interests, began publication. The increase in the volume of business led to the establishment of a second bank, a branch of the Standard Bank of South Africa.[45] The most widely planted crop was coffee, followed by rubber. Cocoa was just emerging as a third important crop,[46] but when its price dropped during the war cultivation ceased.[47] Total plantation acreage fell from 25,184 in 1915–1916 to 19,690 in 1916–1917.[48]

As the end of the war gave way to the slump of 1921, the crisis in the plantation sector intensified. Rail and shipping rates on coffee and rubber exported from Uganda to Britain had increased during the war. At the same time, the rise in the sterling value of the Indian rupee had increased the sterling cost of production in East Africa.[49] Then between 1920 and 1922 certain commodity markets collapsed. The crisis was particularly severe in Uganda because many planters had not even begun to make a profit, due to the fact that the period between planting and harvest for coffee is about three years and for rubber is seven.*

---

* That is, in Uganda. In most rubber-growing areas, at much lower altitudes, the period is four years.[50]

As one of the plantations, Bukona Estates Ltd., explained its dilemma to the Colonial Office:

While the coffee and rubber plantations were just becoming productive, cotton cultivation was increasing by leaps and bounds. From the first few plots in 1904, cotton acreage grew to 50,000 acres in 1912–1913 and 207,000 in 1920–1921.* From 1907 on, cotton furnished the largest single item in the export trade of Uganda.[53]

"The Company was registered on the 23rd June, 1914, with a nominal capital of £15,000 to take over a freehold estate consisting of 14,000 acres. . . .

"The present issued capital consists of 9,152 shares of £1 each held by 12 shareholders all of whom are resident in the U.K. At the outbreak of the war, the company was carrying on its policy of development and had not arrived at the productive stage; consequently it has suffered severely since 1914.

"Its cash resources were exhausted by the middle of 1915 and recourse had to be made to loans granted by the National Bank of India when the normal rate of currency of 15 rupees to the pound was in force. Down to February, 1920, Rps. 84,000 had been so borrowed from the Directors of the Company. In February, 1920, the Government altered the currency from Rps. 15 to the £ to 10 florins to the £ so that instead of the Company having to repay £5,600, being the equivalent to Rps. 84,000 at 15, its liability was immediately converted into £8,400, being the equivalent of 84,000 florins at ten to the £. The present overdraft at the National Bank of India is Rps. 91,000. The bank has refused to advance any further money and the Directors have found it impossible to raise any more money in order to repay the bank. Owing to the new rate of exchange and in common with other undertakings both commercial and planting in Uganda and East Africa, the Company is faced with bankruptcy unless assistance is forthcoming to meet the heavy loss occasioned by the change in the currency. . . . During the war a good deal of coffee was sent home but the Company has suffered from the high rate charged for ocean freight and marine war risk insurance and has also been hampered in its production by the fact that the rubber only came into bearing when it was almost impossible owing to the war to send out machinery for dealing with the crop."[51]

* Specifically, the figures from 1912–1913 to 1920–1921 were as follows:[52]

	Acreage	Bales
1912–13	50,000	20,000
1913–14	110,000	26,000
1914–15	118,000	40,000
1915–16	92,000	26,000
1916–17	129,000	22,000
1917–18	134,000	28,000
1918–19	145,000	27,000
1919–20	155,000	36,000
1920–21	207,000	47,000

The success of cotton and the difficulties of the planters were related. As we have seen, the peasant who grew cotton was not available as a plantation worker. Furthermore, with the dramatic expansion in the acreage of cotton cultivated, many farmers—particularly in Buganda and Eastern Province—began hiring a laborer or two. The conflict between the plantation and the peasant sectors intensified. As D. N. Stafford, honorary secretary of the Uganda Planters' Association, wrote to Col. Amery, under-secretary of state at the Colonial Office, the "prime cause" of the planters' difficulties was "in the first instance . . . the rapid growth of the cotton industry, which absorbed our labour," and, subsequently, "the terrible neglect of the planting interests by the Government." [54]

The position of the planters was supported unabashedly by the locally appointed Development Commission of 1920, which represented the majority of official local, and unofficial European, opinion. The Development Commission castigated the director of agriculture for having "failed to identify himself with the planters' interests as he should have done," thus indirectly chastising him for having supported "native cultivation." The commission described the policy of the department of agriculture as "so disastrous to common welfare" that "the matter calls for immediate action." It demanded that "the Government should issue explicit instructions with regard to the policy of the Agricultural Department" and that these "should at least contain a direction that plantation crops should be encouraged and receive attention equally with native products." [55]

The plantation owners were faced with opposition from several sectors. The revaluation of the rupee had benefited the importing traders while hurting the exporting plantations, and these trading interests were backed by the banks, who refused to grant any further overdrafts to the planters[56] and opposed the planters' demand for a change in the rate of exchange to lower their costs of production. The banks were convinced that the planters' troubles were not just short run, the teething troubles of an infant industry, but that the planters were unable to sell their products not because of any "defect" in exchange but because of the high costs of production.[57] This was a convincing argument, especially once it was expressed *relative* to the cost of the peasant sector.

It was here that the planters met their strongest and most powerful opposition, for the peasant sector was also the cotton sector. In preparing to battle against the cotton interests, the planters were confronting not just the Uganda peasants—scattered, disorganized, and politically powerless—but the main beneficiary of their cotton production, the Lancashire textile industry—a concentrated, well-organized, and politically potent force at the imperial level. In 1914, at the outbreak of the war, when transportation difficulties and high insurance rates discouraged ginners from purchasing the bulk of Ugandan cotton, the British Cotton Growing Association, afraid that the peasants would be "discouraged" as a consequence of the "unremunerative price" offered by the ginners,[58] purchased all the cotton grown that year and promoted the "payment of a higher price than what [was] being paid by the ginning companies." [59] Further, at a time when cotton production in the colony was not yet firmly established, when the peasants could easily revert to producing no more than the amount needed to pay the yearly tax should prices be very low, the BCGA, afraid that "the natives will not receive the encouragement which is so essential at the present juncture," [60] made arrangements to establish control over three ginneries in Uganda so as to "enable us to deal with a considerable portion of the crop." [61]

After the war, the BCGA was joined by other, more powerful, advocates of Empire cotton production. At a meeting in Manchester on December 13, 1916, groups "representing practically the whole of the cotton spinning and manufacturing industries of Lancashire" resolved unanimously:

> A. That the present situation as to the supply of cotton is most serious, and requires the immediate attention of Her Majesty's Government.
>
> B. That it is essential for the future prosperity of this country, and also for the welfare of the colonies, that cotton growing should be developed as rapidly as possible in all suitable parts of the Empire.[62]*

---

* Present at the meeting were the following organized representatives of the Lancashire textile industry:

In 1918, the Committee on Commercial and Industrial Policy after the War noted in its final report that the existing "deficiency" in the supplies of cotton was likely to increase in the immediate future and expressed alarm "that one of the principal industries of the U.K. should be so largely dependent as it is upon one source of supply [the United States] entirely beyond its control." [63]

The report of the Empire Cotton Growing Committee to the Board of Trade emphasized the world shortage of cotton goods and the fact that prices were "already at levels far in excess of anything recorded since the cotton famine in the sixties." [64] It noted that it was of vital importance to Lancashire to obtain increased supplies of suitable cotton. Indian and Chinese cotton, the committee maintained, was unsuitable, and Egyptian cotton was limited in quantity. Thus the committee concluded that the BCGA had "conclusively proved" that cotton suited for use in the Lancashire mills could be "satisfactorily grown in increasing quantities in several parts of Africa, notably in the Sudan, in Uganda, Nigeria, Nyasaland, and also in the West Indies."

By 1920 there was a clear contradiction between the interests of the British rubber and coffee planters and those of a section of the metropolitan bourgeoisie, the Lancashire textile industry and the metropolitan banks in Uganda which thrived on the cotton trade. Despite the entreaties of the Development Commission, the colonial state faithfully served the interests of the

---

British Cotton Growing Association
Federation of Master Cotton Spinners' Association
Cotton Spinners' and Manufacturers' Association
Wiggins and District Cotton Employers' Association
Amalgamated Association of Operative Cotton Spinners
Amalgamated Association of Card and Blowing-Room Operatives
Cotton Spinners' Provincial Association (Bolton)
Northern Counties Amalgamated Association of Weavers
Liverpool Cotton Association
Manchester Cotton Association
Bleachers' Association, Ltd.
Bradford Dyers' Association, Ltd.
Calico Printers' Association, Ltd.
Fine Cotton Spinners' & Doublers' Association, Ltd.
Lancashire and Cheshire Coal Owners' Association

metropolitan bourgeoisie. In 1921, when buyers were "either unable or unwilling to buy all the cotton offered," [65] the governor proposed that the government purchase all the cotton.[66] He emphasized that "the maintenance of the cotton growing industry" was "a matter of importance from the point of view of securing a large supply of cotton from within the Empire to meet future needs." [67] In spite of his early support for the planters, he had no option, for what was at stake here were imperial interests.

A deputation of Uganda planters then sought to bypass the colonial state and take their case directly to the Colonial Office. They complained that "the importance of the planting industry in Uganda had been overlooked by the Government, attention having been centered on the development of cotton," and emphasized that "about £1,000,000 were invested in the planting industry as compared with £250,000 in the cotton industry." In his reply, the colonial secretary bluntly reminded the planters "that the production of cotton was a matter of general imperial interest" [68]—that of the British manufacturer and financier—compared to which the local interests of the British planters were insignificant.

As the crisis further intensified, the unity of the planter class disintegrated. The larger planters attempted to take their cases individually to the Colonial Office. By far the largest was the Mabira Forest (Uganda) Rubber Company, Ltd., launched in London in 1906 with authorized capital of £120,000 and anticipated annual profits of £80,000,[69] and considered the "showplace of Uganda." [70] During the war the company represented to the Colonial Office the "grave loss" it was "suffering through the holding up of our consignments of produce . . . a direct result of the imperial military operations in East Africa" and "respectfully" asked for "temporary financial assistance . . . to meet pressing liabilities and prevent the ruin of the Company's enterprise in Uganda." [71] The under-secretary politely conveyed his "regrets," maintaining that he could not "see his way to apply to the Treasury for financial assistance to be afforded the Company." By 1920, the company's financial position had so worsened that it was reduced to requesting a postponement of "the payment of rent due January next for some little time to enable us to complete our financial arrangements." The Colonial Office note was curt and short: "The government wants its revenue, and although the amount [£300] is small it would be impossible to refuse a similar concession to any other tenant of the Government. Decline, with regret, on that ground." [72] On May 13, 1921, the governor of Uganda telegraphed the Colonial Office that the liquidation of the company was "imminent." [73] The Colonial Office was unmoved, however, and the company went bankrupt.

The majority of the planters decided to appeal to the Colonial Office on grounds of patriotism, making their appeals as "kith and kin." They organized an Ex-Soldiers League, emphasized that they had done their patriotic duty during the war, cited precedents from other colonies where settlers had been granted free titles to land, underlined their "needs as Europeans" for the amenities of life, and asked for "6,000 acres in all." * The governor transmitted their request to the colonial secretary, Sir Winston Churchill, who responded in one sentence: "I regret I am unable to accede to their request."

As the position of the larger plantations became critical, the governor himself appealed to the Colonial Office. He proposed a committee of two planters, with a government official as chairman, to "carefully scrutinise" the position of all estates in order to "determine those of good management and promise,"

---

* Here is the text of their petition:

"We, the undersigned, served with His Majesty's forces during the recent and other wars. Prior to 1914 the majority of us had taken up land in this district, and had spent money in developing plantations.

"We are aware that in many colonies, land has been granted free to ex-soldiers on account of their war services. In many cases to those who previously held, and indeed still hold, large areas.

"We have no wish to obtain extra land in addition to that which we are working. But we feel that owing to the setbacks suffered by our plantations during our absence from service, coupled with the heavy depressions of the last three years, we may reasonably ask for some alternative grant in our favour.

"We are already in occupation of land here, which under our development assists at colonisation, which in other parts of the Empire, free grants of land have been given to aid.

"We therefore respectfully ask that we may be granted our present holdings as free gifts." [74]

and to thus identify and assist those whom a "little judicious assistance may save from reversion to bush." [75] The Colonial Office approved an inquiry but firmly declined to promise assistance. The committee recommended that assistance be given to fifty-one plantations. The request was referred to the British Treasury, which was "not prepared to sanction any expenditure from Protectorate funds for this purpose." [76] The governor expressed "deeply felt disappointment" that his "considered recommendations" were refused and requested a "reconsideration." The Colonial Office, however, remained adamant. Regardless of the arguments the planters used—racial, national, or humanitarian—and regardless of whose support they mustered, the *class* interests of the metropolitan bourgeoisie prevailed. Many of the plantations reverted to bush; some survived, and others were auctioned off to Indian traders (who began to produce sugar, for which there was a large internal market).

Not only did peasant agriculture receive metropolitan support because of the nature of its commodity, cotton, but the commodity market crisis affected it less severely because of the nature of peasant agriculture. The plantations were oriented solely toward export, which tied their fortunes to fluctuations in the international capitalist market, a market they did not, and could not hope to, control. Cotton, on the other hand, was produced by small-scale growers who also produced other crops for their own use. If their export crop failed, they still had their subsistence food crops to fall back on. The *partial* subordination of peasant production to the dictates of the international capitalist market proved to be a source of strength. The crisis of 1920–1922 decided, once and for all, that Uganda was to be primarily a peasant economy.

The production of millions of peasants could not be *directly* sold on the international capitalist market; there had to be an intermediary between the small commodity producer and the metropolitan buyer. This was the small trader. He had his shop in the vicinity of the peasant farm, so he could purchase peasant products for export and sell metropolitan imports in exchange, and yet had institutionalized and regular contacts with the city, so he could resell the raw materials to the large export-import houses and purchase the consumer goods he would resell the peasant. It is to the formation of this commercial petty bourgeoisie, the *dukawallah*, that we turn now.

Notes

1. Harry Johnston, *General Report on Uganda*, July 10, 1901, Foreign Office; quoted in H. M. West, ed., *The Mailo System in Buganda*, p. 57.

2. Johnston to Salisbury, March 17, 1900, FO 2/297; quoted in A. Low and C. Pratt, *Buganda and British Overrule*, p. 94.

3. Memorandum by Johnston, No. 13, East Africa Confidential, London, March 2, 1903; included in H. M. West, ed., *The Transformation of Land Tenure in Buganda Since 1896*, p. 18.

4. Johnston to Salisbury, March 17, 1900, FO 2/297; quoted in Low and Pratt, p. 94.

5. Low and Pratt, p. 11.

6. J. H. M. Beattie, "The Nyoro," in Audrey Richards, ed., *East African Chiefs*.

7. Roscoe, *The Banyankole*, p. 210; see also Charles M. Good, *Rural Markets and Trade*, p. 176. According to Good: "Ganda agents were appointed to two Ssaza chieftainships [in Ankole] as early as 1905, and two years later 3 of 9 Ssaza posts and 22 Gombolola chieftainships were held by Ganda."

8. E. H. Winter, *Bwemba Economy*, p. 6.

9. Ibid.

10. John Middleton, "The Lugbara," in Richards, ed., p. 330.

11. *Uganda Notes*, June 1904, p. 83.

12. See *The Empire Cotton Growing Review* (journal of the Empire Cotton Growing Committee), vol. 1, no. 1 (January 1924), p. 2.

13. Address by J. R. Hutton, Chairman of the British Cotton Growing Association, before the Royal Arts Society on January 26, 1916; enclosure in CO 536/79.

14. The King's Speech, 1904; quoted in Cyril Ehrlich, "The Marketing of Cotton in Uganda," p. 32.

15. Alan Pim, *Economic History of Tropical Africa*, p. 122.

16. Cyril Ehrlich, "Cotton and the Uganda Company, 1903–1909," pp. 162–175.

17. E. W. Nye, "A Short Account of the History and the Development of Cotton in Uganda."

18. Cmd. 4910 of 1909, pp. 10–11.
19. Telegram from Chief Secretary to the P.C., Western Province, September 26, 1924; in *Report of the Ormsby-Gore Commission*, Cmd. 2387 of 1925, pp. 142–143.
20. Letter by Wallis to the Secretary of State for Colonies, January 29, 1914, p. 4, in CO 536/84.
21. The district commissioner in Mbale wrote about the difficulty of spreading cash-crop cultivation "owing to the entire indifference in money matters" so that the people saw no object in growing anything but food products." See A. G. Powesland, *Economic Policy and Labour*, pp. 8–9.
22. M. S. M. Kiwanuka, "Uganda Under the British," in B. A. Ogot and J. A. Kieran, eds., *Zamani*, p. 319.
23. *Uganda Herald*, September 1, 1933, p. 24.
24. Director of Agriculture, Memorandum on Native Coffee Production; quoted in *Uganda Herald*, September 1, 1933, pp. 23–24.
25. See particularly the writings of John Roscoe: *The Baganda, The Bagesu and Other Tribes of the Uganda Protectorate, The Northern Bantu*, and *Twenty-Five Years in East Africa*.
26. Uganda Government, *Report of the Committee of Inquiry into the Coffee Industry*, 1967, p. 2.
27. Governor Bell's Report on the Cotton Industry, Cd. 4910, p. 11.
28. Cmd. 910 of 1902, p. 3.
29. Cmd. 910 of 1902, pp. 2–3.
30. Return of Concession in the East Africa and Uganda Protectorates, Cd. 1628 of 1903.
31. Cd. 4524 of 1909, p. 5.
32. UP, *Annual Report for 1907–1908*, p. 34.
33. Foreign Office, United Kingdom Government, *Kenya, Uganda and Zanzibar*, n.d., p. 87.
34. UP, *Annual Report for 1901*, p. 122.
35. *Proceedings of the Royal Colonial Institute*, vol. 36, 1904–1905, p. 72; quoted in Powesland, p. 13.
36. *Uganda Notes*, June 1904, p. 85.
37. Governor, ESA SMP 2002/08/I/1; quoted in Powesland, p. 18.
38. Kenneth Ingham, *A History of East Africa*, p. 206.
39. See Report of the Committee of Enquiry into the Labour Situation in the U.P., UP No. 3685 of 1938, p. 16; UP, Northern Communications, p. 7; and Walter Elkan, *Migrants and Proletarians*.
40. See Powesland, p. 40; and Walter Elkan, "The Uganda Economy, 1903–1945," in V. Harlow and L. Chilver, eds., *History of East Africa*, vol. 2, p. 428.

41. UP, *Annual Report for 1911–1912*, p. 21.
42. Elkan in Harlow and Chilver, eds., vol. 2, p. 413.
43. UP, *Annual Report for 1913–1914*, p. 11.
44. UP, *Annual Report for 1915–1916*, p. 7.
45. UP, *Annual Report for 1911–1912*, p. 25.
46. Ibid., p. 21.
47. H. B. Thomas and Roger Scott, *Uganda*, p. 143.
48. UP, *Annual Report for 1916–1917*, p. 4.
49. Rise in the sterling value of the Indian rupee to a maximum of 2/8½ resulted in the introduction of the East African florin stabilized at 2/sterling. See UP, *Annual Report for 1920*.
50. Elkan, in Harlow and Chilver, eds., vol. 2, p. 414.
51. Bukona Estates Ltd. to the Colonial Secretary, April 2, 1921, in CO 536/116.
52. Figures from Nye, p. 289.
53. Thomas and Scott, p. 125.
54. D. N. Stafford to Col. Amery, 14 August 1920, in CO 536/108.
55. *Report of the Uganda Development Commission*, 1920; enclosure in CO 536/99, paragraphs 231, 232, 233.
56. Telegram from Deputy Governor to the Secretary of State for the Colonies, March 2, 1920, in CO 536/100.
57. Memorandum from the National Bank of India Ltd., to Secretary, East African Currency Board, Formill Bank, Westminster, February 3, 1921, in CO 536/116. Also see telegram from the Officer Administering the Government of Uganda to the Secretary of State for Colonies, February 25, 1920, in CO 536/100; telegram from the Governor to the Secretary of State, January 5, 1921, in CO 536/109.
58. The Officer Administering the Government of Uganda to the Secretary of State for the Colonies, No. 111, of September 5, 1914, in CO 536/70.
59. Letter from Chairman of BCGA to the Under-Secretary of State for the Colonies, February 18, 1915, in CO 536/79.
60. Letter from Chairman of BCGA to the Under-Secretary of State, Colonial Office, October 6, 1915, in CO 536/79.
61. The BCGA advanced funds to the Bombay-Uganda Syndicate, a British firm, "on condition they pay a minimum price at their ginnery," took over Messrs. Hansing's ginnery, and leased the Bukedi-Uganda Cotton and Trading Company's ginnery. See Chairman of BCGA to the Under-Secretary for the Colonies, March 9, 1915, in CO 536/79; see also No. 111 of September 5, 1914, in CO 536/70.

62. See memo to the Prime Minister, Appendix II of *Report to the Board of Trade of the Empire Cotton Growing Committee*, Cmd. 523 of 1920, London, HMSO, p. 51.

63. *Final Report of the Committee on Commercial and Industrial Policy After the War* (HMSO, London, 1918), CO 9035, p. 16.

64. Cmd. 523 of 1920, pp. 4–5; see also Appendix II, pp. 52–53.

65. Thomas and Scott, p. 132.

66. Telegram from Governor to the Secretary of State for Colonies, March 5, 1921, in CO 536/109.

67. Ibid. As one observer noted: "[The] cost of general administration per 100 inhabitants in Kenya, a white settlement territory, [was] twice that of Uganda, a native state. The exports of Uganda in 1925 were nearly twice the exports of Kenya. 87.5 percent of the value of exports from Kenya [was] consumed in Government expenditures in comparison with only 25.5 percent in Uganda." See R. Leslie Buell, "The Destiny of East Africa," pp. 11–12.

68. Enclosure in "Memorandum on the Uganda Development Commission 1920," minutes of a meeting with a deputation of Uganda planters on August 6, 1920, with the Colonial Secretary, in CO 536/106.

69. Cyril Ehrlich, in Harlow and Chilver, eds., p. 413.

70. Mabira Forest (Uganda) Rubber Co., Ltd., to the Under-Secretary of State, Colonial Office, December 21, 1920, in CO 536/106.

71. Mabira Forest Rubber Co. to the Under-Secretary of State, Colonial Office, April 11, 1916, in CO 536/83; also included is the reply from the CO.

72. Memorandum on the Financial Position of the Company in letter from the Mabira Forest Rubber Co. to the Under-Secretary of State for the Colonies, December 14, 1920, in CO 536/106; also included is the reply.

73. Telegram from Governor to Colonial Office, May 13, 1921, in CO 536/116.

74. See Petition from Ex-Soldier Settlers in Bunyoro District, enclosure in dispatch from Acting Governor Eliot to the Colonial Office, September 5, 1922, in CO 536/120; also included is the reply.

75. Telegram from Governor to Secretary of State for Colonies, January 27, 1921, in CO 536/109; also included is the reply.

76. Governor to Secretary of State, February 22, 1921, in CO 536/109; also see Governor to Secretary of State, March 21, 1921, in CO 536/110. Included is the reply from the Secretary of State.

3

Indian Capital: The Formation of a Dependent Commercial Bourgeoisie

The eventual dominance of Indian over African commerce represented a qualitative change in the very nature of both trade and production in Uganda, a change from *internal* trade that linked domestic production to domestic consumption to an *externally oriented* export-import trade that gradually divorced the two. Let us take but one example, that of Kigezi in Western Province. The Annual Report of 1930 for the district noted:

> There is no doubt that the Indians are capturing much of the trade which was formerly in the hands of natives, e.g. Katwe salt and locally caught fish. Salt is brought to Kabale by lorry and there made into traditional bundles which are retailed at 80 cents instead of the former one shilling. This acts detrimentally in two ways: (a) It is bought for cash, thus eliminating trade in the exchange of goats and sheep for salt, (b) the profits go to the Indians instead of the natives. The goat and sheep trade is thus also affected.[1]

Only a year later, the process had advanced a stage further. The Annual Report for 1931 noted that "the salt trade (with Katwe) is moribund, as it has largely passed into the hands of Indians, through the medium of their lorries. This is reflected in the *export* by the Indians of thirty-two tons of Katwe salt to Ruanda" [2] (emphasis mine). In this chapter, we shall underline the process whereby the Asian commercial bourgeoisie became

65

the principal intermediary in the imperialist exploitation of the colony.

Prior to the colonization of the East African mainland, however, the presence of Indian merchant capital was confined to the island of Zanzibar, which for centuries had been the entrepôt of the triangular trade between the East African coast, the Arabian coast, and India. By the middle of the nineteenth century, Zanzibar was the world's chief market for ivory and gum-copal,[3] as well as being an exporter of slaves.

In spite of its nearness to the commerce of the Indian Ocean, there was an almost total absence of British shipping in Zanzibar. As late as 1856, more American and Hamburg ships visited than did British ships.* And yet the chief part of Zanzibar's imports from India, Singapore, and Hamburg consisted of articles of British manufacture.[5] Obviously, the absence of British capital and shipping did not mean the absence of British interests. This was particularly so given the nature of the class that dominated the commerce of the island, the Indian merchant bourgeoisie. In 1861, Rigby explained the dominant position of this class:

> All the trade of the port is passing into the hands of the natives of India. The ivory is consigned to them from the interior; the gum-copal is purchased from the diggers by the "Banyans" residing on the coast, the entire cargoes of U.S. and Hamburg vessels are purchased by them.[6]

As long as Indian wholesale merchants and financiers monopolized Zanzibar commerce, British capital had little reason to be dissatisfied. It was not just that these merchants were under the protection of British imperialism; far more important, the markets in which Indian merchant capital had a strong base, those on the west coast of India, were already dealing in British manufactured goods. As early as 1820, the two primary commodities Indian merchants brought to the East African main-

---

* From 1855 to 1859, only 12 British ships called at Zanzibar, compared to 154 American, 97 from Hamburg, 89 from France, and 30 from Portugal, Prussia, Spain, Denmark, and Hanover.[4]

land—British iron and British printed cottons—were both imported from Bombay.[7] It was because of this that the British consuls in Zanzibar were content to follow a diplomatic policy that safeguarded and expanded the base of Indian merchant capital. This objective alliance between the British metropolitan bourgeoisie and the Indian merchant bourgeoisie in late nineteenth century Zanzibar foreshadowed the later relation between the two in the East African mainland colonies.

And yet the vast majority of the Indians who emigrated to the East African mainland in the early decades of the twentieth century were neither primarily traders nor previous residents of Zanzibar. They belonged to two different social groups: the indentured laborers and the commercial workers. Although both groups arrived at roughly the same time, the reason behind each arrival must be understood if we are to grasp their importance.

Indentured Labor

When the late-nineteenth-century "scramble for Africa" began, Britain's primary and most populous colony was India. At the same time, the peoples Britain conquered in this period all had precapitalist economies: labor was not yet a commodity. Those who practiced agriculture had access to land, while those who manufactured owned their own tools. Colonial administrators time and again recorded the unresponsiveness of the East African peasantry to wage incentives. As an official report to the Colonial Office recounted in 1904:

> Every possible means were tried to induce the natives to labour, but without avail; even under the pressure of famine in 1898–1899, nothing would pursuade them to work continuously or systematically.[8]

At the outset, when only nominal control had been established over the colonies, it was not possible to extract forced labor from the inhabitants (although the practice was introduced as early as possible, as we have seen). At the same time, slavery was not an alternative, having been abolished in British colonies. Labor had to be brought in from the outside, and for this Britain turned to India. According to Lugard:

From the overcrowded provinces of India . . . we could draw labourers, both artisans and coolies, while they might also afford a recruiting ground for soldiers and police.[9]

In 1834, the year slavery was abolished, the sugar planters of Mauritius began importing labor from Calcutta, and about seven thousand laborers were reported to have been recruited by 1837. According to an official report on emigration from India:

> There can be no doubt that in this manner indentured immigration has rendered invaluable service to those of our colonies in which, on the emancipation of the Negro slaves, the sugar industry was threatened with ruin, or in which a supply of steady labour has been required for the development of the colony by methods of work to which the native population is averse.[10]*

Thus official slavery was replaced by its disguised form.

In East Africa, the need for labor to build the Uganda Railway began the flow of Indian immigrants into the region. Consider the response by Sir John Kirk, His Majesty's Commissioner at Zanzibar, to a question put to him by a parliamentary commission established to investigate "emigration from India to the Crown Colonies":

> Q: We would be rather glad if you, in the first place, will tell us what were the circumstances under which Indian coolies were recruited for the railway.
>
> A: We began by trying native labour, but we found that we could not get enough of it, to begin with, and that it would not go on continuously; that the natives, when the rains began, had to go back to their own grounds for the purpose of cultivation. Then

---

*Between 1842 and 1870, the numbers and destination of indentured emigrants from India were as follows:[11]

Mauritius	351,401
British Guiana	79,691
Trinidad	42,519
Jamaica	15,169
Other West Indian islands	7,021
Natal	6,448
French colonies	31,346

came a time of famine owing to want of rain, and labour was almost impossible to get. Then we appealed to the Indian Government, and the greater part of the work of the railway carried on by means of Indian coolies.[12]

This importation of indentured labor began in 1895, and was at first from Karachi. In 1898 it was decided to establish at Bombay an agency to facilitate the export of both produce and labor to the East Africa Protectorate (Kenya) and Uganda.[13]

Along with the railway workers came soldiers, who were used to quell mutinies within the ranks of the Sudanese troops that had been employed for the initial colonization of East Africa.[14] As the railway advanced, there gradually developed a demand for artisans, not only for the railway itself but also for the newly established mission and government stations. Clerks, carpenters, bricklayers, blacksmiths, and gardeners—they all came from India.[15]* Because of this gradually increasing demand for semiskilled and skilled labor, the importation did not cease, as many authors have assumed,[17] with the completion of the trunk line from Mombasa to Kisumu in 1901 or with the dissolution of the Railway Committee in 1903. It in fact continued until 1922. From the 39,771 indentured laborers who came to East Africa after 1895, however, only 7,278 (or 18.3 percent) remained in 1922. The rest either died or returned home.†

---

* On the motives of those who decided to emigrate as indentured laborers, the official Committee on Emigration from India to the Crown Colonies and Protectorates had this to say in June 1910: "They go because they are uncomfortable at home and welcome any change of circumstances. They have quarrelled with their parents or their caste fellows, or they have left their homes in search of work and have been unable to find it. Many are not recruited in their own villages. The recruiters hang about bazaars and the high roads, where they pick up loiterers and induce them to accompany them to the depots and agree to emigrate, by relieving their immediate wants and by representations, no doubt often much overdrawn, of the prospects before them. The male emigrant more often than not is unaccompanied by any member of his family, and indeed, the family is frequently not even aware that he has left the country until (possibly some years afterwards) he reopens communications. . . . The Indian peasant will not leave home unless under pressure of very dire necessity."[16]

† Points of origin and numbers of indentured Indian labor emigrating to and returning from East Africa were:

Those who remained took to "petty trades." The reason was simple: the government would not sell them land for political and economic reasons.* From the outset, the thrust of colonial

*Importation of Indentured Indian Labor into East Africa,
1895–1923* [18]

Year	From Bombay	From Karachi	Total	Returning Indians
1895–1896	0	1,123	1,123	0
1896–1897	3,900	0	3,900	0
1897–1898	1,383	330	1,713	0
1898–1899	0	9,479	9,479	4,511
1899–1900	28	9,903	9,931	3,632
1900–1901	0	8,032	8,032	6,394
1901–1902	4	0	4	7,117
1902–1903	0	172	172	5,815
1903–1904	0	25	25	396
1904–1905	0	97	97	330
1905–1906	200	238	438	134
1906–1907	0	861	861	122
1907–1908	206	177	383	131
1908–1909	27	52	79	519
1909–1910	20	32	52	188
1910–1911	86	41	127	77
1911–1912	134	249	383	109
1912–1913	0	443	443	103
1913–1914	171	334	505	1,084
1914–1915	196	66	262	180
1915–1916	134	41	175	143
1916–1917	24	224	248	250
1917–1918	20	219	239	123
1918–1919	96	247	343	227
1919–1920	61	145	206	267
1920–1921	551	0	551	368
1921–1923	0	0	0	269
	7,241	32,530	39,771	32,489

* Sir John Kirk, questioned by the Committee on Emigration from India to the Crown Colonies and Protectorates:
Q. Did many of them remain in the Protectorate?
A. Not very many. A certain number remained. They were always entitled to their repatriation during six months after expiry of service; but practically even if it was exceeded the Railway never made any difficulty. But a few remained.

policy was to keep Africans in the agricultural economy and out of the marketplace—thus keeping them away from activities (such as commerce) that would give them the skill, the vision, and the opportunity to organize the colonial masses—while allocating the trading function, through administrative encouragement, to an alien community that could easily be segregated from the mass of the colonized and thus rendered politically safe. The petty bourgeoisie in the colony had for political reasons to be an ethnically *alien* petty bourgeoisie.

It was none other than Captain Lugard who explained the substance of this policy when making a case for the importation of Indians to East Africa:

> Being unaffected by the climate, much cheaper than Europeans, and in closer touch with the daily lives of the natives than it is possible for a white man to be, they would form an admirable connecting link (under the close supervision of British officers), their status being nearly on a par with natives, while their interests are entirely dependent on the Europeans. As they would establish themselves permanently, with their families, in the country, they would have a personal interest in it.[20]

At the same time, this minority would play a vital role in helping to *create* the underdeveloped exchange economy. The spread of Indian commerce would be an extension of the activities of Indian merchant capital based in Zanzibar, activities already based on the export of raw materials to metropolitan markets and the import of British manufactured goods to local markets. It was this function that the Colonial Office singled out in 1920:

> By the extension of internal commerce in which Indian traders take an active part, the natives are gradually familiarized with European products and are led to work, of their own free will, in order to find means to purchase such luxuries and conveniences.[21]

While state policy kept the African out of the marketplace,

Q. What did they remain as—as freeholders?

A. I think they all took to petty trades.

Q. That, we are told, is still the case: that the Indian who remains rather turns to being a trader than being a landowner.

A. Yes. The Government will not sell land.[19]

the Asian was made the link in the export-import exchange economy. All necessary relations between the exploiters and the exploited were mediated through this class. In return for its services, the Indian petty bourgeoisie, without being members of the ruling class, became beneficiaries of the colony's inequalities, and at the same time, like the Baganda landlords, collaborators in the colonial enterprise. While the Baganda landlords helped maintain social peace, the Indian trader extended the hold of the market, and thus of the class that controlled the terms of exchange in the market, the metropolitan bourgeoisie.

The Colonial State and the Small Entrepreneur

Trade was a significant activity in Uganda before the Indians arrived, and the vast majority of traders, large as well as small, were indigenous. What, then, was the concrete historical process that led to their replacement?

African trade was dealt a decisive blow at the very outset of colonial rule. The 1900 Agreement gave land to chiefs who had been traders. Thus assured of sizable incomes from rent, and given the long-run stability of colonial law and order, they had little reason to subject themselves to the vicissitudes of the market to seek commercial gain. Small traders, on the other hand, found structural impediments to their existence in the form of taxes, which quickly destroyed them as a class. Beginning in 1901, every trader was required to purchase a trading license, and the fee was kept high enough (around £10) to be prohibitive to any but large businesses. The purpose, as the secretary fluently stated it in response to a complaint from a British trader, was to nip the African trader in the bud:

> In regard to traders' licenses, this was meant to safeguard the genuine trader, as the small native trader could not trade or undersell the genuine trader, since he had to take out the same license. The Commissioner's object was to remove the small pettifogging traders, whose object it was to undersell the genuine trader. Do you not think that this has been attained? [22]

Those African traders who remained, therefore, did so in spite of the structural impediments and because they found room in the colonial export-import economy.

In those early days, when the peasant economy was synonymous with cotton, the cotton industry allowed breathing room
for two kinds of small entrepreneurs: the hand ginner and the
middleman. Both occupations required little capital, no more
than family labor, rudimentary technical skills, and a knowledge
of local conditions, and so were an ideal stepping-stone for
accumulating both capital and experience. At the same time, as
long as their activities remained indispensable to the export of
cotton, neither were subjected to license fees. And when licenses
were instituted, these were the first of the African traders able
to accumulate sufficient capital to buy them, set up a shop, and
keep sufficient stock.

Both opportunities were short-lived, however, as the state
quickly responded to pressure from the large-scale ginners and
declared both handginning and the work of the independent
middleman buyer illegal. The critical reasons for the colonial
state's actions were the need to ensure quality and the enormous
difficulty of supervising the activities of thousands of small
entrepreneurs.

The question of quality was not independent of the interests
of the metropolitan bourgeoisie. The cotton that Lancashire
needed was not just *any* cotton; it needed cotton of a specific
quality as a substitute for long-staple American cotton. As early
as the Lancashire cotton famine of 1861–1866, the increased use
of Indian cotton had brought the issue of quality to the fore.[23]
As the chairman of the British Cotton Growing Association
explained to the Royal Society of the Arts:

I must draw particular attention to the question of quality. The
Lancashire cotton trade is mainly an export trade, and therefore
has to meet the competition of the whole world, and there is
probably no industry which has suffered more through hostile
tariffs. So far this competition has been mainly met by producing
articles of finer and more superior quality, which were beyond the
capabilities of our competitors. The production of such articles
required not only the greatest skill on the part of the operatives
but also longer, finer, and better qualities of cotton. India, which
produces about 5 million bales, seems to be unable to grow the
quality of cotton required. Out of a total consumption of 4 million
bales, Lancashire only uses about 200,000 bales of Indian cotton,

and this solely for the coarsest cloths. Owing to the attacks of the boll weevil, the States are also unable to produce sufficient quantities of long-staple cotton. The only other country which can produce the quality required is Egypt, but the total annual production of this country is less than a million bales, and unfortunately, the cultivable land is limited in quantity and no large increase in production can be expected in the future. *The problem therefore was not only how to establish and develop new cotton fields but also to discover countries where cotton of good and suitable quality could be grown* (emphasis mine).[24]

As we have seen, Uganda was to become such a country. As the BCGA told the Colonial Office, Uganda cotton "commands a considerable premium above almost all other types of colonial grown cotton, averaging about 1d. a pound over middling American." [25]*

The colonial state's emphasis on quality was thus directly dependent on Lancashire's demand for that particular quality, and was not an attempt to produce what was technically best given the raw material structure of the Ugandan economy. In 1920, when a British capitalist proposed to start a factory in Uganda to manufacture cotton for local use, the Colonial Office referred the project to the Empire Cotton Growing Committee, which rejected it outright, primarily on the grounds that "the quality of Uganda cotton makes it more appropriate for high-class goods than for stout fabrics which are required for the local market." [28] High quality had become a reason *not to* manufacture and *to* export: export demanded a certain quality; once established, the quality justified the export. The tautology became embedded in history.

---

* By 1927–1928, according to the secretary of state for dominion affairs (responding to a question in the House of Commons), Uganda had become the largest grower of cotton in the British possessions, excluding India. According to the secretary, the five largest producers were:[26]

Uganda	138,486 (bales of 400 lbs.)
Sudan	126,115
Tanganyika	24,040
Nigeria	20,930
Union of South Africa and Swaziland	11,013

By 1933, Uganda was producing about 10 percent of world production in its class.[27]

The emphasis on quality led to a plethora of government regulations that mitigated against the existence of small-scale, technically unsophisticated enterprises. Hand gins—relatively inexpensive to purchase, able to handle only a small amount of cotton when at maximum capacity, operated by the grower and his family and therefore requiring little capital—had quickly become popular in the Buganda countryside. Not only did they introduce peasant farmers, with relative ease, into the small manufacturing sector, but they also provided a means of capital accumulation through the use of a simple technology and family labor. As the acting governor wrote the colonial secretary, although the hand gins were of "little importance to the industry," they represented "a class of trade carried on by small proprietors." In order to encourage this class, he proposed a reduction of fees on hand gins.[29] The BCGA, asked by the Colonial Office whether there should be "differentiation in favor of hand ginners," "strongly advised the discontinuance of ginning by such machines as early as possible."[30] The BCGA made it clear that hand ginning was an "unsatisfactory" method because the quality of the ginned cotton could not be easily ensured. In his instructions to the governor, the secretary of state then wrote emphatically:

> On the question of hand ginneries, there can be no doubt that in the general interest of the cotton industry it is desirable that hand ginning should ultimately be eliminated and I am anxious that nothing should be done which would tend to encourage it.[31]

Needless to say, there was no "general" interest here; there were instead two sectional interests, that of the local hand ginners and that of the metropolitan manufacturers. The latter, as sectional as any, possessed the undivided loyalty of the colonial state and thus was able to masquerade as the "general" interest. And so the 1918 Cotton Rules instituted the phased elimination of hand ginning in the colony,[32] in order, as the director of agriculture explained in a memorandum on the subject, to ensure "the reputation of Uganda cotton in Liverpool." To the Buganda Lukiko he stated:

> Cotton hand ginned in villages would be very liable to get dirty and damaged and ginned cotton should be pressed at once, when it

is practically safe from deterioration, and this can only be done at a proper ginnery. Hand gins do certainly divide seed from lint but in the hands of inexperienced people, they are bad because the native would not know whether the gin was damaging the lint or not and the people who buy cotton in Europe are very particular.[33]

One more structural impediment to small enterprise had come into being, justified, as always, on technical grounds.

Like the hand ginners, the middlemen were also a *necessary* aspect of the cotton industry in its early days. Necessary because the middlemen were the only link between hundreds of thousands of peasant growers, whose individual plots were scattered over hundreds of square miles, and a few ginners.* These buyers, requiring but a set of scales and a few hundred shillings' capital, wandered from plot to plot, setting up their scales and buying any and all the cotton offered them. At first, the colonial state and the ginners rejoiced in these few thousand African and Asian entrepreneurs who saved them from the problem of marketing. But while the presence of numerous competing middlemen—provided that the metropolitan demand for peasant cotton remained, which it did—guaranteed a free market and a relatively high price to the grower, from the ginner's point of view, these middlemen not only allowed the peasant to retain a higher share of the value of his total product than would otherwise be the case, but also themselves appropriated another part of the value, diminishing the ginner's share twice. The Buganda Chamber of Commerce wrote the governor complaining of middlemen "who are permitted to come between them [i.e., between the ginners and the growers] and who do nothing but interfere with the proper course of business," and warned:

> Under present conditions there is no security for the ginner. Every Indian in the country buys cotton where and when he likes and many natives do likewise. No company will erect a plant in any of the cotton-growing areas here, so long as these middlemen are not prevented from buying against it even up to the gates of the ginnery, or so long as the price paid to the grower is not in any way controlled.[34]

---

* When not specified, ginner refers to the large-scale mechanized ginner, not the hand ginner.

The result was the Uganda Cotton Rules of 1913, which sought to both limit the area of operation of the middlemen and to restrict their number. First, in order to eliminate the wandering buyer the rules established fixed centers that were to be "open markets," and declared buying elsewhere illegal.[35]* The ginnery and its environs were placed outside the open market, thus giving the ginners a monopoly over cotton buying in their areas.[38] Second, the rules introduced licenses (for ginners) and permits (for middlemen) that entitled the possessors to buy in the open markets.[39] Licenses were then issued free to all "substantial" firms,[40] thus excluding the small middleman, while the licensed firm could obtain any number of permits it wished at one rupee each to issue to its buyers in a particular district.†

The system backfired, however. Because of the keen competition between ginners, each ginner gave out the maximum number of permits to the middlemen, and at the same time, there was nothing to compel the middlemen to sell the cotton they bought to the ginners issuing them the permits. The 1914 amendments to the rules attempted to rectify the situation. A license fee of 150 rupees (£10) was introduced,[42] with free permits to be issued by the licensee, to whom permit holders were bound to deliver their cotton. What the market could not do, the state did, rendering the middlemen legally subservient to and economically dependent on the ginners.

But neither the ginners nor the state were satisfied with these measures since buying licenses were limited to "responsible firms" (rather than just to ginners), and the only criterion for a "responsible firm" was that it could pay the £10 fee. While the poorest of the middlemen were successfully eliminated, the

---

* In the Eastern Province, twenty-nine "open markets" (exclusive of ginneries) were gazetted in 1913.[36] During the 1918–1919 season there were seventy-five of these in Buganda and Eastern Province together. The department of agriculture, however, "found that this number was too large to reduce the operations of the speculative middlemen buyers" and so reduced the number to thirty-five.[37]

† The system was introduced in the Eastern Province in 1913; in Buganda, where the middlemen were better established, this part of the rules (Rule XII) was not introduced until 1917.[41]

trade was lucrative and new entrants were continually pouring in. By 1918 the proliferation of middlemen had led to rising prices,[43] and the state attempted to restrict licenses to ginners alone. Boustead and Clarke, a large British firm employing middlemen, made representations to the Colonial Office through their head office in London and, for a while at least, won some respite.[44] The Colonial Office instructed the governor that licenses to purchase raw cotton must be issued to anyone who could pay the specified fee.[45]

The result was the 1918 Cotton Rules. Instead of attempting to eliminate the entire class of middlemen, they concentrated on thinning their ranks to only the substantial ones. Open markets were replaced by "buying stores." Whereas the market was a large, fenced-in open space divided into plots or stalls, the buying store was a building of "certain dimensions" with an iron roof. For the first time substantial assets became a prerequisite to being a middleman, and thus to entering the cotton industry at all. As the director of agriculture informed the governor, this brought about a "large reduction in numbers of buyers and the elimination of the most unsatisfactory type," with the consequent result that "stores at posts were [henceforth] largely in the hands of ginners, or agents buying for ginners on commission, or at worst, reasonably substantial middlemen who had considerable trade interests and who had perhaps aspirations to become ginnery owners." [46]

Finally, in 1922, representatives of the Lancashire cotton interests, the Uganda ginners, and the director of agriculture met at the Colonial Office in London and resolved that "no more buying licenses be issued to new applicants." [47] The 1922 Rules faithfully legislated that a buying license could be refused "on the ground that a sufficient number of licenses in the area have already been granted." [48] The monopolistic tendencies in the industry were further consolidated; for the small entrepreneur, it was yet another setback.*

---

* While in substance this was a struggle between middlemen and ginners, its political expression was most often in *racial* terms. This was because, even at the time of World War I, the ginners tended to be Europeans and the middlemen Africans and Asians; class domination appeared as racial domination. In

The fact was that the middlemen's services were no longer necessary to ensure the collection of cotton for export. The system did not need them, as it did the ginners and the growers. The state was not constituted to represent their interests, but to represent those of the metropolitan bourgeoisie, to whom it guaranteed a supply of raw materials. To be sure, once in a while the *national* question did come to the fore. Substantial British middlemen, like Boustead and Clarke, did, through the auspices of a metropolitan head office, gain moments to breathe, but only moments. In the final analysis, the middlemen were destroyed, not as a race but as a class—regardless of whether they were black, brown, or white. By 1923, the Governor's Inquiry into the Cotton Industry was told by representatives of the BCGA that in nine cases out of ten the buyers were paid on commission by a ginner and that the genuine middleman was "a rare avis." [53] In 1938, the Commission of Inquiry into the Cotton Industry reported that there were only about forty-four independent middlemen, whose total purchases amounted to 2.7 percent of the crop.[54]

Buganda, where there were many African middlemen, the director of agriculture deplored the proliferation of middlemen as leading to a state of affairs which "shielded them from the usual month's labour per annum," thus "withdrawing them from the labour market" and making of them "rogues and vagabonds": every African trader was one less African producer.[49] In the Eastern Province, where the middlemen were almost solely Indian, the ginners centered their attacks on the "unscrupulous Indian traders." [50] The middlemen's interests were also organized and articulated in racial terms by the Buganda Lukiko and the East Africa Indian Association.[51]

It was only the colonial state that viewed the contradiction simply and purely in class terms. The governor wrote the secretary of state of the need "to eliminate this somewhat unfair competition of men who simply buy in order to resell without taking any substantial part in the process of growing, preparing and marketing the cotton." [52] "Men who simply buy in order to resell"—in other words, traders, or, at best, the merchant capitalists (as opposed to industrial capitalists), that class of people who appropriate a part of the economic surplus not in the process of production but in that of circulation. They were parasitic even so far as the *existing* order was concerned. Even though the governor posed the issue in terms of productive and unproductive capital, the fact was that the class that dominated *within* the underdeveloped economy of Uganda was big unproductive capital, the commercial bourgeoisie. But unlike the middlemen, the services of this class were necessary to ensure the export of raw materials to the metropole and the import of manufactured goods.

The Petty Bourgeoisie

While the trading licenses, the laws against hand ginning and against the independent middleman's activities, applied to the small Indian trader as much as to the small African trader, the former increased in numbers precisely because in the early part of the century he was *not* an independent trader. The legend of the *dukawallah*—the twentieth-century personification of the Puritan ethic, with no capital but ample initiative—contains an important distortion: the early *dukawallah* was a commercial worker or a businessman's agent, rather than an independent entrepreneur.

We have seen that by the time colonial rule was established in Uganda, trade on the East African coast was controlled by a few wealthy Indian merchants resident in Zanzibar, who had set up a string of establishments running from the coast into East Africa. The best known of these was Allidina Visram, whose "empire" extended from Bombay through Mombasa and Baga-moyo to the East African interior.[55] * He followed the British into Uganda and, as the secretary to the governor noted, "opened a store at nearly every government station." [57] By 1900 he had branches at Kampala, Jinja, Kisumu in Kenya, and all along the River Nile. By the time he died, in 1916, Visram had 240 shops in East Africa and the Congo.[58]

At first, as the wholesaler extended his operations he encouraged his poor relations from India to join him as assistants to run his shops; later, as prosperity became plenty, the circle of relations expanded to the community of caste or sect fellows.† The wholesaler also supplied and bought from small but semi-independent *dukawallahs* who acted as his agents. He supplied them with a variety of imports which they sold in return for local produce that he marketed internationally. The agent was tied to the wholesaler not as an employee but by chains of credit. More often than not he too was a caste fellow who had been encouraged to migrate from India to East Africa. As Sir Charles Eliot reported in 1902:

* Other important wholesalers in Uganda were Adamjee Alibhoy and M. G. Puri.[56]

† Here I am referring to Hindu castes (e.g., Patels, Lohanas) and to Muslim sects (e.g., Ismailis, Sunnis). I will henceforth refer to both as castes.

At present, one merchant, Allidina Visram, supplies almost all the small traders with trade goods . . . [and those] traders may repay him by monthly installments, while trading under his name.[59]

Family or caste relations were thus a source of cheap labor. Short of returning to India—and given that the state would not sell them land—these commercial workers had little alternative but to accept the conditions of labor and the terms of remuneration dictated by the wholesaler. The emigration of the nonindentured from India to East Africa was not in search of, but in response to, opportunities.

Once an assistant had saved enough wages or an agent sufficient income to establish his own *duka,* he followed the beaten path. He bought a license and supplies and set up shop. If his operations expanded, he too turned to his caste fellows in India for a source of labor power (shop assistants). So, while Nasser Virjee came to East Africa as an assistant to Allidina Visram in the 1890s, by 1910 he had established his own shop and was setting up branches and importing assistants himself. Karmali Alibhai, brought as an assistant by Nasser Virjee in the 1910s, had by the 1920s set himself up as a *dukawallah.*

This pattern of emigration and the subsequent formation of an Indian petty bourgeoisie meant that the vast majority of the traders came from a small number of castes or sects. Even as late as 1954, while Indian holders of trade licenses in Uganda belonged to thirty-two different castes or sects, nearly 80 percent of them—4,011 out of 5,819—came from three groups: the Ismailis, the Lohanas, and the Patidars.[60] And it was also the case that these were the most effectively organized castes among the Uganda Indians, reflecting, in their demands, activities, and leadership, the interests of their trading members. The remaining castes, made up of nontrading artisanal, clerical, or other working families, confined their organization and activities to the religious sphere.

To be sure, the first organization of the Indian petty bourgeoisie was not as a caste association but as an East Africa-wide political organization, the East Africa Indian National Congress, which was formed in Mombasa in 1914. The attempts by Kenya settlers to fashion that colony's political economy along the

South African model, and the threat of their success spreading to Uganda and Tanganyika, had galvanized petty Indian capital throughout East Africa into coming together and associating politically. The Congress conducted its most intense political struggles in the period between 1919 and 1924, demanding a common electoral role with Europeans.[61] The result was the Devonshire White Paper of 1923, entitled "On the Indian Question," which both rejected the demand for a common role and rebuffed the settler's aspiration for political autonomy and proclaimed the general principle of "the paramountcy of African rights." Since the content of "African rights" was to be determined by the Colonial Office, the declaration in fact proclaimed the paramountcy of the metropolitan bourgeoisie over settler capital. That same metropolitan bourgeoisie, through the Ormsby-Gore Commission of 1925–1926, guaranteed the Indians that Uganda would not pursue the policy of segregation followed in Kenya, and maintained that Tanganyika was protected from such discrimination by the terms of the League of Nations mandate.

The result of this series of events was that by 1926 there no longer existed a material base for an East Africa-wide unity of Indian capital. That same year saw the formation of the Central Council of Indian Associations of Uganda and of the Indian Association in Dar es Salaam; the latter had previously been a local voice of the powerful East Africa Indian National Congress and now became a central organization for Tanganyika. The Central Council of Indian Associations of Uganda was also an organization of Indian capital, but was geographically limited to Uganda. According to H. S. Morris:

> The men of the "upper classes," who were responsible for the formation and management of the Council, were drawn from a small group of prosperous merchants, most of whom were engaged in the cotton and coffee trades.[62]

The first caste organization beyond the sphere of religious or cultural activities took place among the Ismailis, a sect highly centralized under the spiritual and political leadership of the Aga Khan, who lived outside Africa. It had an internal system of taxation which yielded financial resources that, though communal in form, were in actuality controlled by the Aga Khan. As early as 1905, the Aga Khan, in response to a group of seceders who demanded "community control over communal property," had appointed three of his followers to act as his agents in matters of land and property in East Africa. An Ismailia Council was formed in Zanzibar to protect the Aga Khan's material interests. In 1924, when the Uganda government tried to set up a landholding corporation for *all* Indian charitable, religious, and educational properties, it became necessary for the Aga Khan, if he was to maintain personal control over communal assets, to get state recognition of communal property. Under his direction, an Ismailia Provincial Council was set up in Uganda, with similar bodies in Kenya and Tanganyika. Its members were selected by the Aga Khan, who also supervised much of their work.[63]

As Morris has shown, it was the success of the Ismailis in defending and representing "community interests" before the state—particularly in securing state land and monetary grants to establish communal educational and social services—that prompted the rest of the Indian petty bourgeoisie to begin to organize as caste associations in order to secure state assistance for their own children's education and welfare. Equally important was the willingness of the state to grant them recognition, and thus resources, as caste associations. Just as state assistance to African education was mediated through the missionaries so that it might have a religious basis,* so state assistance to Indian education was mediated through the petty bourgeoisie organized in religiously based caste associations. The establishment of these caste associations was thus a response to the traders' need to organize their relations with the state.

The politics of the Indian petty bourgeoisie was the politics of caste associations personalized as the politics of individual leaders. They coincided with the desire of the colonial state to reduce the conduct of politics to personal ambition, and thus to personal (or communal or tribal) rivalries. The individualization of politics meant that the state singled out a few individuals of wealth and culture who were to be recognized as community

---

* See Chapter 6.

representatives. An intricate and well-understood system of patronage existed, with an invitation to a "sundowner" at the governor's mansion as the highest reward. Politics became the glorification of rivalries between the affluent few who had been singled out by the colonial authorities.

In spite of this veneer of culture and respectability, the politics of the Indian petty bourgeoisie remained the politics of the marketplace. It was the political embodiment of the vision of the successful trader who must realize his objective position as that of a middleman, of an agent of exchange who cannot in the long run determine the terms of exchange, who to survive must understand the vagaries of the market and learn to bend his operations in harmony with these changes. The Indian petty bourgeoisie was not a section of the ruling class. It could not expect long-term protection from the colonial state; neither, unlike the African petty bourgeoisie, could it expect to lead a national political movement and aspire to state power. It was rather like the nineteenth-century French petty bourgeoisie that Marx characterized in *The Eighteenth Brumaire*: truly a *middle* class, wedged in between two contending classes, conscious that all that belonged to it was the present, not the future. Indian politics—ambivalent, expedient, ritualized, opportunistic—was the political expression of this highly precarious and insecure objective position. Theirs was the politics of an objectively alien class.

There was one exception to this short-run, opportunistic politics: the Uganda Action Group, formed in early 1960, discarded the racial form of petty bourgeois Indian politics and expressed itself in liberal rhetoric, while attempting to carve for itself a niche in the nationalist movement. The objective base of Indian liberalism was the Indian bourgeoisie, a social grouping of businessmen and industrialists. Although it did not control state power, it was the dominant class in the Ugandan economy by 1960, with a long-run vision that stemmed from its strength in the economy. It is to the historical development of this bourgeoisie that we must turn now.

The Bourgeoisie

The Indian bourgeoisie was located structurally within the processing industries—first cotton ginning, and later coffee processing. Its development was within the cotton ginning industry, which in its early years was dominated by British capital, and only later came under the control of Indian capital. An historical analysis of its development shows the different phases in the development of, and contradiction between, British and Indian capital over control of the industry. Such an analysis also brings to the fore the role of the colonial state in the resolution of this contradiction, and thus further underlines its *class* character.

1. THE ENTRY OF BRITISH CAPITAL: 1906–1916

Grown on thousands of widely scattered small peasant farms throughout the southern half of the Protectorate, all the cotton had to be channeled to the ginneries. Since roughly two-thirds of the seed-cotton produced was "a waste product of no economic value," [64] there was an enormous difference between the cost of transportation of ginned and unginned cotton.* Further, long-distance transportation of unginned cotton increased the chances of its quality being damaged by rain, especially because long distances could only be covered by porters carrying headloads. The establishment of ginneries close to the centers of cultivation was a necessity.

The first power ginnery was established by a British firm, the Uganda Company, Ltd., in 1906.† As cotton production in the

---

* The cotton gin separates the lint from the seed. The lint is later pressed into bales and exported.

† The Uganda Company was the "industrial arm" of the Church Missionary Society. Its list of directors read like an individual representation of the various social forces that constituted the imperial movement. In the words of an apologist for the company, Cyril Ehrlich: "It was at this stage that a remarkable group of men appeared on the scene. They were led by two members of a family whose name is honoured in the history of Africa [sic!]. A distinguished ancestor [Sir Thomas Fowell Buxton, 1786–1845] had been created a baronet in 1840 in recognition of his work for the abolition of slavery; and they combined his philanthropic interest in what was still the 'Dark Continent' with some experience of business. Mr. [later Sir] Thomas Fowell Victor Buxton was the

Protectorate grew in volume and improved in quality, a number of other European firms arrived.[67] By 1914 there were already seven metropolitan-based firms—five British, one French, and one German.[68] That same year the BCGA entered the field.[69]

2. THE ENTRY OF INDIAN CAPITAL: 1914–1918

By this time a new figure had appeared on the scene: rising from the ranks of trade, purchasing but one ginnery through the pooled contributions of many collaborators, Allidina Visram established the first Indian-owned ginnery in partnership with a number of less substantial merchants.[70] Visram's agents, already placed around the country, added cotton buying to their multiple activities.

The beginning of the war and the break in shipping between Uganda and Liverpool provided the Indian ginner with his real opportunity. In the 1914–1915 season, when the cotton crop lay unsold in the fields, the governor urged one and all to buy lest the grower be discouraged from planting for the next season.[71] A number of Indian traders came forward, bought the seed at low prices, and shipped it to Bombay and Japan. The quality found immediate favor in both places, where the local textile industries were going through structural transformations, shifting from the production of coarse cloth to fine counts, and were thus in search of long-staple, fine cotton.*

The immediate result was twofold: capital flowed into Ug-

President of the Anti-Slavery and Aborigines Protection Society and was also the treasurer of the C.M.S. His cousin, Alfred Fowell Buxton, was a well-known London banker. Other members of the group included Henry Carus Wilson, who had spent some time in Uganda, and Henry Edward Miller, Managing Director of an export and import commission firm. They had seen Borup's correspondence and met him in London during his first leave. They were keen to support any scheme which might help to develop Uganda and its peoples." [65]

Prior to 1906, the cotton crop was dealt with either by hand gins or was sent to the British East Africa Corporation's ginnery at Kisumu (Kenya) to be ginned.[66]

* Ehrlich[72] quotes Vera Anstey (*The Economic Development of India*, Table XIC, p. 620) and G. Allen (*A Short Economic History of Modern Japan)* to show the increase of cotton cloth production in India and Japan. Though the figures themselves do not reflect it, the increase was partly qualitative in that it included a turn toward the production of fine counts.

anda from Bombay textile interests and, in conjunction with a multitude of local cash subscribers—various Indians who in the past had been employees of, or commissioned buyers for, European ginning firms in Uganda—supported a second Indian ginnery.[73] At the same time, the BCGA, anxious to prevent the Uganda crop from being diverted from Lancashire, proceeded to buy the entire crop from Indian ginners, thereby guaranteeing them a profitable and secure market.[74] When charged by other European ginners with "reckless and short-sighted support of Indians," and with "steadily creating the position in which these various Indians could be independent of further support from the Europeans," [75] the BCGA responded that the Indians would have had little problem with capital anyway, since the National Bank of India—a British bank founded and based on Indian trade—had decided to give them all-out support.[76]

The problem of money capital, however, was solved once and for all with the arrival in Uganda of Narandas Rajaram and Co., Ltd., a well-known Indian firm with vast monetary resources and considerable experience in the cotton industry. Established

Indian Cotton Textile Industry

Year	Looms (thousands)	Numbers employed in mills (thousands)	Spindles (thousands)
1900–1901	40.5	156.4	4,942
1913–1914	96.7	260.8	6,621
1918–1919	116.1	306.3	6,651
1925–1926	154.6	370.6	8,403

Japanese Textile Industry

Year	Spindles (thousands)	Output of cotton yarn (million pounds)
1903	1,381	317
1913	2,415	607
1920	3,814	727
1925	5,186	975

in 1860, this firm had become the first Indian enterprise to be represented in the Bombay Chamber of Commerce.[77] Beginning by sending a representative to buy and export lint cotton to Bombay, Narandas Rajaram rapidly began to acquire ginneries in Uganda. By 1918, it had become a powerful force in the cotton industry, at one stroke ending the domination of a few English firms and simultaneously forging a strong link between the Uganda and the Bombay market.

3. CONTRADICTION BETWEEN BRITISH AND INDIAN CAPITAL: 1918–1928

The contradiction between British and Indian capital was in substance between better-established capital that was striving to restrict entry into the market and new capital that was attempting to break into that same market. One was striving for monopoly, the other for free trade. In the decade after the war, this contradiction appeared as a racial conflict between British and Indian ginners.

Along with Narandas Rajaram came other Indian ginners, and at the same time the flow of Indian capital to finance the operations of the local Indian ginners increased. By 1918, the governor felt compelled to telegraph the secretary of state:

> Feel it is necessary to state plainly that industry is now so assured that all cotton purchased this season will be sold at full prices whether the three London companies purchase any or not.[78]

The three London companies—the British East Africa Corporation, the Uganda Company, Ltd., and the Uganda Cotton Buying and Ginning Co., Ltd.—faced with keen and deadly competition from Indian capital, turned to the state for political assistance. Their troubles, initially confined to competition from the middlemen, were now further aggravated. Pleading to the Colonial Office that "they may be driven out of the industry," [79] they asked for a legal arrangement whereby they could buy the entire Uganda crop at a price fixed so as to guarantee them at least a minimum profit.[80] The Colonial Office, however, feared that the price would be "so low that . . . it would probably deter [the grower] from sowing cotton again," [81] and it was also clear that the Indian ginner was "able to offer a high price." [82] It thus reasoned that "the main point is the grower. Last year it is perfectly certain that he did not get nearly enough for his cotton, and further, that he is quite aware of the fact." [83]

This argument over minimum prices, which was to recur time and again during the colonial era, provided the grower his only protection against intensified exploitation. Unlike his counterpart, the industrial or agricultural worker, the grower was neither separated from his means of production, nor producing solely for exchange. Every cotton-growing family devoted a few acres to subsistence production, to cultivating bananas and vegetables for their own consumption. They did not have to produce any more cash crops than were necessary to secure cash for taxes. Thus, partly self-sufficient and partly shielded from the tyranny of the market, growers could limit what they produced should the terms of exchange be too unattractive.

So far as the state was concerned, the *supply* of cotton was the first priority, and so the minimal interests of the grower had to be protected. Next came the ginners' interests, while the middlemen were quite dispensable. In the words of the Colonial Office:

> The attitude taken up here as a result of the discussion in August 1922 was that the first importance must be attached to the interests of the grower and of the cotton itself, and that the ginners, who are as essential a part of the industry as the growers, must come second. . . . Our review was that the ginner should be protected from undue competition of the middleman, and, as a result, that the grower should be protected against undue price cutting on the part of the ginners.[84]

To give "first importance" to the grower *as opposed to* the ginner was just another way of saying that the interests of the metropolitan bourgeoisie would have priority over those of local ginning capital, even if British.

The British ginners' problems were caused by their costs of production. Hoping to eliminate the middlemen, they had begun constructing their ginneries at inland "centers of production." With the arrival of new and more powerful ginners from India, this solution turned into a problem.[85] The Indian firms built substantial ginneries at the port, and the inland ginneries had smaller capacities and higher working expenses. As Narandas Rajaram explained to the Colonial Office, while he spent under 5 cents per pound of cotton for ginning and pressing, the English ginner spent 10 to 12 cents per pound.[86]

While the state had been unwilling to grant the British ginners monopoly control over supplies of cotton, when the British ginners came around a second time to request that an area of land around the ginnery be legally declared under the buying monopoly of the ginnery, the state obliged. While the BCGA asked for a ten-mile radius,[87] the state agreed to five miles.[88]

For the large Indian ginneries this posed an immediate dilemma. While the inland ginnery could take full advantage of the new law, for the port ginner the circle became a semicircle and its throughput was disproportionately decreased (since its capacity was much larger). Protesting vehemently to the Colonial Office against such manifestly partial treatment, Narandas Rajaram warned in no uncertain terms:

> We shall not in any event retire from the cotton trade. . . . We shall have to finance the small Indian ginner upcountry who in most cases will be a successful middleman and once these men get a firm with capital to back them I make bold to say there wouldn't be a European ginner left in the country—in two years time.[89]

Thus began the proliferation of the middleman ginner, a local Indian financed from India. The process was aided by the structure of the industry, which made entry possible at various levels, with varying amounts of capital. The middleman ginner could either finance his ginnery himself, or purchase it with a loan from a large ginner, or simply be a paid agent of the large ginner. In all three cases, he sold lint to the large ginner, who exported it.* The rise of the middleman ginner meant a dramatic increase in the number of ginneries. From 11 in

---

* As Banadali Jaffer, a middleman ginner with two ginneries in Buganda, told the Uganda Cotton Ginners' Association, he had £10,000 in cash but still could not expect to export himself. He thus sold all his cotton to Narandas Rajaram.[90] Mr. Kalidas, another middleman ginner, had financed one ginnery himself, but for the second was financed by Mr. Candole of Madhavji Dharamsi and Co., to whom he sold all his cotton for export.[91]

1912–1913, 19 in 1915–1916, and 42 in 1918–1919, the number jumped to 74 in 1921 and 176 in 1926.[92]

The birth and proliferation of middlemen ginners provided the most prosperous among the Indian petty bourgeoisie with a way of entering the ginning industry on the processing side, and then to accumulate enough capital to become independent of the large ginner. The same process that had brought the wholesale trader's agent or assistant into Uganda and permitted him to become an independent trader in a few years repeated itself in another sector of the economy.

Once again, it took state action to check the proliferation of middlemen ginners. In 1920, as a result of pressure from established ginners, Chief Justice Carter informed the secretary of state that pending the return of the governor he proposed "as a general rule" to refuse approval to all applications for ginneries unless recommended by the director of agriculture.[93] In 1922, a lawyer representing fourteen Indian ginners complained to the colonial secretary that the government was hesitating to give licenses to his clients, despite the fact that all fourteen were already ginners, men of capital and familiar with the cotton trade.[94] In his exhaustive report to the secretary of state on the cotton industry in 1923, the governor questioned "whether there is any advantage to be gained by the further competition of new ginneries, which may result in the overcapitalization of the industry." [95] Overcapitalization was the watchword. As to what this meant, the governor was quite candid:

> I adopt the . . . point of view . . . that, if it is necessary to extend to an existing ginnery protection under the 5-mile limit against the buying post or buying center, it is not less necessary to accord the same measure of protection against the new ginnery coming into operation, even though Government is not committed to the principle by any past undertaking. . . .[96]

The governor was simply issuing a reminder that the state was not a neutral referee but an interested party, that it had backed the established ginner before and that it planned to do so consistently.

The secretary of state responded by bringing government officials and ginners' representatives together on a Cotton

Control Board, leaving to it the question of deciding whether or not to permit new entrants into the industry.[97] The verdict was given in the report of the attorney-general on the Cotton Ordinance of 1926: "Stated in briefest terms, the approved policy of the Government is to restrict the number of ginneries in any area in accordance with the cotton-producing capacity of that area." [98]

That same year an African applicant—a Muganda landlord who wanted to erect a ginnery on his own site—was rejected by the Cotton Control Board "on grounds that there were already too many ginneries in the country." [99]* But the point was that whatever the number of ginneries, the profits reigning in the ginning sector remained extremely high, attracting additional capital investment; furthermore, the official ban on constructing new ginneries had boosted the price of existing ones far above their costs of construction. It was a monopoly price aimed at securing a monopoly profit. From 1926 on, no one was able to enter the ginning industry except by buying an already existing ginnery. There were 176 working ginneries in 1926, 177 in 1927, 146 in 1928, and 150 in 1929.[100] By 1926, the structure of the cotton industry was a monopoly structure and its most important guarantor was the state.

By 1926, however, the dominance of British capital had been successfully challenged by Indian capital. As the Ormsby-Gore Commission of 1925 noted, out of a total of 114 ginneries of all sizes, 100 were owned by Indians,[101] and some of the remainder were Japanese. Also, as the following list indicates, the British were not even dominant when small, family-managed enterprises were excluded (that is, those owning less than two ginneries).† The companies owning two or more ginneries in Uganda and their capital bases were:[102]

---

* As we shall see in the next chapter, by 1928 the attractiveness of landholding had drastically diminished in Buganda. Numerous landlords went into commerce and their sons into the professions. Had they not been barred from constructing ginneries, those with sufficient capital—and there were quite a few—would certainly have entered the ginning industry, given its lucrative returns.

† I am aware that ownership of ginneries does not necessarily imply control. In the absence of statistics on the proportion of the cotton crop handled by particular ginneries, it is the only available indicator.

British (capital based in Britain)
Uganda Company 8
British East Africa Corporation 6
BCGA 5
Margach and Margdi 4
East Africa Ginneries 5
Uganda Buying and Ginning Company 3
  Total ginneries 31

British-Indian (British capital based in India)
Bombay-Uganda Company 7

Indian (capital based in India)
Narandas Rajaram and Company, backed by Sir Purshotamdas Thackordas 8
Nakasero Trading Company, Singo-Central Office, and Mubende Cotton Trading Company, all financed by the Mafatlal Gaganlal group of textile industries in India 6
S. C. Parikh and Company and Uganda Cotton Union, both financed by Mafatlal and C. Parikh group of industries in India 7
Uganda Commercial Company, financed by the Sir Homi Mehta group of industries in India; later partly financed by Toyo Menkwa Kabushiki Kaisha of Japan 6
Kampala General Agency, financed by the Ambalal Sarabhai group of industries in India 7
  Total ginneries 34

Indian-Ugandan (Indian capital based in India)
Vithaldas Haridas and Company, later Muljibahai Madhvani and Company 8
Nanji Kalidas Mehta, financed partly by Mathurdas Gokuldas, the one-time cotton king of Bombay, until his liquidation in 1924–1925 6
Damondar Jinabhai 4
Jinja Cotton Buying and Ginning Company 3
Jamal Walji 3
  Total ginneries 24

British-Ugandan (British capital based in Uganda)
Foster Brothers 3

Japanese (capital based in Japan)
Toyo Menkwa Kabushiki Kaisha Ltd. 6
Ramdas Khimji (5) and Iserdas Bhogilal (1), both financed by Gosho Kabushiki Kaisha Ltd. 6
  Total ginneries 12

The primary issue in the ginning industry became the dominance of Indian capital and entry of the Japanese. The decision by the British East Africa Corporation to withdraw entirely brought the issue to the fore. An enterprise called the British Cotton Corporation (BCC), managed by Mr. Cox, a past manager of the BEAC, and financed by "Lancashire and banking interests," [103] was formed in late 1926 in England. The director of the BCC, Mr. Llewellyn, wrote the Colonial Office that "if the [cotton] industry is to be consolidated on economic and British lines, the present system of ownership should be superseded on the lines of our proposals." [104]*

The BCC proposed that all ginneries in Uganda be national-ized by the government, that compensation (£1.5 million) be paid by the British treasury, and that the BCC be appointed as government agents charged with managing the ginning side of the industry.[107] The danger, as the BCC saw it, was not just that the industry "was rapidly passing out of British control," but "that a real and serious menace exists in the activities of the Japanese in Uganda." [108] The Japanese concerns, involved in Uganda through either the direct ownership of ginneries or the financing of Indian middlemen ginners, included the two listed above, as well as the Nippon Menkwa Kabushiki Kaisha (Japanese Cotton Trading Co., Ltd.), which had entered the cotton trade in the interim. Significantly, these comprised the "big three" importers of raw cotton into Japan, handling some 80 percent of total imports. The danger of Japanese competition was further enhanced by the Japanese government's annual £40,000 subsidy to Osaka Shoresen Kaisha, which ran a monthly shipping service to the East Coast of Africa.[109]

The most obvious constraint on any open discrimination against Japanese trade was legal. At the turn of the century the British government had ratified the Congo Basin Treaties (the Berlin Act of 1885 and the Brussels Act of 1890), prohibiting any discriminatory commercial practices either for or against any of

---

* While its operating costs would be financed by Messrs. D. Zoete and Gordon, one of the biggest financial trusts in London,[105] the corporation wrote: "It is unnecessary for us to say that government sympathy is of the greatest importance, as also how best this can find practical expression." [106]

the signatories.[110] The Congo Basin Treaties had been superseded after the war by the Convention of St. Germain-en-Laye, which included the same antidiscriminatory clause, and was signed by Japan as well.[111] There was to be an "open door" to all capitalist powers to the territories covered by these agreements, and these included Uganda—unless Britain chose to violate the treaties.

But before any such drastic step could be taken, it was necessary to size up the extent of the Japanese danger. And it was here that the governor disagreed with the "urgent warnings" of the British Cotton Corporation and saw in their shrill voices nothing but a reflection of their particular interests. As he told the Colonial Office when called for a personal consultation to discuss the proceedings of a meeting held between the Colonial Office, the BCC and their city financiers, it was "more likely that Indians would obtain control over the industry in Uganda rather than Japanese." [112] India, furthermore, was a part of the Empire; Japan was not.

The argument now focused on the question of the destination of Uganda cotton, and how important it was that it reach Lancashire. Since the shipping crisis during World War I, Bombay had been an important destination for Uganda cotton, and from consuming less than 1 percent of Uganda's export in 1914–1915, it became, by 1921, the market for over half. In addition, even cotton destined for Lancashire often went through Bombay. As the 1923 Governor's Inquiry into the Cotton Industry discovered,[113] it was more expeditious to ship via Bombay because of the more regular steamship service over both sea routes. Furthermore, freight from Kilindini in Kenya to Liverpool cost Shs. 96/- per ton dead weight, while from Bombay to Liverpool it only cost Shs. 50/80; the difference of 45/20 provided considerable margin to pay the Kilindini–Bombay freight cost. Also, during the ten-day transit it was possible to effect a more satisfactory sale: if the Liverpool market were better then, the cotton could be sent onward; if not, it could be offloaded at Bombay. The figures quoted in the accompanying table therefore exaggerate the position of India as the ultimate destination of the cotton exported since they are based on the destination of cotton given at the time of loading on the Kenya docks.

Destination of Uganda Cotton as Percent of Total Cotton Exports

Year	To United Kingdom	To India
1906–1907	83	3
1907–1908	90	0–1
1908–1909	71	1
1909–1910	75	3
1910–1911	77	0–1
1911–1912	80	0–1
1912–1913	80	0–1
1913–1914	75	0–1
1914–1915	73	1
1915–1916	74	0–1
1916–1917	62	30
1917–1918	67	33
1918–1919	51	49
1919–1920	66	29
1920–1921	62	32
1921–1922	37	62
1922–1923	29	70
1923–1924	42	56
1924	35	64

Source: Ehrlich, *The Marketing of Cotton in Uganda*, Table 2, p. 150. (Based on annual reports of the Department of Kenya and Uganda.)

At this point we may recall that at the time of the plantation crisis in 1920–1922, there were two sections of the metropolitan bourgeoisie that had supported the production of cotton: the Lancashire textile industry and banking capital, particularly the National Bank of India, Ltd. The National Bank of India, a British bank whose operations were based on the Indian trade, expanded its scope to include within its fold the growing Uganda–India cotton trade. It therefore remained the principal section of the metropolitan bourgeoisie backing the interests of Indian capital in the Uganda ginning industry.

During the crisis, Lancashire was most anxious to keep

Uganda as a future producer of long-staple cotton; at the same time, it showed little interest in consuming Uganda's *existing* production. While the government was trying to keep cotton production up by ensuring the peasant a high enough price, in 1920 Major Leggett of the British East Africa Corporation (the agents of BCGA in Uganda) was writing to the Federation of British Industries complaining of Lancashire's lack of interest in buying the current supply of Uganda cotton:

> You are, of course, well acquainted with the great efforts that have been made during recent years at the instance and on the exaltation of the Lancashire cotton industry, strongly endorsed by the Imperial Government, towards stimulating the utmost possible increase in the quantity of cotton grown within the British Empire. The supplies from America and other existing sources were stated to be inadequate to the needs of the cotton industry and the need for the growing of more and more cotton, especially of the better quality, has been widely advertized to be a patriotic duty as well as sound business. The cotton-growing campaign included many assertions that good demand existed and would continue for all cotton that could be grown within the Empire, especially of cotton qualities superior to middling America stock.
>
> The present position, which we can only describe as highly anomalous, is that the efforts made by the Colonial Office, the Uganda Government, and private enterprise, to increase the growth of cotton in Uganda have been amazingly successful but that the demand for the product itself by the Lancashire cotton interests has been for several months, and still is, practically nil.[114]

These several months stretched into years. Replying to claims by British ginners that shipments to India were "not exactly welcomed," Messrs. Narandas Rajaram argued that these very shipments had been "the salvation of the Uganda crop." [115] The National Bank of India wrote the Colonial Office reminding them that "nearly all the 1920 crop is lying in Liverpool unsold and finds no buyers, and the same fate would seem to await the 1921 crop now in the course of being brought to the market." [116] For Lancashire, the Uganda crop was a form of long-term insurance, "eagerly sought" only when supply of American cotton ran short or dry; otherwise, it was neglected. But the

Uganda crop could be an effective insurance only if in the short run that same crop could find a market other than Lancashire but under the political control of the British state. Such a market was India. Thus the Board of Trade wrote the Colonial Office that it was only necessary to "limit cotton exports to Empire destinations." The Empire Cotton Growing Committee was quite blunt in its insistence that the "prohibition of export of cotton from Uganda to India was unthinkable." [117] It was gradually becoming clear that it was in the interest of Lancashire that the export of Uganda cotton to India be guaranteed. At the end of its investigation on the question of the destination of Uganda cotton, the Colonial Office concluded: "There can be . . . no doubt that, from the point of view of internal as well as imperial policy, the outlet to India must be safeguarded." [118]

It was now clear that attempts by the British Cotton Corporation to secure the reorganization of the ginning industry along "economic and British lines" represented the interests of a few British businessmen (the BCC), rather than the *general* interests of the metropolitan bourgeoisie: both Lancashire and London banking capital were opposed to the scheme,[119] as were the larger companies in Uganda, which showed no "signs of interest" in it.[120]

Just at this time—to be precise, in March 1928—the governor telegraphed the colonial secretary informing him that ginners in Buganda had formed an association with a view to reducing both the number of ginneries and the cost of operating them,[121] a "reorganization" that could be brought about without affecting the destination of the cotton. The Colonial Office immediately resolved to grant the association the two guarantees it had earlier promised the BCC: (1) no further ginneries or markets would be allowed in the area covered by the association, and (2) no licenses would be granted to ginneries erected on freehold or existing estates in the area.[122] In other words, the political power of the state would be used to guarantee conditions that would secure a monopoly for the established ginners. Meanwhile, the Colonial Office wrote the BCC of its final decision:

Mr. Amery [the colonial secretary] has come to the conclusion that it is desirable that any necessary reduction in the number of ginneries in Uganda should be brought about by natural process of competition or by reorganisation from within the industries. In the circumstances he has decided, with the full concurrence of the Governor of Uganda, that the Protectorate Government should not cooperate in any such scheme as that which has been put forward by the Corporation, and the Acting Governor is being informed accordingly.[123]

It is to the content and basis of this "reorganization" that we turn now.

4. THE DECADE OF MONOPOLY ASSOCIATIONS: 1928–1938

The historical backdrop to the "reorganization" was increasing competition in the industry. The number of ginneries grew from 33 in 1922 to 176 in 1926, when the official ban was put on their construction.[124] The ginners claimed—and the government's own Commission of Inquiry agreed—that the increase "had forced down their profits to such an extent that they would be able to carry on no longer." [125]

It was difficult to square this assertion with the fact that new entrants were constantly eager to join the industry, but the fact was that while many ginners were making a handsome profit, some of them—the large European ginners—were less well off. As the Government's Annual Report for 1929 commented, "There was a tendency for European ginners to dispose of their interests" [126] and leave the industry.* The reason for this was their larger capacity in comparison to that of the middleman Indian ginner, and their consequent need for a higher output to run at capacity, coupled with the extremely high costs of European (as opposed to Indian) management.

To all owners of ginneries—but particularly to the large British ginners—the prospect of establishing monopolistic associations to guarantee a minimum level of profit was very attractive. As expected, the British ginners took the lead in setting up the association of ginners, its aim being to reduce

---

* Col. Franklin, of His Majesty's East African Dependencies Trade and Information Office, wrote Sir Bottomley at the Colonial Office on February 3, 1930: "As far as I can make out, some twenty-five of the European-owned ginneries in Uganda have changed hands lately and are now under Indian control—a sad state of affairs." [127]

expenses and increase profits.* The result was an immediate drop in the price offered the grower. As the governor informed the Colonial Office, "It is difficult to deny that the direct result of these combinations was deliberate depression of prices." [129] The growers retaliated by carrying the cotton across the border into Eastern Province, where competition had no obstacles. The next season, 1929, the state again came to the assistance of the ginners. The Colonial Office explained:

> . . . with a view to encouraging the formation of associations of ginners in Uganda, the Governor of the Protectorate has decided during the present season to prohibit the movement of seed cotton between a non-Association area and an Association area or between one Association area and another. [130]

That same year, associations spread to Eastern Province (Busoga) and Northern Province. The Busoga Seed Cotton Buying Association stated its objectives to be: "(a) to check ruthless competition, (b) to decrease overhead charges, (c) to encourage cultivation and ensure good quality, and (d) to obtain fair profit for each member." [131]

Opposition among growers then spread to the Eastern Province, where the Young Basoga Association picketed ginnery sites and persuaded growers to hold back their cotton. [132] "The combination is causing great distrust and dissatisfaction among the growers, who are holding up their cotton in all districts," the governor wrote the Colonial Office. [133] In 1929, afraid "that planting would be much reduced in the Protectorate as a result [of associations]," the government appointed a Commission of Inquiry into the Cotton Industry.† While lamenting the low

---

* The governor wrote the Colonial Office: "If it were not for British ginners in taking the lead in forming an Association in Buganda, we should, I think, be seeing today exactly the same condition—cutthroat competition—as we have seen in the past." [128]

† In his speech to Legco in early September 1929, the governor explained the appointment of a Commission of Inquiry and commented: "The phenomenon of 1928, when the Baganda growers saw that by taking their own cotton across to the East of the Nile where open competition was still in force they could secure a price several hundred shillings higher per hundred pounds than was being offered by the buying associations within Buganda, had a very marked effect upon them. It seemed to me that the point of view of the native population was

prices offered the growers, the commission went through mental gymnastics to give unqualified support to ginners' associations:

> Excessive competition of this kind among the purchasers of cotton is no doubt of financial benefit to the native, for the time being; but it is obvious that an industry cannot go on indefinitely paying more for its raw produce than is economic. The time must come when a halt must be called; and the survivors in the fight will probably come to terms among themselves, with a view to paying such prices only as will compensate them for their past losses. They will obviously have less capital to expand and the position of the grower will suffer accordingly, unless fresh capital from outside is brought into the industry.[135]

And so, in order to ward off the threat of monopoly in the long run the government proposed to create monopolies in the short run! The commission concluded: ". . . but we see no practical method of bringing it [excessive competition] to an end unless one Association or probably two come into existence for the whole Protectorate."

But the same factors that had led to this "excessive competition" made it difficult to maintain a voluntary price-fixing association. Early in 1929, when the harvested crop declined, the incipient disunity between ginners rapidly gave way to open hostility as the associations disintegrated into competition. Both the Buganda and Busoga Seed Cotton Buying Associations, the models the commission had in mind when it recommended government encouragement of associations, collapsed in 1930.[136] Because of the presence of buying stores and open markets near ginnery sites, competition between ginners took the form of providing free transport to growers from their plots to the ginneries. Trucks proliferated. By 1932 the *Uganda Herald* "understood that already every available lorry in Kenya, Tanganyika, the Sudan and Congo has been engaged for the coming season."[137] Price competition gave way to service competition.

The obstacle to an association among all the ginners was the

---

not likely to be dispelled by any reassuring statements made by the ginners or by the Government, and that until native feeling could be reassured there was a very serious danger, in Buganda at any rate, that the native might not only not extend but actually curtail their existing cotton production."[134]

efficiency of the small Indian ginners, who used family labor and had low management costs.[138] With very little capital savings, they were unable to survive any long period of adversity; on the other hand, if the crop was small, they sought short-run profits by bidding up the price of raw cotton. Faced by the slightest adversity, the small ginner was all too willing to break the ranks.

At the same time, the earlier contradiction between European and Indian larger ginners was resolved through an alliance. Indian capital, which already had controlling interests in the industry, saw important political advantages in maintaining the presence of British capital. As the governor explained it to the Colonial Office:

> There is reason to believe that the Indians, who as you know, already control by far the greater portion of the capital involved in the business, do not wish to see British firms disappear altogether. The reason that they wish for a continuance of some British interests is, I think, mainly because they regard the presence of these interests as an influence in favour of the recognition by government of a higher scale of costs than would be expected if all the ginners were under Indian or Japanese ownership and management. It is possible that they would also believe, not altogether without reason, that the representations of the body which contains a considerable proportion of British ginners receive more consideration both locally and by the Colonial Office than were those of a body composed entirely of Indians.[139]

The contradiction among ginners was now between the interests of the large and the small ginner. It was up to the state to create conditions that would leave the small ginner no choice but to combine with the more substantial members of his class. In June 1932 the state—in the person of the director of cotton cultivation—called together a Cotton Lorry Disarmament Conference, "very fully attended by all the ginners," with the object of reaching "complete lorry disarmament." [140] Then, in 1933, the Cotton Zone Ordinance established fourteen quality zones for cotton, legally prohibiting the movement of raw cotton from one zone to another by motor transport.[141] The official reason was to prevent the spread of cotton disease, but the consequence was to put a fetter on service competition. Since the state forbade the ginner from offering transport and higher prices to distant growers, every ginner was now confined to buying within his own zone. By itself, price competition had limited effect in increasing the supply of cotton. Thus, chained to more substantial members of his class, the individual small ginner had little alternative but to cooperate with his class brethren in the name of class interest. As the governor's 1938 Commission of Inquiry predicted, "It was foreseen . . . that it [the Ordinance] would facilitate the formation of local buying associations inasmuch as it provided for the establishment of zones throughout the country into and out of which the movement of seed cotton was prohibited, except by head loads." [142] Representing the large ginners, C. P. Dalal (of Narandas Rajaram), by now the Asian unofficial member of Parliament, publicly "congratulated the Hon. the Director of Agriculture for his sincere effort in trying to help the ginning community." [143]

The state, however, put an upper limit on the future prosperity of this "ginning community." Section 4 of the 1933 Ordinance specified that the government could fix the minimum price to be paid for raw cotton in every zone.[144] Recognizing that it had removed all obstacles to the ginners' lowering the price they would pay the growers—and to the growers reducing production as a response—the state specified the minimum price of cotton, thereby assuring supplies. As early as 1929, the first Commission of Inquiry had warned:

> If prices are paid to the native grower which he regards as unfair, and an inadequate remuneration for his labours, he will become discontented; and production, instead of increasing, will diminish.
>
> Taking these circumstances into consideration, we recommend that as long as Associations and combines unrecognized by the Government exist, the Government should make it an offence to sell cotton below the prices arrived at under the formula recommended.[145]

And the BCGA, when corresponding with the Colonial Office about local attempts at associations, warned: "The only thing we have to watch is that any 'squeezing' of the Native must be prevented . . ." [146]

Once there was a minimum—which turned out to be a

maximum—price for raw cotton, the single most important variable in the cost of production remained management. Once again, it was the Indian ginner, with his relatively low management costs, who was able to make a greater profit.* In the first decade of associations, the price of ginneries multiplied several times. In 1937, several ginneries were sold "at prices ranging from two to three times their original costs." [148] The 1938 Cotton Commission gave as the primary reason for the high price of ginneries the "desire for people to obtain an entrance into the industry," [149] an entry highly prized precisely because of the reigning superprofits.

With their lower costs of management, the Indian ginners further consolidated their hold on the industry during this monopolistic phase.† An industry that was almost solely European owned and managed at the time of World War I was just as completely Indian owned and managed by World War II. When it was time to appoint the first two unofficial members to

---

* The governor explained the situation to the secretary of state: "The figures of ginning which were put forward both in England and locally, and the criticisms of the costs as given by the Carter Commission, were based largely on the assumption that the criterion ought to be a British ginning business with a considerable European staff. Indian firms can, of course, in many cases work far below these figures and the minimum price which is fixed to a large extent on the figures of costs of British firms has the effect of putting a considerable extra profit into the pockets of Indian firms." [147]

† By forming "pools" through voluntary agreements between ginners within each zone with the active backing of the state. Before these voluntary agreements were to expire in 1939, the state appointed another Commission of Inquiry into the cotton industry. While acknowledging the feeling of "the majority" of the members in the industry that it "should be left free to formulate its own scheme for reorganization, when the existing pool arrangement expires in 1939," the Commission recommended statutory pooling arrangements because any voluntary attempts at reorganization would "break down." [150] Given an industry composed of enterprises with vastly varying costs of production, it was no surprise that the relatively efficient but small ginners would resort to competition at the first opportunity. The government, in suppressing the tendency to competition and in creating conditions to sustain monopoly combinations (and, if necessary, enforcing these combinations) was consistently acting in the interests of those who had to lose from competition, that is, the large and established ginners. Before it could take action on the Report of the 1938 Commission of Inquiry into the Cotton Industry, war broke out and the question of statutory pools was shelved until the 1940s.

the Legislative Council, the governor chose C. P. Dalal (of Narandas Rajaram) and P. L. Fenton (of the Standard Bank of South Africa), who represented the two most important sections of capital based in Uganda: processing and banking.[151]

Big Capital Consolidates

The lessons of the cotton industry were learned well. When the department of agriculture introduced new crops into Uganda—particularly coffee, which was to become the leading crop in the Protectorate—it took measures to organize both processing and marketing along monopoly lines from the outset. The governor emphasized "the importance of restricting buyers to reputable firms and individuals of some standing." [152]

In 1930 an ordinance to provide for the "grading of coffee for export" was enacted. A restricted number of coffee factories were granted the right by the director of agriculture to operate as "licensed curing works," and their managers were certified as graders. All coffee bought from growers for export had to pass through these factories. While the purpose was to maintain quality, the result—as the Central Council of Indian Associations reported to a visiting Indian commission of inquiry[153]—was to "drive the coffee trade into the hands of firms who [were] holding licenses for curing works," which were in effect guaranteed a quasi-monopoly position.* In 1932, the government went further and introduced the Native Produce Marketing Ordinance in order to further limit the breathing space allowed small traders.† Section 3 stipulated that buying centers be listed so that buying licenses could be restricted in each area. Section 12 gave the governor the power to grant an exclusive license to a particular producer in any area.[156]

---

* As the director of agriculture noted in the Legislative Council, no further licenses were to be issued until the coffee cured in the licensed works in the Kampala–Port Bell area exceeded 3,500 tons. This was "one of the grounds on which certain applications for licenses from Indian firms were turned down." [154]

† This ordinance was based on the Trades Licensing (Amendment) Ordinance (1932) of Tanganyika. Similar legislation was passed in Kenya (the Marketing of Native Produce Ordinance, 1935) and in Zanzibar (the Clove and Copra Ordinance, 1934).[155]

There thus existed three different systems for the processing and marketing of coffee in Uganda in 1932.[157] In Buganda, where only the Coffee Grading Ordinance was applied, only curing was monopolized; marketing remained open to all traders. In Ankole and Kigezi in the Western Province, the number of buying licenses was restricted by establishing buying centers, while marketing was partially monopolized. In southern Bugisu and the Bwemba country of Toro, which grew the bulk of the valuable Arabica crop, there was a total monopoly at the level of both marketing and curing.[158] While the monopoly was in theory given to the local native administration, it was actually handed over under a management contract to A. Baumann and Co., a local subsidiary of Lever Bros. of London.

In 1936 curing and marketing were monopolized throughout the entire coffee industry when Robusta coffee was brought under the Native Produce Marketing Ordinance. Buying centers were listed throughout Buganda, and exclusive licenses for both purchase and curing were given to the Old East Africa Trading Co., A. Baumann and Co., and Jamal Ramji and Co., the last being an Indian firm.[159] In response to complaints from less substantial Indian capital, the governor wrote the viceroy of India that the Native Produce Marketing Ordinance was "of course entirely non-racial in character." [160] The governor was, in fact, correct. Though the ordinance had a clear bias, it was not a racial but a *class* bias. While it granted buying and curing monopolies to big capital, it left small capital out in the cold.

The Native Produce Marketing Ordinance was not limited to coffee but, as the title says, applied to all "native produce"—that is, to everything produced by the peasants of Uganda. Although cotton and coffee were by far the most important, those less important in value and quantity produced—peanuts, leaf tobacco, sesame, beeswax—nevertheless figured as the most important items of *petty* trade, and, with the exception of leaf tobacco, comprised the bulk of *internal* trade.*

---

* Simultaneous with the Native Produce Marketing Ordinance came the Trading Centers Ordinance. Maintaining that "from the point of revenue it was almost impossible to keep track of the non-native population which was widely scattered and constantly shifting," and arguing that "there is no doubt that

Beginning in 1930, the government had embarked on a policy of agricultural diversification. The purpose was not to get away from export production, but to complete the subordination of internal trade to the export trade, and to produce a variety of cash crops for export. As with coffee, leaf tobacco, peanuts, and sesame were brought under the Native Produce Marketing Ordinance. Four buying licenses were issued in 1933 and 1934, creating a quasi-monopoly in the purchase of leaf tobacco; the most lucrative concession went to the British-American Tobacco Co., Ltd.[163] The reorientation of peanut production "for export" was undertaken following the visit of a representative of Lever Bros., Ltd. of London,[164] and this meant, among other things, that the government took the peanut trade away from thousands of petty traders and gave it to a single exclusive licensee, A. Baumann and Co.[165]

With the Native Produce Marketing Ordinance, the monopolization of both marketing and processing structures was complete. The history of capitalism in Uganda was very different from that of early capitalist Europe. It was not *national*

---

government has lost large sums in rent and licenses from these people," the governor in 1924 called for the concentration of the nonnative trading community to defined trading centers by empowering the government to refuse the issue of licenses except in certain trading areas.[161] The rural "nonnative trading community" was, of course, the small Indian traders who had just been legally barred from purchasing local produce. Given their dispersal into the remotest regions, it was most difficult to supervise their operations and implement the law. Their concentration into "trading centers" solved the administrative problem while ensuring a larger fiscal revenue from trading licenses. At the same time, it solved a political problem by granting the demand of African traders for freedom of competition from Indian traders. But this was, to an extent, an empty gesture, for like the small Indian trader, the small African trader was without a license to buy local produce; at the same time, the agents of the large enterprises granted the licenses were free to move about the countryside making their purchases.

Meanwhile, Indian *dukawallahs*, physically concentrated in "trading centers," developed a strong awareness of their common interest as established traders vis-à-vis the incoming traders. This consciousness materialized into local associations which lobbied in the chamber of commerce for increased trading licenses and more difficult conditions of entry into commerce for "native" traders. For example, the Eastern Province Chamber of Commerce (dominated by Indian traders) passed a resolution asking the government "to introduce legislation to control the new increasing native trading activities." [162]

capitalism but *colonial* capitalism, with its own historical specificity. Its monopoly structures resembled monopoly capitalism in the metropolitan countries not because the domestic economy was controlled by an independent monopolistic bourgeoisie, but because it was an appendage of the metropolitan monopolistic economy. The reign of big capital in the colony was not the result of an internal *class struggle* between small entrepreneurs, with a section emerging as monopoly capital, but the result of the smothering of small capital by the *political* power of a state which consistently served the interests of the metropolitan bourgeoisie. Colonial capitalism was never competitive capitalism.

One result of this process was that, of the class physically located within the colony, the one that emerged dominant by the time of World War II was the Indian bourgeoisie. Unlike the bourgeoisie of capitalist development in Western Europe, this was not an industrial but a *commercial* bourgeoisie—in spite of the fact that its most important investments were in the processing industries, cotton ginning and coffee curing. Processing, however, is not really an industry. It is an adjunct of commerce, and its purpose in Uganda was to facilitate the export of the produce involved. The Indian bourgeoisie was thus an intermediate class; its interests were in harmony with, and subservient to, those of the metropolitan bourgeoisie, which dominated the entire colonial system and was the prime beneficiary of the export-import economy. As it expanded its operations, it depended on British finance capital, principally the National Bank of India, Ltd., as its chief source of credit. In this sense the Indian bourgeoisie was a dependent class.

Among the Indians in Uganda there were thus two distinct classes, the commercial bourgeoisie (the businessmen located in wholesale trade and in the processing industry), small in number but dominant in its appropriation of the territorially retained surplus, and the more numerous petty bourgeoisie (the retail traders). While they formed two separate classes in the economy, the petty and the commercial bourgeoisies acted as one single force at the level of politics, under the hegemony of the commercial bourgeoisie.

The specificity of the Indian commercial bourgeoisie was that it arose under the protective umbrella of the colonial state. That it was a class of non-national origin meant that it shared no common cultural heritage with the masses. That it was a protégé of the colonial state meant that it had no need for—nor did it attempt any relations with—the masses outside the marketplace. Here it was most unlike the African petty bourgeoisie, whose social origin was predominantly from the peasantry and whose method of advance, as we shall see, was through mass political organizations and mass political struggles. So far as the Indian commercial bourgeoisie was concerned, its social distance from the masses was expressed in an intense racial consciousness. It was an *apolitical* class.

Notes

1. Kigezi District, *Annual Report for 1930*, XII, "Trade and Economic Development," ESA; quoted in Charles M. Good, *Rural Markets and Trade in East Africa*, p. 197.
2. Ibid.
3. Lawrence J. Sakarai, "Merchant Trade with and Settlement in East Africa," p. 45.
4. C. P. Rigby (1861), quoted in Sakarai, pp. 24–25.
5. Ibid.
6. Ibid., p. 8.
7. James Bird, *Commercial and Geographical View of Eastern Africa*, quoted in Sakarai, p. 45.
8. Cd. 2164 of 1904, p. 11.
9. Frederick D. Lugard, *The Rise of Our East African Empire*, p. 488.
10. See reports from commissioners, inspectors and others: 1910, vol. 27, *Report of the Commissioners on Emigration from India to the Crown Colonies and Protectorates*, Parliamentary Paper, vol. 10 of 1910, HMSO 5192, p. 21.
11. Ibid., p. 3.
12. Ibid., p. 237.
13. See Foreign Office to India Office, December 22, 1898; in FO 2/431: Agency in India for African Protectorates, 1896–1900.
14. See C. 9841 of 1898 and C. 8718 of 1898, on Recent Events in Uganda Protectorate; see also FO 2/429, FO 2/550, and FO 2/551 on employment of Indian troops in the protectorates, August 1900

to December 1901; see also L. W. Hollingsworth, *The Asians of East Africa*, pp. 39–42.

15. See FO 2/431, Agency in India for African Protectorates, 1896–1900; and FO 2/552, Agency in India for African Protectorates, 1901.

16. *Report of the Commissioners on Emigration from India to the Crown Colonies and Protectorates*, vol. 10, 1910, HMSO 5192, p. 17. See also, in the same, replies by Pitcher (paras. 4728–4729), Bolton (paras. 5405–5406), and Marsden (para. 4890).

17. See, for example, David Apter, *Political Kingdom in Uganda*, p. 164; see also Nigel Oram, "Why Indians Came to East Africa."

18. "Report on the Administration of Bombay Presidency," quoted in Robert G. Gregory, *India and East Africa*, pp. 53, 61.

19. Minutes of Evidence, *Report of the Commissioners, Inspector and Others*, paras. 7581–7584.

20. Lugard, p. 490.

21. Foreign Office, *Kenya, Uganda and Zanzibar* (HMSO, 1920), p. 72. The same policy had been stated in the early 1900s in rather elaborate and generous terms by Her Majesty's Special Commissioner to Uganda, Sir Harry Johnston:

> On account of our Indian Empire we are compelled to reserve to British control a large portion of East Africa. Indian trade, enterprise and emigration require suitable outlets. East Africa is, and should be, from every point of view, the America of the Hindu.

Quoted in Apter, p. 164.

22. Entebbe Archives A/7/Misc., February 13, 1901, quoted in Cyril Ehrlich, "The Poverty of Uganda 1893–1903."

23. J. Watts, "The Facts of the Cotton Famine, 1866," p. 59, quoted in Cyril Ehrlich, "The Marketing of Cotton in Uganda 1900–1950."

24. J. R. Hutton, Chairman of the BCGA, before the Royal Society of Arts on January 26, 1916; in publication of the BCGA, "The Effects of the War on Cotton Growing in the British Empire," enclosure in CO 536/79.

25. Memorandum on the scheme of the BCGA for financing the cotton crop of Uganda in CO 536/171, October 7, 1914. As one writer judged in the *Empire Cotton Growing Review*, an official journal of the Empire Cotton Growing Committee (vol. 1, no. 4, October 1924): "This cotton is of high quality and used against staple American as well as Upper Egyptian. . . ."

26. *Uganda News*, April 26, 1929, p. 29.

27. H. B. Thomas and Roger Scott, *Uganda*, pp. 135–136.

28. The committee also maintained that "the manufacture of cotton of

good quality requires a degree of skill which the native of Uganda, or any imported Indian operatives, could not hope to attain." Letter from manager, Binny & Co. Ltd. to Under-Secretary of State for Colonies and reply by the Colonial Office, both in CO 536/107.

29. In Dispatch No. 335 of July 17, 1914, by Acting Governor Wallis to the Secretary of State for Colonies, in CO 536/70.

30. Letter from the BCGA to the Secretary of State, July 14, 1914, in CO 536/74.

31. Secretary of State to the Governor of Uganda, No. 373 of September 10, 1914, in CO 536/74.

32. Uganda Cotton Rules, 1918, Section C, para. 7. Enclosure in the Uganda Cotton Ordinance, 1908, and The Uganda Cotton (Amendment) Ordinance, 1910, in CO 536/124.

33. Memorandum on Lukiko Resolutions Nos. 21 and 24, Appendix No. 3 to Memorandum on Uganda Cotton Industry by Director of Agriculture to Chief Secretary, Entebbe. Enclosure in dispatch from Acting Governor to Secretary of State of February 8, 1923, in CO 536/124.

34. Chamber of Commerce, Buganda, to Governor. Enclosure in Director of Agriculture to Chief Secretary, Entebbe, of January 4, 1917, in CO 536/84.

35. Director of Agriculture, memorandum on the development of the cotton industry of January 30, 1923, in CO 536/124.

36. Agriculture Department, MP 486 (iii), April 13, 1920, quoted in Ehrlich, "The Marketing of Cotton in Uganda," pp. 175–177. The market was in reality "a large open space fenced around and divided inside into plots or stalls for the buyers." See also CO 536/124.

37. Ibid.

38. This is a correction to Ehrlich, who maintains that it was under the 1922 rules that wandering buyers were eliminated (pp. 167–169). The 1922 rules, in fact, merely reiterated what was instituted in the Eastern Province in 1913 and extended to Buganda in 1917.

39. See Uganda Cotton Rules, 1913, in CO 536/87.

40. Director of Agriculture, memorandum on the development of the cotton industry of January 30, 1923, in CO 536/124.

41. Director of Agriculture's report on the cotton industry of 1917, in CO 536/84.

42. Director of Agriculture, memorandum on the development of the cotton industry of January 3, 1923, in CO 536/124.

43. Ibid.

44. Ibid.

45. Confidential Dispatch of Secretary of State to Governor of January 2, 1914, and response by Acting Governor of February 7, 1914, both in Cotton Rules, 1914, in CO 536/67.

46. Director of Agriculture, memorandum of January 3, 1923, in CO 536/124.

47. The other two subjects discussed at this meeting were the cost of a buying license (renewal), which might be increased, and the market scheme proposed by the director of agriculture, which, it was hoped, would tend to eliminate irresponsible buyers. The meeting was attended by Herbert Reed, G. F. Seel and Mr. Bottomley (Colonial Office), James Curey and Jacey May (Empire Cotton Growing Committee), W. S. Himbury (BCGA and ECGC, representing the interests of Lancashire), D. S. Basen (Uganda Co., the largest British ginner in Uganda), and Mr. Simpson (director of agriculture). See minutes of meeting held August 3, 1922, in CO 536/122.

48. Rule 8, Uganda Cotton Rules, 1922.

49. Report by Director of Agriculture for 1915, in CO 536/79.

50. Colonial Office Minutes on representations by a Uganda ginner, Mr. Chadwick of Lyon, Lord & Co., in CO 536/92.

51. See telegram from the East African Indian Association, Mombasa, on 1913 Cotton Rules to Secretary of State of January 14, 1914, in CO 536/74.

52. Governor to Secretary of State, November 9, 1915, in CO 536/79.

53. Statement submitted by H. Horsley, representing the BCGA, enclosure in confidential memorandum on the cotton industry in Uganda of 1923, in CO 536/127.

54. Report of the Cotton Commission, 1938, p. 53.

55. J. S. Mangat, "Was Allidina Visram a Robber Baron?", pp. 33–35.

56. George Delf, *Asians in East Africa*, p. 3.

57. Entebbe Archives, minutes by Secretary's Office, June 9, 1925, in J. S. Mangat, *A History of the Asians in East Africa c. 1886 to 1945*, p. 52.

58. Helmut Laumer, "Channels of Distribution in Uganda," in Paul Zajadacz, ed., *Studies in Production and Trade in East Africa*, p. 363.

59. FOCP No. 7946, p. 28; quoted in Mangat, *A History of the Asians in East Africa*, p. 153.

60. H. S. Morris, *Indians in Uganda*, pp. 184–185.

61. F. R. S. DeSouza, "Indian Political Organization in East Africa," pp. 9–14.

62. Morris, p. 107.

63. Ibid., p. 79. All details on the Ismailis are from this work.

64. G. F. Clay, in *Empire Cotton Growing Review*, July 1934, p. 174. In fact, the government hoped that no unginned cotton would be shipped from Uganda after January 1, 1917. See Director of Agriculture's report on the cotton industry, 1917, p. 13; in CO 536/84 (File No. 8860).

65. In *The Uganda Co. Ltd.: The First Fifty Years*, p. 6.

66. See Clay, in *Empire Cotton Growing Review*, July 1934, p. 174.

67. Cd. 4910 of 1909, p. 3; see also *Uganda Herald*, September 13, 1912, p. 2.

68. They were: the British East Africa Corporation Ltd., the Uganda Company Ltd., the Uganda Cotton Buying & Ginning Co. Ltd., the Bukedi-Uganda Cotton & Trading Co. Ltd., the Bukedi-Uganda Cotton & Trading Co. Ltd., and the Bombay-Uganda Cotton Syndicate Ltd., all British; Messrs. Hansing and Co., German; and Messrs. Besson and Co., French. See memorandum from British ginners to the Under-Secretary of State for the Colonies, November 24, 1914, in CO 536/74.

69. Letter from the BCGA to Butler, Colonial Office; in CO 536/88 of July 27, 1917.

70. Memorandum by Hutton of BCGA on the Confidential Report on the Cotton Growing Industry of Uganda by Samuel Simpson, 1915, in CO 536/79.

71. Memorandum from Deputy Governor Wallis to Bottomley, Colonial Office, March 26, 1917, in CO 536/88.

72. In "The Marketing of Cotton in Uganda," pp. 149–155.

73. For example, one of the subscribers in the second ginnery—The Allidina Cotton Co., Ltd.—was Mehta, "a man who had been employed by the B.C.G.A. to buy cotton for them on a small percentage" and who was "creditably reported to have invested 15,000 rupees (£1,000) in Dastur's concern." See Letter from BEAC to Bottomley at the Colonial Office, January 2, 1916, in CO 536/88.

74. As Hutton, the chairman of BCGA explained to Bottomley, Colonial Office: "Our main object in buying the cotton is to prevent it going to Bombay, as it is badly needed in this country." May 23, 1917, in CO 536/88.

75. FO 2/431, Agency in India for African Protectorates, 1896–1900, and FO 2/552, Agency in India for African Protectorates, 1901.

76. Letter from Hutton, chairman of BCGA to Bottomley, Colonial Office, January 16, 1917, in CO 536/88.

77. Frank Moraes, *Sir Purshotamdas Thakordas*; quoted in Ehrlich, "The Marketing of Cotton in Uganda," pp. 147–148.

78. Telegram from Governor to Secretary of State, December 3, 1918, in CO 536/91.

79. Telegram from Bottomley, Colonial Office, to the Governor, November 26, 1918, in CO 536/92.
80. Letter from the Board of Trade, Commercial Department, to Messrs. British East Africa Corporation, Ltd., January 9, 1918, in CO 536/92.
81. CO minute, February 22, 1918, on proposed meeting of Colonial Office with three European ginning companies in Uganda on the proposed fixing of prices for the 1919 season, in CO 536/92.
82. CO minute, November 25, 1918, on the purchase of next year's crop by government, in CO 536/92.
83. Ibid. Ehrlich, "The Marketing of Cotton in Uganda," pp. 129–130, presents considerable evidence to demonstrate the effect of competition on rising prices. For example, the following were the prices reported for February, 1917, in Lango and Teso:

	In market (rupees)	At ginnery (rupees)	In market to middlemen (rupees)
Lango	9/71	7/–	11/82
Teso	8/–	7/–	—

84. Minute by CO on dispatch from the Governor on the Cotton Industry, November 9, 1923, in CO 536/127.
85. As the deputy governor complained, "in spite of these disabilities [talking of the competition against middlemen and British ginners] Indian firms now hold very strong positions and new ones coming in." Telegram from Deputy Governor to Secretary of State, July 20, 1919, in CO 536/95.
86. R. Purshotamdas Thakordas of NR to Charles Armstrong of the Colonial Office, February 7, 1919, enclosure in Cotton Rules 1919, memorandum dated August 6, 1919, in CO 536/98.
87. Memorandum from BCGA to Under-Secretary of State, November 1, 1919, in CO 536/98.
88. Telegram from Governor to Secretary of State, September 21, 1918, in CO 536/90. The governor explained his intentions to the secretary of state: "My purpose is to eliminate these [buying posts] and concentrate the ginnery agents and independent buyers in carefully sited central markets at a reasonable distance from the established ginneries." See Confidential Memorandum of the Cotton Industry in Uganda, 1923, by the Governor, in CO 536/127. The

governor received full support from the ginners' association, dominated by the established ginners. In 1922, and then again in 1923, it passed a resolution "that this association urges the Government to maintain its avowed policy of restricting within a radius of five miles from all ginneries, the grant of a cotton buying license." Memorandum by C. O. Dalal representing N.R. & Co. to the Governor. Enclosed in confidential memorandum, in CO 536/127.

89. Letter from Fox of N.R. & Co. to Armstrong of Lyon, Lord & Co. Enclosure in letter from Armstrong to Bottomley at the Colonial Office, January 7, 1919; further enclosure in memorandum on Cotton Rules 1918, of January 4, 1919, in CO 536/99.

90. Jaffer's testimony to the Uganda Cotton Ginners Association, appendix to Confidential Memorandum on the Cotton Industry of Uganda, 1923, from the Governor to the Secretary of State, November 9, 1923, in CO 536/127.

91. Dharamsi's testimony to the Uganda Cotton Ginners Association in CO 536/127.

92. Appendix II, *Carter Commission Report*, 1929.

93. Telegram from Carter to Secretary of State, May 22, 1920, in CO 536/100.

94. The clients were Nanji Kalidas, Mathurdas Nanji & Co., Haji Merali, Damodar Karsanji, Salim Saed Arab, Manishankar Hariram, Sundarji Manji, Mohmed Haji Suleman, Ahmed Harji Suleman, Vithaldas Haridas & Co., Megji Kanji, Naranbhai P. Patel, and Rugenath Keshavji. Dispatch Acting Governor (enclosed letter from CO home to Governor) to Secretary of State, October 31, 1922, in CO 536/121.

95. Confidential Memorandum on the Cotton Industry in Uganda, 1923, in CO 536/127.

96. Ibid.

97. The members of the board were to be as follows: *official members:* director of agriculture, the provincial commissioners of Buganda and Eastern Province, the land officer, the divisional superintendent of the Kenya and Uganda Railway, and the deputy director of agriculture. *Unofficial Members:* three members from the Uganda Cotton Association, two from the Uganda Chamber of Commerce, one from the Eastern Province Chamber of Commerce, and one to be appointed by the *kabaka* and approved by the governor as representing the interests of growers. See the Cotton Ordinance, 1926, in CO 536/145 (File No. 14153).

98. Enclosure to Dispatch No. 168 of March 3, 1926, in CO 536/141.

99. Dispatch from Deputy to the Governor to the Secretary of State, No. 7, January 2, 1930, in CO 536/160 (File No. 20502).

100. *Carter Commission Report*, 1929, appendix II.

101. Ormsby-Gore Commission Report, Cd. 2387 of 1925, pp. 143–144.

102. Compiled from R. R. Ramchandani, "Asians' Role in the Cotton Industry of Uganda," Table 3; Memorandum by the British Cotton Corporation Ltd. on Uganda Cotton Industry, CO 536/144, p. 20 (File No. 14008); and Memorandum on the Development of the Uganda Cotton Industry by the Director of Agriculture, January 30, 1923, CO 536/124, p. 237 (File No. 8998).

103. Memorandum from Cox of B.C.C., Ltd., to the Governor of Uganda, enclosure in file on Merger Scheme for Cotton Industry, No. 14008, December 16, 1927, in CO 536/144.

104. Letter from Llewellyn of the B.C.C., Ltd., to the Under-Secretary of State, May 27, 1927, enclosure in CO 536/144.

105. Letter from Llewellyn of B.C.C., Ltd., to Bottomley at the Colonial Office, February 22, 1928, enclosure in File No. 20024 on Cotton Industry Merger, in CO 536/148.

106. Letter from Llewellyn of B.C.C., Ltd., to Under-Secretary of State, March 14, 1928, in CO 536/148.

107. Memorandum by the B.C.C., Ltd., on the Uganda Cotton Industry to the Secretary of State, in CO 536/144 (File No. 14008). See also CO minute on B.C.C., Ltd., of July 25, 1927, by Bottomley in CO 536/144.

108. CO 536/144 (File No. 14008).

109. Ibid. At the same time, Col. Franklin, H.M. Trade Commissioner in East Africa, wrote to the Colonial Office of the "very distressing news" of Japanese takeovers, and added: "During the past year the Japanese have come into the open and acquired quite a number of ginneries in Uganda and if they continue at this rate, they will largely control the industry before we know where we are." Franklin to Ormsby-Gore at the Colonial Office, April 5, 1927, in CO 536/144 (File No. 14008).

110. See, for example, Articles III of the Convention Between Her Majesty and His Majesty the King of the Belgians, acting as founder of, and in the name of, the International Association of the Congo. Signed at Berlin, December 16, 1884.

111. ". . . international obligations prevented the government from committing any public act discriminating against the Japanese (I find that Japan ratified the Convention of St. Germain-en-Laye on April 6, 1922)"; CO minute on the Merger Scheme by B.C.C., Ltd., in CO 536/144 (File No. 14008).

112. The meeting was attended by Bottomley, Parkinson, and Seel of the Colonial Office; Cox, Higgin, and Llewellyn of B.C.C., Ltd.; and Lyall, Zoete, Gordon, Markby, Stuart, and Wadeson, City financiers, at the Colonial Office on May 4, 1928. The talks between the governor and Bottomley were also held at the Colonial Office on July 11, 1928. See CO 536/148 (File No. 20024).

113. Governor's Inquiry into the Cotton Industry, 1923, in CO 536/127. See also testimony by C. P. Dalal, representing Narandas Rajaram in the inquiry, and *Empire Cotton Growing Review*, vol. 4, no. 3 (July 1927), p. 277.

114. Major Leggett to the Director, Federation of British Industries, November 16, 1920, in CO 536/108.

115. Fox, manager of Narandas Rajaram to Charles Armstrong, enclosure in Colonial Office Memorandum on Cotton Rules 1918, letter dated December 23, 1918, memorandum dated August 6, 1919, in CO 536/98.

116. Memorandum from National Bank of India Ltd. to Under-Secretary of State, Colonial Office, June 10, 1921, in CO 536/116.

117. Colonial Office notes on testimony by Fountain of the Board of Trade and Todd, Secretary of the Empire Cotton Growing Committee, November 12, 1918, in CO 536/92; see also letter from the Board of Trade, Commercial Relations and Treaties Department, to Under-Secretary of State for Colonies: "The Board understands that a substantial portion of the Uganda crop is marketed to India and that it is necessary that no restriction should be imposed to its export to that destination." December 11, 1918, in CO 536/92.

118. Minute by Colonial Office on Export of Uganda Cotton, November 5, 1918, in CO 536/92.

119. "Disposal of British-Owned ginneries to Japanese and Indian Interests," January 1930, in CO 536/156 (File No. 20490).

120. From Colonial Office to Rt. Hon. Sir Robert Horn, Personal and Confidential X20024/28 Uganda, September 29, 1928; in CO 536/148 (File No. 20024).

121. Telegram from the Governor to the Secretary of State, March 27, 1928 in CO 536/148.

122. On the two guarantees, see memorandum by Cox of the B.C.C., Ltd., to the Governor, William Gowers, of July 26, 1927, and reply from Governor Gowers to Cox, July 28, 1927, both in CO 536/144 (File No. 14008).

123. Colonial Office to Chairman, B.C.C., Ltd., X20024/28 Uganda, of July 25, 1928, in CO 536/148.

124. The figures are from UP, *Carter Commission Report*, 1929, p. 4.
125. Ibid.
126. UP, *Annual Report for 1929*, p. 13.
127. Franklin to Bottomley, February 3, 1930, in CO 536/159 (File No. 20490).
128. Governor to Colonial Office, March 9, 1930, in CO 536/159 (File No. 20490).
129. Gowers to Bottomley, March 12, 1929, in CO 536/115 (File No. 20345).
130. Perkinson to British Cotton Co., June 27, 1929, in CO 536/156 (File No. 20355).
131. Memorandum from the Busoga Cotton Buying Association, in CO 536/144 (File No. 14008).
132. Agricultural Department, Jinja File 2124 in Ehrlich, "The Marketing of Cotton in Uganda," p. 256. See also letter from "A Muganda" to *Uganda News*, August 23, 1929, p. 10.
133. Governor to Bottomley at Colonial Office, March 12, 1929, in CO 536/155 (File No. 20345).
134. *Uganda News*, September 6, 1929, p. 27.
135. See paras. 96 and 98 of UP, *Carter Commission Report*, 1929, p. 17.
136. *Report of Cotton Commission*, 1938, p. 17.
137. *Uganda Herald*, June 17, 1932, p. 26.
138. Reynolds, Director of BCGA in Uganda to Managing Director, BCGA, Manchester, December 21, 1927, in CO 536/144.
139. Gowers to Bottomley at Colonial Office, March 9, 1930, in CO 536/159 (File No. 20490).
140. *Uganda Herald*, June 17, 1932, p. 26.
141. *Uganda Herald*, July 7, 1933, p. 25.
142. *Report of Cotton Commission*, 1938, p. 17.
143. *Uganda Herald*, August 4, 1933, p. 21.
144. *Uganda Herald*, July 7, 1933, p. 25. Section 6 also fixed a maximum price for ginning and baling cotton.
145. *Carter Commission Report*, 1929.
146. BCGA to Colonial Office, January 16, 1928, in CO 536/144.
147. Gowers to Bottomley at Colonial Office, March 9, 1930, in CO 536/159 (File No. 20490).
148. Ehrlich, "The Marketing of Cotton in Uganda," p. 268.
149. *Report of the Cotton Commission*, 1938, p. 49.
150. Ibid., p. 81.
151. *Uganda Herald*, March 17, 1933, p. 17.
152. Bourdillon to Secretary of State, Confidential of February 21, 1934, in CO 536/181 (File No. 23560).

153. Memorandum from the Central Council of Indian Associations to K. P. S. Menon in *Uganda Herald*, October 10, 1934, p. 16.

154. Report of K. P. S. Menon in *Gazette of India Extraordinary*, June 24, 1935, p. 201.

155. *Uganda Herald*, August 26, 1932, p. 17.

156. Ibid., p. 15.

157. Ibid.

158. M. Yoshida and D. G. R. Belshaw, "The Introduction of the Trade Licensing System for Primary Products in East Africa," p. 17.

159. Ibid., p. 18.

160. *Gazette of India Extraordinary*, June 24, 1935, p. 234.

161. "Non-Native Trading in the Buganda Province," in CO 536/179 (File No. 3653).

162. See, for example, an Eastern Province Chamber of Commerce resolution and account of the preceding debate "asking Government to introduce legislation to control the now increasing Native Trading Activities," in minutes of Eastern Province Chamber of Commerce meeting, Jinja, December 26, 1926. Report in *Uganda News*, January 14, 1927, p. 7.

163. For information on the number of licenses issued for leaf tobacco, peanuts, and sesame, see memorandum by the Central Council of Indian Associations to K. P. S. Menon in *Uganda Herald*, October 10, 1934, p. 16; report of K. P. S. Menon in *Gazette of India Extraordinary*, June 24, 1935, pp. 202–205; and Yoshida and Belshaw, pp. 17–18.

164. Acting Governor Scott to Under-Secretary of State for Colonies, No. 178 of April 30, 1932, in CO 536/172 (File No. 22103).

165. Ibid.

4
Landlords, Tenants, and the Colonial State

The Baganda landlords were a creation of the colonial state. Their ownership of land, the most important means of production in an agricultural economy, was the basis of the commonality of interest between the landlords and the colonial state in upholding colonial law and order. But this shared interest was only one aspect of the relationship. Control over land gave the landlords control over the producers on the land, and thus over the agricultural surplus product. This same product was the source of the state's revenue. As the landlords became conscious of their structural position and began to appropriate an increasing share of their tenants' surplus product, the contradictory aspect of the relation between the landlords and the state came to the fore. The resolution of this contradiction was in the favor of the state, leaving the landlords with but formal control over their land and the peasantry substantially free. This fundamentally affected the process of rural class formation in the rest of the colony. Here we shall trace the process in detail.

Buganda

The Buganda Agreement of 1900 provided for the grant of freehold miles to about 1,000 chiefs. By the time the allotment was completed in 1909, over 3,700 title holders had been registered. By 1926, these had multiplied to some 10,000, primarily as a result of inheritance or sale.[1]

The two decades after 1900 saw not just an increase in the number of landlords, but an increase in their power as a class. The landlords began to use their ownership of land to increase their control over the economic surplus produced on it. Their appropriation took several forms. Initially, they simply extracted a land rent *(busulu)* from the tenants. With an increase in the production of cotton on tenant farms, however, the Buganda Lukiko (a legislative body comprised solely of the landlord-chiefs) stipulated that some percentage (or tithe) on the quantity of cotton grown by each tenant should be paid over to the landlord.[2] This percentage, a form of tribute on cash crops, came to be known as the *nvujjo*.* As the amount appropriated from the tiller increased, so did the value of the land. In 1912–1913, the annual report for the Protectorate noted a rise in the price of land from 4 shillings to over 30 shillings an acre.[3]

The state's share of the surplus came in the form of taxes, and for this purpose the agreements concluded with the various kingdoms of the south specified the taxes that could be collected from the producers and institutionalized the office of tax collector.† Since they were imposed by the head, however, these taxes treated tenants and landlords the same, thus permitting substantial accumulation by the landlords, who used their funds for their own consumption. This fact did not go unnoticed by the state for long. As early as 1914, an official committee "appointed

---

* While the individual landlord appropriated his share of the surplus in the form of *busulu* and *nvujjo*, the landlords *as a class* did so in the form of *luwalo*, or forced labor. Although this was but another form of material appropriation by the landlords, the contradiction between the state and the landlords over *luwalo* took a form distinct from that over *busulu* and *nvujjo*, so we shall analyze the case of *luwalo* later.

† The Buganda Agreement of 1900 specified a "hut tax" of 4 shillings per annum and a "gun tax" of 4 shillings per annum.[4] The 1909 Poll Tax Agreement substituted a poll tax of Shs. 6/8 for the hut tax, but retained the gun tax. A similar poll tax was instituted in the Eastern Province (excluding Busoga, which had yet to recover from the severe famine of 1908–1909). For the rest of the Eastern Province, a poll tax was instituted in 1910–1911, in place of the existing mixed system of hut tax and poll tax.[5]

to enquire into and offer suggestions for raising additional revenue" complained of "the injustice of the poll tax," whereby "the wealthy chiefs who own from ten square miles up to one hundred and have large herds of cattle pay the same indirect taxation as the ordinary peasant." [6] The legal obstacle to increased taxation of the landlord class was removed in August 1920, when the government convinced the Lukiko to pass a resolution "voluntarily agreeing to further taxation." [7] In the subsequent Buganda Taxation Agreement of 1922, the Lukiko agreed to (1) an annual tax of 20 shillings on every Muganda with five or more acres of land; (2) an annual tax of 2 shillings on all other Muganda; and (3) an annual tax of 10 percent on the *nvujjo* collected by every Muganda landlord.[8]* But the Buganda Development Tax, as it was called, was at best an indirect way for the state to appropriate surplus peasant production. As state taxation on the landed class increased, there was nothing to stop the landlord from extracting an increased *nvujjo* from his tenants—which was precisely what he did.

In 1925 a government committee was appointed to investigate the increasing share of the surplus being siphoned off as land rent. The committee report maintained that "as much as one-third of the crop [was] frequently taken by the landlord," and that the Lukiko had drafted a bill in order to legalize the increased rent. The committee described the Lukiko proposals as "monstrous," the existing *nvujjo* system as "an oppressive burden on the landless class," and concluded: "It will thus be seen [that] under the new regime the ruling or upper class have benefitted enormously at the expense of the serf class." [10]

The result of increasing ground rent *(busulu)* and tribute on cash crops *(nvujjo)* was not just that the landlords appropriated a greater share of surplus produce, thus setting a limit on what the state could appropriate as taxes from the tenants, but that it also resulted in a qualitative change in the conditions of production. As fruits of increased cultivation were appropriated

---

* As a later committee appointed by the governor "to consider certain matters affecting tenure and rents of native land in the Buganda Province" admitted, the *kabaka* and the Lukiko had agreed to the 1922 agreement "as a temporary and experimental measure and with considerable reluctance." [9]

in the form of *busulu* and *nvujjo*, the tenant lost all material incentive to extend his cultivation of cash crops. In fact, in the second decade of colonial rule, cotton acreage declined in Buganda from 27,380 acres in 1911–1912 to 20,100 in 1916–1917, while it increased in the Eastern Province from 29,720 to 97,961 acres in the same years.[11] As the acting governor later explained to the colonial secretary, "The levying of excessive rents and of tribute on produce was seriously endangering the production of economic crops and creating a sense of insecurity in the minds of their tenants."[12] The social relations of production had become a fetter on production itself.

The problem was not just a relative decline in the share of the economic surplus available to the colonial state, but an absolute decline in the total surplus, a decline more in the production of cash crops produced for exchange than of subsistence crops produced for use. The supply of raw materials to the metropolitan bourgeoisie was threatened, and nothing short of a fundamental change in the very class relations of production could solve the problem. It was necessary to attack the structural position of the landlord; that is, the class relation between landlord and tenant that enabled the landlord to appropriate the surplus product from the tenant.

At the same time, the class position of the landlords had given rise to a political problem, known as the "*bataka* controversy." In creating a class of landed gentry, the 1900 Agreement had undermined the position of both the traditional *bataka* (the clan heads who controlled ancestral lands, counted in terms of villages) and the *kabaka* (who, as we saw in Chapter 1, had previously centralized his power over the entire kingdom at the expense of both the hereditary *bataka* and the appointed *batongole*). When Daudi Chwa, the young prince, took over the duties of the *kabaka* from the three landlords appointed as regents, the *bataka* formed the Bataka Association to ask for a revision of the 1900 Land Agreement, and appealed to the governor to intervene on their behalf. Though numbering only 2,000,[13] the *bataka* successfully articulated the grievances of the Baganda tenant peasantry and thus won considerable popular support and political importance. While the *kabaka* gave them limited support,[14] the Lukiko—which politically represented the landed class—totally rejected any attempt at revising the 1900 Agreement.

The claims of the *bataka* were investigated and upheld in principle by a commission of inquiry. From the point of view of the state, the *bataka* issue was but one aspect of a multiple problem: the landlords were getting fat on their appropriation while the tenants were responding by reducing their cash-crop production; economically, the appropriation of the landlords jeopardized both the supply of raw materials to the metropolitan bourgeoisie and the revenue of the state while politically, the *bataka* organized the grievances of the tenant peasantry. The problem, however, was also an opportunity, one that the state seized when it passed the 1928 Busulu and Nvujjo Law. The law put a limit on the *busulu* and *nvujjo* the landlord could appropriate from his tenant, while guaranteeing the tenant complete and hereditary security of tenure *so long as* he continued the effective cultivation of his land, in other words, so long as he continued to grow cash crops.[15] The effect of the law was to render the relation between landlord and tenant by and large formal, substantially robbing it of its class content. At one stroke the state had achieved several goals: (1) it severely limited the material basis of the power of the landlord-chiefs; (2) it gave the peasants security of tenure provided they cultivated cash crops for export; (3) it guaranteed the metropolitan bourgeoisie its supply of raw materials; (4) it deprived the Bataka Association of the popular basis of its support;* and finally, (5) it made it possible for the state to increase its share of the economic surplus.† Not surprisingly, the state justified

---

* The governor informed the Lukiko that although the commission of inquiry had upheld the claims of the *bataka* in principle, the secretary of state had "definitely decided not to intervene in this dispute."[16] At the same time, the passage of the Busulu and Nvujjo Law removed the immediate grievances of the tenants; in subsequent years the Bataka Association died a natural death.

† A memorandum from the agricultural land officer to the chief justice, chairman of the 1927 Finance Committee, made clear that the imposition of a land tax in Buganda was "inopportune" without a "drastic alteration in the relationship between landlord and tenant."[17] But the official committee that devised the specifics of the law advised an increase in taxation of peasants, considering it "equitable and advisable." It pointed out that "the abolition of *nvujjo* will cause a fundamental redistribution of wealth throughout the

the law as a measure "safeguarding the interests of the native tenants." [20]*

In their appropriation of the tenant peasantry, the landlords had not just confined themselves to demands for *busulu* and *nvujjo*, but had demanded surplus labor, or *luwalo*, which was due to them as a class and not as individuals. Written into the 1900 Agreement, *luwalo* took the form of a communal obligation whereby each town, village, or settlement was obliged to provide one laborer for every three huts to work on the upkeep of local roads for a month every year. The labor was controlled and its use directed by the Lukiko. In 1920, under pressure from the government, the Lukiko made *luwalo* an individual obligation, requiring all males over eighteen to work eight days in every quarter. In order to encourage the supply of "free" labor, the law stipulated that the *luwalo* obligation could be commuted for 10 shillings by men employed on contracts for more than three months each year.[22]

The 10-shilling commutation led to the building of a sizable fund. Since it was a part of the Buganda Treasury, it was removed from government control and was under the direct supervision of the Lukiko, which controlled treasury funds. By 1924, the commutation was estimated at £50,000 annually,[23] the

---

Province," that "cultivators will gain enormously," and that "the small additional direct taxation will hardly be felt." [18] The state passed a Native Taxation Law that same year. The governor, while countering the claims of the chiefs that the *nvujjo* was justified because it was "traditionally sanctioned," made it clear that what mattered was not the exploitation of the peasant, but whether it was the state or the landlords who benefited: "Supposing the Buganda Province produces 100,000 bales of cotton in the near future, this means something like £150,000 from the 10 percent levy going into the pockets of 'landowners'—to say nothing of the yield from other crops. If this 10 percent was native custom, surely it was also customary for the chiefs to be called upon to pass on to the Central Government in one form or another, a considerable proportion of what may be gotten out of the cultivator." [19]

* This ideological justification was reflected in the writings of bourgeois historians who sought to explain the law. Low and Pratt interpret the political events of the late 1910s and the 1920s as the result of the "increased concern in this period to promote the well-being of the ordinary subject." They cite the "more important" reason for the passage of the law as "a very strong desire to protect the *bakopi* [peasants] from exploitation by their landlords." [21] Such an explanation is no more than an apologia for the colonial state.

largest source of Buganda government revenue (which, apart from the *luwalo*, amounted to £36,000 in 1925).[24] Besides being the source of revenue for government expenditures, the funds were also used for extravagant consumption by the prominent members of the landed gentry (for instance, for car loans).[25] In 1925 the governor wrote to the secretary of state of "the necessity for a far closer supervision and control of the headquarters organization of the native government, especially of the native treasury, than has hitherto been possible." [26] The Lukiko, of course, bitterly resisted any encroachment on its financial independence. It took ten years, from the 1919 Protectorate Government Financial Rules, meant as guidelines, through the partial and later complete audits of 1921 and 1923, before a complete reorganization of the Buganda Treasury under "loyal" management finally gave the colonial state effective control.[27]

Once the landlords' economic base had been undermined, it remained to politically undermine their position by altering the hereditary nature of chieftainship and the automatic congruence of landlordship and chieftainship.

The struggle over the Buganda government's right to appoint chiefs reached a climax in 1926 with the resignation of the Baganda *katikiro* (prime minister), Sir Apollo Kaggwa.* This

---

* Sir Apollo Kaggwa's resignation was the result of a conflict with the acting provincial commissioner over the right of a minor chief to contact the Protectorate government *without* going through the Buganda government. The rule that minor chiefs did not get to the colonial state except through the intermediary of the Lukiko had considerably strengthened the political position of the major landlords, who were also the prominent officials of the Buganda government.[28] At issue, then, was the political solidarity and power of the chiefly class itself.

The Colonial Office file on Sir Apollo Kaggwa describes him as having "rendered invaluable help to the British during the perilous days of the mutiny, as well as, finally, against the remnant of the Sudanese, who had been joined by both Mwanga and Kaberega in the wild unknown country of Bukedi, to the East of the Nile. It is no overstatement to say that had his prestige and authority been cast at that time into the balance against the British raj, European influence would have been entirely, if not temporarily, eclipsed." Despite such "invaluable" collaboration, the minute Kaggwa became a political liability, the same British raj threw him overboard.

was but a prelude to the dismissal of the vast majority of the chiefs, including their leading members. For initiating a debate on the British control of Buganda's finances and introducing a resolution "asking that the kabaka's powers over approving the budget be restored," Yusufu Bamuta, secretary to the Lukiko and a full member, was immediately dismissed.[29] Also dismissed, in the process of the "reorganization" of the Buganda Treasury, was the *omuwanika* (treasurer). Between 1921 and 1933, 145 of a total of 212 chiefs were replaced.[30]

The chiefs and officials that remained were put on salary and made transferable—in other words, they were without any independent political base. Most had worked as clerks or interpreters for the central government. The new *katikiro* was Martin Luther Nsibirwa, a former clerk in the Protectorate government, and the new *omuwanika* was Servano Kulubya, an interpreter, an inspector of schools, and one of the members of the 1927 Commission of Inquiry into the funds of the Lukiko.[31] Kulubya proceeded to centralize the control and use of Lukiko funds, taking away from *ssaza* and *gombolola* chiefs whatever financial control they had over *luwalo* monies. During his term of office from 1929 to 1945, the Lukiko estimates note a steady increase in deposits handed over to the center.[32] At the same time, the Buganda Treasury began to take over a number of expenses previously met by the Protectorate government.[33]

The subjection of the Baganda landlords was now complete. Once again politically and economically dependent on the colonial government for their prosperity and position, individual members of this class gladly ran a rubberstamp administration in return for individual favors. Most importantly, however, the entire class structure of Buganda had undergone a transformation. Whereas prior to 1928 the chiefs were landlords and their positions were hereditary (that is, they had an objective base in the economy and a measure of political independence from the colonial state), after 1928 they were without effective control over either their land or their position. Whereas before 1928 they were a class of landlords, after 1928 they were an intermediary state bureaucracy, a collaborating class that was dependent on, and identified with, the colonial state.

Meanwhile, the colonial state had learned some important lessons, lessons which were to have a decisive impact on land policy and rural class formation in the remaining provinces. The question of land policy in the rest of the Protectorate had occupied the attention of the colonial state since a committee was first appointed to make concrete recommendations on the subject in 1914.[34] It was another decade, however, before the issue could be resolved in the minds of the colonial authorities. The reason for the delay was that the resolution of the question of land policy was not possible without a prior resolution of the question of production. Was the surplus to be produced on plantations or on peasant farms? Should land policy provide security of tenure to the peasant or right of alienation to the landlord?

As we have seen, by 1920 the question of whether the Uganda economy would be based on peasant or plantation production was clear, and henceforth colonial policy actively discouraged the transfer of land from "natives" to "nonnatives." In 1920, while approving the draft of a land settlement plan for Ankole, Bunyoro, Toro, and Busoga, the secretary of state specified that the settlement specifically preclude "the right of disposing of any part of them [estates] to nonnatives."[35] In 1922, the Buganda Lukiko passed a bill prohibiting the alienation of *mailo* land to nonnatives. The following year, the secretary of state decreed that the alienation of Crown Land in freehold to nonnatives would be discontinued.[36]

A second issue that had yet to be resolved was whether the traditional ruling classes in the other kingdoms of the south should be granted freehold estates. The 1900 Agreement in Buganda had secured the political support of a powerful, well-organized feudal class. In the rest of Uganda, however, this class was not as powerful; furthermore, in those places where it did possess significant power—as in Bunyoro—it had been brought to heel by Baganda agents and their armies. There was thus no political need to create a class of landlords outside of Buganda. Furthermore, by the 1920s the foremost consideration for the British was the potential danger of a powerful and parasitical indigenous class, which would become a fetter on production and would at the same time compete with the state for the existing surplus.* In a dispatch to the secretary of state noting the political troubles that had arisen in Buganda as a result of the *mailo* system, the governor concluded: "It has become clear that this system is a dangerous one." [38] The 1922 Conference of the Provincial Commissioners, the final in a series of official conferences on land policy beginning in 1914, noted "the social and political troubles which have arisen in Buganda during the past year on the question of the allotment of land under the Buganda Agreement, 1900" and recommended that

> the Provincial Commissioners consider that it is a matter for deep regret that the ideas of "freehold" and "landlordism" should have been introduced into the Protectorate by the Uganda, Ankole, and Toro Agreements, and would urge that this disastrous mistake should not be perpetuated in districts where the Government has not committed itself by any such unfortunate contracts.[39]

This became the basis of colonial land policy in the rest of Uganda in the interwar years. The main objective was to nip in the bud any aspirations or demands for landlordship among the traditional ruling classes by forbidding any intermediaries between peasant producers and the state in the agricultural economy—in other words, the state sought a monopoly of control over the agricultural surplus.

---

* Commenting on the demand by the precolonial ruling class in Toro for land grants similar to those in Buganda, an official committee wrote: "The interested parties have apparently no doubts as to the equity of living upon the labour of others, and it is a noteworthy illustration of the conception of the purpose of land grants entertained by the 'landlord' class in Toro that, since the Agreement areas were allotted, there has been a total absence on the part of the beneficiaries of any attempt to develop these estates, and they have been content to draw rents without consideration of their obligations as large landowners." [37]

What the committee was objecting to was the existence of a parasitic landed gentry totally divorced from production and appropriating its share of the surplus as rent, not a capitalist landed class that would itself supervise and manage production, appropriating its share of the economic surplus not as rent but as *profit*.

The Southern Kingdoms

The above policy was arrived at, however, only in the 1920s. Needless to say, social relations in the countryside had not remained at a standstill during the prior two decades. In the absence of an official land policy, the traditional ruling class, especially where it still possessed a measure of organizational strength, took the initiative.

In those kingdoms with land agreements, Toro and Ankole, where the small chiefly class had already been granted land as freehold, the landlords began extracting rent from their tenants. In Bunyoro, where there was no agreement, the *mukama* (king) began making *kibanja* grants "not only to chiefs still active or retired but to members of the peasant family, to servants of Mukama's household, and to more substantial peasants who had succeeded in asserting some small degree of local ascendency." [40]* Considering the process rather "natural," the local British administrative officers quietly acquiesced. Side by side with official *kibanjas* granted to a chief for the duration of his term, there were private *kibanjas* granted to him for life. By 1930, some 18,549 of the 22,000 poll-tax payers in Bunyoro also paid *busulu* to the holders of *kibanja*.[41] The *busulu* payment, originally 4 shillings per adult male, was increased to 7 shillings in 1914.[42] In Busoga, the primary form of the surplus was that of labor performed by peasants on the chief's farm.[43]

In the 1920s, the colonial state gradually eliminated all attempts by landlords to extract surplus from the peasantry. In Toro, *busulu* was outlawed.[44] In Bunyoro, the government accepted the recommendations of an official commission of inquiry that any landlord and tenant system be rejected and that "the interests of actual cultivators should predominate." [45] In Busoga, the labor tribute a chief could extract from a peasant was drastically curtailed from fifty-two to twelve days in 1926,[46] and was abolished altogether in 1928.[47] In each case, the change was introduced in phases for political reasons: it was necessary that the authority and allegiance of the chiefs not be disrupted

---

* In Buganda, a *kibanja* may refer to a peasant's holding; in Bunyoro, the use of the word is restricted to describing the private holding of a chief.

by too rapid a change in their relations to the peasant producers.* The crux of the policy, however, remained the same: "An arrangement by which the chiefs and peasants alike would be tenants of the Crown, the chiefs being renumerated by fixed salaries and not by the labour or payments of the peasants." [49]

As in Buganda, in all these southern kingdoms, the Crown granted the peasant security of tenure as long as he was in effective occupation of his piece of land.[50] Unlike in Buganda, however, the peasants in these kingdoms became Crown tenants.† The surplus they had previously paid the landlord as

---

* Thus, a Colonial Office minute on Busoga noted: "As regards Busoga, the Provincial Commissioner, Eastern Province, considers that our proposal goes too far in the direction of breaking down the authority of the chiefs. Changes such as we propose must be made gradually . . ." [48]

† While the system in these provinces was, on the whole, different from that in Buganda, there were some similarities.

In Bunyoro, from the funds collected by the native administration, it was decided that "life annuities will be [provided] to persons who now benefit by the *kibanja* system, as it is not intended that they will suffer loss financially from the introduction of the present proposals." [51] In the rest of the Western Province (Toro and Ankole), the system underwent many changes until it finally stabilized in the 1930s:

1. In 1923, tribute was abolished on all but the estates officially granted to chiefs under the Toro and Ankole agreements. Peasants not living on official estates paid "Crown Land Rent" of 6 shillings per annum to the Native Administrations; the proceeds were utilized for the payment of lower-grade chiefs.

2. In December 1927, the poll tax was increased by 6 shillings a year to be paid to native administrations, while rent on official Agreement estates was abolished. It was intended that the higher chiefs be paid the same fixed salaries as the rest of the chiefs, except that the payment "would take into consideration the tribute paid by the tenants" on their land. The governor also approved "the refund for life of all native freeholders who were not salaried officials of the tribute paid by their tenants." Thus all landlords, whether appointed as chiefs or not, now received a fixed sum from the state while the amount paid bore some relation to the number of tenants on the land. Furthermore, the intention was that the above rights would disappear as the land was sold or inherited. This change was announced in the beginning of 1929.

3. As a result of combined opposition from missions, planters (many of whom were also landlords), and chiefs, it was decided a month later, in February 1929, that the above right of receiving a fixed salary in lieu of rent would not be reserved to the original owner alone; it could also be transferred to another through sale or inheritance. The only reservation was that the per capita rate

busulu, they now paid into the native administration treasury as Crown rent.[53] Out of these funds, the state paid salaries to the chiefs.[54] While peasants were still stripped of their surplus produce, the state had gained an important political objective: the chief, instead of being a landlord with private control over land, appropriating rent or labor from tenants, was now a salaried official who could be hired, transferred, or fired. The governor wrote the secretary of state about the political change in the colony: "The peasant now looks to the Protectorate Government through the Mukama for the preservation of the right of occupation instead of to the Mukama through a local overlord." [55]

---

not exceed 6 shillings per annum and that such a right not be attached to any new freehold.

4. In April 1933, the report of the provincial commissioner, Western Province, showed that "30 percent of the native population of Toro and Ankole were nominally living on private land which amounted to less than 10 percent of the area of the district." Instances were given of persons paying poll tax in areas remote from their actual homes in order to secure for the landowner, on whose estate they retained but a nominal house or cultivation, the refund of the tribute paid as part of the poll tax. One of the missions was found to have evolved a plan whereby all its teachers, wherever they might be living, paid poll tax in the area where the mission estate existed; a refund of tribute was then claimed. The provincial commissioner thus formed the opinion that "it might only be a matter of time until every tax payer became a nominal tenant of some landowner, thus diverting the entire amount of the tribute from the native administrations to the pockets of the estate owners."

5. Two important changes were instituted in the Western Province land policy as a result: (a) the tribute as part of the poll tax was reduced from 6 shillings to 4 shillings per annum; and (b) the government decided that the state should not "continue in the invidious position of rent collectors for private interests." It was thus decided that official Agreement landlords will collect their own rent, legally fixed at 4 shillings per annum.

Furthermore, the tenant was given legal security of tenure. It was held that "there is ample public land available for any who are discontented with their lot as tenants." The planters and the missionaries were compensated once and forever in lieu of their regular rent from tenants. The planters' tribute was compounded by a regular sum, while the missionary societies' tribute was replaced by an additional grant-in-aid.[52]

Thus, in that part of Western Province which was Agreement land, that is, in less than 10 percent of it, there was a return to the Buganda system.

The Rest of Uganda

In the first two decades of colonial rule, commodity production for export, encouraged by state taxation and land tenure policies, spread in the south. The same process, however, was limited in the north, where the state sought to discourage cash-crop cultivation and encourage labor migration as a means for earning cash to pay taxes. While commodity production spread in the south, the north (and parts of the west) were turned into a labor reservoir.

The 1920s, however, saw a dramatic change in the policy of the state in these labor-supply areas: for the first time there was a concerted attempt to encourage and spread cash-crop cultivation, particularly of cotton and tobacco, because of the availability of an alternate source of labor for southern agriculture. By World War I, a trickle of immigrants from Ruanda had begun coming into Buganda. In 1924, the Belgians, overzealous in their attempts to extract the maximum from the indigenous population, introduced heavy taxes and compulsory cultivation of food and cash crops, thereby accelerating migration into Buganda.[56] The trickle of immigrants turned into a flow, and soon the Banyaruanda became the bulk of the agricultural laborers in the south.

While certain regions of the north, such as parts of West Nile, did remain a labor reservoir for southern agriculture, the process in most of the area became qualitatively different: the peasants were transformed, through state action, into petty commodity producers. This process, begun in the late 1920s, gathered momentum in the 1930s and 1940s. As in the south, the relations of production on the land provided the peasant security of tenure as long as he cultivated the land effectively. The rent was nominal and the state was the landlord.

By 1932 the Colonial Office was able to "crystallize" what it called the cardinal points of land policy in Uganda:

1. No one to have grants of land in freehold.
2. No grants of "official estates" from the occupants of which tribute can be expected by the holder of office. Introduction of a

system of payment of tribute to the Protectorate government by which it is returned to the native administration and used together with the normal rebate of poll tax as a fund for the payment of salaries and pensions to chiefs.

3. Peasants to be secured in their holdings.[57]

The lessons of Buganda had been well applied in the rest of the Protectorate. Not only was the substance of the 1928 Busulu and Nvujjo Law stretched to the limit through the total elimination of *busulu,* but surplus labor was also eliminated. In fact, landlordship itself was rooted out. Whereas the salaried Buganda chief was still likely to own land and derive at least nominal tribute from his tenants, his non-Buganda counterpart was a civil servant whose only source of income was the salary he received from the state. Thus were created the objective conditions for the existence of a "loyal" class of bureaucrats, junior partners in the colonial enterprise.

Notes

1. Dispatch from Acting Governor Jarvis to Secretary of State for Colonies on "Security of Tenure Enjoyed by Muganda Peasant," August 28, 1926, in CO 536/143.
2. See memorandum from Daudi Chwa, *kabaka* of Buganda, to the Governor and Chief Secretary of Government, June 25, 1926, in CO 536/143.
3. UP, *Annual Report for 1912–13,* No. 787 of January 1914, p. 13.
4. Para. 12, Buganda Agreement of 1900; see Appendix II in A. Low and C. Pratt, *Buganda and British Overrule.*
5. UP, *Annual Report for 1910–11,* No. 708 of February, 1912, p. 4.
6. Report of the commission appointed to inquire into and offer suggestions for raising additional revenue to meet the increasing expenditure of the Protectorate. Enclosure No. 1 in Dispatch No. 178 of April 24, 1914, in CO 536/68.
7. Buganda Taxation Agreement, 1922, of October 17, 1922, in CO 536/121.
8. Ibid.
9. See enclosure in minute by Governor Gowers of July 15, 1925. Enclosure No. 1 in file on Butaka Lands, in CO 536/141.

10. Report of a commission appointed by the governor to consider certain matters affecting tenure and rents of native lands in Buganda Province, enclosure in minute by the Governor, SMP 880, Minute 1 of July 15, 1925, in file on Butaka Lands in CO 536/141. As a 1925 report from the deputy director of agriculture stated, in Bamunanika and Bukoba (Kyaggwe) something like 250 tons of cotton valued at £8,000 had been collected as *nvujjo* from the *kabaka*'s *mailos*, an average of about Shs. 20 per grower. See J. V. Wild, "Note on 1928 Busulu and Nvujjo Law," in H. M. West, ed., *The Transformation of Land Tenure in Buganda Since 1896*, pp. 79–86.

11. Memorandum from Simpson to Chief Secretary, Entebbe, January 4, 1917, in CO 536/84.

12. Dispatch from Jarvis to Secretary of State for the Colonies, August 28, 1926, in CO 536/143.

13. Wilson to Sadler, January 2, 1903, BRA General, 1902; quoted in Low and Pratt, p. 144.

14. Low and Pratt, p. 235.

15. Report of a committee appointed by the governor to consider certain matters affecting tenure and rents of native land in the Buganda Province, in CO 536/141.

16. Confidential Dispatch of October 17, 1926, announcement by Acting Governor Jarvis to a special meeting of the Lukiko, in CO 536/141.

17. H. B. Thomas, "Memorandum on the Taxation of Land and Survey Office," Entebbe, April 4, 1927, in West, ed.

18. In CO 536/151 (File No. 20258).

19. Quoted in J. V. Wild, "Note on the Busulu and Nvujjo Law," March 10, 1948, in West, ed.

20. Confidential Dispatch from Acting Governor to Secretary of State, Enclosure No. 1 of October 7, 1926, in CO 536/141.

21. In *Buganda and British Overrule*, pp. 231, 237.

22. See CO 536/104. The commutation was also open to private traders, to those who owned more than a square mile of land, and to *batongole* chiefs and their deputies. See also *Buganda Annual Report, 1920–21*.

23. *Buganda Annual Report, 1924*.

24. Governor to Secretary of State, November 9, 1925, in CO 536/137.

25. See Protectorate Government, Commission of Inquiry Following the Auditor's Report of 1926 into the Buganda Treasury, quoted in John Crysostom Ssekamwa, "The Development of the Buganda Treasury," p. 124.

26. Governor to Secretary of State, November 9, 1925, in CO 536/137.

The governor, writing of the need for "continual financial supervision" of the Buganda treasury, proposed to the secretary of state that "should, however, an adverse majority opinion prevail [in the Lukiko] I would ask for your authority as a final resort to inform the *kabaka* and his advisors that you have carefully considered the proposals, that you have decided that they are essential to the efficient administration of Buganda for the conduct of which their loyal cooperation with the Protectorate Government is expressly required by Paragraph 6 of the 1900 Agreement. . . ."

27. See Ssekamwa, "The Development of the Buganda Treasury," pp. 65, 80, 84, 98–101, 157.

28. File on Apollo Kaggwa in CO 536/141.

29. Letter from Yusufu Bamuta in *Time and Tide*, January 18, 1929. See also enclosure in File No. 20269 on Yusufu Bamuta, CO 536/151; and *Uganda News*, April 20, 1928.

30. List of chiefs in Buganda for 1922, Makerere Main Library, Africana Section. See also John Crysostom Ssekamwa, "Submission and Reaction in Buganda," pp. 443–444.

31. See Ssekamwa, "The Development of the Buganda Treasury," pp. 115, 161.

32. Buganda Lukiko Estimates, 1928–1945; quoted in ibid., p. 187.

33. For example, from 1930 on, social services in Buganda were financed by the Buganda government from *luwalo* funds. By 1941, the Buganda government was lending the central government £5,000 yearly, to be repaid after the war without interest. Also in 1941, on the advice of the Protectorate government, the Buganda government lent £10,000 to the East African War Bonds operated from Kenya at an interest of 2½ percent. Beginning in 1940 also, the Buganda government took over the financing of primary education in the province. Ssekamwa, "The Development of the Buganda Treasury," pp. 187–188, 215.

34. V. Harlow and L. Chilver, eds., *History of East Africa*, vol. 2.

35. Memorandum on Land Settlement in Ankole, Bunyoro, Toro, and Busoga from Secretary of State to Governor of Uganda, February 22, 1921, in CO 536/104.

36. Colonial Office Memorandum on Alienation of Land in Uganda, in CO 536/166 (File No. 21082).

37. Inquiry into the Grievances of the Mukama and the People of Toro, Report of the Committee, in CO 536/143, pp. 5–6 (File XF 7438).

38. Minute by the Governor, enclosure to dispatch to Secretary of State by Acting Governor on land policy, November 7, 1922, in CO 536/121.

39. Appendix to the minutes of the Provincial Commissioners' Conference, 1922, Native Land Policy, September 12, 1922, in CO 536/120.

40. UP, *Kibanja System in Bunyoro*, p. 19.

41. The remainder were made up of chiefs and lesser officeholders, of *kibanja* owners and their agents, and of residents in townships and on certain freehold and leasehold estates. Ibid., p. 21.

42. Beattie, "The Nyoro," in Audrey Richards, ed., *East African Chiefs*, p. 169.

43. Colonial Office, minute on land tenure in Toro, May 9, 1929, in CO 536/154.

44. Colonial Office, minute on land tenure in Toro, in CO 536/155.

45. UP, *Kibanja System in Bunyoro*, p. 24.

46. Colonial Office memorandum on Busoga land policy, in CO 536/149.

47. Wrigley, in L. A. Fallers, ed., *The King's Men*, p. 41.

48. Colonial Office, Land Settlement in Ankole, Toro, Bunyoro and Busoga, August 9, 1917, in CO 536/86 (File No. 49903).

49. Colonial Office, minute on land tenure in Toro, CO 536/155.

50. See, e.g., circular distributed among the people in Toro. Enclosure in dispatch from Governor to Secretary of State, May 9, 1929, in CO 536/154.

51. Report of the Commission of Inquiry into Land Tenure and Kibanja System in Bunyoro, 1931 (Entebbe, 1931). Enclosure in No. 77 of February 12, 1932, Governor to Secretary of State, in CO 536/171 (File No. 22057).

52. A. W. Place and H. B. Thomas, "Memorandum on Busulu Payment to the Native Governments of Toro and Ankole in Western Province." Enclosure in dispatch from Governor Mitchell to Secretary of State, April 3, 1936, on Toro and Ankole Agreements, in CO 536/190 (File No. 40148).

53. Colonial Office memorandum on Busoga land policy, in CO 536/149; and dispatch from Governor to Secretary of State on Land Tenure in Toro, May 9, 1929, in CO 536/154. See also Governor to Secretary of State, March 23, 1923, in CO 536/124.

54. Ibid.

55. Dispatch from Governor to Secretary of State on Land Tenure in Toro, May 9, 1929, in CO 536/154 (File No. 20296).

56. Archie Mafeje, "The Fallacy of Dual Economies Revisited," p. 6.

57. Memorandum by Colonial Office on the report of Commission of Inquiry into Land Tenure and Kibanja System in Bunyoro, 1931, in CO 536/171.

5
On the Colonial State and the Articulation of Modes of Production

What are referred to today as the underdeveloped countries were incorporated into world capitalism in the last four centuries. The resulting world capitalist system can be conceptualized as the product of an articulation of various modes of production, with the capitalist mode dominant and the precapitalist modes dependent. The substance of the domination is that it is the accumulation needs of the capitalist mode that determine the nature of production in the precapitalist modes. At the level of analysis of national economies, the territories that capitalism came to control in this period can be divided into two separate groups. In the first are the territories that capitalism *populated*, the settler colonies, and here the primary process was that of the destruction of existing modes of production and the prevalence of the capitalist mode. In the second are the territories that capitalism *dominated;*[1] here it neither simply nor primarily destroyed the precapitalist modes by appropriating the producers and making wage laborers of them, but rather restructured and conserved them in a dependent relation. While the precapitalist modes lost their independence, they were conserved in their *forms.*[2] While precapitalist relations (forms) were conserved, their content, the productive forces, now functioned strictly in the interest of capitalist accumulation. In the resulting social formation, the capitalist mode dominated, though it did not prevail. Such was the case in Uganda.

The specific nature of the domination, and thus of the articulation of the capitalist with the precapitalist modes, is the result of concrete historical circumstance and can only be grasped through concrete historical analysis. This articulation is a process that must be looked at in its different phases. Let us first examine the nature of the articulation in the first phase of colonial capitalism, the phase of its consolidation.

The Feudal Mode of Production

In Uganda, the autonomy of this mode was lost with the destruction of the feudal state. But while the unity of the *class* was undermined, a section of the feudal lords were reconstituted as landlords, subordinated to the colonial state. Whether legal or not, this process took place wherever the feudal mode prevailed in the south of Uganda. Where the precolonial ruling class had been the most powerful, in Buganda, the landed class retained a measure of autonomy from the colonial state until the second phase of colonial capitalism, the phase of its hegemony.

Feudal forms of appropriation—labor service, tribute in kind and cash—remained, but the serf became a tenant producing commodities *for export*. His production was integrated into the world market through the intermediary of the trader, and the surplus also took the form of trader's profit, appropriated by both the small trader and the metropolitan-based export-import company.

The Communal Mode of Production

Here there were two distinct forms of articulation, which should be considered separately: in one case, the communal mode was transformed into the petty commodity form, and in the other it retained its communal form.

In the case of *petty commodity production*, the communal cultivator, whose production had been for use, now became a petty commodity producer. While the process of production retained its precapitalist nature, the *purpose* of production underwent a radical transformation: the producer remained united with the means of production, the unit of production remained the family, and the technology of production was still the hoe, but the peasant now produced raw materials for metropolitan industry, and exchanged them at prices dictated by the metropolitan market. The small commodity producer was not just dominated at the level of exchange (the market), but also lost a measure of autonomy at the level of production. As we shall see, the change in what the peasant produced could only be brought about through the coercive agency of the colonial state. Once this change was accomplished, the petty commodity producer became enslaved to metropolitan capital through the intermediary of merchant capital. Here, the surplus predominantly took the form of the trader's profit.

In the case of *surplus labor production*, which occurred in the so-called subsistence areas of the colonial economy, two processes coexisted side by side: the proletarianization of the peasantry and communal production for use. The region of Uganda where this tendency was most pronounced in the first phase of colonial capitalism was the north. Commodity production was actively discouraged, and male members of a household were sent to work in the pockets of capitalist production (plantations, processing industries) while the rest of the family (the wife and children) remained on the land to carry out "subsistence" production. The male member was a migrant worker seasonally employed when the plantation or processing industry needed him. For the remainder of the year he returned to his family, whose production met his cost of subsistence: his wage, the price of his labor power, was sufficient to maintain one person (himself) for six months, not one family for twelve months. Because communal production coexisted with the capitalist mode of production, labor power was paid drastically below its value; the communal form, even when producing for use, was subordinated to and subsidized the cost of production of the capitalist mode. Just as petty production supplied cheap raw materials to the capitalist mode internationally, the communal form provided cheap labor to the capitalist mode nationally. Once its relations with the capitalist mode are examined, the communal mode loses its "subsistence" character.

In the second phase of colonial capitalism, the phase of its hegemony, the process of articulation underwent a qualitative change. Those sections of the precolonial feudal classes that had remained as landlords were now destroyed and feudal forms of appropriation were eliminated. (Only in Buganda, once again for political reasons, did they retain a nominal existence.) The only form to survive from the feudal era was superstructural: the institution of the kingship.

The almost total destruction of the feudal form did not, however, lead to the generalization of the capitalist mode. In fact, capitalist production suffered a decline as the plantations shrank in importance: the critical factor here was the accumulation need of metropolitan capital. What did become prevalent was petty commodity production. When Indian capitalists proposed to extend the scope of capitalist production by expanding sugar plantation agriculture, the secretary of state argued against plantation production, which would necessitate the creation of wage labor, and for peasant cultivation, which would supply the raw material to the sugar-processing industry.* In fact, the colonial state attempted to freeze the process of class formation in the countryside at the level of petty commodity production, so as to prevent the emergence of a capitalist landed class and its correlative, a rural proletariat. The producers became Crown tenants who had hereditary rights to land as long

---

* In 1940, the governor wrote the secretary of state asking for permission to alienate two plots, one of 2,400 acres (at Lugazi) and one of 2,560 acres (at Kakira), for the expansion of cultivation by the two sugar plantations. The secretary of state responded: "The grant of these additional leases would seem to indicate a step in the direction of wholly capitalistic sugar production in the Protectorate. Such a policy has been found to be undesirable in the other sugar producing dependencies, where much effort has been devoted to the building up of an industry based on cooperation between large capitalistic units which . . . manufacture, and small holders (including tenants) who grow the raw material but do not manufacture." [3]

Only when the governor made it clear that the small holders were already involved in the manufacture of the other raw materials (cotton and coffee) and that the labor for the plantations would be coming from existing "nonproducing areas" did the secretary agree.

as they cultivated it effectively, but could neither sell it nor buy it. The predominance of petty commodity producers provided the necessary social base for the absolute rule of the colonial state.

Although the capitalist mode was confined to small pockets within the colonial political economy, diminishing in importance in the second phase of articulation, it was nevertheless the dominant mode. The laws of accumulation of the capitalist mode determined the motion of the dependent precapitalist forms. While the capitalist mode dominated internationally, its domination in Uganda was not the result of its physical prevalence but of the dominant position of the colonial state, which was thus the national expression of the internationally dominant capitalist mode.

Colonialism is the implantation of a state apparatus in the conquered territory. The colonial state was a geographical extension of the metropolitan state; it was directly subordinate to the latter. Empirically, this appeared as the subordination of the colonial governor to the colonial secretary, and of the colonial bureaucracy to the Colonial Office. Simply put, the colonial state represented an *absentee* ruling class, the metropolitan bourgeoisie, and it performed the functions of both state and ruling class in an "independent" nation.*

The colonial state created the structures of the underdeveloped economy at both the levels of production and exchange. The very purpose of the peasant's production was altered—he now produced commodities for the metropolitan market—and the system of cash taxation, backed up by the coercive apparatus of the colonial state, was instrumental in generalizing this change. Although pockets of commodity production and export had existed in precolonial East Africa—for instance, the production of food crops on the Tanganyikan coast and their export to the plantations of Zanzibar, and the production and export of ivory from Uganda to European markets—on the whole, production in the territorial economy had been for internal consumption, trade had been in surpluses, and the nature of production determined the nature of trade.

---

* I refer here to *nonsettler* colonies in Africa.

With colonialism, the relationship between trade and production was reversed: the very purpose of production became trade, and the demands of the metropolitan market determined what would be produced. The change in the nature of production went hand in hand with a change in the *basis* of trade, from internal to export-import. The state's consistent preference for the Indian over the African trader had an objective basis: the operations of Zanzibar-based Indian merchant capital were already based on the export-import trade, particularly in British manufactured goods, whereas the African trader's activities were located in internal trade. The subordination of the African to the Indian trader was objectively the subordination of internal to export trade, a process in which the colonial state played a critical part.

Just as it created the structures of the underdeveloped economy, the colonial state destroyed and created entire classes. It destroyed the political autonomy and the material base of the precolonial ruling classes, at first partially and then totally. As it undermined the indigenous traders whose activities were located in internal trade, it also destroyed that class which produced manufactured goods for internal exchange, the artisans. As we have noted, the most important technology of production in the agricultural economy, the hoe, previously manufactured internally, was now imported from the metropole. In the first phase of colonial capitalism, all labor was reduced to the lowest common denominator, that of unskilled labor producing raw materials on the land. The class that the colonial state created was the working class, the wage laborers, first through forced labor and later through prohibition of cash-crop production and the requirement of cash taxes. While creating labor power as a commodity, it also attempted to limit this process for political reasons. The vast majority of producers in the colonial political economy were petty producers on land, united to their means of production. Underdeveloped capitalism is a peasant society.

Central to the process of articulation of these modes of production was the role of the colonial state. Whatever the forms this articulation took, at a certain level of abstraction we can identify the similarities and extract what may be called the general characteristics of underdeveloped capitalism, thereby bringing out its historical specificity.

First, with colonialism, metropolitan capital penetrates the process of production in the colony; as a result, the structure of production in the underdeveloped economy is subordinated to the accumulation needs of metropolitan capital. The productive activity of the people is redirected to the production of cash crops. The determination of these crops—cotton, coffee, tea—is by the colonial state, and its production is for export to the metropolitan market. While capitalism generalizes commodity production, underdeveloped capitalism generalizes commodity production *for the metropolitan market*. Thus, Clive Thomas posits as an "iron law" of an underdeveloped economy that the structure of production bears no direct relation to the structure of consumption.[4] ("We do not produce what we consume, we do not consume what we produce.") The underdeveloped economy is first and foremost an export-import economy.

Second, circulating (unproductive) capital dominates production. The commercial capital that dominates production is that capital whose operations are based on export-import. The primacy of commercial capital—the decisive role of the trader and the merchant—within the territorial economy reflects the primacy of metropolitan capital at the level of the colonial system.

Third, commercial capital possesses a monopoly base which is not a result of a class struggle between different sections of capital (monopoly is not the outgrowth of a competitive economy), but is a result of the political actions of the colonial state. Colonial legislation secures a monopoly base for territorially based capital. In turn, this base is not an expression of internal strength but an expression of the monopoly base of metropolitan capital to which it is tied in a dependent relation. It is on the basis of this inherited monopoly base that it builds up its strength in the territorial economy. (The case in point in Uganda is the Indian commercial bourgeoisie.)

That the monopoly base of dominant capital is not a result of an internal class struggle within capital, with one section emerging as a monopolistic bourgeoisie, has enormous consequences for the development of productive forces in the territorial economy. "The essence of the 'productive forces' in the capitalist mode of production is to be constantly *in the process of transition* from manual labour to mechanized labour,"[5] a process that is the objective result of the class struggle, the competition between enterprises that necessitates a continual replacement of variable by constant capital and a continual expansion in the size of the productive enterprise. The absence of this struggle in underdeveloped capitalism is also the absence of a tendency internal to it that leads to the constant revolutionizing of the forces of production. Also, precisely because territorially dominant capital possesses a monopoly base, the premise of its appropriation is not as much an expansion in the productive base as the exchange of unequal values made possible by the same monopoly base.

Fourth, the surplus that is retained internally takes predominantly the form of merchant's profits. Agricultural surpluses are not reinvested in agriculture but are siphoned off into commerce. The social consequence of this is both the pauperization of agricultural producers and an attempt by its most advanced members to go into trade. This dictates the very process of class formation in underdeveloped capitalism. The propertied class that develops from among the indigenous people is a class that forms in the very interstices of the externally oriented export-import economy: in commerce, in cash-crop agriculture, and within the state apparatus itself. The historical process creates within the colony mediating economic structures and social classes that have an objective interest in maintaining the process of underdevelopment.

Notes

1. The distinction is made by J. Banayi, "The Mode of Production in Indian Agriculture."
2. See Charles Bettelheim, Appendix I to Arghiri Emmanuel, *Unequal Exchange*, pp. 297–298.
3. Governor to Secretary of State and reply from Secretary of State,

Confidential, Acquisition of Land by Non-Natives, March 18, 1940, in CO 536/207 (File No. 40266).
4. In "Issues of Transition to Socialism in Tanzanian-Type Economies."
5. Etienne Balibar, "The Basic Concepts of Historical Materialism," in L. Althusser and E. Balibar, *Reading Capital*, p. 237.

6
The Formation
of the Petty Bourgeoisie

The political and economic demise of the Baganda feudal landlords meant an end to the political cohesion of the class. The Lukiko was no longer the political representative of this landed oligarchy. Although a number of individual landlords remained members, and although new members either had or were granted titles to land, the change was fundamental; the leadership of the Buganda Parliament was now in the hands of a new social group, comprised of men who had been trained in the womb of the colonial state. Educated in missionary boarding schools, having worked their way up as interpreters or clerks in the Protectorate government, these individuals formed the nucleus of a new breed of appointed chiefs. Together they faithfully administered colonial policy. It could not be otherwise, for structurally they had little independence from the colonial state, which was now the surest safeguard of their political position. Even though they "owned" land, the source of their income was their salaries as chiefs, not their rent as landlords. This political fact, however, was seldom reflected in their ideology. On the contrary, they thought of themselves as "modernizers," the bearers of a new and progressive order. Objectively, however, as personified by the new *katikiro* (prime minister), Nsibirwa, and by the *omuwanika* (treasurer), Kulubya, they were the collaborators par excellence.

It should thus be no surprise that in the interwar period

opposition to the colonial order organized as opposition to the Lukiko, the expression of the colonial state in Buganda. During the 1930s numerous organizations and groups petitioned the *kabaka* and even the Protectorate government against the "Nsibirwa-Kulubya clique," later turning to the peasant producers for support against what they termed the "feudal exploiters." In the 1940s these protests reached a crescendo, culminating in the assassination of Nsibirwa and the enforced resignation of Kulubya during what have come to be known as the 1945 and 1949 riots.

These riots actually comprised two related but separate aspects: the rural violence, which was confined to Buganda, and the general strike, which was nationwide. The social forces that coalesced in this historic and mass opposition to the colonial order included various interests, some of which were in harmony only over the short run: bureaucrats upset about racial discrimination in pay scales, cash-crop farmers full of resentment against ginners and state marketing boards for creaming off a substantial part of their surplus product, traders demanding an end to state-protected monopoly privileges, and urban workers demanding better wages. What was later called a "nationalist" movement was in fact a coalition of groups, each with its own specific interest. If we are to understand the response of the state to this movement, and its own development, we must locate each strand that composed this coalition in terms of its social origin, trace its historical development, identify its organizational form, underline its political consciousness, and finally, grasp the objective position and *particular* interests of each before it merges into the general flow that became the "national" movement. It is the purpose of the following two chapters to present such an analysis.

While this national movement was in its composition a coalition of various social groups, its political leadership came primarily and increasingly from one social class, the petty bourgeoisie, which formed rapidly on the heels of the 1928 Busulu and Nvujjo Law. Unlike the landed gentry, the petty bourgeoisie was seldom politically cohesive. In fact, its formation was in three distinct sections of the export-import economy: as traders, as kulak farmers, and as civil servants. The nascent working class, the only indigenous social group to organize its interests independently of the petty bourgeoisie, was rapidly subsumed under that heading. Here we will analyze the early formation and politics of the petty bourgeoisie and working class.

The Workers

The precolonial economy of Buganda was also a precapitalist economy: there was no market in labor. No social group depended on the sale of its labor power for gaining access to the social product. The worker, dependent on a wage income, was the creation of the colonial state. While the state initially depended on forced labor, in time it created a class of "free" laborers through taxation. At the same time, however, the state did not want a class of workers exclusively dependent on wages, but a social group that would be available for employment in the capitalist economy for temporary periods but would otherwise return to and remain a part of the precapitalist agricultural economy. The precapitalist mode of production was thus to be preserved in a perverted form, as a labor reservoir for the capitalist mode of production.

We have seen how colonial policy divided the country between "producing" and "nonproducing" areas, with the north being the labor exporting and "nonproducing" area.[1] Accordingly, the job of the department of labor was to "ensure the welfare of native labour . . . [by] rendering the labour more mobile";[2] or, as the governor put it more explicitly in recommending the formation of a department of labor to the Colonial Office, its "primary object [was that] of increasing the flow of voluntary labour from outlying districts to the cotton producing areas."[3] When the planters were faced with an extreme labor shortage, the governor assisted the planters' association in setting up "an organization for recruiting labour in the less productive areas and conducting it to their plantations."[4]

In the 1920s the colony found an alternative supply of labor in Ruanda. By 1948, over a quarter of the population of Buganda came from Ruanda and West Nile, in that order of importance.*

* In the words of the provincial commissioner, Northern Province: "Although the district as a whole grows a considerable quantity of cotton and tobacco

The largest section from among them, the Banyaruanda agricultural laborers, were employed by the Baganda kulaks. The northern workers, on the other hand, were primarily employed by the two sugar plantations in the south (which employed 12,000–14,000 laborers) and by the government's public works department.[6]

The dominant characteristic of this labor was that it was "target labor": individual workers came to get enough money to pay their yearly taxes or to meet the costs of a particular social commitment, such as marriage.[7] Migrant, short-term, and highly mobile, this type of labor was least susceptible to being organized to defend its working interests. Common interests born out of temporarily shared working conditions were themselves temporary, and could at best beget temporary organization. Even the most highly concentrated of these workers, the plantation laborers, did not form a union until 1962. The agricultural workers employed by the Baganda kulaks, on the other hand, were both temporarily employed and geographically scattered, two to three on a farm, and were concentrated in neither time nor space.

As the number of these workers increased, the government's 1938 Commission of Inquiry into the Labour Situation in Uganda recommended that "the formation of a class of workers exclusively dependent on wages should be encouraged—but cautiously," [8] the reason being that migrant labor was economically costly, both in terms of providing for the transport and, in the course of transport, for health supervision and shelter. But the governor disagreed. Migrant labor, he maintained, "suited the needs of Uganda"; it might be "uneconomical" for

---

planting is making headway, it is perhaps fortunate that no really satisfactory economic crop has yet been found suitable for those areas with the highest population density. As a result of this perhaps there is, as yet, no conscious feeling of land hunger.

"The District is a valuable source of manpower, for the Lugbara and to a lesser extent the Alur are amongst the best manual workers in the Protectorate. Numbers travel to central Uganda of their own volition to seek employment with the Railway, sugar plantations, and on various industrial concerns and the district is an important source of contract labour, which is only taken from the highly populated areas." [5]

the government to transfer labor from one area to another, but it certainly was "beneficial." [9] First, the employers benefited *economically* because they paid the laborer a wage substantially below its value—that is, its cost of reproduction. Second, the system had *political* benefits: the objective conditions of migrant labor militated against effective political organization.

In spite of this, a migrant labor force could be maintained only as long as objective conditions of work allowed for it, that is, only as long as the labor required was seasonal and unskilled. This was possible when labor was needed on plantations and farms (both practicing agriculture with a low level of technology, needing unskilled labor for periods of intense employment, such as harvesting, weeding, and sowing, which alternated with periods of low activity), in state construction projects, and even in the processing industries, which operated at a peak in the three months following the cotton and coffee harvests.

Although manufacturing proper did not become a significant part of the territorial economy until after World War II, as a result of changing needs of metropolitan capital, the beginnings of a stable labor force can be traced to World War I, when a Buganda section of the East African Transport Corps was trained as motor car drivers and was later employed both in government service and by ginners and hullers as truck drivers.[10] Along with the domestic servants employed by the colonial bureaucrats and the commercial bourgeoisie, they formed the first stable elements of an urban wage-labor force. The Buganda African Motor Drivers Union was the first union to be formed in Uganda, in 1939. Along with the domestic servants, the motor drivers formed the only organized and the most articulate section of the workers in the 1940s. We shall return to this later.

The Petty Bourgeoisie

Let us now examine the historical development of the three sections of the petty bourgeoisie: the kulaks, the civil servants, and the traders.

1. KULAKS

A kulak is to be distinguished on the one hand from a self-sufficient middle peasant who may produce for the market but relies on family labor for production (though he may occasionally employ a laborer), and on the other hand from a capitalist farmer who is no longer a cultivator but a manager who relies solely on hired labor. A kulak is a rich peasant who *regularly* supplements his family labor force with hired labor; he is thus both a cultivator and an employer.

The 1928 Busulu and Nvujjo Law, by robbing the landlord-tenant relation of its economic substance, created the conditions for the emergence of a numerically large and powerful coffee- and cotton-cultivating kulak class in Buganda. The law gave security of land tenure to the Muganda peasant and his children as long as they cultivated it effectively. Although his children could inherit the land, he could not sell it. Furthermore, the law limited *busulu* to 10 shillings per annum and *nvujjo* to 4 shillings per annum, but the legal limits on the payment of *nvujjo* applied to the maximum of three acres per cash crop;[11] beyond this, the landlord could ask for as high a payment as he wished. On the other hand, the landlord was not allowed to evict the tenant as long as the latter was cultivating the land, even if the landlord wished to farm it himself. Thus, the landlord was legally kept from becoming a capitalist farmer, while the tenant had little initiative to increase the cultivation of a particular cash crop beyond the protected limit of three acres. The result was twofold: the market in land in Buganda was minor, and productive land units were seldom larger than three acres per cash crop. Had there been a free market in land, the class that would eventually have dominated the agricultural economy would have been a capitalist farming class owning large tracts of land and employing numerous laborers. The class that did emerge, however, was a kulak class, large in numbers but employing a few laborers on small plots of land. Capitalist farmers with "undertakings which extend over as much as 150 acres [and] . . . a regular labour force of perhaps 50 workers" were, according to Wrigley, "altogether exceptional." [12] In other words, they did not become a social class but a collection of individuals, both politically and economically insignificant in the larger political economy.

Small groupings of such capitalist farmers also flourished outside Buganda, particularly in Bunyoro. They had developed from the early *kibanja*-owning chiefs who, in the decades before 1933, had managed to accumulate some wealth from their appropriation of *busulu*.* Their numbers, however, were few, the land they controlled was of marginal importance in the regional political economy, and whatever political power they wielded stemmed not from their position as capitalist farmers but from their political appointment as chiefs administering colonial policy.

With the exception of Busoga, which we shall discuss later, there were no kulak formations outside of Buganda. In the remaining areas of peasant production, peasants held the land as Crown tenants and paid nominal rents. There was no market in land, nor was there any shortage of land. In Bunyoro, a study showed not only that there was "no land shortage," but also that there was no "evidence that any money or goods [were] demanded from prospective tenants." [14] In fact, as late as 1953, "only about a quarter of the available cultivable land" in Bunyoro was in use, while in Toro, a 1960 survey concluded that "there is plenty of land" and that "as long as he [the peasant] continues to cultivate that land it is his to use." [15] Neither was there any agricultural wage labor in these regions. As a result, wherever there were plantations—the African tobacco plantations in Bunyoro and the non-African sugar and tea plantations in Busoga and Toro—the labor came from the West Nile district in the north.

Commodity production began in the Northern Province in the

---

* It should be noted that after 1933, even though the colonial state decided to issue certificates of occupancy to actual cultivators in Bunyoro, in fact the certificates were issued to the previous landlords. The land allotted thus contained peasants who were barred from taking out certificates of occupancy over the areas they actually cultivated. Nevertheless, the landlords, even though in possession of titles of occupancy, were not allowed to extract *busulu* from the tenants. The landlord-tenant relation thus remained a purely formal one—a status relation, not a class relation. Even this formal relation had become a barrier to the advancement of production by the 1950s. Beattie noted: "I should add that signs are now beginning to appear that an attempt by a tenant to develop his holding on modern lines, by planting permanent crops, etc., is coming to be regarded as grounds for eviction." [13] In other words, the *relations* of production had become a fetter on the advancement of the forces of production, as happened in Buganda.

1920s. The arrival of migrant labor from Ruanda, which reduced the importance of the north as a labor supply area, coincided with attempts by the state to introduce cash-crop cultivation, particularly in Lango and Acholi. Henceforth, the north was divided into two economic regions: West Nile remained a source of migrant labor, while Acholi and Lango reemerged as important centers of cotton production. As in the Western Province, in Acholi and Lango there was no legal ownership of land by the peasantry, but cultivation established undisputed rights of use. Peasants breaking new land were not required to pay an entry fee (in either money, goods, or services) to the chiefs.* Peasant production of cash crops in the Northern and Western provinces was based on the use of family labor. In other words, kulak formations did not emerge in these regions.

The one exception outside of Buganda was Busoga. Although here too there was no legal ownership of land and the peasants were Crown tenants, land was not in plentiful supply. Commodity production in Busoga had begun in the early part of the century and by mid-century the scarcity of land was pronounced. Cultivation was no longer sufficient to establish the right of use and prospective cultivators had to pay a *nkoko* (entry fee) to the chiefs.† Once he had paid, however, the peasant could occupy the land indefinitely for as long as he continued to cultivate it effectively. From the ranks of these peasants there emerged small groups of more prosperous peasants who employed other peasants. Though similar to that in Buganda, the process was on a much smaller scale, and lacked the effective organization of the Baganda kulaks. The Busoga kulaks remained a regional social group of marginal consequence to the national political economy. Nonetheless, the

---

* A 1953 survey by the provincial commissioner concluded that in Acholi there was "no land shortage" and that "demarcation for the purpose of cultivation establishes ownership." Similarly, in Lango, "cultivation gives undisputed right to the use of land as does occupation of a house to the land around the compound." [16]

† By 1960, the *nkoko* had become "a definite payment of money which has grown steadily as the years have gone on. It varies in size from several thousand shillings for large plots near urban centers, particularly around Jinja, to some fifty or more shillings in distant rural areas." [17]

content of their politics and the nature of their organization, as we shall see, really made Busoga seem a Buganda writ small.

The bulk of the kulaks were thus situated in Buganda.* The emergence of rich peasants from the ranks of the cash-crop growers coincided with a dramatic shift from cotton to coffee production. Coffee was a much more attractive crop because an average yield of two tons per acre paid the grower ten times more than seed cotton yielding 400 pounds per acre.[19] At the same time, the requirements of coffee production put it beyond the reach of the middle or poor peasant, making it a kulak crop. For one thing, unlike cotton, which matured in seven months, coffee could not be harvested for four years. Also, unlike cotton, coffee required greater skills, and could not be grown in rotation with subsistence crops, thus requiring an adjustment in the life of the peasant grower.[20] The expansion in coffee cultivation thus went hand in hand with the emergence of the kulaks.†

The labor employed by the Buganda kulaks came from Ruanda. As we have seen, the trickle of immigrants turned into a flow in the 1920s. The figures for 1924 showed that of 4,834 immigrants all told, 1,394 (28.8 percent) were from Ruanda. More came in the years between 1931 and 1948, when the non-Baganda people in Buganda increased by over 28.5 percent to some 441,000. In 1948, 34.0 percent of the African population in Buganda was made up of immigrants from outside the province, most of them Banyaruanda agricultural laborers.[22]

In the late 1950s, Wrigley classified the population of Buganda as comprised of: (1) large farmers (2 percent) who "may employ as many as 100 labourers, though 12–20 is more common"; (2) well-to-do peasants (19 percent) who "generally employ one or two porters [laborers] fairly regularly, and one or two more occasionally, but . . . nearly always [do] some manual

---

* As late as 1954, the government's White Paper on Mechanization in Agriculture declared that "in all areas, except Buganda, the majority of farmers run their farms with family labour." [18]

† By 1958, coffee was grown on 22,700 acres in Buganda whereas cotton covered only 20,800 acres. The figures for 1962 were 26,300 acres for coffee and 13,500 for cotton. The kulaks consolidated, as we shall see, in the period after 1949. Buganda produced about 92 percent of Uganda's total Robusta coffee exports.[21]

work [themselves]"; (3) middling peasants (27 percent) who "rarely employ hired labour"; (4) poor peasants (32 percent) who use only family labor; and (5) landless laborers (20 percent).[23] The core of the kulaks were the well-to-do peasants, who employed the bulk of the landless laborers.

2. CIVIL SERVANTS

The European officer in Africa is expensive, and if his numbers were multiplied beyond a certain point, the burden of his renumeration would weigh too heavily upon the population. Only from the African race can sufficient qualified men be obtained at an economic cost.[24]

The first recruits to the group of functionaries of the colonial order were inevitably the petty clerks and artisans working for the government, the railway administration, and the missions. At the outset, when Europeans were in short supply and Africans only marginally within the control of the colonial state, most employees were recruited from India, along with the railway labor. Later phases of recruitment concentrated on creating a local supply of skilled and clerical labor. Local recruitment of government employees came in three phases, each the result of a different impetus. As government administration expanded, the need for clerical and artisanal service increased. By 1920 the governor was warning the Colonial Office of "various shortages in carpenters and bricklayers" and seeking permission to employ Chinese labor,[25] in order to get away from Indian labor, which he found "too inefficient and costly." That same year, the governor wrote the secretary of state that the ultimate object of his policy was "the substitution of natives of the Protectorate for the many aliens at present employed in the civil clerical staff and in all grades of skilled government employment." [26] The Imperial Treasury, in turn, was quite clear in its instructions: "We of course would welcome any reasonable and feasible scheme likely to result ultimately in the substitution of native for Asiatic labour at substantially less cost." [27] The problem, however, was that "mission schools turned out only a few natives capable of effectively replacing a Goan or an Indian on the Protectorate's clerical staff." [28]

To remedy the situation, the government offered Indian artisans bonuses if they would "successfully train native carpenters," [29] but not a single Indian volunteered "owing to the opposition usually encountered from [their] fellow countrymen," who had no desire to assist in speeding their own redundancy.[30] Provision was then made in the yearly budget for an instructor of native artisans,[31] and within a year Makerere College was founded, "mainly for the training of artisans." [32] Classes began in 1922, with a staff of two; seven carpentry and seven mechanical pupils attended.[33] But despite these attempts to create a supply of local artisans, the governor reported in 1925 "that essential public works cannot be undertaken unless artisans are obtained from outside the Protectorate." [34] The recruitment of Indian artisans continued, though at a lesser rate.

The second impetus for local recruitment coincided with the expansion of the peasant economy. If peasant cash-crop production was to be organized for export, if the product was to be subjected to vigorous quality control, and if the returns on the product were to be taxed, the government needed an extensive administration that would supervise both production and marketing, and organize the collection of taxes. In other words, the prerequisite to appropriating a substantial surplus from the peasant economy was an expanded civil service, composed of a

Africans and Asians Employed by
the Government, 1923
(excludes categories with employment below 100)

	Asian	African
Clerks, general	223	68
Dispensers, dressers, compounders, vaccinators	—	295
Motor drivers and mechanics	2	100
Masons	2	362
Carpenters	—	136
Blacksmiths	139	11
Agricultural instructors and gardeners	1	141

Source: N. A. Motani, "The Growth of an African Civil Service," Table 3.

general clerical staff and a specialized technical cadre. The 1915–1916 Annual Report of the Protectorate speaks of "native agriculture" as being "fostered by a body of specially trained native instructors, who specialize in the crop adapted to the several districts." [35]*

The third impetus to civil service expansion followed the 1928 Busulu and Nvujjo Law, which reduced the landlord-chiefs and hereditary chiefs to a collection of state-appointed, salaried, civil servant chiefs.

By 1929, the need for an expanded technical staff was effecting the educational structure of the colony. A technical school was opened near Kampala and others were under construction. Makerere College gradually became a professional school with important veterinary and agricultural faculties. Successful candidates became junior secondary school teachers or entered government service as assistant medical officers, assistant agricultural officers, and engineering assistants. Those who failed became dispensers, police subinspectors, clerks, and so forth.[37]

State-run technical or professional institutions provided only a small number of civil servants, however. The bulk were trained in mission schools, which were financially assisted by the state. A religious consciousness was an important part of the ideological baggage carried by the civil servants in particular, and by the petty bourgeois intelligentsia in general.

Both the state and the missions had excellent and complementary reasons for this close collaboration. Colonial education first made inroads into Uganda under the aegis of the missionaries. From very early on, the missions concentrated on building

---

* Besides this social infrastructure, another prerequisite to appropriating this surplus was a developed economic infrastructure, especially a network of roads and railways that could effectively bring the exports into the city and take the imports out to the countryside. Thus, the first railway lines to be built in Uganda (after the completion of the Uganda Railway in 1902) were those to Toro in 1928 and Soroti in 1929, the years when the thrust to expand "native" production was bearing rich fruits.[36] Baganda transport, on the other hand, relied primarily on a vast network of roads. The road system radiated from Kampala, the commercial capital, to the cotton- and coffee-growing areas. The result was that at independence the country possessed, as did the peasant economies of Ghana and Southern Nigeria, one of the best road systems in Africa.

schools. The Rev. H. A. Brewer, headmaster of the Kamuli School in Busoga in 1920, explained:

> For many years it has been the unusual feature of Uganda that the schools have fed the church—that is, that it has been through the appetite for education that the Africans have come to us and so, in our schools, have been introduced to Christ.[38]

The missionaries understood that it was not piety but material benefits that drove the colonized to the church. But the problem was that the establishment of an extensive network of schools cost money, and the missions were not financially equal to the task. Their financial troubles were exacerbated after World War I, when there was a crisis of confidence in the assumed superiority of Western Civilization and nagging doubts about the justification for the "White Man's Burden." Intellectuals revived the concept of the "noble savage," while anthropologists romanticized the "sanctity of tribal institutions."

Closer to home, the poor and the pious, who had donated their pennies for "the salvation of mankind," were becoming noticeably hesitant to continue their generosity. Oliver has shown the consequences of this crisis for the missions, both Protestant and Catholic. The Catholic Church suffered heavily from its loss of financial contributions: in only five years, from 1931 to 1935, contributions to the Central Missionary Fund declined by 50 percent. The Protestants, on the other hand, suffered a decline in the number of missionaries willing to work abroad.

In Uganda, the lack of money and personnel was acutely felt. It coincided, curiously enough, with Papal pronouncements, Lambeth encyclicals, and the resolutions of missionary conferences, all stressing the "importance of preserving so far as possible the fabric of indigenous societies and of encouraging appropriate varieties in liturgy and devotions."[39] Though couched in esoteric language, this was no less than a call for indirect rule. Beginning in the 1920s, an African petty clergy made its appearance on the religious scene in Uganda. It was, for one thing, cheaper to maintain: the estimated annual cost of a married European missionary was £650; the stipend for an African clergyman ranged from £10 to £25.[40] At a time of nascent nationalism and increasing racial consciousness, he was also far more convincing: his color was black.

The church, like the state, practiced "indirect rule,"—and both did so for pragmatic purposes and when necessary; equally, both found adequate "moral" justifications to legitimate their practice.

For its part, the state needed not only an "educated native," but a "loyal educated native." As the official "Scheme of Development for African Education" emphasized:

> If we are to avoid the disastrous consequences which elsewhere have followed the forcible divorce of religion and education, it is clear that, although the right of conscience will remain inviolate, religious instruction and observance must, within the competence of established and accredited religious bodies, continue to be available for the children of all parents who so desire it.
>
> The principle just enunciated is as valid in its future application to nonmission as to mission schools.[41]

The missionaries understood this ruling-class anxiety. In 1920, American missionary societies working in Africa had convinced the Phelps-Stokes Fund to finance a commission of missionaries and educators "to try and apply to the African scene the results of experience in Negro education in the United States." The commission made "detailed suggestions as to how education could be adapted to the needs of African society so as to promote its development *without causing its disruption*" (emphasis mine).[42] British missionaries submitted a memorandum to their government that emphasized that there was "an overwhelming weight of competent testimony that if education was not to be disruptive of morality and the social order it must have a religious basis." [43]*

---

* A rather more detailed presentation of this position was made by the Advisory Committee on Native Education in the British Tropical African Dependencies in its memorandum to the secretary of state: "Since contact with civilization and even education itself must necessarily tend to weaken tribal authority and the sanctions of existing beliefs, and in view of the all-prevailing belief in the supernatural which effects the whole life of the African, it is essential that what is good in the old beliefs and sanctions should be strengthened and what is defective should be replaced. The greatest importance must therefore be attached to religious teaching and moral instruction. But in schools and in training colleges they should be accorded an equal standing with secular subjects. Such teaching must be related to the conditions of life and to

This alliance of interests was buttressed by financial considerations. The missions did not fail to emphasize their unique advantage: that they were able to attract the services of qualified men and women at a lower cost than any government. Figures were quoted from India showing that "the cost to the government of a pupil in an aided mission school could be as little as one-fifth of his cost in an identical government school." [45]

So most schools in Uganda were run by missionaries and largely financed by the state, as shown in the table on the following page. With the spread of the peasant economy in the 1920s and the subsequent expansion of the educational structure, the state established a department of education and made further grants to missions "sufficiently important to enable the mission to undertake a vastly superior educational programme and to facilitate control of educational policy by government." [46] By 1950, of the fifty-three secondary schools in Uganda, forty-seven were mission run, three privately run, and the remaining three run by the state. [47]

The political usefulness of missionary education, it should be clear, stemmed from its *dual* nature: that it was technical as well as ideological, that it imparted skills such as reading, writing, and arithmetic as well as values such as loyalty to the existing order and disciplined self-sacrifice in the interest of that order. Lord Lugard was clear in his appreciation of this in a discussion of the education of the sons of Fulani chiefs in Nigeria:

I hope that they would thus be taught not merely to read and write but to acquire an English Public Schoolboy's ideas of honour, loyalty, and above all responsibility. It is by such means that I hope the next generation of Fulani rulers may become really efficient, reliable, and honest co-operators with the British in the administration of the Protectorate. [48]

---

the daily experience of the pupils. It should find expression in habits of self-discipline and loyalty to the community. With such safeguards, contact with civilization need not be injurious, or the introduction of new religious ideas have a disruptive influence antagonistic to constituted secular authority." [44]

The statement, in other words, is a call for a mutually benefiting coexistence between church and state.

Government Grants to Missionary Societies
for Education
(amounts in pounds)

Year	CMS	White Fathers	Mill Hill Mission	Verona Mission
1906–1907	150	—	—	—
1911–1912	850	300	100	—
1912–1913	850	300	100	—
1915–1916	850	300	100	—
1916–1917	850	300	300	—
1917–1918	850	300	100	—
1918–1919	1100	750	250	—
1919–1920	1750	950	300	25
1920	1900	950	300	25
1921	4750	3075	1650	100
1922	4750	3075	1650	100
1923	5688	3645	2038	125
1924	5688	3645	1888	125

Source: Uganda government annual reports from 1906 to 1924.

This was not education, but training; not liberation, but enslavement. Its purpose was not to educate a person to understand the objective limits to the advancement of individual and collective welfare, but to train a person to accept and even administer the limits in an "efficient, reliable, and honest" way. Such training could most effectively be imparted in a controlled environment. Thus Hattersley, headmaster of the Mengo Day School, argued for its conversion to a boarding school: "If the nation is to be reborn, the children are far better removed entirely from their surroundings and shown how to make a fresh start." [49] The boarding school was a total environment, much like a jail or an insane asylum. Its purpose was to turn out a particular breed of men, "loyal" Afro-Saxons—the collaborating class. A woman from the north whose husband was recruited into one of these schools lamented in a folk song:

Bile burns my inside!
I feel like vomiting!

For all our young men
Were finished in the forest
Their manhood was finished
In the classrooms
Their testicles
Were smashed
With large books! [50]

Enrollment in these schools was not open to everyone but confined to the sons of chiefs—that is, to future "leaders." The education scheme for Uganda passed by the Board of CMS in 1909 was explicit: "We aim specially at gaining the attendance at our schools of chiefs who are still minors and sons of chiefs." [51] The best-known of these schools—King's College (Budo) and Kisubi College—became the Eton and Harrow of Uganda.*

Two characteristics of the civil service were the result of this colonial educational system. First, Baganda students were the dominant graduates from the mission schools. This can be seen from the enrollment at Makerere College. In or before 1953, a total of 1,698 African students were admitted from Uganda, Kenya, Tanganyika, Zanzibar, Ethiopia, Nyasaland, Northern Rhodesia, and the Sudan. Of these, 671 (40 percent) were Baganda. Compared to the Kikuyu of Kenya, who numbered 14 college students per 100,000 population, for every 100,000 Baganda, 80 were at Makerere. [53] Furthermore, E. Goldthorpe's interviews with old students show that "Makerere was in the past filled from a relatively narrow privileged class of chiefs and other wealthy and educated people" and that this was "especially true of the Baganda tribe." [54] Given that schools were for "sons of chiefs," the social origin of the Baganda bureaucrats in

---

* King's College, Budo, was the boarding school which replaced Mengo Day School, which opened in 1904. The women's counterpart of King's College, Budo, was Gayaza High School for Girls, while its Catholic counterpart was Kisubi College. While these institutions were confined to the children of higher chiefs, their material advantages were not lost upon the lower chiefs. The Annual Report for 1909–1910 stated: "Minor chiefs are now banding together, and, with the help of the county chiefs, putting up school rooms at the centers of the counties where their children may have special teaching in a better equipped place with a better paid native teacher." [52]

the central government was from among the chiefs, not the kulaks.

Second, in spite of the dominance of the Baganda within it, the civil service was the first colonial institution truly national in its scope and recruitment. But like the school system, the civil service was racially structured: pay scales were different for Europeans, Asians, and Africans. The African civil servants became the first social group among Uganda Africans to organize along both national and racial lines. The Uganda African Civil Servants Association was established in 1922 in response to the official exclusion of African civil servants from government war bonuses granted to both Europeans and Asians.[55]* The association spread rapidly from Kampala to Masaka, Jinja, Mubende, Mbarara, Masindi, Kabale, Arua, Fort Portal, Mbale, Soroti, Gulu, and Lira[56]—in other words, to every single urban center in Uganda, north and south.

The association was preceded by another group: the Young Baganda Association (YBA), which was set up in 1915. Its organization reflected the dominance of the Baganda in the civil service, and of the *Protestant* Baganda at that. Most of the founder members of the YBA either were or had been clerks and interpreters in government offices. Products of the Protestant King's College, Budo, and mainly sons of ruling chiefs,[57] including some members of the royalty, they petitioned the governor, requesting that the standard of education in the schools be upgraded so the graduates could obtain good jobs.[58] The demands of the YBA did not just articulate the interests of potential civil servants, however; they also reflected the interests of those who were already attempting to enter a far more lucrative enterprise—trade. Confronted by an increased monopolization of the economy, they called for "free trade [as] necessary for the welfare of the natives." [59]

3. TRADERS

As we saw, a combination of the carrot and the stick—the 1900 Buganda Agreement and the 1901 Trade Licensing Act—

---

* The first meeting of civil servants dissatisfied with racially differential treatment was held on July 9, 1919. The actual formation of the association, however, did not come until 1922.

dealt a decisive blow to African trade in Uganda. The gradual monopolization of the cash-crop economy under state auspices and the abolition of hand ginning and middleman buying closed off the most promising avenues to the small African entrepreneur. By the 1930s both the trading petty bourgeoisie and the commercial bourgeoisie—traders and businessmen—were dominantly Indian.

In the later years, state policy continued to consolidate the position of big commercial capital and undermine that of the small traders. We have seen that the ripest fruit that came the way of the large established enterprises was the 1933 Native Produce Marketing Ordinance, which at one stroke delivered the bulk of the produce trade into the coffer of big capital by restricting the issue of purchasing licenses to one or a few "reputable" firms. Not satisfied with this, the Uganda Chamber of Commerce asked for further state control over "itinerant traders":

> Although the number of these itinerant traders may be small at present, the volume of business obtained by them is large and by their indiscriminate trading they have ruined the *legitimate wholesale trade* of Uganda which has a very detrimental effect on the customs revenue of this country.
>
> Unless these people contribute something towards the revenues of Uganda they are in a position *to compete unfairly with the established traders* in Uganda, who pay heavily for the privilege of trading in this country (emphasis mine).[60]

The state, equally hypocritical in its pronouncements, contended that there is "no justification for racial discrimination in township and trading centers," and passed the 1938 Trading Ordinance, which did away with the distinction between wholesale and retail shops by imposing the same license fee on both. Formally equal treatment of those substantially unequal—the basis of bourgeois equality—protected the privileged position of the strong. The result was that the formation that emerged among the Africans in the commercial sector was that of traders, not businessmen. By a trader, I refer to an individual member of the petty bourgeoisie; by a businessman, to an individual member of the commercial bourgeoisie. The trader's operations, however substantial, are confined to retail. The businessman's activities are located within wholesale trade. While the African traders emerged as a social group with common interests and a common organization, the African businessmen, as we shall see, were few and far between. They remained as individuals, never begot a common political organization, and thus cannot be seen as a class.

The first of the African traders in Buganda came from that section of the precolonial ruling class which was excluded from the terms of the 1900 Agreement *and* was already involved in the export-import trade in the precolonial period. These were the Muslim chiefs with strong commercial ties with the coastal Arab and Swahili traders. From their ranks came a number of the independent African middlemen in the cotton industry. When phased out of cotton buying by limits on the number of buying posts and buying licenses, those with sufficient savings went into trade. Added to their numbers were a few tenants who had enough savings to seek relief in commerce from the weight of the landlord's demand for *busulu* and *nvujjo*.

The 1928 Busulu and Nvujjo Law gave a substantial boost to African commerce. The small landlord, denied sufficient income in the form of rent, was compelled to turn to the next best alternative, trade. With the proceeds from the sale of his land, he was able to purchase a license, premises, and sufficient stock. He soon became a businessman.* His social origin was from the landed class, not the peasantry. These businessmen, few in number, were confined to Buganda in the years before World War II.

The 1928 Law also created the conditions for the emergence of a cash-crop-growing kulak class. Given the nature of the underdeveloped economy, with the siphoning out of agricultural surpluses as commercial profits, trade appeared a far more lucrative enterprise than production. The social consequence was that the prosperous peasant, too, sought to go into trade.

---

* The best-known of these African businessmen was Micheal Kawalia Kaggwa, the grandson of Sir Apollo Kaggwa, the *katikiro* of Buganda until his resignation in 1926. He was burned to death in 1972 when he attempted to drive tenants off his land so he could convert it into a plantation.

The social origin of the vast number of small African traders, preponderantly in Buganda, was the rich peasantry.

In the north, the cash-crop economy did not gather momentum until the 1930s and 1940s. Here the commercial entrepreneur was most often a hawker rather than a trader. (While both are retailers, a trader's material assets include a shop and its stock; he is physically situated in a particular location. The hawker's resources, on the other hand, are so meager that establishing a shop is precluded. He travels with a wheeled carriage and buys and sells in extremely limited quantities.)

Hawkers were concentrated where commodity production was the most advanced: in Lango and Acholi. In 1940, Steiger-Hayley listed six pursuits of a Lango trader. What is most interesting about the list is that it reveals the position of the hawker in the export-import economy: like a commercial worker, his "profit" is fixed and is in reality a wage; furthermore, he performs the indispensable function of bringing together at a low cost small articles of little value for export (cowhides, goatskins, simsim) and at the same time does the marketing of imported items such as the indispensable hoe and the more expensive bicycle.* He buys these from, and sells them

---

* From T. T. Steiger-Hayley's list of pursuits

1. Cowhides: The Lango trader goes around to any village from which news comes that a bull is to be killed. He buys hides from the Langi at –/50 to 2/– and sells them to the Indians for 1/50 to 5/–. These hides are exported by the Indians.

2. Goatskins: The Langi trader buys skins from the Langi at –/50 and sells them to the Indians for 1/–. These are also exported, but the demand is not great.

3. Ghee or clarified butter *(mo dyang)*: . . . The Langi trader buys *mo dyang* from the Langi at 2/– a gallon and sells it to the Indians at 2/50 a gallon. They retail it locally.

4. Simsim: There are a few simsim stores about the country and simsim is exported by the Indians when the price is good. But it is usual for a Langi trader to go to the remoter villages to buy simsim for resale to the Indians.

5. Bicycles: Should our Langi trader have collected a little money at the more modest trades, he might invest in a new bicycle in one of the Indian shops. This he will ride to the villages and exchange for cattle. The cattle he will resell at one of the monthly cattle auctions organized by the government, and so he will be able to invest in more bicycles, until he has made enough for his needs.

6. Spears, bells, and knives: These are made by local smiths and sold for money. Hoes are bought from the Indians.[61]

to, the trader, who is another link in the chain that ties the hawker to the exporter and the importer in the city. What also emerges from Steiger-Hayley's list is that even the few items that remain the objects of *internal* trade, such as ghee, are still sold by the hawker to the Indian trader, who retails them. As internal trade became marginal, its operations were subsumed under those of export-import trade.

Gradually, of course, the hawker saved money. As Steiger-Hayley reported: "Those who have served in the Indian shops may be tempted to set up shops of their own." [62] In other words, the hawker attempted to follow the route of the early Indian trader, who came from India as a commercial worker, accumulated savings, and then set up as an independent trader. But there was one important difference. The hawker came late. Even when in possession of a trading license, premises, and stock, he found that others had preceded him, and he entered into bitter competition to secure a share of the going trade. Furthermore, trade was for the export-import market and its very structure—centralized, hierarchical, externally oriented—ensured the dominance of the established Indian retailer over the incoming African retailer, just as it did that of the Indian wholesaler over the Indian retailer. Fortunately, we have an excellent description of the credit chain that provides the connecting links in the export-import economy, from the metropolitan bank to the African retailer in the village, in an unequal relation:

> The Asian importer works on credit and it is incredible how much can be guaranteed on a single consignment of goods. The order given to a British firm is covered by the conforming house in London, giving credit of three to six months, during the actual time of the sea and rail journey. The goods are then sold to a wholesaler who never pays in cash, but signs a promissory note payable in three months. The importer discounts the note at a bank and collects his money. The wholesaler sells to a series of sub-wholesalers who pay him by promissory notes which are likewise discounted and the sub-wholesalers sell to retailers who also sign notes. Some retailers also sell to other retailers.[63]

The "other retailers" were primarily Africans who had neither an account nor a loan arrangement with a bank; they signed debit notes to the supplying Indian retailer, remaining in constant debt to him. In the long run, this debt materially cemented the supplier–buyer relation between the two. This relation was described in detail in the Report of the Commissioners on Africanization of Commerce and Industry in 1968:

> Even in the more rural areas, the African traders have found it difficult to compete with the Asian traders only a few miles away. The African traders still tend to buy from these same Asians because, though not wholesale, they are their nearest sources of supply. The Asians must make a profit on their wholesale/retail sales and so the African traders must charge higher prices than the Asians. Thus the consumers are attracted back to the Asian centres. At worst the African traders' prices are governed by the Asian prices and in consequence the Asian retailer/wholesaler prospers at the expense of the poor African trader.[64]

Certainly there were important and significant changes between 1940 and 1968. In fact, the most substantial addition to the *numbers* of African traders came in the wake of World War II. At the same time, there was a substantial increase in the *volume* of trade carried on by African traders. But, as we shall see, these changes were not the result of *individual* competition at the level of the economy but of *political* action by the class as a whole, a lesson not lost upon the petty bourgeoisie in the years after independence.*

---

* The lesson was learned in small steps, gradually but surely. For example, in 1946 an African trader, exasperated by his condition, which seemed almost fated in spite of all his efforts to alter it, wrote the editor of a British paper in Uganda: "We Africans are anxious to start trading among our own people but are at a loss to know how to buy on a basis that will allow of a margin of profit. Many have tried and failed owing to sheer ignorance. Those with sufficient capital to start trading are entirely at the mercy of Indian traders, who know that if they sell goods to Africans for resale, they are defeating themselves. On the other hand, to buy goods at retail prices does not allow of a margin of profit. Many who have returned from military service with a balance of cash could with the help of some advisor start a small shop, if he knew where to buy at wholesale rates. Could someone not tell us where the traders buy their goods?"[65]

The editor gently reminded the correspondent that his was not a problem of ignorance, an individual problem, but a *structural* problem: "Small traders, whether African or British, have great difficulty in obtaining goods direct from manufacturers; at present almost the only way for them to obtain stocks is to purchase through local wholesale firms."

Thus, *all* sections of the petty bourgeoisie found the path to further development blocked: traders were subordinate to Indian commercial capital, civil servants found themselves at the lower rung of a three-tiered, racially structured government service, and kulaks found themselves subject to the political rule of the Lukiko chiefs.

Not only was the development of the petty bourgeoisie blocked in its infancy, but there was uneven development within the class. The kulaks were the most advanced. The traders, although they emerged as a distinct social group, had neither the organizational independence nor the economic strength of the kulaks, and in Buganda both their organization and interests became subsumed under those of the kulaks. The small trader there found it paid much more to be a farmer while running a retail shop in the front room of his mud-built, iron-roofed house. In other words, even at the level of individual existence, the bulk of the traders were kulaks first and traders second. In the north, on the other hand, there was no regional formation of kulaks, and the traders arose as an organizationally distinct social force—but not until after World War II.

In the interwar period, the politics of the petty bourgeoisie were the politics of the kulaks, a social group dominantly situated in one region: Buganda. But the politics of the Buganda kulaks were also the politics of tribalism, a politics whose class content was obscured as the tribal form became its battle cry.

The Politics of Tribalism

The politics of Uganda from 1900 to 1949 can be divided into three distinct historical periods: 1900–1928, 1928–1938, and 1938–1949. The transition from one period to the next is informed by a qualitative change in the class structure, and therefore the class leadership and base of political organization. In the first phase, 1900–1928, political leadership stemmed from those precolonial ruling classes which were successful in securing a measure of popular support. In the second phase, political organization was undertaken by the landlords, whose material base had been undermined in the late 1920s. Their organization was most conspicuous for failing to acquire support from beyond its narrow class confines. In the third phase, we see the rise of mass-based politics under the direction of the kulaks. It remains for us to detail political activity in each period.

Politics in early colonial Uganda was the exclusive preserve of the precolonial ruling classes, and centered on the issue of control over the most important means of production: land. Where there was no formal agreement with the colonial state, and thus no land grants awarded to precolonial oligarchies—as in Bunyoro and Busoga—politics took the form of petitions and personal representations from the chiefs to the state asking for land grants similar to those provided by the Buganda Agreement of 1900. But in spite of the absence of official land grants in Bunyoro and Busoga, the chiefs succeeded in securing control over a measure of the economic surplus, either by controlling the peasant surplus labor (in Busoga) or by unofficially controlling land that gave them the power to extract rent from the peasant producers (in Bunyoro). In neither case were these chiefs, who were already appropriating a share of the peasants' product or labor, able to organize these same peasants in support of their demands for official grants of land. Their politics remained confined to ineffective formal petitions and polite personal presentations.

In the Agreement kingdoms (Buganda and Toro), where land grants were made to sections of the precolonial ruling classes, political activity was of a different nature because it involved significant participation by the exploited tenant peasantry. The political leadership that organized the tenants' grievances came from those sections of the precolonial ruling classes that were *excluded* from the formal grants. Both the Bataka Association of Buganda and the Young Men of Toro were able to incorporate as part of their demands the grievances of the tenant peasantry over rent and forced labor, thereby gaining a popular base.

The changes in British land policy in the 1920s dramatically altered the material underpinnings of political activity in most of the colony. As soon as the state granted the peasantry effective immunity from the control of a parasitic landed class, the material basis of popular support for the traditional ruling classes vanished. Given the paucity of their numbers and their

lack of control over any means of production, their political
demise was immediate.

Whereas this process led to a sudden and a long-term decline
in organized political activity over most of the colony, the
situation was somewhat different in Buganda. Although the
Bataka Association lost its popular base, it was the landed
oligarchy which moved onto the political stage. This oligarchy
had existed for over two decades and controlled the bulk of the
productive land. It had been organized through the Lukiko *as a
class*, and had acquired political maturity through long battles
against both the *bataka* and the colonial state. The individual
leaders of this class owned miles of tenanted land and possessed
considerable political experience. They were not about to leave
the political stage gracefully when the 1928 Busulu and Nvujjo
Law drastically reduced their income from rent and stripped
them of their political position as chiefs.

The years after 1928 saw an attempt by these Baganda
ex-landlords—or, more correctly, "formal" landlords—to organize to regain their lost material and political base. Their first
important political organization was the *Bulunge Bua Buganda*—the Common People of Buganda—which attempted to
emulate the Bataka Association in organizing peasant grievances, hoping to score the same degree of political success. The
Bulunge Bua Buganda was organized by Yusufu Bamuta, who,
it will be remembered, was dismissed as the secretary to the
Lukiko for having initiated a debate on the Protectorate
government's proposed audit of Buganda government finances.
While Yusufu Bamuta toured England hoping to publicize the
grievances of the landlords, the party organized mass petitions
asking for its primary political demand, the introduction of an
elected assembly in place of the appointed Lukiko, now dominated by the salaried chiefs.[66]

The Bulunge Bua Buganda failed to secure a mass base for
one simple reason: the changes that had undermined the
landlord's position had also removed the tenant's oppression.
This failure resulted in a number of political changes. The
demand for an elected Lukiko began to reflect more precisely
the specific interests of the ex-landlords: they were opposed not
to the general privileges of the compradore class in the Lukiko,

but to their own exclusion from the ranks of these compradores. They now hoped to secure their demands not through a popular political organization but through petitioning the colonial state and enlisting its sympathy. In 1934, the Bulunge Bua Buganda gave way to the Uganda African Welfare Association (UAWA); what had hoped to be a populist political organization became a self-consciously colonial pressure group.

The demand for an elected Lukiko was made more specific: "That the service of the leading Ministers [referring to the *katikiro* Nsibirwa and the *omuwanika* Kulubya] be limited to a number of years." [67] By the end of the decade, a UAWA petition to Lord Hailey, His Majesty's Special Commissioner on Native Administration Affairs, included a series of complaints: (1) government opposition to the establishment of a People's Representative Council; (2) neglect of traditional customs; (3) disregard of the *kabaka;* (4) the low price of cotton; (5) confining higher education to a few; (6) low wages of labor; and (7) lack of free trade.[68]

These complaints reflected a general change in the class composition of Buganda society, particularly the rise of such new social groups as kulaks, traders, and urban workers. Just as importantly, it reflected an accommodation and adjustment to the rise of a new political organization, the Descendents of Kintu, whose demands embodied the particular grievances of the kulaks (and the traders). In a few years the UAWA passed into obscurity and the Descendents of Kintu emerged as the primary political force in Buganda. Gradually the politics of the court were giving way to the politics of the marketplace; the politics of the notables to those of the petty bourgeoisie.

Before we can examine the organizational form of these politics (the Descendents of Kintu), we must examine the content of the interests of this rising class in Buganda, the petty bourgeoisie, and in particular of its dominant section, the kulaks.

The antagonistic relations of the kulaks, who emerged as a social group in the 1930s, was not just confined to the Banyaruanda laborers they employed, but extended to the ginners and the chiefs as well. As we have seen, in the 1930s the kulak cotton grower found his income whittled down by a powerful, state-supported, ginners' monopoly buying association. The growers attempted to transport their cotton to the Eastern Province where no such policy existed in the early days, protested individually through letters to the European press, and organized collectively to pressure the *kabaka*'s government to represent their interests before the colonial state—all without much success. The fact was that the *kabaka*'s government was in reality the Lukiko which, in the person of its members, the individual chiefs, administered the economic policy of the colonial state, and thus could give no more than rhetorical support to the cotton growers. The kulaks and the traders dubbed these chiefs "alien" and "anti-Baganda," in the same category as Indian ginners and Banyaruanda land laborers.

At the same time, the centralization of the political power of the Lukiko in the hands of two individuals—the *katikiro* Nsibirwa and the *omuwanika* Kulubya—had rendered the *kabaka* more akin to a figurehead than a political power. The *omuwanika*'s policy of rigidly centralizing Lukiko finances, of removing any local or *kabaka* control over the budget, and of creating large surpluses deposited with the central government[69] further exacerbated the antagonism between the *kabaka* and the Lukiko leadership. By 1939, the conflict was in the open and the *katikiro* and *omuwanika* were both writing to the governor claiming that they were greatly perturbed at the drinking that was going on at Salema (the lake residence of the *kabaka*).[70] When the *kabaka* died that same year, the colonial state bypassed the claimant to the throne and appointed the fifteen-year-old Mutesa as the new *kabaka*, at the same time delegating his authority to three regents: the *katikiro*, the *omuwanika*, and the chief justice.[71] The rule of the compradore chiefs was complete.

The conflict between the *kabaka* and the compradore chiefs provided the objective base for an alliance between the rising Baganda petty bourgeoisie and the *kabaka*. This alliance was, however, on an ideological level. In their campaign against the Lukiko, the growers and traders used the chiefs' "violation" of the *kabaka*'s "traditional respect and dignity" as the basis for an ideological alliance, and this call for "traditionalism"—or "tribalism," as it is referred to now—became the dominant ideology of kulak politics. There were two excellent reasons for this. First, an anti-alien "traditional" ideology excluded at one stroke all the social groups with whom the kulaks had antagonistic relations: the Banyaruanda laborers, the Indian ginners, and the compradore chiefs who had violated "tradition." Second, because of the uneven development of the regions in Uganda, the kulaks had not developed as a national but as a regional social group, fighting their bitterest political struggles not against the colonial state at the national level but its regional expression, the Buganda Lukiko. Thus the ideology that the kulaks employed in their political struggle was also regional—the ideology of tribalism. This was not a simple "return to tradition"; it was the result of very concrete and contemporary objective circumstances. Neither was it the politics of the Buganda people. It was the politics of a particular social group in Buganda, the kulaks, and its political target included another social group in Buganda, the compradore chiefs.

The organizational birth of this "tribal" politics was marked by the establishment of the Descendents of Kintu. It stepped up organized opposition to the compradore chiefs, particularly to the *katikiro*,[72] and at the same time deplored the disregard for tradition by the ruling chiefs. For the growers, it demanded high cotton and coffee prices. From the colonial state, it demanded free trade and free education.*

---

* The first of the Baganda commercial entrepreneurs who sought to expand beyond retail trade had of necessity to turn to enterprises other than the monopolized cotton industry or the wholesale trade of the Protectorate. The trade that they concentrated their capital and energies on was motor transport. By 1937 there were 197 buses on the roads of Uganda. Of these, 157 were owned by Asians, 3 by Europeans, and 37 by Africans—most of the latter being Baganda.[73]

With the coming of depression and active state assistance to big capital in establishing monopoly control over various branches of the economy, competitive conditions in the motor industry became the target of state action. In 1936, the Overseas Motor Transport Co., Ltd., of London, after successful applications in Kenya, wrote to the government of Uganda asking for "an exclusive license for the carrying of passengers" on the major roads of Uganda. The reason, as always, was technical—to guarantee road safety—but the precondition was that: "We propose nothing until competition on these roads is eliminated. We hold the view most strongly that competition does not work for efficiency in this

Though primarily articulating the grievances of kulaks and traders, the Descendents of Kintu brought within its organizational fold all the disaffected social groups in Buganda. Its chief organizer and secretary was Ignatius K. Musazi, a former

---

type of business." [74] The Colonial Office Minute considering the application deliberated: "The trouble with African and Indian owned passenger services [is that] . . . they cut each other's throats in competition for passengers, neglect to make proper provision for maintenance and depreciation of their vehicles, and tend to compete at lower rates whenever the traffic is heaviest without any schemes of things." On the other hand, the European company "could provide a better service with better vehicles and there is equally little doubt that it must have a monopoly if it has to pay its way." [75] Needless to say, the Asian and African owners were synonymous with small capital and the European with large capital. In 1938, the government's traffic control board unanimously recommended "the grant of an exclusive license to the Overseas Motor Transport Co., Ltd., for a period of ten years from the 1st January, 1939, with an option of extension for a further five years." The criteria on which the board made its decisions as to whom should be granted an exclusive license were: (1) financial stability, (2) experience in operating bus services, and (3) general reliability—as based on two important factors from the point of view of the public, namely, efficiency and safety.[76] The rationality of the system itself militated against small capital and in favor of big capital. In late 1938, the Uganda Transport Co., Ltd. (UTC) was formed in accordance with the terms of agreement between the Overseas Motor Transport Co., Ltd., and the governor of Uganda.

The birth of the UTC spelled the death of the most substantial of African commercial enterprises, bus owners and operators. The Descendents of Kintu articulated the specific grievance of this social group: "It is futile to base the reasons for the employment of a foreign commercial body to rob the local people of their own trade upon the fact that motor bus casualties are frequent in this country. We hear that three deaths occur daily in London at an average rate. We are not aware that a body of foreign, say German, commercial people has ever been invited to bring their public service vehicles and use them in London for their own profits.

"Therefore we would submit that all Buganda-owned buses that have been off the road for no other reason except for the reduction of buses in order to give room to the Overseas Motor Transport Co. be allowed to run on our roads again subject to the prevailing regulations of the Traffic Code." [77]

The second demand of the Descendents of Kintu reflected its opposition to the chiefs who had successfully used their political position to monopolize access to higher education. This was the demand for "free education": "Now shall we, Baganda, be given free education therein [at Makerere College] or only sons of chiefs, whose fathers or guardians draw high salaries from the taxes, which we poor people have to pay, alone study in the new college?" [78]

inspector of schools who was closely associated with the cash-crop farmers. His associates were Shem Spire Mukasa, a prominent Mutaka who had had some of his land appropriated by the government to expand Mulago Hospital;[79] Father Spartus Mukasa, head of the African Hellenic Church,[80] established in opposition to progovernment missionary churches; Yusufu Bamuta, the ex-secretary of the Lukiko and organizer of the Bulunge Bua Buganda, who later established the Bamuta Cotton Company but failed in his bid to enter the cotton industry; and James Kivu, who founded the Baganda Motor Drivers' Association in 1939.

The Baganda motor drivers, trained during World War I and employed in government services, were strictly only quasi-urban workers. Carrying crops from the cotton and coffee farmers to the Indian and European ginners and hullers, they provided a most important link in the system of social communication among and between the farmers and traders. The Baganda Motor Drivers' Association, though, was not strictly a working class organization. It included both those employed as drivers and those driving their own vehicles:[81] it was a workingmen's organization that also included individuals from the petty bourgeoisie. This was reflected in the petitions the association directed to the Fabian Colonial Bureau in England, calling for freedom of operation for African enterprise in the transport business, the "right of Africans to enjoy the fruits of their own labour," and the freedom of farmers to sell their own products—"simsim, groundnuts, and so on"—directly to the government without having to go through the intermediary of any monopoly company.[82] The organization of these workers' grievances was neither in opposition to, nor distinct from, those of the petty bourgeoisie. In fact, although it was ostensibly a workers' association, the workers' interests were at times subordinated to those of the petty bourgeoisie—precisely because these interests had not yet emerged as distinct. Their point of unity was their opposition to the colonial order.

Besides the motor drivers, the only other workers to possess a measure of organizational solidarity were the domestic servants: they lived in the city and in the towns and worked in the houses of state bureaucrats or wealthy merchants, those who were the personification of colonial rule. They were both objectively exploited and personally humiliated. Their hours of work were long and irregular. At night they returned to their shanty dwellings, a sharp and a daily reminder of the difference between employer and employed, and between colonizer and colonized.

The crisis of 1945 was sparked off by an event that provided a specific issue around which opposition to the colonial order coalesced. This was a "traditional" issue, in itself of little practical significance, but ideologically of the utmost importance in highlighting the collaboration between the colonial state and the Lukiko hierarchy in an anti-Buganda policy. Contrary to "tradition," the *namasole* (queen mother) had decided to marry a commoner. She was supported by both the Anglican Church and the *katikiro* Nsibirwa. From the Native Hellenic Church to the lower chiefs to the cash-crop-growing peasantry *(bakopi)*, including the Descendents of Kintu, opposition was vocal and widespread.[83] The sporadic political ferment of a decade found its focal expression in this one event. Confronted by such strong opposition, the governor asked the *katikiro* to resign. But the resignation, a partial concession, merely strengthened the opposition's determination to seek a realignment of forces within the Lukiko.

The new *katikiro*, Wamala, one of the few higher chiefs of kulak origin, set about appointing a number of kulak farmers and traders to positions of power. Opposition to the subservient role played by the chiefly hierarchy in its relations with the colonial state then built up within the Lukiko, where the secondary contradictions among the chiefs began to come into the open and intensify. These were conflicts between the chiefly hierarchy and the lower chiefs,* and even between the re-maining member of the Nsibirwa-Kulubya "ruling clique"— *omuwanika* Kulubya—and the *ssaza* chiefs. With Nsibirwa already replaced by Wamala, the *ssaza* chiefs petitioned the *kabaka* asking that Kulubya be dismissed.

In 1943, the colonial government sought to circumvent the

---

* The increasing concentration and centralization of power in the hands of the big chiefs, and especially the three regents, had given rise to contradictions between the chiefly hierarchy and the lower chiefs.

Land Alienation Law and acquire land for the Empire Cotton Growing Research Centre and the proposed Makerere College. In order to maintain legal niceties, it proposed that the Lukiko buy the land. The proposal was resoundingly defeated by the smaller chiefs, led by *katikiro* Wamala in the Lukiko and supported in the country at large by the newly organized Bataka Union and the Bakopi Bazukulu (Baganda Common People). When he persisted in his opposition, Wamala was forced to resign by the Protectorate government, and Nsibirwa was reinstated. At the same time, the Dundas Reforms of 1944 gave British officials a more advisory capacity, leaving direct rule to the Lukiko—which meant Nsibirwa and Kulubya. To the united opposition of kulaks, traders, lower chiefs, and workers it seemed as if the status quo ante had been restored and the political work of an entire decade nullified.

Such was the background to the general strike and the rural violence of January 16–19, 1945, and to the assassination of *katikiro* Nsibirwa on September 11 of the same year.[84] At the organizational core of the strike were the domestic servants. They were to light the spark at Entebbe on January 1, after which wave after wave of strikes, from urban center to urban center, began. The domestic servants were also instrumental in consolidating these sporadic uprisings at Kampala on January 14, the beginning of the countrywide general strike.[85] The strike spread to government workers, to those employed in factories, hospitals, public transport, and plantations.[86] Every urban center in the colony was paralyzed.* Domestic servants provided leadership in the urban areas, kulaks in the countryside, and the motor drivers acted as belts of communication, spreading the news of the crisis from town to town and district to district.

---

* Beginning with a meeting of domestic servants in Entebbe on January 1, there was a strike of public works department (PWD) laborers and tailors at Masaka on January 5, township and PWD laborers at Entebbe on January 8 and 9, township authority labor in Kampala on January 10, East African Tobacco Co. labor on January 11, and PWD labor on January 12. A meeting of Kampala domestic servants on the fourteenth resolved to continue the strike, which then spread to post and telegraph, railway, bus, and power in Kampala on the fifteenth, to Koja, Jinja, and Mbale on the seventeenth, to Iganga, Kisubi, and Mubende on the eighteenth, to Masaka on the nineteenth, and to Mbarara on the twentieth.[87]

Rural violence ensued throughout Buganda. The targets were the Baganda chiefs and the Indian traders and ginners. While the monopoly position of the wholesaler and the ginner was sanctified by law, the very nature of the export-import economy protected the position of the small Indian retailer. The guarantor of the system was the colonial state itself although it did not seem to play a direct role in this chain of exploitation. There was one exception, however: the state marketing boards, established to control the export of the two principal crops in the colony, cotton and coffee. The crisis was followed by attempts to organize against these boards.

In theory, the boards were granted monopoly rights over the export of both cotton and coffee and were supposed to shield the grower from the fluctuations of the world market by guaranteeing him in advance a stable price for the duration of the season. Any surplus accumulated in one season was then to be used to boost the price offered in the next. Over the long run, the board price and the market price were supposed to even out. In fact, however, since the boards were able to fix the buying price of both raw and ginned cotton, they were able to keep a substantial margin between the price they paid and that collected for exported cotton, thus accumulating a substantial surplus. Deposited in the Bank of England, this aided the British war effort.

The importance of the boards was accentuated because of the spectacular rise in the price of both cotton and coffee during and after the war. The price of cotton rose from Shs. 70 per hundredweight in 1938–1939 to Shs. 280 in 1949–1950. Coffee that fetched £41 a ton in 1938 fetched £100 a ton in 1946.[88] The prices received by the growers rose nowhere near as much as the world market price.* According to the calculations of one of

---

* The information I have gives the price of cotton and coffee accruing to the growers as a percent of their world market price for the years 1950–1952:

	1950	1951	1952
Cotton	50	39	45
Coffee	27	31	43

Source: C. C. Wrigley, *Crops and Wealth in Uganda*, p. 69.

the few economists to consider this phenomenon, the marketing board skimmed off 38 percent of Uganda's total earnings.[89] By the end of 1958, Uganda growers had "contributed" £30.8 million to the cotton and coffee Price Assistance Funds,[90] and about £30 million in various export duties.[91]

The growers' grievances were vociferously articulated by the newly established Bataka Party. Unlike its 1920 predecessor, the 1946 Bataka Party was firmly a kulak party. While it criticized the increased taxes, the acquisition of land at Makerere, and the leadership of the chiefly hierarchy in the Lukiko, the brunt of its attack was reserved for the marketing boards. In 1948, mass party meetings were held monthly and attended by up to 8,000 people.[92] The Kiganda press openly denounced the surpluses accumulated by the marketing boards and the resulting low prices to the growers:

> We the growers are aggrieved to see that the Protectorate Government refuses to free our cotton for which we sweat. Probably the Government is so shy that it has been so far unwilling to inform us of the fact that we the producers are its labourers to whom it pays a wage or gift of Shs. 30 on every 100 lbs. and reserves for itself Shs. 47/70 on every 100 lbs. Once again we implore the Government to understand that it has no right whatsoever to save for itself any money that would accrue to us from our cotton.[93]

On April 2, 1941, the Uganda African Farmers' Union (UAFU) was registered. It was intended to be an umbrella organization representing the growers' groups that had mushroomed all over Buganda. At its center was Ignatius Musazi, the organizer of the Descendents of Kintu. On May 18, 1948, a general meeting of "African produce growers" called by the Uganda African Farmers' Union asked

> that next year's [i.e., 1948–1949] cotton crop be collected by the African Produce Growers and request the Governor to help us in arranging the ginning of our raw cotton on the nearest ginneries to every buying post on reasonable charges.[94]

This was a highly specific demand, and the UAFU was sufficiently well organized to carry it through. It collected the cotton crop from its member growers, and then approached the government and the ginners for ginning facilities. It was flatly rejected. "The Uganda Company have refused to gin our cotton and the growers have refused to part with their cotton in the same way as the Nigerians did with their cocoa," a growers' representative said in explaining to the *kabaka* why the union decided to store its cotton rather than sell it to any of the ginners.[95] The state responded by fixing a legal marketing period after which no cotton could be sold, but this failed to coax the union to part with its cotton. The state then declared it illegal to store cotton at any but licensed premises (ginneries), thus making it mandatory for the union to sell its cotton to these licensed premises.

A few weeks later—in April 1949—the second major wave of kulak-led rural violence spread across Buganda. Strikes in the urban areas followed, though they were neither as general nor as effective as in 1945. Attempts were made to set *omuwanika* Kulubya's house on fire.[96] The wrath of the kulaks consumed the property of most of the compradore chiefs. The first houses to be put on fire were those of the minister of finance and the minister of justice of the Buganda government.

In Kibuga a total of 115 buildings were burnt, consisting of 12 belonging to the Buganda Government, one social welfare center at the Technical School at Makerere, 75 belonging to the officials of the Buganda Government, 10 houses of Africans employed by the Protectorate Government, and 17 houses of private individuals.[97]

Violence spread beyond the chiefs to the Indian ginners and traders. Pamphlets distributed throughout the countryside attacked the "Indian millionaire ginners." Ginnery owners found groups of people requisitioning their trucks, cash, and petrol,[98] and Indian shops in semiurban trading areas were sacked.[99] The growers' representatives pointed out to the *kabaka* the collusion between the chiefs and the ginners: "These chiefs receive money from the Indians as a return for the assistance given to them." [100] In the first week, over 110 people were arrested.[101] On May 27, the governor told the colony that "formal government [had] broke[n] down and the situation was out of control." [102] The growers' representatives made five demands to the *kabaka:*

(1) that people elect their own chiefs; (2) that the number of elected representatives in the Lukiko be raised to sixty; (3) that the present government resign; (4) that growers gin their own cotton; (5) that growers sell their agricultural products directly wherever they like.[103]

In 1945, an astute Muganda observer from Katwe, an African trading center on the periphery of Kampala, wrote the editor of the *Uganda Herald* about "the problem of the new African middle class":

> A new class is being born before our very eyes. Those of us who prefer the proverbially advantageous position of the onlooker are watching with an ever increasing interest the growth of this class. This class is taking form and shape with a speed that is to some people terrifying. Certainly the war has helped to speed this growth. This class becomes increasingly self-conscious and excessively vocal every day; and all this to the end that it may acquire for itself a position (together with the attendant privileges) in the social and political life of the country.
>
> It is not for . . . anyone to ignore its existence. Certainly the first thing about any social phenomena is to recognize it as a fact. Then we shall be in a position to understand its nature and its results. That knowledge will help us in the solution of our many post-war problems, be they medical or educational. The official will know what class of African he is dealing with; and the African will understand the limitations imposed upon him by the size of the class he represents.[104]

The point was that the 1949 rural violence, just as that of 1945, could not be dismissed as a "disturbance," for these were *political* events. And as political events they represented the demands of a class, the African petty bourgeoisie (specifically, the Baganda kulaks). This class found that the very nature of the organization of social production and appropriation set limits to its own growth, and that either room had to be made for it in the existing system of appropriation or the whole system was in danger. For this to happen, a fundamental shift in the political relations between the colonial state and the African petty bourgeoisie was necessary. The colonial state understood this very well.

184 *Mahmood Mamdani*

Notes

1. Governor to Secretary of State on Labour Policy. Enclosure to dispatch No. 433 of November 4, 1924, in CO 536/133.
2. Colonial Office memo on forced labor, in CO 536/162 (File No. 20580).
3. Dispatch from Governor to Secretary of State, August 21, 1924, in CO 536/132.
4. Dispatch from Governor to Secretary of State on Recruitment of Labour. Facilities Accorded to Planters, enclosure to dispatch No. 397, October 4, 1924, in CO 536/132.
5. R. M. Bere, "Northern Province: Uganda," pp. 9–10.
6. Governor's notes on postwar economic development in Uganda, in CO 536/209 (File No. 40287 of 1943).
7. T. T. Steiger-Hayley, "Wage Labour and the Desire for Wives Among the Lango," p. 15.
8. See para. 157 of the report, enclosure in dispatch from Governor to Secretary of State, No. 13, January 14, 1939, in CO 536/203 (File No. 40208). The governor in his dispatch disagrees with this recommendation of the report maintaining that the time is not yet ripe for creating a permanent wage-labor force, even "cautiously," but the purpose here is only to show the *late* development of an urban stable proletariat in Uganda.
9. Ibid.
10. Memorandum from Acting Governor to Secretary of State, The Organization of the Native Civil Service, January 15, 1920, in CO 536/99.
11. "The Economic Development of the Kingdom of Buganda, Part 1: Economic Survey," a report to the *kabaka*'s Council of Ministers by the Buganda Planning Commission, p. 17.
12. C. C. Wrigley, in L. A. Fallers, ed. *The King's Men*, p. 48.
13. J. H. M. Beattie, "The Kibanja System of Land Tenure in Bunyoro," p. 8.
14. Ibid.
15. M. L. Perlman, "Land Tenure in Toro," p. 8.
16. Bere, pp. 6–7.
17. J. T. Fleming, *Recent Developments in Kisoga Land Tenure*, p. 42.
18. UP, "White Paper on Mechanization of Agriculture," May 1954, p. 1.
19. W. Senteza Kajubi, "Coffee and Prosperity in Buganda: Some Aspects of Economic and Social Change," p. 143.
20. Ibid., p. 140.

21. Ibid., p. 136.
22. Audrey Richards, *Economic Development and Tribal Change: A Study of Immigrant Labour in Buganda*, p. 77.
23. C. C. Wrigley, quoted in A. J. Manners, "Social Stratification and Political Change," p. 102.
24. Commission Established to Examine and Report on Makerere College, Colonial No. 142, p. 15.
25. Governor to Secretary of State, July 22, 1920, in CO 536/101.
26. Acting Governor to Secretary of State, January 15, 1920, in CO 536/99.
27. Treasury to Colonial Office, August 6, 1921, in CO 536/116.
28. Colonial Office memo on forced labor, in CO 536/162 (File No. 20580).
29. Deputy Governor to Secretary of State, July 21, 1921, in CO 536/121.
30. Acting Governor to Secretary of State, May 11, 1920, in CO 536/100.
31. Memorandum from Governor to Secretary of State, September 11, 1920, in CO 536/102.
32. Colonial No. 142, pp. 76–77.
33. *Uganda Herald*, December 21, 1963, p. 13.
34. Telegram from Governor to Secretary of State, September 23, 1925, in CO 536/136.
35. UP, *Annual Report for 1915–1916*, p. 7.
36. A. M. O'Connor, *Railways and Development in Uganda*, p. 44.
37. E. Goldthorpe, *An African Elite*, pp. 10–13.
38. Busoga High School, Sixteenth Annual Report for 1926, Busoga College Archives, quoted in Tom Watson, "A History of C.M.S. High School in Uganda."
39. Roland Oliver, *The Missionary Factor in East Africa*, p. 232.
40. Ibid., p. 235.
41. UP, "Scheme of Development for African Education, 1944–1954," p. 1.
42. Oliver, p. 264.
43. Ibid., p. 268.
44. "Education Policy in British Tropical Africa," memorandum by the Advisory Committee, March 1925, Cmd. 2374 of 1924–1925.
45. Oliver, p. 268.
46. Dispatch by Governor to Secretary of State, No. 247 of June 17, 1929, on native civil service, in CO 536/156 (File No. 20396).
47. Colonial Office, *The British Territories in East and Central Africa 1945–1950*, p. 114.

48. Quoted in A. Low and C. Pratt, *Buganda and British Overrule*, p. 171.

49. Hattersley, Annual Letter, February 12, 1912, CMS G3 A7/09; quoted in Watson, p. 39.

50. Okot p'Bitek, trans., *Song of Lowino*.

51. Quoted in Watson, p. 20.

52. UP, *Annual Report for 1909–1910*, p. 17.

53. Goldthorpe, pp. 25, 28.

54. Ibid., pp. 39, 45.

55. "History of the Uganda African Civil Servants Association" (typescript), 1947, in Maini Papers AR MA 5/12, Railway Advisory Council, 1952.

56. Ibid.

57. Memorandum from C. F. Andrews to Secretary of State, January 10, 1920, in CO 536/107.

58. Memorandum from C. F. Andrews to Secretary of State, December 22, 1919, in CO 536/107.

59. Ibid.

60. Resolution of the meeting on March 14, 1933, in *Uganda Herald*, March 17, 1933, p. 17.

61. T. T. Steiger-Hayley, pp. 15–18.

62. Ibid., p. 18.

63. John Stonehouse, *Prohibited Immigrant*, p. 91. Stonehouse, an English Fabian socialist, worked with the cooperative movement in Uganda in its formative stage in the late 1940s.

64. Commissioners on Africanization of Commerce and Industry, *Report of 1968*, p. 5.

65. *Uganda Herald*, December 25, 1946, p. 18.

66. The petition is in a dispatch from Governor to Secretary of State on Representations of Bulunge Bua Buganda Party regarding affairs in Uganda, February 13, 1930, in CO 536/157 (File No. 20409).

67. Petition from the Uganda African Welfare Association to Hailey, Special Commissioner on Native Administration Affairs, April 2, 1940, in CO 536/208 (File No. 40006/13).

68. Ibid.

69. Enquiry by Treasurer on Revenue and Taxation, para 5, in CO 536/189 (File No. 40101).

70. Governor to Colonial Office, Confidential of July 15, 1939, in CO 536/202 (File No. 40080/1).

71. Reuters news dispatch, enclosed in File No. 40080/9 on Buganda Affairs, in CO 536/202.

72. Petition by the Descendants of Kintu to Secretary of State, December 17, 1938, in CO 536/202 (File No. 40080/7).

73. "Omnibus Services," in CO 536/194 (File No. 40156).

74. Chairman, Overseas Motor Transport Co., Ltd., to the Chief Secretary Uganda Government, May 1, 1933, in CO 536/190 (File No. 40156).

75. Colonial Office minute, enclosure in ibid.

76. Deputy Governor to Secretary of State, No. 34 of February 10, 1938, in CO 536/199 (File No. 40156).

77. Petition by the Descendants of Kintu to Secretary of State, December 17, 1938; in CO 536/202 (File No. 40080/7).

78. Ibid.

79. Apter, *The Political Kingdom of Uganda*, p. 203.

80. Colonial Office note on Spartus Mukasa, enclosure in Petition by Descendents of Kintu to Secretary of State, December 1, 1938; CO 536/202 (File No. 40080/7).

81. For an analysis of the Motor Drivers' Association, and of the workers' movement in general, see I. K. Musazi, "Strikes and Disturbances in Uganda: Their Origins and Results," in Milton Obote Foundation, *Labour Problems in Uganda*.

82. Memorandum from the President-General of the Uganda African Motor Drivers' Association to Dr. Hendon, Fabian Colonial Bureau, September 14, 1943; in CO 536/210 (File No. 40310).

83. See E. M. K. Mulira, *Troubled Uganda*.

84. *Uganda Herald*, September 12, 1945, p. 1.

85. UP, Report of the Commission of Inquiry into the Disturbances Which Occurred in Uganda During January 1945, pp. 14–15.

86. Ibid.

87. Ibid.

88. Colonial Office, *The British Territories in East and Central Africa, 1945–1950*, Cmd. 7987, p. 36.

89. A. Hazelwood, "Trade Balances and Statutory Marketing in Primary Exporting Countries," p. 74.

90. D. Walker, "Balanced Social and Economic Development of Uganda," quoted in Simeon Gor, "Country Study of Uganda," pp. 93, 95.

91. C. C. Wrigley, *Crops and Wealth in Uganda*, p. 70; see also G. B. Masefield, *Agricultural Change in Uganda*, p. 113.

92. Report of the Commission of Inquiry into the Civil Disturbances in Uganda During April 1949, pp. 72–73.

93. *The Gambuze* of April 2, 1948, quoted in A. B. Mukwaya, "The Rise of the Uganda African Farmers' Union in Buganda," p. 4.

94. Stonehouse, pp. 74–75.

95. Ibid., p. 23.

96. *Uganda Herald*, April 27, 1949, p. 1.

97. Kingdom Report, pp. 31–32; quoted in Horace Campbell, "And the Africans Organized to Enter the Marketplace."
98. *Uganda Herald*, April 30, 1949 (special edition), p. 1.
99. *Uganda Herald*, April 29, 1949 (special edition), p. 1.
100. Report of the Commission of Inquiry into the Civil Disturbances in Uganda During April 1949, p. 23.
101. *Uganda Herald*, May 5, 1949, p. 1.
102. *Uganda Herald*, April 29, 1949, p. 1.
103. Report of the Commission of Inquiry into the Civil Disturbances in Uganda During April 1949, p. 22.
104. A. B. Mukwaya to the editor, *Uganda Herald*, January 3, 1945, p. 13.

7
Petty Bourgeois Politics:
The Period of Consolidation

Mr. Lennox-Boyd, the Colonial Secretary, said in the House of Commons in London that an African property-owning middle class would be "one of the stabilizing factors in that continent". He said he would regard himself as "pretty inefficient" if, at the end of his period of office, he had not encouraged a sense of private profit and public service among the Africans.
—*Uganda Argus* (July 1956), p. 1.

The significance of the 1945 and 1949 crises was not lost on the British government. The effect on colonial policy was immediate and decisive. To understand the political consequences of these changes, it is necessary that we isolate different aspects of state policy as it affected the classes that played the leading roles in these events, the working class and the petty bourgeoisie.

State policy toward the working class, the propertyless class, had two distinct aspects: the short-run and the long-run, or the economic and the political. The object in the short run was to placate individual members of this class by granting their immediate economic demands, particularly those that had sparked the two general strikes. War bonuses were thus issued, "not only [to] those in the higher established grades of government service but also in the lower ranges of labour." [1] At the same time, the state announced its intention "to fix in the different parts of the country minimum wages for labour which would be binding by law on all employers, whether government or private." [2] (Though announced on January 31, 1945, it took another general strike for this to become the practice.)[3]

The long-run strategy was political. Its purpose was twofold: to secure state supervision over union finances (and thus activity), and to fragment the working class organizationally by promoting intraunion rivalry.

Even before the general strikes, as early as 1942, the government had appointed English labor officers who, the Colonial Office explained,[4] had "long experience of trade union administration to make the development of the new unions their particular care and to make sure that the growth of trade unions among Africans took the right line." The "right line" was to ensure that unions "not fall into the hands of unscrupulous persons anxious to exploit it for their own ends"; that is, that the unions be developed strictly as economic organizations to promote wage demands, not as organizations that might articulate political demands. The Office added: "There can be no doubt as to the value of these officers." *

Despite such care, the proletariat played a vital role both in the general strike of 1945 and that of 1949. The response was the Trades Unions Ordinance of 1952.† Chapter 2 of the

---

* In recommending the appointment of such official "advisors," Major G. St. J. Orde Browne, sent from London to carry out an investigation of the emerging labor movement in Uganda, wrote: "The need for this appointment is to ensure that the growth of a trade union movement—already perceptible in East Africa—should be on sound and well-proved lines, and that it should not fall into the hands of unscrupulous persons anxious to exploit it for their own ends. For such a part, the selection of an experienced official of an English union has proved a very satisfactory solution." [5]

† The 1952 Trades Unions Ordinance was preceded by the ordinances of 1937 and 1942. Both of these, however, were put on paper for international diplomatic reasons—because Britain was a member of international bodies such as the League of Nations. The 1952 Ordinance, on the other hand, was the legislative response of the colonial state to the internal development of working class organization.

Ordinance explained how the earliest unions (particularly the Uganda Motor Drivers' Association) were used as instruments of political protest. Its stated purpose was to ensure that this would not recur. To control the scope of union activities, the Ordinance specified objects for which union funds could be used and required unions to submit annual financial statements. To undermine the political strength of unions, the Ordinance attacked the very bases of their organizational solidarity: it required unions to provide representations for separate sectional interests.[6] Proletarian solidarity based on the *general* interests of the working class was henceforth declared illegal.

The 1952 Trades Unions Ordinance became the great barrier erected to stem the tide of working class organization. Immediately after the 1949 strike a new union, the Transport and General Workers Union, was registered. Once again, its hardcore members were the Kampala taxi drivers. This time, though, the recruitment was also successful among workers in Busoga. The intent of this union was "to form a comprehensive union for all workers in Uganda," [7] but general unions had been declared illegal by the 1952 Ordinance, and after eight months of protesting against the Ordinance the Busoga drivers finally registered separately as the Busoga African Motor Drivers' Union.[8] While the number of unions increased, the membership of individual unions declined as each sectional interest received its own separate organizational expression. By 1957, the only remaining union with a membership larger than 500 was the Railway African Union, with 3,000 members.[9]

State action was directed not just against the organizational unity but also the organizational autonomy of the union movement. The union as the guardian of the interests of labor was now displaced by work committees which, established in every place of work and closely supervised by the department of labor, mediated between the workers and their employers in case of dispute. In their first major strike after the 1952 Ordinance, the rank-and-file workers—dustmen, hedgecutters, sweepers, hospital assistants, laboratory technicians, and council employees, 2,300 in all—protested the Salaries Commission Report which excluded them from retrospective wage raises granted skilled workers. They circumvented the official work committees and organized wildcat strikes.[10] Increasingly, workers' demands were being expressed outside the formal structure of representation.

Within the established union movement, leadership passed from the motor drivers, the domestic servants, and other unskilled or semiskilled workers to the better-established, state-employed, white-collar civil servants organized in 1955 as the General Clerical Union *and* to the skilled and clerical members of the Railway African Union. In other words, leadership within organized labor shifted from the ranks of the working class to the lower echelons of the petty bourgeoisie (the lower civil service). The most vociferous demand from both these unions was for "Africanization," a reflection of their hopes for sharing the fortunes of the emerging petty bourgeoisie.

The Petty Bourgeoisie

The eclipse of working class politics and the rise of petty bourgeois politics were in fact two sides of the same coin. Following the events of 1945 and 1949, state policy was aimed at consolidating or creating (depending on the part of the country) a class whose interest was in maintaining the status quo and guarding the stability of the country. A propertied class, whatever specific privileges it might seek, would never question the general rule of property. In the words of the Royal Commission of 1953–1955:

> We endorse the majority view of the Carpenter Committee that "the ultimate solution to the problem of supervision in this country lies . . . in the emergence of a foreman class from amongst the Africans themselves." [11]*

---

* The commission was appointed after the general strikes and violence in Uganda, the Meru land case and the dock workers' strike in Tanganyika, and the Mau Mau resistance in Kenya. A much longer section from its report explains the recommendation in detail: "The theme that those who possess an advantage have attained it merely because they belong to a more favored racial community runs like a pathological obsession throughout the daily life and work of the community. This gives rise, in the last resort, to the belief that all would be well if, by a stroke of the pen or of the sword, the African could be rid of the presence of the non-African or could obtain complete political domination over him.

Such a class would be a rural and urban petty bourgeoisie, made up of kulaks, traders, and civil servants.

But the rise of the petty bourgeoisie as a "foreman class" was not possible without the liquidation of the compradore chiefs. In Buganda, they were organized in the Lukiko and in the 1945 and 1949 crises they had proved to be a major liability to the colonial state. Changes in the electoral law, first after 1945 and then after 1949, made forty of the eighty-nine members of the Lukiko *elected* nonofficials; twenty of these were to be "persons of special qualifications elected directly by the *ssaza* councils." [13] The *kabaka* explained to the Lukiko who these might be:

> The time is ripe for the introduction to this legislative assembly of people who would be of great value to this Lukiko by virtue of their education or by their prominence in various occupations. For certain reasons such people have hitherto found difficulty in being elected to this assembly according to the terms of the electoral law of 1945.[14]

The Buganda Lukiko, which had hitherto given political unity to the chiefs as a compradore social group by giving them control over the state apparatus, was thus opened to the rising petty bourgeoisie.

Once begun, the process continued in the following years. In 1953, the governor and the *kabaka* held "a series of discussions about constitutional and local government development in Buganda, with a view to giving increased responsibilities to the Buganda Government and a greater part in the system of Government to the people of Buganda." [15] Concretely, this meant, a further increase in the number of elected members of

---

Conversely, the non-African population seeks their security in measures which would prevent such an occurrence and often seek that security in the political domination of the African. . . . It has to be understood that the isolation of the races in East Africa must be overcome. . . . This implies that the pattern of economic relationships, at present confined merely to an association of interests between the races on the fringes of activity, typified by the European employers on the one side and the African labourers on the other, and by the purely transient contacts provided by commerce, must be replaced by a common objective in which the members of every race clearly understand that they have common interests. . . . Only thus can the economic and political dangers which threaten East Africa be avoided." [12]

the Lukiko to sixty out of eighty-nine; that the *kabaka* would henceforth consult members of the Lukiko before appointing ministers; and that the *kabaka* would "put forward to the Lukiko proposals for a system of local government to be established at *ssaza* level to which the Buganda Government would devolve certain of its functions." * Furthermore, for the first time since 1928 the Buganda government's financial projections were to be debated in the Lukiko before being approved, and elected members were to be appointed to the financial committee itself.

As it became more of an elected body, the Lukiko came increasingly under the control of the section of Buganda society that possessed the most effective mass political organization. This was the petty bourgeoisie, particularly its kulak section, which had in the previous decade successfully organized a mass peasant base in its struggles against the chiefs. In sum, the Lukiko after 1949 was increasingly an expression of the political unity, not of the chiefs, but of the Baganda petty bourgeoisie.

Outside Buganda, where the chiefs dominated local district councils, the change was initiated by the African Local Government Ordinance of 1949, which established a minority of elected members on the councils.[17] Following the Wallis Inquiry into Local Government of 1953, the state introduced the District Administrations (District Councils) Ordinance of 1955, whereby a majority of the members were directly elected.† The newly elected members were primarily petty bourgeois intellectuals (teachers) or traders. In Bunyoro, for example, the first direct elections were held in 1960 and totally undermined the chief-

---

* In addition, it was decided that:

"1. The responsibility at the Protectorate level and below for the operation of certain departmental services will be transferred from the Protectorate Government to the Buganda Government. [These included services in education, medicine, veterinary, and agriculture.]

"2. There will in consequence have to be financial adjustments.

"3. H. H. the Kabaka had decided that there will have to be an increase in the number of Senior Officers of the Buganda Government." [16]

† Under this ordinance, four districts (Bugisu, Kigezi, Teso, and Maoli) immediately introduced directly elected majorities while five (Ankole, Acholi, Bunyoro, Lango, and West Nile) kept approximately the same proportion of elected, appointed, and ex-officio members for an interim period.[18]

dominated district council: over half of the new members were teachers. Similarly, the Teso district council, elected in 1956, was dominated by a coalition of teachers and traders.[19]

Comparable changes were taking place in the central government, where the first African members of the legislative council were nominated after the general strike of 1945. The process was accelerated after 1949 when the first African was appointed to the executive council of the governor.[20]

Gradually the new "foreman class" made its appearance at the political level. At the same time, also through the efforts of the colonial state, this group was expanding its economic base. Whereas the political consolidation of the petty bourgeoisie required the liquidation of the chiefs, its economic consolidation necessitated the liquidation of the class dominant at the level of the economy in the colonial export-import exchange system: the Asian commercial bourgeoisie and petty bourgeoisie. This process was far more gradual, however, because of the strong economic base of the Asian commercial bourgeoisie (unlike that of the chiefs). The kulaks, traders, and civil servants who made up this class each followed different paths of economic development, which we will now trace separately.

1. KULAKS

The report of the 1953–1955 commission emphasized that "agrarian policy must occupy a key position in the general scheme of development in East Africa," [21] and recommended the spread of individual ownership of land and the encouragement of the "progressive farmer"—that is, the kulak. In its own words:

> Customary communal tenure is not only African: It is world-wide. The trend towards individualization has likewise been world-wide and it has the virtue of developing a political as well as an economic sense of responsibility.[22]

Following the commission's report, and on the recommendation of the secretary of state, representatives of the governments of the East African colonies, Northern Rhodesia, and Nyasaland held a conference on African land tenure.[23] The conference resolved that all the governments concerned "would be well advised to encourage the emergence of individual tenure in areas where conditions are ripe for it." *

By 1960, the Uganda government had already begun promoting "individualisation of land ownership" in three "pilot" districts in Kigezi, Ankole, and Bugisu.[25] In theory, the land was available for all. In practice, "registration" was conducted by a committee with the parish chief as chairman, along with fifteen to twenty-five male taxpayers who had been elected at a meeting of males in the parish, called together by the county chief. Before adjudication could begin, a deposit was required, and the claimant was asked to pay survey and title fees ranging from Shs. 50 for less than two acres to Shs. 610 for 400 acres.[26] In theory, everyone possessed "equal" rights. In practice, those with Shs. 610 were more "equal" than those with only Shs. 50. The resulting protest in these districts led to the appointment of a commission of inquiry which recorded the following complaints: (1) the chiefs take advantage of the scheme to snatch land for themselves and their friends; (2) the survey fees are too high and only the rich can afford them; and (3) the appeal procedure is too expensive and too lengthy.[27] Although these protests came to naught in Ankole, the policy was not extended to those parts of Uganda where private ownership had not yet

---

* The conference report divided the area between the Sudan and the Limpopo into three regions on the basis of population density and production system:

1. Pastoral areas where the population is that of communal nomads. Here the conference encouraged plans "to transform that pattern into a modern ranching pattern which, if successful, will disrupt the existing communal tenure and demand its gradual replacement by a form of individual tenure." Singled out were the Masai districts of Kenya and Tanganyika, the Northern Frontier district of Kenya, and the Karamoja district of Uganda.

2. Areas of sparse population, subsistence agriculture, and shifting cultivation, where communal tenure "is well adapted to subsistence need." These areas included much of the plateau country lying south of Lake Victoria, the Masai plains, and most of the Central African Federation.

3. The areas of high productivity and dense population, where customary tenure is fast giving way to forms of individual tenure. Reference was made to the Lake Victoria basin, including much of Uganda, and areas about the highlands of Kenya and Tanganyika.

The conference's recommendation was that governments accelerate the tendency to individualization in the third region, which included much of Uganda.[24]

come into being. (It did not, however, deter the state from promoting the kulaks where they already existed, in Buganda.)

Before undertaking measures to expand the economic base of the kulaks, the state sought to control their organizational expression—the cooperative—and direct it into politically safe channels. As early as 1920, Buganda cotton growers had attempted to associate and market their crop collectively so as to protect their immediate material interests. The Buganda Growers' Association, formed by five farmers in 1920, faltered in the face of stiff opposition from the ginners and the state. In the 1930s, the decade of the ginning pools, growers' marketing societies again proliferated throughout Buganda. In 1935, representatives of these societies met and formed the Uganda Growers' Cooperative Union. By 1938 it comprised twenty-six societies, fifteen of which were active.[28] When, in 1944, the Registrar of Cooperative Societies in Ceylon (also the League of Nations Advisor on Cooperation) visited Kenya to report on the situation there, the Uganda government invited him to submit a preliminary report on cooperation in Uganda. This report "urged that immediate action should be taken to control and assist the numerous quasi-cooperative societies already in existence by the enactment of legislation and the appointment of a Registrar." [29] The Cooperative Societies Ordinance of 1946 declared the formation of cooperatives legal, but subjected them to a series of regulations and controls. That same year, a registrar of cooperatives was appointed to run a department of cooperatives.[30] The cooperatives, like the trade unions, were to be cultivated under the protective eye of the state and steered clear of political involvement. A government minister, Mr. Maini, explained the reason for the establishment of the ordinance to hostile representatives of Uganda commercial capital:

> The question in discussing this bill is not as to whether cooperative societies are good or bad *per se*, but the discussion of the mode in which the activities of cooperative societies should be directed and controlled.[31]*

---

* The first approach by the Protectorate government to the Colonial Office for permission to enact cooperative societies legislation on the grounds of "the

The immediate effect of the ordinance was to put cooperatives under the tutelage of colonial administrators who "guided" them into assuming their proper "roles." Perhaps the best-known of the cooperatives was the Busoga Growers' Cooperative Union established in 1952. Considered "a most creditworthy cooperative union," in the words of an official report,[33] the members' contribution of Shs. 3.5 million was augmented by a Shs. 7 million contribution from the government. The union "benefitted from and thrived on government patronage and assistance." From its very inception to independence in 1962, British cooperative officers "managed" its accounts and "advised" its leaders on matters of policy.

Having secured the political framework within which the cooperative movement was to grow, the state proceeded to expand its economic base. Immediately after the 1949 riots, the Uganda government made arrangements to purchase the Ngongwe Ginnery from Liverpool Uganda Company and lease it to the Uganda Growers' Cooperative Union, thereby opening the door to cooperative participation in the ginning industry.[34] In 1951, a second ginnery was leased to the union,[35] and in 1952 the government passed a cotton bill giving itself the legal power to acquire ginneries in order to transfer them to the cooperatives. If the latter could produce one-third of the purchase price, the remainder would be loaned by the state.[36]* By 1960, coopera-

---

general necessity for legislation of this nature to control African cooperative societies," was made as early as 1937. At the time the colonial secretary declined, maintaining that such legislation was premature. With an eye to the future, however, he added: "At the same time I am interested to see from the Solicitor General's memorandum that there are already distinct signs of a movement towards cooperation among the native producers, and if this is the case and if such a movement begins to develop, then it will be necessary to enact legislation, to regulate and control cooperative societies, and the existence of vested interests, however powerful, cannot be allowed to stand in the way.

If societies are properly controlled and regulated, there should be no tendency for them to be politically powerful or as a source of embarrassment for the government, but if societies are allowed to grow up uncontrolled that may well be the case." [32]

By 1949 a movement toward cooperation among "native producers" had indeed begun and it was necessary for the colonial state to properly control and regulate them.

* The arrangement was later institutionalized when it was decided that the

tives controlled fifteen cotton ginneries and ginned 16 percent of the crop.[37]

Explaining the rationale behind such a drastic reorganization of the ginning industry, an official report stated:

> If Africans had not been assisted to enter this industry, the effects both on cotton production and marketing, and on the general state of affairs in the country, would have been exceedingly serious in view of the very strong and widespread demand among Africans for a part in cotton ginning.[38]

The cooperatives were similarly assisted in their efforts to enter the coffee industry. A reorganization of the coffee industry was begun in 1953 when the government announced a plan to promote "participation by Africans in both the primary marketing and processing of coffee and to remove the present differentiation between the methods in marketing of African and non-African coffee." [39] The Coffee Industry Ordinance provided for the establishment of six new African-owned curing works,* the arrangement being once again that the government would loan two-thirds of the cost[41] (from the price assistance fund, which by now totaled £14 million[42]). Whereas in 1953 there were six licensed curing works and seven licensed hullaries, all owned by non-Africans, in 1960 the cooperatives owned five curing works, two estate coffee factories, and a number of coffee pulperies.[43]†

As the accompanying table shows, the cooperative movement, the organizational vehicle of the advancing petty bourgeoisie, had taken giant strides by 1961, the year before independence.

---

two-thirds loan would come from the Credit and Savings Bank under a government guarantee.

* It should be noted that coffee curing works and hullaries were primarily owned by British metropolitan capital and that, unlike in the cotton industry (primarily owned by Indian capital), there was no provision for the compulsory (or voluntary) acquisition of existing curing works, but only for the cooperatives' ownership of *additional* works.[40]

† Besides this, legislation was introduced in 1957 to enable private associations of African growers to establish "estate" coffee factories so as to process *and* market coffee in the open market. In 1959, a price support scheme was introduced to subsidize these private estates. The result was that by 1960 the private associations controlled eight curing works and thirty estate factories.[44]

Where there were no kulak formations, it was the traders who took control of the emerging movement. As early as 1946, there were seventy-five organizations of a "cooperative nature" and they encompassed not only agricultural marketing societies but also shopkeepers' and supply societies and consumer stores.[45]

Uganda: The Growth of the Cooperative Movement,
1951 to 1960

Year	Societies	Members	Unions	Total tonnage of all crops handled
1951	401	36,620	5	14,300
1952	574	53,968	10	23,675
1953	799	71,458	12	24,268
1954	1,025	94,315	11	31,948
1955	1,099	114,047	11	37,623
1956	1,256	126,962	12	36,176
1957	1,408	135,014	15	47,453
1958	1,534	147,421	15	58,012
1959	1,583	187,860	15	80,630
1960	1,622	211,214	16	89,308
1961	1,622	252,378	21	(not available)

Source: UP, *Commission of Inquiry into . . . Cotton-Ginning Industry,* 1962, Appendix 8, p. 80.

2. TRADERS

We feel that it is from this class of Africans [the traders] that a large proportion of the new middle class will arise which is essential to political and economic stability. We recommend that accordingly Government should pay close attention to the development of Africans in private enterprise.[46]

The numbers of African traders was swelled by the soldiers returning from active duty in World War II. Out of some 60,000 returning soldiers,[47] only 6.6 percent were offered paid employment in the technical trades and as government drivers.[48] From those who remained there emerged, in the words of the 1953–1955 Royal Commission, a "new class of small African capitalists." They used their war gratuities to set up small shops and to establish themselves in the transport business, buying second-hand lorries and buses.* Their entry into the transport sector was made possible by a change in government policy toward the small African entrepreneur, whereby more and more routes were given to Africans.[50] The result was that substantial African-owned companies, such as the Buganda Bus Service Company and the Masaka-Bukedi Company,[51] were granted exclusive licenses on some of the major routes, and licenses on minor routes were granted to a number of smaller entrepreneurs.† Since many of the soldiers came from the north, their return there meant a boost to the northern trade. As a government study on the advancement of Africans in trade confirmed, the largest pockets of African trade in Uganda were within Buganda in the south and Lango and Teso in the north.[53]

Although by 1955 Africans had entered trade in large numbers, the problem quickly became their place in the trading hierarchy. This same government study reported that in 1955 there were approximately 12,000 African traders in the Protectorate.[54] Although they constituted over 70 percent of all traders in numbers, they controlled only one-third of the retail trade;[55] further, 18 percent made no annual net profit at all, 62 percent made £50 or less, and 20 percent only made up to £250.[56] The study concluded:

---

* The commission reported: "The war gratuities which were paid to [the returning soldier] enabled his emergence as a new class of African small capitalists. He invested in the transport business conducted often with second-hand buses and lorries and he put his money into small shops throughout the country. Lack of business knowledge, insufficient capital and the competition of the Indian trader, however, caused large numbers of failures, with the result that these men, who owing to the wider knowledge of the modern world which they had acquired were potential leaders, emerged frustrated and dissatisfied. . . . These are the new leaders of Africa and they are in many cases embittered men." [49]

† For example, the following notation appeared in the *Uganda Herald*: "Last September, a group of Africans from Kioga (mostly ex-soldiers) applied for a license to run bus services from Lira to Soroti (via Aloi and Urungo) and from Lira to Parango. The group was originally styled the Kioga Co., but the name was later changed to the Lango Bus Co.

"The routes applied for have now been allocated to the company by the Traffic Control Board. . . . This will be the first time that an African company of this kind has ever operated in Lango District." [52]

The survey demonstrated that the problem was not to assist Africans to enter trade, but to assist those who had already engaged in trade during the period when skill in trade was not all-important, to acquire the necessary trading techniques in order to maintain their position and to develop further under competitive conditions.[57]

As a solution, the study proposed to teach the necessary skills for trade, provide credit facilities, and strengthen the traders organizationally.

The department of commerce vigorously set out to implement these recommendations. Simple books on how to run a shop, keep accounts, deal with a bank, and so on, were published and distributed to shopkeepers.[58] Courses for traders were held at the local government and community development center in Entebbe, where the demand exceeded available space.[59] A fund of £400,000 was established for financing a program to build shops for rental to Africans in major townships and trading centers.[60] Wholesale showrooms were established in areas remote from the wholesale supply center.[61] To make it possible for the African retailer to become independent of his better established Indian counterpart, the legal ban against mobile wholesalers was removed.[62]

To confront the problem of the lack of credit facilities, a land bank—the Uganda Credit and Savings Bank—was established in 1950 with a capital of £600,000. In contrast to other land banks, it gave loans to farmers *and* traders.[63] By 1953, £100,000 in loans had been extended for tile- and brick-making, fishing, printing, the purchase of trucks and buses, the erection and repair of buildings, and to assist in the discharge of encumbrances on land.[64] In 1954, an African Loan Fund of £150,000 was set up for the farmers outside of Buganda who did not "own" land.[65]

To promote the development of small manufacturing enterprises, the Uganda Development Corporation (UDC) established in 1955 a subsidiary called the Small Industries Scheme, designed to help finance new enterprises or the expansion of existing ones.[66]

It was not long before it was time to count the harvest. The number of the African retail traders increased from 11,600 in

1952 to "approximately 14,000" in 1956.[67] By 1958, the *Uganda Argus* was commonly reporting such items as the following:

Plans for the creation of a new trading company calculated to bring more trade into the hands of Africans were announced at a meeting of traders and businessmen at Mengo Blue Gardens by Mr. L. C. B. Bassude, promoter of the project. Several hundred attended the meeting, including the Muganda Minister of Health and Works, Mr. A. K. Sempa.

Mr. Bassude is a representative member of the Buganda Lukiko (and a former leader of the Bataka Union).[68]

The changes were not just quantitative, but were also qualitative. Previously unorganized and scattered, tied individually to Indian retailers who were their source of supply and credit, African traders were now beginning to show a measure of organization. This organization, independent of and in opposition to the Indian retailers, was given a boost by the colonial state. Earlier, their lack of organization had presented problems to the state when it attempted a controlled distribution of consumer goods (particularly cotton piecegoods) to various retailers during the war. This had been relatively easy in the case of the Indian retailer, whose trade interests were well organized and whose various associations acted as intermediaries between the state and the retailer, but it proved most difficult in the case of the African retailer. Attempts among the traders themselves to organize mutual assistance societies had left them at the mercy of Indian retailers. The state responded by encouraging the formation of associations by offering them a source of supply independent of the Indian retailers. By the end of the war many such groups were in operation, their membership varying from a few individuals to hundreds. The most important of these were the Masaka-Buganda Cooperative Society, the Lango Shopkeepers' Association, the Teso Traders' Association, and the Buganda Cooperative Society of Wandegeya, which had over 600 members and, among other activities, ran its own press.[69] For the first time, the traders had bypassed the Indian retailer and wholesaler to deal directly with the state.

The end of the war was not the end of official interest in the organization of African traders. Following the Advancement of Africans in Trade report, the department of commerce started planning associations of traders throughout the country.[70] The object was not just to organize widely scattered *local* associations. According to the committee recommendation accepted by the government, "the formation of a local traders' association at county, township, or other appropriate levels should be encouraged and that each local association should send representatives to district associations which, in turn, should send representatives to a Protectorate chamber of commerce." [71] In 1958, 130 such representatives from all parts of the Protectorate met for four days in discussions on trading questions and voted to hold another convention in Kampala the following year.[72] From one trader to a group of traders, from local associations to regional associations, and from the regions to the capital city, these representatives associated as a national convention discussing common strategy. In 1959, the Uganda Traders' Convention held its second annual meeting.[73] Gradually this section of the petty bourgeoisie was attaining self-consciousness, a consciousness that was above all national.

3. THE CIVIL SERVANTS

The march of the petty bourgeoisie onto the national political scene carried with it the state bureaucrats, although they trailed in the rear. This could not be otherwise, for as long as state power remained in the hands of the colonial authorities, there was a limit to the "Africanization" of its higher personnel. The changes in the preindependence period were changes in salary and personnel at the intermediate and lower levels. A standing finance committee minute in 1952 noted:

> Members are well aware that it is Government's intention to encourage the admission of Africans to the higher branches of the Civil Service as Africans capable of carrying higher responsibilities become available.[74]

By 1955, the number of Africans at the "higher" level had increased from "no more than five" to "well over fifty." [75] The proportion of Africans in the higher grades of the civil service climbed from 18 percent in 1956 to 28 percent in 1961.[76] The 1954 report of the salaries commission recommended an end to racial pay scales in the civil service.[77] Significant "Africanization" of the state bureaucracy, however, had to await the transfer of state power to an indigenous class, the African petty bourgeoisie.

The Politics of Independence

The decade from 1952 to 1962 saw the rise and fall of a bewildering number of political parties in Uganda. Large or small, all of them were located within one section or another of the petty bourgeoisie. In the struggle for state power, however, the only ones of political significance were those that acquired support from beyond their narrow class confines. Thus, although their leadership stemmed from a particular section of the petty bourgeoisie, all of the important political parties had a base in a particular section of the peasantry. These mass-based petty bourgeois parties were further distinguished from one another by their differences in ideology. Not one of these parties was able to emerge and capture the leadership of the independence movement: nationalist parties vied for support against parties that were tribal or religious in their ideological orientation. This failure was both a consequence of the failure of the petty bourgeoisie to emerge as an integrated and unified class, and a result of the fact that its most advanced section was the kulaks, a group that was regional in its formation, and whose politics was regional in its articulation.

The mass-based petty bourgeois parties—whether nationalist, tribal, or religious—were each based in a different section of the petty bourgeoisie. In the commodity-producing regions of the country, where there were significant kulak formations, political organization took a predominantly *tribal* expression. Where kulak formations were absent but commodity production was carried on by peasant farmers, traders provided the political leadership for organizations that were *nationalist* in their orientation. *Religiously* oriented parties were successful in capturing a peasant base in the noncommodity-producing regions, where trading formations were in their infancy. The advanced section of the petty bourgeoisie in these regions were the intelligentsia, teachers and civil servants, all educated in—and the teachers employed in—church-affiliated schools. The churches and the denominational schools acted as recruiting agents for the religiously based parties.

In identifying the social base of each political party, we must understand clearly that the leadership of the tribal parties did not come solely or even primarily from the kulaks, or that of nationalist parties from the traders. In both, leadership came to a large degree from the intellectuals, but—and this is the critical point—in the ideologies they produced these intellectuals seldom went beyond the material interests of the class, or the section of it with which they were allied. As Marx explained in *The Eighteenth Brumaire of Louis Bonaparte*:

> Just as little must one imagine that the democratic representatives are indeed all shopkeepers or enthusiastic champions of shopkeepers. According to their education and their individual position, they may be as far apart as heaven from earth. What makes them representatives of the petit bourgeoisie is the fact that in their minds they do not go beyond the limits which the latter do not get beyond in life, that they are consequently driven, theoretically, to the same problems and solutions to which material interest and social position drive the latter practically. This is, in general, the relationship between the *political* and *literary representatives* of a class and the class they represent (pp. 50–51).

It is thus that we can identify tribal, nationalist, and religious intellectuals in Uganda. Like the petty bourgeoisie itself, the intelligentsia was highly fragmented in their ideological formation. The first section of the petty bourgeoisie to organize was the kulaks, first in Buganda and then in Busoga. In each case, these were local organizations with a local consciousness. In their conflict against the state-supported chiefs the kulaks had built up local (tribal) organizations and rallied mass peasant support for king and tradition and against the chiefs who had forsaken tradition by collaborating with the colonial state. In Buganda, the various political organizations, from the Descendants of Kintu to the Bataka Union and the Bakopi Bazukulu, were dominated by kulaks. In Busoga, it was the district council, filled with appointed chiefs, that became the object of kulak hostility. When the councils were democratized and the kulaks given access to local political power, one objective circumstance that might have compelled them to ally with other social groups at the national level was prevented. While the chiefs organized as Abataka Abasogo, or Basoga Elders, and continued their earlier demands for land grants from the colonial state, the kulaks organized as the Young Busoga Association and the Busoga Farmers' and Traders' Association.[78] Their grievances included cotton prices and soil conservation policies, but their most vociferous demand was for "complete and unlimited control of local government finances." [79]

The Basoga "tribalists" attempted consciously to emulate their Baganda counterparts. They demanded that the Basoga flag fly over the Lukiko Hall and that the registration plates be removed from the *kyabzinga*'s (king's) car, as was the same privilege granted the *kabaka* in Buganda. In effect, they were demanding that the colonial state recognize the separate interests of the Basoga kulaks, and guarantee that the local territory, the district of Busoga, would remain their political base after independence—just as the state seemed to have guaranteed the Baganda kulaks. And so Basoga "tribalism" attempted to rival that in Buganda:

> Busoga is a very important country among the countries of Uganda; what measures are being taken by the Busoga District Council to safeguard the position of the Kyabazingaship when Uganda achieves self-government? [80]

In both Buganda and Busoga, it was the political dominance of the kulak farmers, along with their early use of tribal ideology and organization to mobilize peasant support against the colonial state and its appointed chiefs, that explained the failure of the subsequent nationalist parties to organize a mass base among the peasantry. By the time the "nationalist" politicians came around, the peasant base had been preempted by the "tribalists."

The only exception was the temporary success of the Uganda National Congress in Buganda from 1953–1955.

1. UGANDA NATIONAL CONGRESS, THE UGANDA PEOPLES' CONGRESS, AND THE KABAKA YEKKA

The Uganda National Congress (UNC) was founded in 1952 by members of the Buganda petty bourgeoisie. Its central committee consisted of three full-time politicians, five shopkeepers and traders, two clerks, two lawyers, four journalists and newspaper editors, two schoolmasters, and one student abroad.[81] Nonetheless, the UNC in its early years found little support in Buganda. Though Musazi, the leading figure in the party, was also the founder of the Federation of Partnerships of Uganda African Farmers (which followed the banned Uganda Farmers' Union after the 1949 crisis), the vast majority of federation members did not join the UNC; nor did the kulak-traders or the kulaks in the rural areas. Party support was almost exclusively confined to the independent traders in Mengo, Katwe, Wandegeya, and Bwayise.[82] What were the reasons for this?

In Buganda, the political consequence of the events of 1945 and 1949 was the British-supervised democratization of the Lukiko: increasing numbers of elected members entered the Lukiko in 1945, 1949, and again in 1953 as a result of the constitutional reforms. By then, elected members numbered sixty out of eighty-nine. Between 1951 and 1953, 67.5 percent of the elected members listed themselves as "cultivators" and 22.5 percent as traders.[83] The character of the Lukiko had changed from being a citadel of chiefly power to a representative of kulak-trader interests. It was this political success of the kulak-led Baganda "tribalism" that explained the lack of success of the "nationalist" UNC outside of the trading townships in its early years.

The social base of the UNC, in spite of the fact that its individual leaders came from Buganda, was in those regions where there was a cash-crop-growing peasantry but no significant kulak formations. This included Teso, Bukedi, and particularly Lango and Acholi, where party members organized mass meetings of 500 to 600 people.[84] Here, traders, teachers, and civil servants comprised the petty bourgeoisie. It was also from among their ranks that the new members of the district councils were elected. Their political expression was the UNC. In both

Lango and Teso, local traders' organizations—the Lango Shopkeepers' Association and the Teso Traders' Association—already existed and provided some of the early organizers for the local UNC branch. In Lango, for example, Cherry Gertzel describes the social background of the founding members of the UNC: Engur, secondary-school educated, had worked as an interpreter for the district commissioner and had been trained as a medical dresser; Ben Otim, also secondary-school educated, had become in 1948 the secretary of the Lango Shopkeepers' Cooperative Society, which had unsuccessfully tried to provide wholesale facilities for African traders to enable them to break into the local retail trade; Ngwenge, a small trader, primary-school educated, had become the president of the Shopkeepers' Cooperative; finally, Olyech had been a clerk in the Lango local government and then a storekeeper.[85] In Acholi, on the other hand, traders were few in number and teachers and civil servants primarily comprised the petty bourgeoisie.* Here UNC organization came in response to workers' and peasants' oppression by the chief-dominated district council. In 1951 and 1952, the council's standing committee approved forced labor of up to a month a year, fines of Shs. 10 for failure to plant famine-reserve food, and wages of Shs. 18 a month for urban workers. Local UNC leaders organized a strike among Gulu workers in 1953 directed against both the district council and the *lawir-wode*, the head of the chiefs and thus of the tribe.[87]

In 1953, the UNC entered its second phase in response to altered political circumstances in Buganda. This led to a burst in its membership in Buganda, going beyond independent traders to include kulak-traders (individuals with both occupations) and even kulaks.

Once the Buganda kulak traders came to dominate the Lukiko, they gradually moved to demand that the colonial state consider their interests as separate from those of the non-Buganda petty bourgeoisie. The occasion the Lukiko seized to advance this demand was the aftermath of a speech by the colonial secretary, Mr. Lyttleton, before the East African

---

* In 1963, there were 445 African traders and 7,074 teachers and civil servants in Acholi, which had a population of 340,000.[86]

Dinner Club, in which he made reference to the "possible" federation of the "whole East African territories." The theme was enthusiastically taken up by the settlers' paper in Nairobi, the *East African Standard*. In response, the Lukiko drafted a memorandum deploring the secretary's remarks and declaring that the Lukiko "was compelled to take steps to safeguard their future." They demanded that the affairs of Buganda be transferred to the Foreign Office and that a time limit be set for the independence of Buganda within the Commonwealth. Already in control of the Lukiko, and not content with just a separate consideration of their interests by the colonial state, the Baganda petty bourgeoisie was demanding independence, not as much from the colonial state (they were willing to accept independence "within the Commonwealth") as from the other sections of the rising petty bourgeoisie in Uganda, particularly the "nationalist" traders. In response, the colonial state demanded that the *kabaka* sign a statement of total allegiance to Her Majesty's government and inform the Lukiko accordingly. When he refused, the *kabaka* was exiled.

The resulting constitutional crisis was a major political crisis for the Buganda kulaks. There was a real possibility that the Lukiko would revert, through the initiative of the colonial state, to the control of the chiefs. For the first time since 1949, kulak control over the Lukiko was uncertain and their political future insecure. In the ensuing battle to rally public support for the *kabaka*'s return, the UNC took the lead. And the Baganda kulaks (from leaders in the Lukiko to cultivating members), their very political position at stake, without any organization outside of the Lukiko, joined the ranks of the UNC and plunged themselves into the battle.

In the following years, both the political organization and the ideology of the Buganda UNC was increasingly dominated by the Baganda kulaks. In many areas UNC and Farmers' Federation (FUAF) personnel were the same. Of the UNC branch chairmen in Buganda, 34 percent were traders and 29 percent farmers,[88] while others came from various sections of the petty bourgeois intelligentsia. Unlike in the rest of Uganda, the Buganda UNC had become an alliance of kulaks and traders, with the kulaks increasingly setting the political tone.

Ideologically, kulak dominance of the Buganda UNC was reflected in the increasingly "tribal" orientation of the party branches. The kulak demand for the independence of Buganda became the demand of the Buganda UNC. At a meeting that was reported to have a "colossal and unprecedented attendance," with no non-Baganda speakers invited despite customary practice to the contrary, and with two elected Lukiko members among the invited speakers, the following resolution was passed:

We disagree with being united with those territories which have different customs, ways of living, and agreements which are entirely different from ours. For that reason, we, the members of the UNC, Buganda branch, have met and decided that Buganda as a separate kingdom should be removed from the Colonial Office into the Foreign Office. . . . In this determination to move from the Colonial Office to the Foreign Office we know that all our brothers who are in the areas surrounding us, such as Toro, Ankole, Teso, Lango and other areas of Uganda, approve of this move and have the same determination. They are ready to hand in the same resolution. The reason why we have not mentioned them in this resolution is that Ssabasajja Kabaka of Buganda does not rule those areas. However, we confirm that in a few days they will hand in their resolutions so that this decision . . . includes their areas as well. This decision . . . will be presented to Ssabasajja Kabaka and his government so that it can be discussed in the Lukiko.[89]

In 1955, the *kabaka* was allowed to return. As part of the bargain, the Lukiko signed the 1955 Agreement with the colonial government. In the process of securing the *kabaka*'s return, important because he was the key symbol in kulak "tribal" ideology, the kulak-led Lukiko truly managed to reduce the *kabaka* to a mere symbol. The 1955 Agreement changed his position from that of ruler to that of "constitutional monarch." In one attempted justification, the Lukiko wrote:

This is the core of the fabric of our culture and traditions to which must be adapted the new conception of constitutional monarch whereby the king is immunized from conflict with his people on matters political, but his traditional prerogative to advise his people on these matters is not impaired.[90]

That is, the *kabaka* must be a symbol, set apart from political conflicts, and therefore stripped of political power. In the name of tradition, tradition had been revoked! With the *kabaka* turned into a constitutional monarch, the kulak Lukiko now set itself on the road to monopolizing political power in Buganda.

The objective circumstance which had precipitated kulak participation in a "nationalist" political party and reoriented the ideology of that party to Baganda "tribalism" no longer existed. The *kabaka* had returned; the Baganda petty bourgeoisie was once again firmly in control of the Lukiko; and the chiefs were no longer a political threat. The result was the disintegration of the kulak–trader alliance that had become the Buganda UNC. Membership in the UNC, which had climbed to a peak of 50,000 during the *kabaka*'s exile, dropped to 10,000 after his return.[91] There were mass defections from the party to Baganda "tribalism." As prominent a member as Abu Mayanja, the UNC secretary-general and a man of Baganda kulak origin, joined the *kabaka*'s government as minister of education.

For the UNC, the *kabaka*'s return created an acute political crisis that it was unable to survive. Its constituent elements, the kulaks and the traders, assumed organizational independence from one another. The kulaks went the way of the Buganda Lukiko, later to reemerge as a political party, the Kabaka Yekka (KY); the traders, after a short life as the Uganda Peoples' Union (UPU), donned the cloak of the Uganda Peoples' Congress (UPC), both with their allied intellectuals. The only significant change was that the UPC gradually brought within its fold a section of the latest emerging fraction of the petty bourgeoisie, the state bureaucrats. What was in appearance a regional and tribal split—between Baganda and non-Baganda—was in essence a split between the two fractions of the petty bourgeoisie, the kulaks and the traders. And it was the traders, the national group par excellence, with the sole national grievance—the dominance of a nonnational petty bourgeoisie—who now proceeded to occupy the national political stage.

2. THE TRADERS' MOVEMENT

With the contradiction between the kulaks and the chiefs resolved by the colonial state (as the kulaks assumed control over the Lukiko and the *kabaka* was neutralized into a constitutional monarch) in Buganda, as in the rest of Uganda, the contradiction between the African and the Indian traders came to the fore.

The objective basis of this conflict was that it was not possible for the state to promote the consolidation of the African petty bourgeoisie without at least partially liquidating the existing Indian petty bourgeoisie. When the government passed the Cooperative Societies Ordinance in order to boost the organizational strength of the African kulaks and traders, the loudest opposition came from the Indian Merchants' Chamber, the Indian member of the legislative council (Sir Amer Maini, a representative of cotton-ginning interests and soon to be appointed a minister), the Central Council of Indian Associations in Uganda, the Uganda Cotton Association, and the Indian Association of Kampala and Jinja—all organizational representatives of Indian trading and ginning interests. With one voice, they declared as "premature" the setting up of African cooperatives and opposed any hint of state assistance to them.[92] In the civil service, Asian railwaymen employed by the Kenya and Uganda Railway met in Uganda to draft petitions to safeguard "Asian" privileges.[93] While the African Civil Servants' Association sought equal pay for Africans and Asians, the Asian Civil Servants' Association demanded parity with Europeans, "equal pay for equal work." [94] No matter which section of the African petty bourgeoisie attempted to advance, it collided head-on with its Asian counterpart: the class struggle assumed the form of a racial conflict.* There was one difference, however: while the

---

* An unsigned pamphlet distributed during the 1949 crisis declared: "I am requesting the Buyer/Customers who may buy some goods from Indian shopkeepers who are scattered outside the township to stop buying from them . . . We are losing the wealthiness of our nation because of their [the Indian traders'] being scattered in each and every village. Now there shall be a loss of life because of the Indians."

Another pamphlet maintained: "The Indian cotton ginners get loans amounting to millions of shillings from the bankers which money is being paid by the poll-tax payers of this government. This accumulated sort of deluding makes every Indian to be rich and after the cotton season all interest accrued. The buyer makes his own enormous profits, the ginner also makes his own enormous profits and thirdly comes the Indian shopkeeper who trades in clothes through black marketeering.

consciousness of the African trader was *both* national and racial, that of the Indian trader was simply racial. The Asian petty bourgeoisie had become an objectively *alien* class.

Changes after 1949 exacerbated this contradiction. The entry of returning soldiers into trade, the expansion in the number and scope of operation of the African traders, their organization into associations by the department of commerce—all served to strengthen the organization and consciousness of African traders *as* traders. As they consolidated their position, gained increased confidence, and prepared for further advances, they refused to accept the barrier of the Indian trader. Unable individually to compete at the level of the market, they prepared to use their newly found collective political strength to ensure their economic advance. The weapon they wielded was that of the trade boycott.

In 1954, when there was heightened political activity in Buganda because of the *kabaka*'s exile, the UNC introduced a total boycott of non-African trade and transport in order to press for the return of the exiled *kabaka*.[96] As the boycott intensified, physical threats were made and measures taken against both the rural Asian traders and those Africans who frequented Asian shops in the urban areas.[97]

The *kabaka* returned in 1955, but his exile had been only the *occasion* for the boycott, not the *reason* for it. The reason, the established Indian trader, remained. While the UNC declined in the following years, the local traders' associations that had implemented the boycott formed a common front under a common organizational umbrella: the Uganda National Movement (UNM). Augustine Kamya, the trader who led the UNM at its mass rally on March 9, 1959, announced a second boycott: "From now, ten minutes to six, all trade is put into the hands of Africans. From this hour no African should enter a non-African shop."[98]

The boycott quickly spread beyond Buganda to Jinja and Mbale, and so did the government's attempts to suppress it.

"Let every Muganda who is interested in this policy join with in advancing and see that the growers gin their cotton, and, by working together the Indians will be compelled to return to Bombay empty-handed."[95]

Restrictions were placed on mass meetings, the UNM was declared illegal, and all its leaders were arrested; six were even deported.[99] Yet the boycott continued and in fact gained strength with each passing day. A few months later, the chairman of the Uganda Traders' Association publicly told a meeting of prominent Asians that "Asian traders in Uganda must, willingly or unwillingly, yield all retail trade into African hands." [100] By March 1960, four months after the boycott began, the Indian Merchants' Chamber estimated that "nearly half the Asian traders in the rural areas of Buganda have been forced to remove business elsewhere." [101] Many of the displaced traders were said to be "moving from place to place," even going "to the Western and Eastern Provinces." By April 1960, the African townships of Buganda seemed cleared of Asian traders. As the *Uganda Argus* reported for one township:

> The only remaining Asian trader in Bwayise Bazaar, near Kampala, had his premises burnt down on Friday night while a crowd of Africans, who refused to help him or call the police, stole his property, while he and his wife dragged it from the house.[102]

Every single organized political force in the country was compelled to voice support for the boycott. Whether Baganda or non-Baganda, kulak, "respectable" professional citizen, or chief, every political organization fell into line. In confronting the Asian petty bourgeoisie, the African trader was highlighting the most visible link between metropolitan capital and the direct producers, rural or urban. The fact that the African trader sought to replace the link and not break the chain, to become the intermediary himself by re-forming the system, was of little political relevance at this historical juncture. The traders' grievances, however limited and partial, reflected the demands of every social group in the colony. Opposition to the Asian trader became a *national* opposition and the grievance of the African trader a *national* grievance. For the time being, no other differences mattered. Every party stood in line and paid homage.

With the flight of Asian traders from the rural areas of Uganda, the boycott seemed to have exhausted itself. Independence was near, and whether peasant, worker, or trader, all expected that independence—the assuming of state power by an indigenous social group—would solve the problem of Indian control over trade, and much more easily. The question for the moment was: Who was to control the state?

3. THE DEMOCRATIC PARTY (DP)

The successful organization of kulaks and traders provided the impetus for the organization of other social forces, the chiefs and the civil servants, at the national level. To understand the nature of the organizations they evolved, it is necessary to grasp the objective conditions of their social existence. Among the chiefs, particularly in Buganda and generally in the rest of Uganda, the most important circumstance of their existence was religion. Ever since the 1900 Agreement, which had parceled out both land and the position of chiefship on the basis of religion, the chiefs in Buganda had been predominantly Protestant and the population predominantly Catholic. Catholics were barred from holding the posts of prime minister and treasurer, and were allowed only eight county chiefs, as opposed to ten for the Protestants. Likewise, in the southern kingdoms the Protestants predominated, as the accompanying table shows.

Chiefs by Religious Affiliation

Kingdom	Religion	Percent of county chiefs	Percent of sub-county chiefs	Percent of parish chiefs
Ankole	Protestant	87.5	86.0	77.4
	Catholic	12.5	14.0	22.6
Toro	Protestant	85.9	87.0	65.5
	Catholic	14.3	13.0	33.6
Bunyoro	Protestant	100.0	88.0	63.4
	Catholic	0	12.0	36.6

Source: Audrey Richards, ed., *East African Chiefs*, pp. 143, 171.

The north, colonized much later, was spared some of this religious strife. There the colonial state, having consolidated its rule over the south, considered it prudent to come to terms with the Roman Catholic missionaries. Chiefly appointments were therefore carefully divided among Protestant and Catholic converts in most of the north.[103] Among the Alur, the Catholic chiefs were even permitted to dominate; this, however, was balanced by assuring Protestant domination among the Gisu.[104] But while the state attempted religious parity, religion still conditioned access to chiefship from the traditional ruling groups.

The civil servants, on the other hand, gained religious consciousness through the educational system that trained them. Furthermore, the social origin of the vast majority in the higher ranks of the civil service was from the chiefs. Education being the preserve of the missionaries, and the most educated being by and large the sons of chiefs, there was more than a family resemblance between the particular religious consciousness of the chief and that of the civil servant. Goldthorpe's interviews with students at Makerere in the 1930s showed that Catholics generally came from Catholic schools and Protestants from schools run by Protestant missionaries, as the accompanying table shows.

Religious Affiliation of College Students and
Secondary School Attended

| Religion preference of students at Makerere | Secondary school attended | | |
	Roman Catholic mission school	Protestant mission school	Government school
Roman Catholic	31	—	2
Protestant	1	52	26
Muslim	—	—	1
Undecided	—	1	1

Source: E. Goldthorpe, *An African Elite*, p. 51.

However, access to civil service positions, unlike access to chiefships, was not conditioned by religion.

Religious consciousness was only one of the ideologies permeating the civil service; the other was nationalism. The Catholics among the civil servants were more likely to belong to a religiously based party, while the Protestants, seldom the object of religious discrimination, were far more likely to join a secular and "nationalist" party.

Driven out of the Buganda Lukiko by its democratization and the subsequent control of the petty bourgeoisie, the chiefs attempted to organize at the national level. They were assisted by the fact that a similar transition had taken place in the rest of the country because of the democratization of the district councils. In contrast to the tribal ideology of the kulaks and the national and racial ideology of the traders, the organizing ideology of the chiefs was religious. Using either Catholicism or Protestantism, they attempted to organize both among civil servants and among the mass of people. In the first case they met with relative success; in the second with relatively little. The reason was simple: the religious contradiction was real among chiefs, relative among civil servants, and had no basis in any other social group.

The only important party the chiefs organized was the Democratic Party (DP). The president was Mr. Mugwanya, the unsuccessful Catholic candidate for the Buganda Lukiko's katikiroship.[105] To the Baganda tribalism of the kulak-dominated Lukiko, the DP counterposed an Uganda-based religious orientation. Its leadership was overwhelmingly Catholic; Catholic priests and the Catholic Action Movement assisted its organization.[106] In Buganda, the archbishop sent a pastoral letter to all the parishes on the subject of elections, political parties, and the monarchy.[107] In popular parlance, the DP was known as *Dini ya Papa* (Religion of the Pope). But even though the vast majority of the Baganda were Catholic, the DP failed to secure a mass base among the Baganda peasantry. The "religious" DP failed, as did the "nationalists," because the Baganda peasants had already been organized by the "tribal" kulaks; furthermore, kulak organization of the peasantry had historically been in opposition to these same chiefs.

While in Buganda the DP was a party of the Catholic chiefs, outside it was an expression of secondary contradictions within the petty bourgeoisie.* The DP was important because it gained

---

* The Protestant counterpart of the DP was the Progressive Party (PP), which failed to secure a mass base in any part of the country. Its smaller,

a mass base among the noncommodity-producing peasantry in Ankole, West Nile, and Kigezi—where the market was limited to a few staples, traders were insignificant, and the church was the best-organized institution. It organized primarily through teachers in Catholic schools, as well as through civil servants. For example, in Acholi, the only DP hardcore base among commodity-producing peasants, all but two of the DP's district councillors were teachers.

Given that its active members came primarily from the Catholic intelligentsia, it was no surprise that the central objective of the party was the Africanization of the civil service. Its 1958 policy statement declared:

> [The civil service] must be Africanized as quickly as possible. But we will take care to see that only people of quality are given responsible positions. The idea of reserving certain positions for Europeans must be done away with. Appointments at the present moment should go by merit only. We recognize that at the moment all posts of the civil service cannot be filled by Africans, but we say that these which can be should be taken over at once.[111]

---

limited, and short-lived organization reflected two important facts: that religion had been historically a far more potent organizing ideology among the Catholic minority chiefs than among the Protestant majority chiefs, and that it was a loose coalition of emergent individual interests that failed to find any significant social base. This coalition was made up of Baganda Protestant chiefs who were still members of the Lukiko; a few of the big landlords, who were able to convert their large personal holdings into sizable estate farms after the 1928 Busulu-Nvujjo Law; Baganda businessmen (not traders) who were sufficiently advanced to consider all of Uganda as their potential market while viewing the tribalism of the Lukiko with contempt, and whose social origin was from among the chiefs; and individual Baganda professionals who were attracted to the "respectable" armchair politics of the PP and were loathe to join any popular movement. The thirty-nine-member plenary body of the PP consisted of twenty-one landlords, chiefs, and businessmen; two farmers; one newspaper proprietor; nine teachers; two full-time party leaders; two housewives; one doctor; and one lawyer[108]—that is, it consisted of the few capitalist farmers or chiefs, not kulaks; of businessmen, not traders; of newspaper proprietors, not journalists; and the teachers were "the leaders of the Uganda Teachers' Association and others who had been on various public bodies, township authorities, school boards, and church organizations."[109] These were the responsible leading citizens who aspired to the posts occupied by the colonial governing class. If the UNC resembled the CPP of Ghana in its organizational and class base, the PP was akin to the lawyer-businessman-dominated UGCC.[110]

In Buganda, the DP was the only political force to oppose the secessionist tendencies of the kulak Lukiko. The kulaks, meanwhile, attempted to ban any other political force in Buganda. When they failed to do this, they opposed direct elections in the province, seeking "indirect" elections whereby the Baganda representatives to the central parliament would be selected by the Lukiko sitting as an electoral college. When this strategy also failed, the kulaks made a further desperate bid. On September 24, 1960, the Lukiko passed a resolution declaring Buganda an independent state. It succeeded only in demonstrating its powerlessness without the support of the colonial state.

In March 1961, direct elections were held all over Uganda. The Lukiko boycotted them, but the DP ran candidates, all of whom were unopposed and elected. With its technical victory in Buganda and the support of its mass base in the noncommodity-producing areas outside of Buganda, the DP formed the majority party in the preindependence "elected" Legislative Council. Faced with a successful organization of the chiefs, the kulaks finally organized as a political party, the Kabaka Yekka (the *kabaka* only!).

In Buganda, the victory of the DP was a victory for the chiefs, specifically for the Catholic chiefs. The kulak–chief contradiction, the principal contradiction in Buganda politics in the 1930s and 1940s, once again came to the fore. Outside Buganda, as we have seen, the DP was an expression of secondary contradictions within the petty bourgeoisie: its popular base lay in those areas where the traders were not significant, and where the Catholic Church and denominational schools were a local political force. Here, the DP, a party of the "religious" petty bourgeois intelligentsia, was the only organized opposition to the "nationalist" UPC.

Faced with the DP, the kulaks and traders once again joined forces. The alliance that had characterized and torn asunder the Buganda UNC was reborn on the national stage in the form of a UPC–KY alliance.

Independence

Although independence meant that control over the state apparatus would be exercised by a class located physically within the borders of the colonial territory, it was not simply a result of processes internal to the colony. There had been no open struggle between the colonial ruling class, the absentee metropolitan bourgeoisie, and what was to be the postcolonial ruling class, the petty bourgeoisie. In fact, in the decade preceding independence the petty bourgeoisie was carefully groomed for its historic mission—as Fanon termed it, "that of the intermediary"—by the colonial state. What, then, was the meaning of independence?

In Britain, they said that independence had been granted; in Uganda, that it had been won. Both are partly true. In Uganda's case, the event is best understood in the context of a larger process, the worldwide dismantling of the colonial systems of the old imperial powers. This dismantling was itself the result of a twofold process. In some of the colonies, national liberation movements, through sustained armed struggle based on mass mobilization (as in Vietnam, Algeria, and Kenya) brought to the fore the question of the stability of the colonial order, an order riddled with contradictions. While colonial rule reduced all contradictions between classes *within* the colony to secondary significance, the rise of national liberation movements was testimony to the fact that the contradiction *between* the colony and the imperial power was of principal significance. Was it possible to reconstitute the content of the colonial system, the relation of appropriation between developed metropolitan and underdeveloped peripheral capitalism, in a new form? Could the colonial form of control be discarded but the exploitative relation perpetuated?

At the same time, the dismantling of colonies in the brief space of a decade, almost as if one domino followed another, was a result of contradictions between ruling classes in the advanced capitalist world, contradictions that matured in the wake of the second imperialist war—in particular, the rise of American and the decline of British and French imperialism. Thus, the United States supported independence *except* when it would mean the transference of state power to the producing classes and the abrogation of that most fundamental of bourgeois freedoms, freedom of enterprise. The example that stands out clearly is that of American response to the hasty withdrawal of French colonialism from Vietnam. We can see an historical parallel in

British support for "liberation" movements in the nineteenth-century Latin American countries that sought independence from Spanish and Portuguese imperialism. Independence would end the monopoly control of a single colonial power and give all the imperial countries equal rights over the exploitation of the colonial peoples. It would *multilateralize* the dependence of the colony. Equality of opportunity, an "open door" to every imperial plunderer, was objectively in the interests of the strongest of them. Thus it was that the United States, in its support for the independence of most of the colonial countries in the mid-twentieth century, demanded an "open door" to the exploitation of these peoples.

It was in response to this specific process of decolonization that Nkrumah coined the word "neocolonialism." What was old about it was the system of appropriation: the economic structures of underdeveloped capitalism, formed during the colonial period, remained, as did all the institutions of the colonial state, which were simply handed down to the new ruling class. What was new about it was that political power was transferred to an internally based class. And yet this was not a ruling class in the classical sense. It could not use its control over the state apparatus to appropriate the economic surplus primarily for itself. With independence, while colonialism ended, imperialism remained. As Lenin showed in *Imperialism: The Highest Stage of Capitalism*, "The struggles of the great powers for the economic and political division of the world give rise to a number of *transitional* forms of state dependence. Not only are there two main groups of countries, those owning colonies and the colonies themselves, but also the diverse forms of dependent countries which, politically, are formally independent, but in fact are enmeshed in the net of financial and diplomatic dependence, typical of this epoch." [112] The petty bourgeoisie was a *dependent* ruling class. It could not rule independently of imperialism.

The ascendance to power of the petty bourgeoisie was primarily a result of the crisis of British capitalism and secondly a result of political struggles within the colony. Though their leadership was captured by the petty bourgeoisie, these were in fact the struggles of the working people, the workers and peasants. Nonetheless, the violence of 1945 and 1949 marked the youth of the petty bourgeoisie, when it demanded a place in the system of appropriation, the right to be the sole national intermediary in the relations with the metropolitan bourgeoisie. This contradiction between the metropolitan bourgeoisie and the petty bourgeoisie was resolved when the colonial state helped expand the latter's economic base and consolidate its hold over organized politics, finally leading it by the apronstrings into the legislative council. Such was the political baptism of the petty bourgeoisie. The few awkward moments in its relations with the metropolitan bourgeoisie receded into the background as the identity of interest between the two came to the fore. Cold indifference turned into warm smiles as the hour struck midnight, a new flag was raised, and a new anthem played. The people cheered from the stands and the petty bourgeoisie prepared to execute its new-found responsibility as the guardian of bourgeois property within the newly independent country.

Notes

1. *Uganda Herald*, January 31, 1945, p. 1.
2. Ibid., p. 10.
3. *Uganda Herald*, December 24, 1949, p. 1.
4. Colonial Office, "The British Territories in East and Central Africa," pp. 141–142; see also J. W. Owens, "Insight into Labour," p. 39.
5. Colonial Office, "Labour Conditions in East Africa," report by Major G. St. J. Orde Browne, Colonial No. 193, 1946, p. 34.
6. Roger Scott, *The Development of Trade Unions in Uganda*, pp. 36–37, cites the law in its entirety.
7. Ibid., p. 10.
8. Ibid., p. 12.
9. Walter Elkan, *Migrants and Proletarians*, p. 59.
10. Scott, *The Development of Trade Unions*, p. 14.
11. East Africa Royal Commission, 1953–1955 Report, presented by Secretary of State to Parliament, Cmd. 9475, June 1955, p. 152.
12. Ibid., pp. 191–194.
13. UP, *Annual Report for 1950*, p. 4; see also *Uganda Herald*, April 29, 1950, p. 4.

14. UP, Memorandum on the Report of the Commission of Inquiry into Civil Disturbances in Uganda During April 1949, p. 2.
15. UP, Memorandum on Constitutional Development in Buganda, p. 1.
16. Ibid.
17. Cherry Gertzel, *The Development of Political Parties in Uganda*, p. 2.
18. Ibid.
19. Fred G. Burke, *Local Government and Politics in Uganda*, pp. 111–112, 158–159. For similar changes in the northern districts, see pp. 238–239.
20. UP, *Annual Report for 1946*, p. 2; *Annual Report for 1952*, p. 3; *Uganda Herald*, October 24, 1945, p. 6, and December 22, 1949, p. 4.
21. Colonial Office, Dispatches from the Governors of Kenya, Uganda and Tanganyika and from the Administrator, East Africa High Commission, commenting on the East Africa Royal Commission 1953–1955 Report, Cmd. 9801, p. 145.
22. East Africa Royal Commission, 1953–1955 Report, p. 323.
22. Report of the Conference on African Land Tenure, 1956, pp. 1, 4.
24. Ibid., p. 3.
25. By the end of 1961, grant of titles in these three districts covered approximately 170 square miles. See UP, *Annual Report for 1961*, p. 11.
26. UP, *Report of a Commission Appointed to Inquire into the Operation of the Land Tenure Scheme in Ankole, 1961*, pp. 9–11.
27. Ibid., pp. 13–16.
28. UP, *Annual Report of Registrar of Cooperative Societies for the Year Ended 31 December 1946* (Government Printer, Entebbe, 1947), pp. 2–4.
29. Ibid., p. 4.
30. Ibid., p. 1.
31. Maini's speech and memoranda from the Indian Merchant's Chamber of Kampala, Central Council of Indian Associations, Uganda Cotton Association, and Indian Association, Kampala and Jinja, are in the Maini Papers AR MA 5/33; Standing Finance Committee, 1944–1947.
32. Governor to Secretary of State, No. 69, February 19, 1937. See also Secretary of State to Governor, Confidential, October 20, 1937. Both in File No. 40184, CO 536/195.
33. UP, *Report of the Committee of Inquiry into the Affairs of the Busoga Growers Cooperative Union Ltd.* (Government Printer, Entebbe, 1965), pp. 6–9.
34. *Uganda Herald*, November 17, 1949, p. 1.

35. *Uganda Herald*, January 11, 1951, p. 1.
36. *Uganda Herald*, January 10, 1952, p. 5.
37. See G. B. Masefield, *Agricultural Change in Uganda*.
38. Colonial Office, *Dispatches from the Governors*, Cmd. 9801, p. 116.
39. *Uganda Gazette Extraordinary*, "Proposals for the Reorganization of the Coffee Industry," vol. 45, no. 42 (July 18, 1952), p. 365; see also *Uganda Herald*, July 19, 1952, p. 1.
40. *Uganda Herald*, June 18, 1953, pp. 1, 8.
41. Ibid., August 18, 1953, p. 4.
42. Ibid., June 18, 1953, p. 1.
43. UP, *Sessional Paper on the Proposals for the Future of Coffee Processing and Marketing*, no. 8, 1960, p. 2; see also Masefield.
44. Ibid.
45. UP, *Annual Report of Registrar of Cooperative Societies, 1946*, p. 6.
46. Committee for the Advancement of Africans in Trade, *Uganda Herald*, March 6, 1954, p. 1; see also UP, *The Advancement of Africans in Trade*, 1955, p. 7.
47. UP, *Report of the Civil Reabsorption and Rehabilitation Committee*, 1945, p. 1. UP, *Annual Report for 1946*, p. 3, gives the numbers of these soldiers as "some 54,900."
48. UP, *Report of the Civil Reabsorption and Rehabilitation Committee*, 1945, p. 4.
49. East Africa Royal Commission, 1953–1955 Report, Cmd. 9475, pp. 26–27.
50. Minutes of a meeting between a subcommittee of the Traffic Control Board and representatives of the Eastern Province Bus Co., March 16, 1948, in Maini Papers, AR MA 5/29; Traffic Control Board 1942–1949, Transport Board 1942–1949.
51. District Commissioner to Province Commissioner, Eastern Province, Jinja, April 20, 1948, and minutes of the first meeting of the subcommittee appointed under minute of the 129th meeting of the Traffic Control Board, both in Maini Papers AR MA 5/29.
52. On December 4, 1946, p. 14.
53. UP, *The Advancement of Africans in Trade*, March, 1955, p. 13.
54. Ibid.
55. UP, *Annual Report for 1953*, p. 6.
56. *Uganda Herald*, March 31, 1955, p. 3.
57. UP, *The Advancement of Africans in Trade*, p. 14.
58. For example, *Kutumia Hisabu, Kitabu Cha Kuwasaidia Waafrica Katika Biashara: Using Accounts: A Handbook to Assist Africans in Trade* (The Eagle Press, Kampala, 1956); *Banki Na Jinja Itakavyowasaidia Waafrika: The Bank and How It Will Help*

Africans (The Eagle Press, Kampala, 1955); *Okutunda Edduka, Akatabo akayamba abafrica mu Bsuubuzi: Keeping Shop: A Handbook to Assist Africans in Trade* (The Eagle Press, n.d.); *Mwuza Vyakula Dukani, Kitabu cha kuwasaidia waafrika katika Biashara: The Grocer: A Handbook to Assist Africans in Trade* (The Eagle Press, 1955).

59. UP, *Annual Report for 1953*, p. 6.
60. UP, *Annual Report for 1955*, p. 9.
61. Ibid.
62. Colonial Office, Dispatches from the Governors, Cmd. 9801, p. 115.
63. Ibid., pp. 119–120.
64. UP, *Annual Report for 1953*, p. 10.
65. Masefield, p. 119.
66. G. R. Bosa, "African Businessmen in Uganda," p. 18.
67. Colonial Office, Dispatches from the Governors, Cmd. 9801, pp. 114–115.
68. *Uganda Argus*, July 4, 1958, p. 3.
69. UP, *Annual Report for 1946*, p. 49.
70. *Uganda Argus*, March 28, 1955, p. 3; see also speech by the provincial economic officer to the African Chamber of Commerce, *Uganda Argus*, April 18, 1955, p. 5.
71. UP, *The Advancement of Africans in Trade*, p. 25.
72. *Uganda Argus*, October 11, 1958, p. 1.
73. Ibid., October 12, 1959, p. 3.
74. Standing Finance Commitee, SMPC 2330/3, Senior Posts for Africans in the Administration, Entebbe, October 21, 1952, in Maini Papers AR MA 5/35.
75. UP, *Standing Committee on the Recruitment, Training and Promotion of Africans for Admission to the Higher Posts in the Civil Service*, Final Report, August, 1955, p. 1.
76. *Report of the Commissioner for Africanisation*, 1966, Appendix A, part 1.
77. *Uganda Herald*, July 8, 1954, p. 1.
78. B. D. Bowles, "Nationalism in Uganda," pp. 40–41.
79. Minutes of the Busoga District Council, April 23, 1957, cited in ibid., p. 121.
80. Minutes of the Busoga District Council, February 18–21, 1957, cited in ibid.
81. David Apter, *Political Kingdom in Uganda*, p. 317.
82. Ibid., p. 312.
83. Ibid., Table 1, p. 369.
84. Gertzel, *The Development of Political Parties in Uganda*, p. 8.

85. Gertzel, *Party and Locality in Northern Uganda, 1945–1962*, p. 35.

86. See Colin Leys, *Politicians and Policies*.

87. Minutes of the Standing Committee of the Acholi District Council, November 12–14, 1951; August 8–12, 1952; UP, *Annual Report* on the Northern Province, 1953; cited in B. D. Bowles, pp. 32–34.

88. Apter, p. 321.

89. *Uganda Post*, September 25, 1953, and *Uganda Herald*, October 24, 1953; quoted in Bowles, pp. 61–62.

90. Quoted in Apter, p. 353.

91. Ibid., p. 332.

92. All these petitions in Maini Papers, AR MA 5/33.

93. Petition from Railway Asian Union to Secretary of State for Colonies, July 22, 1946; in Maini Papers AR MA 5/9, Railway Advisory Council, 1946–1948.

94. Memorandum from Asian Civil Servants Association to Civil Service Commissioner, Nairobi, in Maini Papers AR MA 5/9.

95. "Be Content as Your Forefathers Were" and "The Indian and the Wealth of Uganda: How the Indian Has Become a Millionaire in Uganda." Both pamphlets in Luganda original and English translation in Maini Papers AR MA 5/12.

96. *Uganda Herald*, June 5, 1954, p. 1.

97. *Uganda Herald*, June 10, 15, and 17, 1954, all p. 1.

98. *Uganda Argus*, March 9, 1959, pp. 1, 3.

99. *Uganda Argus*, April 25; May 7, 23, and 28; June 1; July 8; all 1959 and all p. 1.

100. *Uganda Argus*, February 2, 1960, p. 4.

101. *Uganda Argus*, March 9, 1960, p. 6.

102. *Uganda Argus*, April 4, 1960, p. 1.

103. John Middleton, "The Lugbara" (p. 342) and P. T. W. Baxter, "The Kiga" (p. 308), both in Richards, ed., *East African Chiefs*.

104. Audrey Richards and A. W. Southall, "The Alur" (p. 324), J. La Fontaine, "The Gisu" (p. 275), both in ibid.

105. Apter, p. 375.

106. Leys, p. 5.

107. Peter M. Gukiina, *Uganda*, pp. 82–83.

108. Apter, p. 337.

109. Ibid., p. 338.

110. On the CPP and UGCC, see Bob Fitch and Mary Oppenheimer, *Ghana: End of an Illusion*.

111. Handbill of the DP; quoted in Apter, pp. 340–341.

112. Lenin, *Collected Works*, vol. 22, p. 263.

8

From Independence to the Coup: A Fragmented Petty Bourgeoisie

The formation of the petty bourgeoisie was not as a consolidated class, either at the level of the economy or at the level of politics, but included three distinct social groups: the kulaks in the agricultural sector, the traders in the commercial sector, and the bureaucrats within the state apparatus. Economically, these social groups were unequally developed: both the traders and the bureaucrats were less developed than the kulaks. The traders were subordinate to the Indian commercial bourgeoisie and the bureaucrats to the members of the metropolitan civil service, who occupied the higher positions in the colonial state apparatus. Furthermore, the uneven development of the economy gave rise to the localization of the most advanced section of the petty bourgeoisie, the kulaks, who were primarily situated in Buganda. Politically, these groups were also organized as separate sections and not as one class. The Baganda kulaks organized tribal associations and articulated a tribal ideology; their success in gaining control over the Lukiko ensured the spread of the same ideology in the ranks of the remaining petty bourgeoisie in Buganda, particularly the traders. The ideology of tribalism was materialized in the power of the Buganda state at independence.

The politics of the non-Baganda petty bourgeoisie had been set by the traders and allied intellectuals. Its composition, however, underwent a change at independence as the transfer of state power allowed for an expansion in the size and power of the bureaucracy. Furthermore, the political bureaucracy was in direct control of the state power; it was transformed into a governing bureaucracy. The traders could not expand in a similar way because the Indian commercial bourgeoisie was nationally based and remained so after independence. The result was a gradual shift in the core of the non-Baganda petty bourgeoisie from the traders to the governing bureaucracy.

Unlike Kenya and Tanzania, Uganda did not emerge after independence with *one* ruling petty bourgeoisie, a section of it controlling state power. Instead, two separate petty bourgeoisies came forth, one Buganda and one non-Buganda, the kulaks at the core of the former and the governing bureaucracy at the core of the latter. The political expression of this fact was the emergence of two states—Buganda and Uganda—each with separately defined powers. This separation, however, was only relative, because the Buganda petty bourgeoisie failed to secede at independence. Confronted by a successful organization of the chiefs, the two petty bourgeoisies formed a *class coalition* at independence.

Though it controlled political (state) power at independence, the petty bourgeois coalition did not yet dominate at the level of production. In fact, its most important political battles thus far had been waged less against the colonial state than against the class that controlled the bulk of the nationally accumulated surplus, the Indian commercial bourgeoisie. Independence thus brought forward two contradictions among the propertied classes in Uganda: one within the petty bourgeois coalition, and one between the petty bourgeoisie as a whole and the Asian commercial bourgeoisie. Of these, the principal contradiction— the one that informed the politics of the period under considera- tion—was the former. The struggles within the petty bourgeoi- sie, with shifting alliances and changing issues, occupied the political stage until their resolution in the *coup d'état* of 1971. Only then did the contradiction between the ruling petty bourgeoisie and the Indian commercial bourgeoisie assume principal significance.

The Petty-Bourgeois State

To understand the internal base of the state that emerged after independence, we abstract for the moment from imperialist oppression and examine the nature of its relations with various classes and strata within the neocolony. As it facilitated the expansion in the economic base of each of its three sections—the kulaks, the traders, and the civil servants—the state acted as the state of the *whole* petty bourgeoisie. At the same time, it decisively smashed attempts at any organization of the workers independent of the petty bourgeoisie. In effect, this meant a continuation of postwar colonial policy.

1. KULAKS

In those parts of Uganda where communal agricultural production was still dominant, state policy attempted to create and consolidate a group of "progressive farmers" (in other words, kulak farmers), vigorously pursuing the recommendations of the 1953–1955 Royal Commission to further the spread of private property in land. This was most successful in Kigezi, where 7,000 private freehold titles were issued after independence under the Registration of Titles Act.[1]

Where private property in land already existed, the object of state policy was to subsidize the large farmer's costs of production by providing him with a "tractor hire service." The tractor hire service began in the postwar period, when colonial economic policy was attempting to consolidate an indigenous propertied class, but whereas there were only twenty tractors in Uganda in 1954,[2] after the 1955 Royal Commission Report, the state earmarked £1 million "for the expansion of mechanical cultivation."[3] At independence, forty tractors were run by the government and by 1964, the program was running 390 tractors and had another 215 on order.[4] In the third Five-Year Development Plan, the tractor hire service received the largest allocation.

While the average size of a farm in Buganda is five acres (in the relatively less populated north it is about nine acres), the tractor hire service only helped farmers with twenty acres or more, or group farms.[5] At the same time, as the 1967 report of the Mechanical Cultivation Officer in Busoga showed, the actual cost of running a tractor was Shs. 111/90 an hour but the farmer was only charged Shs. 43/42.[6] This amounted to an hourly subsidy of Shs. 68/48—over 150 percent.

State assistance also took the form of state support, both political and financial, for the kulaks as a social group. The kulaks' organizational base, the cooperative movement, increased its share of the marketing and processing of high-grade Arabica coffee and of cotton.* The bulk of the Arabica was grown and processed by the growers of Bugisu, who were organized as the Bugisu Growers' Cooperative Union. The cooperatives' share in the marketing and processing of cotton increased dramatically. The number of cooperatives in 1963–1964, with the ginneries they owned and the percent of the seasonal crop they controlled, is shown in the accompanying table. By 1966, the cooperatives controlled 42 ginneries (out of a total of 115) but had been allocated 75 percent of the total crop by the government.[8]

Cooperative Share of the National Cotton Crop, 1951–1965
(percent of total crop)

	Total collected	Total ginned
1951	3.2	1.3
1955	10.7	6.6
1960	22.5	16.0
1965	62.5	52.7

Source: UG, *Report of the Commission of Inquiry into the Affairs of All Cooperative Unions in Uganda,* 1967, p. 107.

A cooperative, like a political party, is an organizational form; to understand its political significance it is necessary to analyze its social content. In other words, which social groups control the cooperative? Whose interests are materialized in its organization?

---

* Low-grade Robusta coffee remained an exception. It comprised 86 percent of the total coffee export and until 1966 was primarily processed by private hulleries; cooperatives processed only 17 percent of the total in that year.[7]

Ginneries Owned by Registered African Cooperative Societies and Unions in Uganda, 1963–1964

Zone	Specified percent by season 1963–1964	Name of society or union	Number of ginneries owned
Mengo	25	The Uganda Growers' Cooperative Union	4
		Buruli Growers' Cooperative Union	1
Masaka	65	Masaka-Bwavu Federates Cooperative Union	1
Mubende	35	The Uganda Growers' Cooperative Union	1
		Mubende District Growers' Cooperative Union	1
Busoga	50	Busoga Growers' Cooperative Union	7
Mbale	55	Bugisu Cooperative Union	2
		North Mbale Cooperative Union	2
		South Bukedi Cooperative Union	2
Teso	35	Iteso Cooperative Union	1
Lango	60	Lango Cooperative Union	2
East Acholi	60	East Acholi Cooperative Union	1
West Acholi	65	West Acholi Cooperative Union	1
West Nile	100	West Nile Cooperative Union	1
Bunyoro	78	Bunyoro Growers' Cooperative Union	2

Source: Uganda Cotton Association files; quoted in R.R. Ramchandani, "Asians' Role in the Cotton Industry of Uganda," Appendix 4.

The control over cooperative policy was vested not in the members but in "entrenched committees." [9] And as E. A. Brett wrote in his study of cooperatives: "At the society level committees are usually composed of the 'big men' of the village —those who are already relatively well placed in terms of the local social situation." [10] As our analysis of the inquiries into the affairs of a host of cooperatives will show, they had become the organizational means of capital accumulation for the rich farmers (and, in some cases, the traders) who controlled the committees and thus the use of surplus funds.

The Uganda Growers' Cooperative Union,[11] the oldest and largest single union in the country, was also the first to take control of a cotton ginnery (in the 1949–1950 season). By 1959–1960, it controlled four ginneries and a coffee factory. Its total turnover was valued at Shs. 42,675,480; its yearly surplus came to Shs. 3,869,680. By the 1964–1965 season, however, although its control had grown to eight ginneries and two coffee factories, its turnover had only increased to Shs. 46,618,840, while the surplus had turned into a deficit of Shs. 526,422. The most important reason for this situation, according to Brett, was "gross mismanagement." Between 1963 and 1966, for example, the union paid out Shs. 3,120,509 in advance bonuses to members, yet produced a loss of Shs. 2,174,957. Although cotton production was declining, the union acquired four new ginneries in 1964. By 1966, it had lent Shs. 205,000 to members of its staff, including Shs. 116,752 to a former ginnery manager. One cashier had embezzled Shs. 34,331. Furthermore, the cooperative's management committee was paying itself about Shs. 35,000 per year more than the amount laid down by the cooperative department, and had made incorrect reports of the amount of coffee in stock to the bank. As Brett concludes:

> These figures merely indicate the most obvious forms of financial mismanagement and misappropriation; local informants made it clear that these practices were commonplace on a smaller scale at every level of the organisation. And although the amounts involved in each instance were no doubt small, their cumulative total was almost certainly very large.

The Bugisu Cooperative Union had had a monopoly in the

buying and processing of Arabica coffee on the Mount Elgon slopes since 1955. By 1958, its management had been brought under the direct supervision of the cooperative department. The official commission of inquiry into its affairs noted that sales had gone unrecorded and that, even when given ten days, the cashier could not balance the cash. The commission concluded: "The general financial condition of the union is not good. In fact, it is in serious difficulties, the causes of which are two-fold: extravagance, and laxity of control." [12] Between 1958 to 1961, when it was under the direct supervision of the cooperative department, the union's surplus soared to Shs. 6,568,600. In 1961, the union reverted to control by a committee. That same year, a trading loss of Shs. 120,000 was incurred. Brett's list of "problems" in this union in later years includes:

> . . . excessive expenditure by committee members, inadequate control over staff, massive irregularities in the awards of tenders, and attempts to maintain the support of members by paying prices which trading conditions did not justify.[13]

The Busoga Growers' Cooperative Union dominated the marketing and processing of cotton in the Eastern Province.[14] In 1961 the union had three ginneries, but by 1964 its assets included seven ginneries and one coffee factory. At the same time, the union's 1960–1961 net surplus of Shs. 1,769,106 had turned into a deficit of Shs. 326,380. Members who had been accustomed to receiving bonuses of from 4 to 5 shillings per 100 pounds of coffee received no bonus from 1963 onward. The government commission listed the following malpractices in the union's relations with its members:

> . . . frauds appear to have been perpetrated by falsifying weight notes, the stealing from and subsequent reselling to the union of raw cotton and the pilferage of lint and cotton seed, through collusion at all levels, and we are particularly disturbed that such allegations appear to involve the officers of member societies, staff and committee members.[15]

It was the "curse of an entrenched committee" that the commission found at the root of the problem:

> Practically all powers of control have been vested in the committees, a number of which have lacked competence or honesty, often

both; and through the very limitations of the law the department has been as powerless as the members to institute any preventive measures against incompetence and malpractices.[16]

Affairs in the smaller unions were no different. According to L. Stevens, the Teso District Annual Report for 1960 stated openly that loans were given to members for "unproductive" purposes and were seldom repaid.[17] In 1964, the Iteso Cooperative Union reported the embezzlement of Shs. 55,920/26. Its 1967 annual report stated that some cotton growers had not been paid between 1965 and 1967 due to the embezzlement of funds. The report concluded:

> Dishonest[y] had spread far and wide. Cash thefts and produce thefts prevail in this area and seem to grow due to the fact that even though the culprits are reported to the police, they escape unpunished.[18]

In Lango, the Shafiq Arain Commission of Inquiry into the cooperative unions uncovered similar instances of corruption and private embezzlement. In Mengo, the cooperative leaders bought a Mercedes-Benz for their own use, to supplement a Land Rover the cooperative already possessed.[19]

But this accumulation would not have been possible without critical assistance from the state. The purchase of private ginneries by the cooperatives was not from funds accumulated from market operations or from members' contributions but was from government loans at below-market rates of interest. By 1961, the state had lent Shs. 11,539,236 for ginnery acquisition, Shs. 9,802,268 of which was still outstanding; by 1966, the equivalent figures were Shs. 44,191,370 and Shs. 29,247,286.[20]

The difference between the pre- and postindependence days was not just in the magnitude of sums involved. The colonial state had kept strict control over the financial operations of the cooperatives through the Cooperative Societies Legislation of 1946 (amended in 1952). Following independence, the petty bourgeois state repealed the 1946 act and replaced it with the Cooperative Societies Act (1963), which reduced the cooperative department to an advisory capacity and granted financial autonomy to the cooperatives. In other words, while the flow of state funds to the cooperatives increased, state control over the expenditure of these same funds declined.

Furthermore, government subsidies came from the cotton and coffee price assistance funds, surpluses that had been accumulated from the state marketing of cotton and coffee grown by all the peasants in the country. Peasant surpluses were thus being transferred to the petty bourgeoisie through the intermediary of the state marketing boards—all in the name of "cooperation."

2. TRADERS

State policy toward the traders was also basically a continuation of postwar colonial policy: their organization, both as individual commercial enterprises and as a class, was encouraged. The African trade development section of the department of commerce continued in its attempts to organize local traders' associations and then bind them together at the regional and national levels. By 1963, it had helped form about 315 traders' associations, with a total membership of over 3,000.[21] In 1963, the local associations formed the Uganda National Traders' Association, a powerful voice for the class interests of the traders.

The activities of the trade development section were not confined to enhancing trader consciousness and organization; the section also lent material assistance to individuals. It helped form 30 buying groups, 41 partnerships, and more than 130 private and public retail and wholesale companies. In addition, it helped erect, supervise, and administer over 158 trade premises, worth more than Shs. 4 million, which were let to African traders. The result was an expansion in the numbers and volume of trade carried on by Africans. Of the 20,000 trade licenses issued in 1965, 16,000 were taken out by African traders. While in 1958 only some £10 million—or 18 percent—of the retail trade was handled by Africans, by 1966 this figure had gone up to some £23 million, or 42 percent.[22]

Besides expanding the base of African retail trade, the neocolonial state also attempted to facilitate the entry of the most advanced section of the trading petty bourgeoisie into that wholesale trade hitherto controlled by Asian commercial capital, thus attempting to create the nucleus of an African commercial bourgeoisie. In order to "train and develop entrepreneurs," and on the advice of the World Bank, the state created African

Business Promotions Ltd. (ABP, Ltd.), established as a subsidiary of the Uganda Development Corporation.[23] With authorized capital of £250,000 in 1964, ABP, Ltd. offered four main kinds of assistance to African businessmen: credit guarantees, discounting, hire purchase, and confirming.[24] Credit purchases made by African businessmen from wholesalers were guaranteed on a 1 percent commission basis, payable by the supplier, if ABP, Ltd. staff were convinced that both parties were reliable. By 1966, £500,000 worth of transactions had been so guaranteed. Under the discounting scheme, ABP, Ltd. assisted African businessmen in bidding for lucrative tenders from government institutions by discounting 90 percent of the value of a tender upon presentation of a delivery note, thereby preventing losses of tied-up capital because of the time lag between delivery and payment. Through its hire-purchase scheme, ABP, Ltd. guaranteed financing for the purchase of vehicles by "qualified traders" hoping to use them as transports. By 1966, twenty-two vehicles, with a total value of £41,898, had been so guaranteed. Finally, the confirming scheme was designed to facilitate the direct importation of goods by African businessmen. By March 1966, twelve such deals had been approved, with a total value of £13,250.

Complicated as they may sound, these efforts were nonetheless quite limited. With a staff of one general manager, an assistant manager, and two field officers, ABP, Ltd. was able to give limited assistance to only a small number of African entrepreneurs:

ABP, Ltd. programs	Numbers assisted
Credit guarantee scheme	324
Discounting scheme	53
Hire-purchase scheme	28
Confirming scheme	13

When ABP, Ltd. was discontinued in 1966, control over the commercial sector still remained substantially in the hands of Asian commercial capital. We shall examine the reasons for this later.

3. CIVIL SERVICE

In the civil service, as in agriculture and trade, the object of state policy was Africanization, the replacement of non-African members of the bureaucracy by Africans. At independence, the government appointed commissioners for Africanization charged with mapping out a detailed and immediate strategy.[25] At the same time, a minister of state for Africanization, George Magezi, was charged with implementing the policy. Since the vast majority of the metropolitan civil servants departed with independence, the task proved relatively easy, especially at the higher levels of the civil service. Civil servants retained their colonial salaries and benefits, befitting their objective position as members of the ruling class.

4. WORKERS

While the state confined its assistance to the petty bourgeoisie, the fruits of independence were demanded by other classes as well, particularly the workers. To understand working class political activity, it is important to grasp both the nature of existing trade union organization and the economic conditions of the working people at the time of independence.

The 1950s saw the establishment of the first manufacturing industries in Uganda, particularly in textiles,* as well as the disruption of manufacturing in neighboring Kenya because of the Mau Mau movement. Kenyan workers fled to Uganda looking for jobs in the newly built manufacturing industries, where their prior experience and skills guaranteed them employment. By independence, Kenyan workers constituted over 10 percent of the Ugandan labor force. They brought with them traditions of militant unionism.

The preindependence period saw the rise of two trade union organizations: the Trade Union Congress (TUC) and the Uganda Federation of Labour (UFL). The former was the finest fruit of the labor department's efforts to ensure the development of a workers' organization along "proper" lines, while the latter reflected the militant traditions among the Kenyan workers in

---

* See section on the Indian commercial bourgeoisie below.

the Jinja manufacturing industries.* Under the watchful guidance of the colonial state, control over the trade unions had gradually slipped away from the semiskilled and unskilled workers (motor drivers and domestic servants, respectively) into the hands of a section of the petty bourgeoisie, the white-collar civil servants. The leadership of the TUC came from the Railway African Union and the Baganda Clerical Workers' Union. Reflecting the care and supervision of the labor department and its advisors, the TUC took a staunch "economist" line, dissociating itself from any political activities or organizations.

The UFL was formed in 1961 when the militant manufacturing unions broke from the TUC. Although the split within the TUC appeared to be a struggle for leadership position, it in fact reflected a conflict between two different conceptions of trade union activity. The Jinja unions argued for a close alliance with the nationalist movement and against the "economism" of the TUC. Thus, on its formation the UFL allied with the UPC. While the TUC affiliated with the "free world" ICFTU, the UFL allied with the Nkrumah-inspired AATUF. While TUC leader Humphreys Luande entered parliament as an "independent," both leaders of the UFL, Reich and Kibuka, formally joined the UPC.

Independence came at a time of worsening conditions for labor. While the percentage of the African population in industrial wage-earning employment rose from 3.2 percent in 1948 to 3.7 percent in 1957, it declined to 3.1 percent in 1962.[26] When total employment is considered,† it has been estimated that between 1954 and 1964 this figure decreased by 1.4 percent a year.[27] In spite of these deteriorating conditions, the union leadership (including that of the UFL) opposed using the "political" weapon of the strike after independence. Party and union were opposed to what they considered to be the pursuit of sectional interests that were in opposition to what they viewed as the general interests of the nation.

* Although the TUC was formed as the direct result of a visit by Kenyan unionist Tom Mboya to Uganda, its formation was really much more the logical culmination of the process that began after the 1945 and 1949 general strikes.

† Total employment includes those in industrial wage employment, domestic servants, those seasonally employed in crop-processing industries, and those employed in peasant agriculture.

The worsening conditions of the workers and the continuing opposition of union leadership to strike action gave progressive individuals within the UPC an opportunity to organize and articulate the interests of labor. In 1963, the Youth League of the UPC organized a series of unofficial wage strikes throughout the country. In the first, in the motor-trades industry in Kampala, the workers remained out in spite of union instructions to return to work. In Soroti, where there was no official union organization, the Youth League organized a general strike in the cotton ginneries around the town and in the commercial enterprises within. A similar general strike was organized among nonunionized workers at Fort Portal in March 1963.

The response of the state was threefold: first, it chose to exploit the ethnic divisions within the laboring class and blamed the strikes on militant Kenyan unionists in Uganda, accusing them of "trying to sabotage the new nation." The minister concerned, Nekyon, threatened to deport all the "troublemakers" to Kenya. Secondly, it passed the 1964 Trades Dispute (Arbitration and Settlement) Act, which made it an offense to strike without first exhausting the existing official disputes procedure, thus entrenching the position of the established unions. Finally, it further backed the official union leadership by imprisoning four of the strike leaders "on charges of trespass, intimidation, and assault." All four held offices in the UPC Youth League and were members of the UFL.[28] Jailing the leaders, however, brought only temporary respite because the rank-and-file members of the league refused to be intimidated by such tactics.* In its attempt to establish political hegemony

---

* Immediately after the arrest of its leadership, the Youth League called in Mr. Onama, the minister of internal affairs and the deputy secretary-general of the party, for "consultations" and demanded to know why he had personally instructed the police to make the arrests. Dissatisfied with his answer, they detained him in the party office, demanding the release of those jailed, cessation of antiparty activities by the minister, and a free hand in dealing with "deviations."

Further, the league condemned the government and the MPs for awarding themselves higher salaries and allowances, and demanded from the government a clearer definition of socialism.[29]

over the working class, the petty bourgeois state was no different from the colonial state. In 1964, the government banned the UFL for its insubordination to official directives, and set up the Federation of Uganda Trade Unions (FUTU). The "cooperative" leaders within the UFL—both Reich and Kibuka from the Jinja unions—were appointed president and secretary-general of FUTU. In other words, the FUTU was the UFL purged of its progressive members and of its organizational autonomy.

At the same time, the UPC government banned its youth league, establishing in its stead the National Union of Youth Organizations (NUYO).[30] The six members of the NUYO national council were appointed by the minister in charge, and officials elected at the grassroots level were no more than "advisors" to the minister. Furthermore, a scheme was instituted that required youth to leave the towns "on tasks of national service." State control over politicized youth was to be as firm as that over the politicized workers.

These changes led to the defeat of the "left" faction within the UPC. At its annual conference at Gulu in 1964, Kakonge, his base of power in the league and the UFL destroyed, was ousted from the post of secretary-general of the party and replaced by Grace Ibingira.[31] The league banned, its most prominent members were expelled from the party.

By 1965, the two organizations that had maintained some autonomy from the petty bourgeois state and articulated the grievances of the working class had either been dissolved or banned. In their stead, the state had established its own "representative institutions." Purged of its progressive members, the UPC moved to the right; after 1964 it was a party without a base among the urban workers.*

---

* Official response to the workers' demands was articulated in one case by a commission of inquiry "into relations between management and workers in the sugar industries." The commission was appointed after a series of seven strikes in one sugar plantation, all of them unofficial and together resulting in a loss of 13,000 days' work.[32] The commission's report stated: ". . . there are workers who have exaggerated ideas about "Uhuru" [independence] and its full implications. It is necessary that the Union should explain to the workers certain basic facts of life in this country which independence has not changed and

5. THE ARMY

The weapon of the strike was also wielded by the armed forces. A strike by the army, however, is by definition an armed strike, an immediate threat to the power of the state. Army mutinies for higher pay and for "Africanization" took place in all three East African countries in early 1964, but the response in each was different. In Tanzania, the state power responded by dismissing the leadership and attempting to establish immediate political control over the army by channeling recruits through the TANU Youth League (TYL) and giving each soldier a dose of political education to fill him with the ethos of the ruling class. In Kenya, an entire corps of British officers was imported to keep the rank and file in check while a group was rushed off to Sandhurst for training. In Uganda, however, the state power responded to the mutinous soldiers *by granting all their demands*. Such a response can only be understood in the light of the fact that the army mutiny coincided with a serious split within the ruling petty bourgeois coalition, to which we will turn now.

The Buganda Crisis: 1966–1967

We have seen that at independence the state power in Uganda was dual. Though the constitution was called "federal," only one region—Buganda—was given separate and substantial powers independent of the center. The Buganda Lukiko controlled public services, local government, its public debt, and had separate powers of taxation; furthermore, its revenue was supplemented by grants from the state, as specified in the constitution. It had its own court system, and subject to the control of the Uganda inspector-general, its own police force. It selected its twenty-one representatives to the National Assembly indirectly, through the Lukiko, rather than by popular vote.

---

which, for the best interest of the country, need not change. These are the facts: that we must pay our way by our work, that we must not only demand to live but also demand to pay for our living and that in short we must know that every right has a corresponding duty." [33] Here was a solemn declaration of rights and duties: the rights of the state and the duties of the working class!

None of these powers could be altered by the Uganda Parliament without the two-thirds concurring vote of the Lukiko.[34]

The Lukiko thus had substantial control over the economic surplus in Buganda and was granted political and legal powers to safeguard its economic base. But the Lukiko was an expression of the power of the Baganda petty bourgeoisie. While it had failed in its early attempts to gain total autonomy for the Buganda state, it did succeed in gaining substantial autonomy at independence. The privileged position of the Buganda petty bourgeoisie was thus enshrined in the constitution.

Whereas Buganda was granted substantial autonomy, the other kingdoms in the south were granted semifederal status and the north was ruled directly by the central government. The "rights" that had been granted to the local petty bourgeoisie in the non-Buganda south and to the various assemblies and district councils they controlled were annulled by the central government at independence. The Western Kingdoms and Busoga Act of 1963 stated that none of these areas could "introduce any bill in their Assemblies before the Minister of Regional Administration of the Central Government approved it." [35] The passage of the act was a prelude to an open struggle between the Baganda and the non-Baganda petty bourgeoisie over the control of the economic surplus in Buganda.

The conflict began over the issue of the "Lost Counties," the two important cash-crop producing areas that had been taken by the British from Bunyoro in the early part of the century and given to the *kabaka* in appreciation of his collaboration with the colonial state. The Uganda (Independence) Order in Council of 1962 called for a referendum of the voters in the two Lost Counties, which had a clear Banyoro majority, after October 9, 1964, to determine their future affiliation: to Bunyoro or to Buganda. The issue was simple but crucial: as parts of Buganda, the producers in the Lost Counties would pay the bulk of their taxes to the Buganda state; as part of Bunyoro, they would pay them to Kampala. It was also clear which way the Banyoro peasants would vote. Not being Baganda, and thus not protected by the 1928 Busulu and Nvujjo Law, the tenant peasantry was sure to vote for freedom from its lord, the *kabaka*. The *kabaka* made various attempts to prevent the vote, and when that failed, to sabotage it. He went on an "expedition" to the Lost Counties with 8,000 ex-servicemen, demonstrated his "royal prerogative" of being above the law by one morning shooting nine Banyoro peasants gathered in a marketplace, and finally settled 4,000 Baganda families in the two counties, demanding they be allowed to vote. The High Court in Kampala ruled against it. Over the bitterest objections of the Kabaka Yekka, the UPC held the referendum on October 9, 1964. As expected, 75 percent of the peasants voted to join Bunyoro, and the territory Buganda controlled was diminished by two counties. It was over this issue that the KY–UPC coalition broke up.

The political importance of the Lost Counties referendum was that it provided a powerful argument *against* the regional orientation of the Baganda petty bourgeoisie. But the ideological orientation of a class does not mechanically follow a shift in its material base. While it is true that a class produces its own ideology, and that this ideology changes over time, it is also true that the ideology can in turn capture the class, making it the victim of its own history. The Baganda petty bourgeoisie was such a case. Nevertheless, 1964 saw the beginning of a process whereby it gradually but painfully shed its tribal ideology. After the Lost Counties issue the Kintu government in Buganda fell and was replaced by one led by S. S. Mayanja-Nkangi, who had been a minister in the Uganda government before the break-up of the KY–UPC alliance. In 1965, aware of the factional struggle within the UPC and the defeat of the "left" faction at the Gulu conference, the Kabaka Yekka decided to disband as a party and instructed its members to join the UPC in an attempt to consolidate the reaction nationally. In early 1966, new elections were called for chairman and a string of other offices in the Buganda branch of the UPC at the initiative of the new secretary-general, Grace Ibingira. The federal attorney-general, Godfrey Binaisa, a pro-Obote Muganda and a representative of the governing bureaucracy, was ousted as chairman by Dr. Lumu, an ex-KY minister and a representative of the Baganda petty bourgeoisie. The KY now masqueraded as the Buganda UPC.

Once the KY had disbanded and its members had joined the ranks of the UPC, the struggle between "center" and "right"

factions—between the representatives of the governing bureaucracy at the center and the petty bourgeoisie proper (the
small property-owning traders and kulaks, henceforth referred
to as the petty bourgeoisie) came to the fore. The "right," in
control of both the post of secretary-general and the Buganda
branch of the party, was at the pinnacle of its power and
prestige. With a majority in parliament, it sought to control
state power through a parliamentary coup. The issue it chose
was that of behind-the-scenes government support in men and
material to the Gbenya (Lumumbist) forces in the Congo.[36] The
charges were those of corruption, the confiscation of monies
captured during the Congo turmoil for personal use. The plan
was to appoint a parliamentary commission of inquiry and
compel the government to resign.* But when the cabinet met
formally to appoint the proposed commission and study the
charges, five of its members were arrested, including Grace
Ibingira. The backbone of the "right," it seemed, was crushed.

These events merely served to intensify the struggle between
Buganda and the state at the center. The substance of the
conflict, as it had always been, was over who would control the
economic surplus in Buganda. The issue was now formulated in
terms of the right of taxation in Buganda. What has become
known as the 1966 crisis began when the central government
reduced its annual grant to the Buganda government by the
amount of the non-African tax collected by the latter.[37] The
Lukiko took the case to the privy council in London, which
decided in its favor, underlining the privileged position of the
Baganda petty bourgeoisie in the existing constitutional framework.

In the aftermath of the arrest of the leadership of the "right"
faction, the Obote government introduced a "unitary" constitution that abrogated all of Buganda's "federal" powers—at one
stroke ending the financial and political autonomy of the
Baganda petty bourgeoisie. The Lukiko refused to pass the new
constitution and demanded the withdrawal of the central

---

* The only person in the party hierarchy in parliament to vote against the
motion setting up a commission of inquiry was the minister of planning, the
lonely member of the pre-1964 "left" faction, John Kakonge.

government from Buganda soil by May 30, 1966. In other words, it revived its old demand of total independence. The crisis was resolved when the central government used its armed might to physically crush the Buganda state. The "revolutionary" constitution of 1967 outlawed all kingdoms in Uganda and declared the state supreme. The 1966–1967 crisis, begun over the issue of taxation, ended with the elimination of the Buganda state.

During the crisis, the governing bureaucracy was able to take decisive action against the Baganda petty bourgeoisie in spite of the fact that the latter possessed a much stronger economic base in the Baganda kulaks, by far the most advanced section of the African petty bourgeoisie. The bureaucracy owed its success first to the growth of its own economic base in the partly state-owned manufacturing industry built by the colonial state in the 1950s, and second to the objective support of the class that was still dominant at the level of the economy, the Indian commercial bourgeoisie.

Indian capital appropriated its share of the nationally produced economic surplus through its control over the wholesale export-import trade. What is significant is that between 1962 and 1967 state assistance to African traders attempting to capture the wholesale trade from Indian capital was confined to the operations of ABP, Ltd., and this, as we have seen, was token assistance. The fact was that from independence to 1967 the contradiction between the petty bourgeoisie and the Indian commercial bourgeoisie was submerged and remained secondary while that between the Buganda petty bourgeoisie and the governing bureaucracy reached maturity and was resolved through an open political struggle. Not only did the Indian commercial bourgeoisie maintain its monopoly control over the wholesale trade, but it expanded its economic base, its strongest section developing manufacturing investments in partnership with the state.

The Indian Commercial Bourgeoisie

After the events of 1945 and 1949, the colonial state initiated a process of acquiring cotton ginneries from Indian capitalists and transferring them to cooperatives. This trend was continued with added vigor by the postcolonial state. Expelled from the processing sector of the economy, Indian capital looked for other profitable investment opportunities. After World War II, the metropolitan British state had initiated a series of qualitative changes in colonial policy whose purpose was to alleviate Britain's postwar economic problems, but whose result was to create a manufacturing sector in Uganda. It was here that Indian capital found the solution to its search for profitable investment opportunities.

Britain's economic problems did not begin on the eve of World War II. As the colonial secretary admitted, the general decline "had really started in 1914" with World War I.[38] According to an analysis prepared for the Empire Marketing Board,* British

---

* The following tables summarize the declining position of British manufacturing capital in world and regional markets.

Exports to South America
(millions of pounds)

Year	British exports	U.S. exports
1913	56.4	28.7
1924	57.2	69.4
1926	52.8	89.8
1927	57.6	88.5
1928	63.8	97.1

Exports to Northwest Europe[a]
(millions of pounds)

Year	Germany	Britain	U.S.
1913	68.4	35.6	33.8
1924	73.4	61.4	54.4
1926	102.4	41.6	52.0
1927	103.4	48.1	56.5
1928	110.4	49.2	55.3

[a] Includes Denmark, Norway, Sweden, and the Netherlands.

Exports to Western Europe
(millions of pounds)

Year	Britain	U.S.	Germany
1913	64.5	64	93.8
1914	92.3	148	29.2
1926	52.1	121	85.5
1927	63.6	113	77.9
1928	66.2	123	90.7

Exports to the Far East [a]
(millions of pounds)

Year	Britain	U.S.
1913	38.8	22.5
1924	59.2	108.2
1926	41.9	96.5
1927	37.2	91.6
1928	44.1	111.6

[a] Includes China, Japan, the Dutch East Indies, Siam, and the Philippines.

Exports to the Far East (Excluding Japan)
(millions of pounds)

Year	Britain	Japan
1913	24.3	16.7
1924	32.5	43.5
1926	28.0	53.3
1927	22.1	46.0
1928	29.6	48.1

Exports to the Southern Dominions
(millions of pounds at approximate 1913 price levels)

Year	Total imports	British exports	U.S. exports
1913	141	67.5	13.3
1926	180	65.8	40.5
1927	185	68.2	40.5
1928	—	66.4	37.8

manufacturers in the period between 1913 and 1928 lost their dominant position in the world market to American capital and their dominance in specific regional markets to American, German, and Japanese capital. While the position of British exports underwent an overall decline in relation to that of other capitalist powers, the decline was the least marked when it came to the colonies.* The value to British traders of the preferential treatment accorded them in colonial markets was emphasized in the Final Report of the Balfour Committee on Trade, convened to deliberate over the problem of Britain's declining position in international trade. The report stated: "In view of the facts it cannot admit of doubt that the preservation and development of these advantages must be one of the cardinal objectives of British commercial policy." [40]

It is in the decade and a half after World War I that we can trace a qualitative shift in British economic policy after a century of free trade. While the state attempted to protect national (British) capital from international competition with a shield of protective tariffs, it sought to strengthen the control of this same national capital over its colonial markets through the

Exports to India
(millions of pounds)

Year	Britain	U.S.	Japan
1913	70.3	2.2	2.9
1924	90.5	7.9	13.5
1926	81.7	10.3	15.5
1927	85.0	13.0	16.7
1928	83.9	11.0	14.6

Source of all tables: F. L. McDougall, *The Growing Dependence of British Industry upon Empire Markets*, London HMSO, Empire Marketing Board Publication No. 23, December 1929, pp. 16–24.

* For example, as was pointed out by the Empire Marketing Board, in 1928 India and China bought about equal amounts from the world but British exports to India were valued at £83,921,000, whereas those to China were a meager £15,717,000. [39]

introduction of Empire preferences and colonial aid. Beginning with Austen Chamberlain's 1919 budget, which for the first time gave preferences to Empire products, the transition was complete with the Import Duties Act of 1931, which declared a general *ad valorem* duty of 10 percent while granting preferences to Empire goods.

"Aid" to the colonies began with the 1929 Colonial Development Act, which established a fund of £1 million a year specifically with the object of "aiding and developing of agriculture and industry in their [colonial] territories, and the promotion thereby of commerce with and industry in the U.K." [41] The development of productive forces in the colonies was to be encouraged *only* if this encouraged accumulation in the metropole. In Uganda, the governor noted that the fund could be used for infrastructural expenditure for the production and export of primary products to the United Kingdom: cash crops, fishery products, timber, and minerals.*

Britain's economic crisis intensified with World War II. Beginning in 1945, the colonial secretary prepared a series of confidential memoranda for distribution to colonial governors on the "economic crisis and the colonial empire." The "economic crisis" was explained as the "reversal in the financial position of the United Kingdom, which can only be described as revolutionary." The document summarized: "In the six years of the war, the U.K. has changed from one of the major creditor countries of the world to the world's principal debtor nation." [43] The immediate problem was that the "drain of the U.K. gold and dollar reserves was accelerating at an alarming rate." The

---

* The governor wrote the colonial secretary: "I note that the purposes for which assistance may be given from the fund fall under the following heads: (a) Scientific research, (b) Improvement in agricultural and industrial methods including the extended use of machinery, and in the growing and marketing of produce, (c) Improvement of transport and communications (including harbours), (d) Development of fisheries, (e) Development of forest resources, (f) Surveys, (g) Drainage and irrigation, (h) Water supplies and development of water power, (i) Supply of electricity, (j) Development of mineral resources, (k) Promotion of public health including medical research, (l) Acceleration of existing program of public works." [42]

solution, as the Colonial Office saw it, existed at two different levels. In the short run, it was necessary to cut down consumption in the colonies:

> . . . control . . . may necessitate some degree of continued austerity in the colonies as in the U.K. itself and the disappointment of the natural expectations of colonial populations for more ample supplies of consumer goods.[44]

In particular, this meant a policy designed "to reduce imports from hard-currency areas and to secure essential supplies without payment of gold or dollars."[45] In Uganda, immediate cuts in the consumption of petrol and rubber were called for.* At the same time, the import of cotton piecegoods from nonsterling areas was limited and a Piecegoods Buying Pool of retailers and wholesalers was formed to distribute the limited supply.[48]

In the long run, the Colonial Office recommended two strategies: to increase exports of primary commodities, particularly to hard-currency areas; and to increase production in dollar-earning and dollar-saving industries.[49] The under-secretary of state for the colonies, visiting Uganda, emphasized the "importance of increased production."[50] The governor concurred:

> During these three or four years [too] we must produce every ton of primary products or raw materials that can possibly be won from our land or our waters with the limited means, human and mechanical, that we possess or can acquire or contrive.[51]

---

* The colonial secretary directed: "Any reduction in consumption of petrol to save dollars as British companies' production is insufficient to meet their trade requirements and has to be supplemented by purchase from U.S.A. or American companies. I trust, therefore, in view of the serious dollar position you will take effective steps to reduce local consumption by 10 percent and to ensure any reduction in supplies from British companies is not nullified by additional imports from dollars sources. . . . These considerations apply equally to gas oil."[46] And further: "It is therefore essential that the greatest possible economy in the use of natural rubber continues to be maintained and that every step be taken to increase the amount of natural rubber available to the United Kingdom."[47]

At the same time, the most important of these raw materials were sold in bulk at subsidized prices to the U.K. government. In the case of Uganda cotton, negotiations were concluded between the Uganda Lint Marketing Board, the British Raw Cotton Commission, and the government of India* in October 1950, stipulating the bulk sale of two-thirds of Uganda's cotton or 300,000 bales (whichever was greater) to the Raw Cotton Commission and the government of India.[52] As an investigator sent to Uganda by the U.S. National Cotton Council noted, the price of cotton sold by the Protectorate government to England and India was considerably lower than the price obtained for the same cotton in the open market.[53] Sales of cotton to the U.K. kept the profit margin at 11 cents (American) per pound and to India at 14 cents per pound, whereas the profit margin in open market transactions was 37 cents per pound. At the same time, the Protectorate government, through its marketing boards, skimmed off a substantial part of the actual export earnings. (We have already seen that in the years 1950–1952, the grower of cotton and coffee in Uganda received less than half the value his crop realized on the world market.) Arrangements were also made to establish a Tobacco Marketing Board to faithfully duplicate the operations of the existing boards by limiting the returns to the grower for the sale of his crop and thereby accumulating reserves in the hands of the state.†

But Uganda had produced raw materials for the metropole from the early days of colonization, and a part of the surplus had always been skimmed off by the state. The changes in agricultural production and marketing in the postwar period were primarily *quantitative*. *Qualitative* changes came in the nonagricultural sector. For the first time in the history of the colony, it was considered advisable to plan a number of industries. The governor calmly explained the reasons behind this historic change to the Chamber of Commerce:

---

* Historically, India was the primary consumer of Ugandan raw cotton and a major consumer of raw cotton within the sterling area.

† Government officials explained to manufacturers' representatives that it was "not necessarily the intention to raise the cash return to individual growers, but that any difference payable between the cash price and the full price should be credited to a betterment fund." [54]

Britain's need is Uganda's opportunity. A great opportunity to demonstrate by effort and sacrifice what Britain means to us in Uganda and always will mean; a great opportunity so to develop the latent resources of Uganda as to benefit Britain and in so doing greatly benefit Uganda; and a great opportunity so to integrate our economy with that of Britain as to ensure greater prosperity and economic security for the people of this protectorate.[55]

Even Uganda's opportunity was a function of Britain's need.

Thus began the first major spurt of manufacturing activity in the history of colonial Uganda. At the same time, Uganda's first "development plan," called the Worthington Plan, was formulated in 1947,[56] and the second bill for British colonial aid passed. In order to finance dollar-saving and dollar-earning industries in the colonies, the Colonial Development and Welfare Act of 1940 was amended in 1945 and £120 million was reserved for the "development of the resources of the colonies and the welfare of their peoples." [57] Unlike the Colonial Development Act of 1929, the new act did not stipulate that its funds only be used in the colonies to promote "commerce with and industry in the U.K." But then there was now an added purpose to "colonial aid": to establish dollar-earning industries in the colonies in order to accumulate dollars in the metropole. In spite of the bill, however, the bulk of the monies for manufacturing investment in Uganda came from the surpluses accumulated by the marketing boards—by December 9, 1950, these amounted to £12.96 million.[58]

The immediate impact of the new policy on Uganda's economy was both infrastructural (the Owen Falls Dam in 1952) and institutional (the Uganda Development Corporation, also in 1952). The Owen Falls Dam was designed to fill a need pointed out by the Worthington Plan: "The only satisfactory solution to the problem of industrial power in Uganda is by hydroelectric development." [59] The Uganda Development Corporation,[60] established initially with authorized capital of £5 million (later increased to £10 million) followed Colonial Office guidelines for the establishment of "colonial development companies." * Its

---

* According to the colonial secretary: "An interesting possibility for us to consider is that of colonial development companies, perhaps run by the colonial

purpose was to promote private British manufacturing enterprise in the colony by having the state guarantee the initial risk capital.*

The first and major UDC investment was the establishment of the first spinning and weaving mill in East Africa—Nyanza Textile Industries, Ltd.—in Jinja in 1955. British textile importing merchants had suffered losses as far back as 1932 and had earlier attempted to get state backing to establish a local spinning and weaving factory but had been opposed by Lancashire.† By 1950, Britain had lost the textile market in East

---

governments, which will be able to assist the local investor and be able to enter into partnership with the investor from outside—not with the idea of itself going into industrial businesses and running those industries permanently, but with the idea of filling this gap, to give enterprise a start, and gradually to be able to pass over to the private investor in the colony both capital burden and the managerial responsibility in the industries—the same sort of thing which is to be done by those Corporations to which the Chancellor of the Exchequer has recently been referring to in this House." [61]

* The historical origin of the public corporation, which was to proliferate in the postcolonial period, lies in the colonial period. The analysis of its historical origin and actual functioning underlines the necessity of going beyond its "public" form to lay bare its actual substance. It also clarifies that the antithesis between individual and public ownership is only relative. As long as the state remains bourgeois, public ownership remains no less private (that is, materializing the interests of a particular class) than individual ownership. To posit an absolute antithesis between the two and identify "public" with "social," as was common in the post-1969 period in Uganda, is to indulge in obscurantism.

† In 1932, a proposal came before the Colonial Office to build a cotton weaving and spinning factory in Uganda. The sponsors were Reid Overman, a British import merchant in Mombasa whose business was "seriously impaired by Japanese competition in the East African textile market," and John Dodd, "one of the leading manufacturers of cotton machinery in Lancashire."

As was customary, the Colonial Office queried the "interested or concerned parties" for their views on the matter, these parties being the Uganda government and Lancashire. The Uganda government took both a short-run and a strictly parochial view. Manufacture of cloth within the colony, the acting governor maintained, would "have a very adverse effect on the Protectorate's revenue." Furthermore, he added: "I also view with misgivings the prospect of the industrialization on any extensive scale of the native tribes of the Protectorate. The indigenous races are agriculturists by tradition and inclination. Large areas of fertile land await cultivation and conditions are ideal for the development of tribes as agricultural communities producing raw materials for export. This development can only be hampered by the diversion of labour to manufacturing centers. . . ." [62]

Africa. Out of a total value of £3.295 million worth of cotton and synthetic fabrics imported into Uganda in 1950, only £838,000 worth, or a little over 25 percent, came from the U.K.[66] Lancashire now saw things differently. Nyanza Textiles was established with capital shares of about £1.5 million, of which UDC subscribed £600,000, the Bleachers Association of Manchester £1,000, and the Calico Printers' Association, Ltd. (of Manchester) £750,000, while management lay in the hands of Calico Printers.[67] These were followed by a number of other joint investments in manufacturing, mining, and finance.*

"So far as the response of Lancashire was concerned, the Colonial Office wrote the governor: "We were informed that Lancashire is contemplating two things: (i) a distinctly overdue movement to obtain cooperation between the manufacturing and merchant sections of the industry in a determined effort to find new markets; the African market for the strong coarse kind of cloth will be one of the objectives, (ii) a definite approach to the Government in advocacy of the withdrawal of the U.K. from the Congo Basin Convention." [63]

Thus, the Colonial Office concluded: "If once a cotton factory were started in Uganda, it would operate not only against Japan, but also against the potential interests of Lancashire. Of course, you will understand that all this about Lancashire is highly confidential."

So far as the Mombasa merchant was concerned, the Colonial Office wrote the governor: "All this has been explained verbally to Mr. Overman under a pledge of secrecy." In writing, however, Mr. Overman was simply informed that "while the Secretary of State thanks you for having communicated information as to your plan, it is not possible to give you any promise or assurance of any kind and that anyone who invests in the enterprise must realize that he is doing so at his own risk." [64] A few months later, Mr. Bottomley at the Colonial Office sent a "personal and confidential" dispatch to the governor: "Mr. Overman called on me a few days ago to say that on Lancashire's advice he had decided to give up the scheme." [65] Such were the inner workings of colonial decision-making.

* UDC partnered British capital as follows:[68]

Manufacturing

1. In Concrete Constructions (Ug.), Ltd., which manufactured reinforced concrete products. The partners were UDC, Ltd., British Steel Reinforcement, Ltd., and A. Baumann & Co., Ltd.

2. In the Uganda Grain Milling Co., Ltd., flour and maize millers and manufacturing of animal feeding stuff, oil, seed crushers, and soap. The partners were UDC, Ltd., Unga, Ltd., and A. Baumann & Co., Ltd.

3. In the Universal Asbestos Manufacturing Co. (E. Af.), Ltd., manufacturer of cement asbestos products. The partners were UDC, Ltd., Universal Asbestos Manufacturing Co., Ltd. of Watford, England, and Tanganyika Cotton Co. (Holding), Ltd.

Even more than in manufacturing, foreign capital dominated in the spheres of banking and insurance. Three British banks— Barclays Bank D.C.O., The National and Grindleys Bank, and the Standard Bank of South Africa, Ltd.—accounted for approximately 80 percent of the total commercial bank assets in Uganda.[69]* The remaining foreign banks controlled 10 percent

---

4. In East African Distilleries, Ltd. The partners were UDC, Ltd., and Duncan, Gilby & Mathieson, Ltd.

5. In the Crown Cork Co. (Ug.), Ltd. The partners were the Crown Cork Co. (E. Af.), Ltd., and UDC, Ltd.

6. In Uganda Meat Packers, Ltd. The partners were UDC, Ltd., and A. Baumann & Co., Ltd.

7. In the Chillington Tool Co. (E. Af.), Ltd. The partners were Chillington Tool Co., Ltd. of Wolverhampton, England, UDC, Ltd., and Mitchell Cotts (E. Af.), Ltd.

8. In the Uganda Fish Marketing Corp. Ltd. The partners were UDC, Ltd., and A. Baumann & Co., Ltd.

Mining

1. Kilembe Mines, Ltd., miners of copper and copper cobalt. The partners were UDC, Ltd., Frobisher, Ltd., and the Colonial Development Corporation of U.K.

2. Sukulu Mines, Ltd., miners of apatite and pyrochlore. The partners were UDC, Ltd., Frobisher, Ltd., and Olin Mathieson Chemical Corporation.

3. Tororo Exploration Co., Ltd., researchers into mineral deposits. The partners were UDC, Ltd., and Frobisher, Ltd.

4. Tororo Chemicals and Fertilizers. The partners were UDC, Ltd., International Ore and Fertilizer Corp., Falconbridge Nickel Mines, Ltd., and Turga Chemical Industries, Ltd., a subsidiary of ICI (U.K.), which was also the managing agent.

Finance

1. Ugadev Bank, Ltd., a finance and hire-purchase company. The partners were UDC, Ltd., and Lombard Banking of London.

2. Development Finance Company of Uganda. The partners were UDC, Ltd., Colonial Development Corp. (U.K.), and Deutsche Geselschaft (Industrial Development Corp., West Germany).

* The extent of British control over internal savings gave the expatriate banks important control over the pattern of investment in the economy. Except for the early 1960s, when big Indian capital moved into manufacturing, bank loans were made primarily to commercial enterprises.[70]

The pattern shown in the table is the natural result of underdeveloped structure of the Uganda economy and of the banks' interest in maximizing profits in the short run. The lending policy to the agricultural sector further serves to underline this point. Agricultural credit in Uganda consisted predomi-

of these assets, leaving about 10 percent in the hands of the two state banks, the Central Bank of Uganda and the Uganda Commercial Bank.* The insurance companies were almost all foreign, mostly British and a few Indian. In 1958—the last date for available figures—only 7 out of 143 companies registered (not all those registered were in operation) were domiciled in

---

nantly of crop financing. "Crop financing" refers to seasonal credit provided for the purchase of export crops for farmers and their movement to places where primary processing takes place. As one observer clarifies: "Credit for this purpose . . . is the only form of agricultural lending [in which] these banks [the expatriate banks] are extensively engaged. It is a lucrative—because quantitatively large—and comparatively safe form of lending which has the added advantage of being annually recurrent. The loans are in the form of heavily fluctuating overdrafts, are outstanding for a few months only, and are renewable at the banks' discretion." [71] It would be far more accurate to term such loans commercial, not agricultural.

Commercial Bank Loans and Advances by Individual Sectors in Uganda, 1960–1966
(percent of total loans and advances)

	1960	1961	1962	1963	1964	1965	1966
Agriculture	13.6	13.0	15.7	14.6	11.4	06.3	8.0
Industry	48.0	41.7 ·	40.9	32.4	26.6	24.0	28.0
Commerce	—	—	22.6	26.3	28.8	34.7	43.5

* The East African Currency Board, responsible for controlling the supply of currency in Uganda as well as in the other three East African colonies, stayed on after independence, ensuring the automatic convertibility of Uganda shillings into sterling. With the "move to the left," the Central Bank of Uganda was established in 1966. It was not until 1969, however, that commercial banks in Uganda were required to have paid-up capital, in cash, with the Central Bank of Uganda. This capital amounted to at least 5 percent of total deposit liabilities of the bank in Uganda and, in any case, not less than 2 million shillings.

On the Uganda Commercial Bank, established by an Act of Parliament, Gershenberg has written: "No attempt was made by the bank to either attract deposits by offering higher rates of return on accounts, nor to attract accounts by offering to charge lower rates of return. In fact, the Commercial Bank of Uganda is a signator to the 'secret' banking agreement, enacted before independence, which binds banks to charge no lower than a minimum rate of interest on loans nor to pay more than a maximum stated rate of return to deposits." [72]

East Africa, one in Uganda and six in Kenya. Further, "most surplus premiums over and above claims and expenses [were] remitted for reinvestment in England." Between 1959 and 1962, £3,604,655 left East Africa for reinsurance in England.[73]

Independence checked the trend toward a close integration of the Ugandan economy with that of the United Kingdom. Uganda's ties with international capitalism became diversified. The flow of British capital into Uganda was reduced to a trickle, and the most substantial British investments in manufacturing began leaving. The change began with the sale of the single most important British investment, in Nyanza Textiles, to UDC (though the Calico Printers' Association continued to hold the management contract), closely followed by Uganda Meat Packers, Ltd., and Ugadev Bank, Ltd.

Those departures were paralleled by the entry of manufacturing capital from a number of the smaller advanced capitalist economies—Japan, Italy, Switzerland—whose most important investments were in partnership with the state or local capital, or both.

The local capital was Uganda Indian capital, which, as we have seen, had gradually been edged out of the processing sector by state action in the postwar period. By 1966, more significant than the state's investments in manufacturing were those of Uganda Indian capitalists, the most important being Muljibhai Madhvani, N. K. Mehta, and the Industrial Promotion Services.*

---

* Their most important partnerships with the state were as follows:[74]

1. Associated Match Co., Ltd. The partners were Muljibhai Madhvani & Co., Ltd. (80 percent), UDC (15 percent), and Sikh Saw Mills & Ginners, Ltd. (5 percent).

2. Associated Paper Industries, Ltd. The partners were UDC, Ltd., Uketa Development Corporation (of the Mehta Group), and Muljibhai Madhvani & Co., Ltd.

3. Steel Corporation of East Africa, Ltd. The partners were Muljibhai Madhvani & Co., Ltd., UDC, Ltd., Societa in Accomandita Luigi Pomini, P. Bonomo, Esq., Societa Per Azioni Fratelli Orsenigo, and V. V. Radia, Esq.

4. United Garment Industry, Ltd., shirt manufacturers. The partners were United Commercial Agencies, Ltd. (Uganda Indian capital), UDC, Ltd., Marubeni-Ida Co., Ltd. (Japan), and Yamato Shirts Co., Ltd. (Japan).

5. Uganda Fishnet Manufacturing, Ltd. The partners were Pyaralli Abdulla

Their investments were made in partnership with the state, with multinational capital, or—less often—independently.*

By 1966 the strongest section of the Indian commercial bourgeoisie had expanded into the manufacturing sector, further solidifying its position as the dominant nationally based capital.

Whereas the manufacturing investments in the 1950s were the result of the crisis of British capitalism, those in the 1960s were the result of the birth of the neocolonial state. High tariff structures, a protected market, and a legally assured monopoly position were partly responsible for this burst of manufacturing activity. Its character was that of *import-substitution*, the production within the national market of those consumer goods that had previously been imported. The most important investments were thus in luxury consumption items (alcoholic beverages, shirts, household appliances made of glass), food processing (grain milling), packing materials (cardboard and metal boxes), and construction materials for offices and houses (concrete and cement blocks).

By 1966, while multinational capital maintained control over the economy through control over finance, in the manufacturing

---

Ltd. & Family (Uganda Indian), UDC, Ltd., Industrial Promotion Services (Ug.), Ltd., Nippon Rayon Co., Ltd., and sundry others.

Industrial Promotion Services (IPS) confined its operations to encouraging manufacturing investment from one particular Indian sect, the Ismailis, in the three East African countries. As early as 1955, the Aga Khan, the spiritual leader of the Ismailis, had declared his goal: "To turn the Ismailis of Africa from a nation of shopkeepers to a highly industrialized nation." [75] Accordingly, in 1963 IPS was founded and financed by the Aga Khan and two other Ismaili enterprises, the Diamond Jubilee Insurance Company and the Diamond Jubilee Investment Trust. It was intended that IPS would act as a catalyst in bringing local Ismaili capitalists in partnership with the state or foreign capital to invest in manufacturing. In Tanzania, for example, the IPS invested in a pharmaceutical factory and a textile mill.[76]

* While it is not possible to provide a complete list, it is possible to cite the case of the Madhvani Group, the most important Indian capital in Uganda, whose vast empire, grown around the nucleus of the sugar estate and factory, included such investments as a textile industry, a brewery, a metal box plant, and a glass works. The annual turnover of the Madhvani Group, £900,000 in 1947, had grown to £26 million by 1970.[77]

sector local capital, invested in partnership with both multinational capital and the state, had become increasingly important. The political limitations of this local capital, the Indian bourgeoisie, permitted the governing bureaucracy considerable autonomy in its relations with the Baganda petty bourgeoisie.

The 1969 Crisis

The 1966–1967 crisis had a marked impact on both the Baganda petty bourgeoisie and the governing bureaucracy. The Baganda petty bourgeoisie, persuaded by the "Lost Counties" issue to shed its ideological parochialism and organize nationally, was compelled to do so by the abolition of the Buganda state.

Meanwhile, the governing bureaucracy was stronger than ever. Once the KY dissolved in 1965, its members entered the UPC, which made possible a collusion of the "right" forces at the national level: the petty bourgeoisie proper, kulaks and traders, organized as the "right" faction of the UPC and were in control of the party after the 1966 election of officers in its Buganda branch, but were unsuccessful in their attempted parliamentary coup against Obote that same year. The result, as we have seen, was the imprisonment of the petty bourgeois opposition. The "right" faction of the UPC, at least for the time being, was in disarray.

The conclusion of the 1966–1967 crisis saw a marked shift in economic policy. With the political autonomy of the Baganda petty bourgeoisie destroyed, the state directed its attention at liquidating the economic base of the Indian commerical bourgeoisie. What had previously been token attempts at creating an African commercial bourgeoisie became the central focus of state economic policy, only now state assistance was not to go to the most advanced section of the petty bourgeoisie as it had in the pre-1966 period, but the few existing African businessmen (politically separate from the petty bourgeoisie) were to be integrated with the individual members of the governing bureaucracy. The method of resolving the contradiction with the Indian commercial bourgeoisie remained the same: the use of state power to create an African commercial bourgeoisie. The change in state policy concerned the *social composition* of the emerging African commercial bourgeoisie: *its core would be none other than members of the governing bureaucracy.*

The ideological groundwork for such a shift was prepared by state commissions charged with conducting investigations into the affairs of the cooperative unions. These commissions reported rampant corruption in the ranks of the cooperatives, submitting detailed accounts of how they had been used for private accumulation by individual members of the petty bourgeoisie.[78] Government ministers charged the cooperatives with "exploiting" the people:

> We used to think that once Indians were out Africans will not cheat Africans. Unfortunately, the unions this year are operating in such a way that we must begin to think again and I am, therefore, praying the Government that at least in new crops we are intending to buy unions should be kept out.[79]

These reports formed the historical justification for creating state-controlled organizations, known as parastatals, that would supersede the cooperatives and supervise the economy directly. The first two parastatals were the National Trading Corporation (NTC) and the Produce Marketing Board (PMB).

The National Trading Corporation was created because of the "need for a substantial share of trade in this country passing into the hands of Africans." [80] The NTC was to ensure that Africans "participate fully in [the] import and export trade." Although it replaced the ABP, Ltd., which was dissolved in 1966, the NTC directed its attention primarily at assisting members of the governing bureaucracy to organize businesses. Accordingly, the minister of planning and community development established a service to assist the formation of new African companies.[81]

At the same time, state assistance to the trading petty bourgeoisie dried up. Requests in parliament for loan programs to traders were rejected because "loan facilities exist in commercial terms in the banks and other financial institutions which traders can avail themselves of." [82] As the minister of commerce and industry explained to the petty bourgeois parliamentary opposition:

What we feel is lacking is for the traders themselves to inculcate in themselves integrity in trade. If they have integrity, they would be able to have at their disposal credit facilities from other traders or wholesalers.[83]

In other words, the failure on the part of a small trader to gain access to commercial credit was explained as a personal failing —the ideology of big capital.

Besides the NTC, the state established the Produce Marketing Board, whose purpose was to assist state control of the internal marketing of food items. Section 9 of the 1968 law establishing the PMB stated: "No person shall buy any controlled minor crops (a) unless he has a license, (b) except in a declared market."[84] Since the state both issued licenses and declared marketing areas, it now had the power to allocate trade in essential commodities to African wholesalers.

The wholesaler, appointed by the PMB, was generally a member of the governing bureaucracy. He was to undertake both the buying and selling of essential food commodities in the national market, two functions hitherto carried out by two different sections of capital and defining the separate economic base of each: buying by the cooperatives and selling by the Asian commercial bourgeoisie. While the PMB's agents were to buy locally grown foodstuffs through the cooperatives, the cooperatives' share was reduced to that of being the agent of the parastatal in the marketplace. The Asian commercial bourgeoisie's role in food distribution, on the other hand, was simply taken over by the agents of the PMB.

Both the Asian commercial bourgeoisie and the cooperatives did whatever they could to safeguard their economic base, and the nature of their resistance highlights the specificity of each class, its strengths and weaknesses. Lacking political power, the opposition of the Asian commercial bourgeoisie had necessarily to be economic. Using the power of their accumulated capital and their existing monopoly control over the distributive sector of the economy, Asian wholesalers responded with economic sabotage. While the law forbade their buying directly from the grower, there was no prohibition against their buying from the PMB wholesale agent. Their sabotage consisted of buying the supplies of the local agent in bulk, storing them for as long as necessary to create a scarcity and ensure a monopoly position, and then selling the stock at a marked-up monopoly price.

In December 1967 the NTC Chief Executive Manager's report listed the following distributive problems: "Interference of non-African wholesalers who offer higher prices to subdistributors to induce them to sell their entire stock of goods sent to them by the Corporation," and "competition from non-African firms who do not wish to see the Corporation take over what has hitherto been their monopoly." [85] The February 1968 monthly report for Bunyoro/Mubende stated that "sugar distribution is in choas. Every Asian can buy and stock sugar like any other sugar distributor." [86] In October 1968, a circular was issued to all subdistricts warning them against selling commodities for distribution outside their districts:

> It has been reported and noticed that some of our distributors have cultivated a habit of flooding through non-African bodies markets that are outside their area/district with commodities they are appointed to distribute. . . . We have received some reports from our field officers reporting some of the Asians in their areas who have filled their godowns with NTC goods purchased through our subdistributors in Kampala and Jinja—some of these Asians have been underselling our legitimate subdistributors of the areas concerned.[87]

But the PMB subdistributor/wholesaler was as much a capitalist as the Asian wholesaler. He too operated by the rules of the marketplace: maximize profits and minimize losses. Without sufficient capital to hold his stock for a long period, he had to sell in the face of declining prices. In the long run, the Asian wholesaler successfully established his monopoly position and reaped monopoly profits. The price of basic foodstuffs monopolized by the state went up, salt[88] from 0/20 to 0/50 and in some places even 0/70, and rice[89] of the first grade from 1/20 to 1/70.

Rising food prices led to political discontent among the most exploited classes in the country, the urban workers and the working peasants. For the peasant growers of foodstuffs, however, there was a twofold catastrophe. Not only did the price of the basic commodities they bought (such as salt) rise, but the price of the commodities they sold declined. We have seen that the PMB agent was not intended to replace the local cooperative as much as to augment it; at the same time, he failed to replace the Asian wholesaler. All three sections of capital—the cooperative, the parastatal, and the Asian wholesaler—extracted their income from the peasants' surplus. The result was a decline in the price the PMB offered the peasant in comparison to what the market had previously offered him, or to what the black market currently offered. The PMB offered the grower Shs. 18 per 200-pound bag of maize, whereas the private trader had offered him Shs. 30. The board's minimum price for millet was Shs. 40 per 200-pound bag, whereas the market price had been Shs. 80.[90]

Growers' opposition was organized by the petty bourgeoisie. The cooperatives refused to buy produce on behalf of the PMB at prevailing prices. A refusal to buy on the part of the petty bourgeoisie and economic sabotage by the Asian commercial bourgeoisie were the substance of the 1969 crisis. But the crisis had external aspects that contributed to its intensification. The Ugandan economy was an underdeveloped economy, integrated into the world capitalist market as a dependent economy. The crisis of underdevelopment manifested itself as the crisis of accumulation.

The years from independence to 1969 demonstrated the shortcomings of a strategy that advocates economic development based on expansion of export production and on foreign private and public capital transfers. The 1961–1966 Development Plan relied for 48 percent of its total financing on foreign assistance;[91] the remainder was to come from the expanded export of primary commodities. But reality did not conform. Instead of an inflow of capital, each year witnessed an increased outflow to the advanced capitalist economies, resulting in a balance-of-payments crisis. The monetary outflow took two forms: an indirect transfer of values through unequal exchange in international trade, and direct money transfers. While the production of coffee doubled and that of cotton increased by half between 1962 to 1969, the international prices for both declined and, these being the principal export commodities, the terms of trade for the economy as a whole worsened.[92] At the same time, these years saw the net outflow of private capital from East Africa. In spite of exchange controls imposed in 1965 on residents' monetary transactions, the process could not be reversed.* The net private capital inflow of Shs. 73.6 million in 1966 turned into an outflow of Shs. 19.6 million in 1969 and Shs. 294.6 million in 1970. At the same time, between 1966 and 1969 the net official capital inflow declined from Shs. 183.9 million to Shs. 133.4 million. After the positive trade balances of Shs. 133.5 million in 1966, Shs. 150.1 million in 1969, and Shs. 402.0 million in 1970, the balance of payments in 1970 registered a deficit of Shs. 7.7 million.[93]†

The 1969 crisis manifested itself at the level of economy and polity, as a result of factors that were national as well as international. The international aspect of the crisis could only be checked in the short run by a special drawing rights allocation from the International Monetary Fund equivalent to the sum of Shs. 38.4 million.[96] The internal economic crisis, however, could only be averted by a *political* solution. At the same time, the opposition of the petty bourgeoisie transcended the limits of the marketplace, where cooperatives had organized peasant discontent: at the conclusion of the 1969 UPC conference there was an assassination attempt on President Obote.

With prices soaring and political discontent spreading, the governing bureaucracy was compelled to act. Continued rule without a mass political base and in the presence of opposition from the Indian commercial bourgeoisie and the petty bourgeoisie, exacerbated by the crisis of accumulation of the neocolonial economy, was proving impossible. Immediately, the government outlawed all but the ruling party, making it illegal for any social

---

* There was a twofold limitation to the effectiveness of the exchange controls: first, they only applied to residents, thereby exempting multinational capital; second, they checked monetary transfers by the petty bourgeoisie but not by the commercial bourgeoisie, which traded directly with multinational capital and thus could resort to such indirect means as the overinvoicing of imports and the underinvoicing of exports to achieve the same ends.

† To be sure, the crisis of accumulation was evident as early as 1965 and had partly informed the 1966–1967 struggle between the state of Uganda and Buganda. Uganda, a country the Colonial Office had singled out for being "alone of the East African territories . . . [to] maintain a substantial favorable trade balance," [94] faced its first balance-of-payments deficit in 1965.[95]

force to organize. In control of the single party, the UPC, the governing bureaucracy was now poised to act decisively.* Such was the background to the "move to the left."

The "Move to the Left," 1969–1970

We recognise that a country cannot depend upon capital from outside because this, apart from being unpredictable, is subject to variation by various factors and has always got strings attached to it. . . . We are fully convinced that the economic future of this country depends on local capital formation and local savings and investment.[97]

1. MULTINATIONAL CAPITAL

The crisis of accumulation necessitated that the state take a more active part in the productive process, increasing its control over the nationally retained economic surplus and its role in determining the level of investment in the economy. Such an expansion was only possible if the public sector was expanded and if some degree of state control over monetary institutions, such as banks, was established.

We have seen that three British banks controlled nearly 80 percent of the commercial bank deposits in Uganda, and that the first attempt by the state to control monetary transactions between the national and the international capitalist market— the exchange control regulations of 1965—had proved largely ineffective. A national currency and a national banking system were now enacted. The March 1969 Banking Act gave the Bank of Uganda the ability to regulate the foreign-exchange holdings of the commercial banks and credit institutions. In October, an amendment to the act required that companies carrying on

---

* As early as January 7, 1964, in the throes of the "Lost Counties" crisis, Obote had articulated his preference for a one-party state. This preference reflected the desire of the governing bureaucracy to give itself, and no other social group, the right to organize politically. But it was only after the expulsion of the "left" faction in 1964, the imprisonment of the "right" faction in 1966, and the elimination of the Buganda state in 1967, that the governing bureaucracy was able to achieve effective control over the UPC. The petty bourgeoisie, having lost its control over the UPC and barred legally from organizing as a political party, was left with the cooperatives as its remaining organizational base.

banking and credit institution business be locally incorporated, which meant that they were required to have, in their own funds, a minimum paid-up capital of Shs. 20 million for a bank, and Shs. 5 million for a credit institution.[98]

As long as the economy remained within the confines of world imperialism, an expansion of the public sector could not be against the multinational corporations but had to be in partnership with them. The nature of this partnership is revealed by the nationalizations decreed by the Obote government in May 1970. In practice, nationalizations are not necessarily antithetical to the interests of capital—in fact, some months before they were decreed in Uganda the state was approached by the oil companies "with proposals for participation in equity to the extent of 50 percent by government." [99] A year earlier, the most important Uganda Indian industrial capitalist, Madhvani, had offered the government 50 percent participation in all his holdings.[100] Why would a multinational corporation invite a host government to "nationalize" 50 percent of its assets? Precisely because such a nationalization would give the corporation access to state capital (since it would be "compensated" for the assets nationalized), keep all management in its own hands, and give it the political advantage of being known as a national company.* The state, on the other hand, gained little more than formal ownership. But while its control over the process of accumula-

---

* In a private conference on United States and European investment in Africa held at Paris in 1969 under the auspices of the African-American Institute and the European Center for Overseas Industrial Equipment and Development, an Italian participant made the following revealing comment: ". . . too often we profess our faith in private enterprise and attack state-owned enterprise. State-owned enterprises often come into being because private enterprise has failed. Moreover, private enterprises often benefit from the existence of state-owned enterprises. . . . Nationalization, as usually done, is not desirable. State-owned enterprises have an obligation 'to play the game' and cooperate with private firms. . . . Africa must have state enterprises—not foreign-owned but locally owned. Reasons for this include the fact that Africa lacks capital; in the absence of private savings the state must intervene. If the state 'plays the game'—abides by the rules—this offers the best possible guarantee for private firms interested in investing in the country since they can enter into partnership with the state. But everyone must behave correctly." [101] The behavior of the UPC government was therefore most correct.

tion would be marginal, it too would reap political support for having nationalized; at the same time, its members would gain access to various directorships, nominal in power but substantial in monetary gain, through a program of "Africanization." The result would not be a nationalization but a partnership—an unequal partnership to be sure, with the state the junior partner.

This was precisely what the Obote government offered multinational capital. In his 1970 May Day speech, Obote announced his intention to take over 60 percent ownership in all the means of production. The following day, the National Assembly enacted a bill "providing government control over eighty-five companies operating in Uganda." [102] The practice, however, was different. The government entered into negotiations with individual corporations, not on the *process* of transfer to the state, but on the *terms* on which international capital would permit the governing bureaucracy the role of a junior partner. Most of these negotiations were incomplete at the time of the January 1971 coup. The oil companies were "nationalized" on a fifty-fifty basis, just as they had offered earlier.[103] National and Grindleys Bank, the only British bank with whom negotiations for a 60 percent state takeover were completed, was granted the right to establish an international merchant banking subsidiary in which state ownership would be limited to 40 percent. Brookbond-Liebig, manufacturers of tea, agreed to a 60 percent government takeover of packing and distribution, but not of manufacturing.[104] The only multinational to agree to a 60 percent state takeover of *all* its operations was a Canadian copper concern. (Interestingly enough, in 1965 it had been projected that "the known copper reserves at Kilembe are sufficient to permit mining only until 1971 at the present rate of working." [105] Nationalization thus gave the multinationals much-needed insurance against losses at a time of high-risk operation.) Finally, a number of multinationals were simply dropped from the list in the coming months.[106]* In fact, only a

---

* Songo Bay Estates, the Development Finance Co. of Uganda, Ltd., East African Distilleries, Uganda Solutea, Tororo Industrial Chemical Fertilizers, East African Batteries (Uganda), Ltd., and Ugationers, Ltd.

week after proclaiming the nationalization decree, the foreign minister was announcing in the National Assembly: "It [is] quite obvious . . . that there [is] still a lot of room for foreign initiative and group and private individual enterprise to play a meaningful role in the country's economy." [107]

All the governing bureaucracy was asking was that room be made at the top. Nationalization was a political catchword for what was in fact a negotiable demand for partnership.

2. THE COMMERCIAL BOURGEOISIE

Just as it need not be against the interests of international capital, an expansion of the state sector in an underdeveloped economy need not be against the interests of that section of the ruling class located outside the state apparatus—in Uganda, the petty bourgeoisie. In fact, the expansion of the state sector in Uganda could have been an expression of the interests of the entire petty bourgeoisie, precisely because state ownership was confined to manufacturing and banking, the sectors the petty bourgeoisie was too weak to enter. Yet such was not the case.

The local incorporation of the banks and the nationalizations of 1970 were an attempt to come to terms with only one aspect of the 1969 crisis, the crisis of accumulation. The contradictions with the Indian commercial bourgeoisie and the African petty bourgeoisie, which had resulted in rising prices and mass unrest in 1969, still remained unresolved. The critical question, then, was whether the expansion in the state sector, in partnership with multinational capital, could be undertaken in opposition to domestic capital—the Indian commercial bourgeoisie and the petty bourgeoisie. In other words, would Uganda's "move to the left" be substantially similar to Tanzania's Arusha Declaration of 1967? [108] It was not, and the reasons highlight certain important differences between the two countries.

The nationalist movement in Uganda, unlike that in Tanzania, was both weak and fragmented, and had been from its formation in the 1950s. The rich peasants in Buganda were the strongest kulak formation in East Africa and the strength of their political organization meant that the nationalist movement had no base in the most populous part of the country. Outside of Buganda, it was split into the UPC and the DP. While the relatively stronger UPC came to control state power in the 1960s, the expulsion of its "left" faction at the 1964 Gulu party conference deprived the party of its base among urban workers. By 1970, the UPC was but an empty shell, a formal organization whose function was limited to being a pipeline for patronage. The weak mass base of the ruling party influenced the very method of introduction of the "move to the left." In Tanzania, on the other hand, the kulaks were the weakest section of the petty bourgeoisie, and TANU, the party of traders and civil servants, possessed a strong peasant base.

"The Common Man's Charter," the document that sought to justify the move, was issued as a personal directive by the president, a marked contrast to the Arusha Declaration, which was debated and issued as a party document. Further, in sharp contrast to Tanzania, in Uganda there was no attempt by the party to organize popular demonstrations to celebrate what had been proclaimed as a march to socialism. The absence of a mass base did not just make a ceremonial difference. It affected the very substance of the "move to the left." Before we can discuss this, we must first grasp the specificity of the Indian commercial bourgeoisie and the African petty bourgeoisie at the level of both economics and politics.

The Indian commercial bourgeoisie in Uganda possessed a much stronger economic base than the same class in Tanzania and Kenya. In fact, its industrial wing was also responsible for a number of important investments in neighboring Kenya and Tanzania. And yet, as we have seen, although dominant at the level of the economy because of its total separation from the masses, it could never aspire to control the state. As long as its economic base was secure, it had no choice but to support the political rule of another class. In contrast, the petty bourgeoisie was capable of organizing peasant discontent, as it had shown in the 1969 crisis, and aspired moreover to control the state apparatus in place of the governing bureaucracy. It was a clear and present *political* threat, which the Asian commercial bourgeoisie was not.

The decisive factor in the "move to the left" was that while the governing bureaucracy lacked a mass base, the petty bourgeois opposition had one, particularly in Buganda. Furthermore, the only way the governing bureaucracy could resolve its political crisis was by taking the wind out of the mass discontent organized by the petty bourgeoisie. But to do this the economy, and with it prices, had to be stabilized, and it was this that dictated the relations of the governing bureaucracy to both international capital and the commercial bourgeoisie. Nationalizations were not contrary to the interests of either. In fact, there was a dramatic reversal in the attitude of the state to the commercial bourgeoisie: the contradiction between the two was resolved through an alliance. So far as the "move to the left" was concerned, established sections of the Indian bourgeoisie found ample reason to cheer it.

In the wake of the 1969 crisis, the PMB reversed its policy of appointing African distributing agents to undermine Indian wholesalers and began to appoint joint African-Asian companies, or simply Asian wholesalers, as its distributing agents. The parliamentary opposition protested that while at one time the NTC had declared that it would not support "any African company with shares held by nonindiginous people," the corporation had "turned around and accepted" all of them.[109] Further, the export-import sector, through which the Indian bourgeoisie primarily accumulated capital and which had been decreed totally nationalized,[110] was now merely to be supervised by the state-established Export-Import Corporation. The director and chairman of the corporation, appointed by the president, was none other than the most important Indian capitalist in Uganda—Jayant Madhvani. Its other five directors, according to the minister of commerce and industry,[111] were all "persons of fully proven business experience." In fact, an executive committee of the commercial bourgeoisie now sat and presided over the export-import trade. Predictably, it decided to let existing export-import firms continue with their business provided they gave the corporation a 1 percent commission on all transactions. So anxious was the governing bureaucracy to consolidate its alliance with the Indian commercial bourgeoisie that the foreign minister, speaking on behalf of the president, found it necessary to assure Parliament immediately after the nationalization decree that "he had spoken with Mr. Jayant Madhvani and his brother and their reaction to the measure had been a welcome one." [112] With the 1970 nationalizations, the governing bureaucracy had not moved to the left; it had simply moved against the right.

3. THE GOVERNING BUREAUCRACY

The alliance with the Indian bourgeoisie isolated the petty bourgeoisie and allowed the governing bureaucracy greater room for maneuver. It utilized this opportunity to create conditions that would give it greater political freedom in the long run. Expanded freedom for the governing bureaucracy, however, was not possible without independence from the petty bourgeois opposition, kulaks and traders, historically its economic base. The "move to the left" was thus meant to realize this independence by creating an expanded public sector: the state would control certain sectors of the economy and the governing bureaucracy would control the state. Contrary to its rhetoric, the bureaucratic state did not seek control over the "commanding heights" of the economy; it only sought to consolidate its control over *intermediary* activities in the economy. With an economic base independent of the kulaks and the traders, the governing bureaucracy would be transformed into a bureaucratic petty bourgeoisie—not a bureaucratic *bourgeoisie*, because it did not seek to undermine the economic base of the commercial bourgeoisie. We say "would be" precisely because the process of transformation was cut short by the coup of 1971.

The pre-1970 governing bureaucracy was a section of the petty bourgeoisie. The post-1970 governing bureaucracy, on the other hand, sought to become the *core* of the petty bourgeoisie. Hence, the petty bourgeoisie, hitherto located primarily outside the state, was to be a *bureaucratic* petty bourgeoisie located within the state apparatus. While the economic base of the pre-1970 petty bourgeoisie would disintegrate, the post-1970 petty bourgeoisie, located dominantly within the state apparatus, would be a new formation, with its own distinctive manner of appropriating surplus, its own ideology, and its own process of formation.

The result of the nationalizations was the creation of an economic bureaucracy. Positions within it, located in particular parastatals, became its most important sources of material gain. The economic bureaucracy supplanted the party as the most important source of patronage. But private enrichment through the public sector, unlike private accumulation through individual ownership, took the form of corruption, not profit. An "unofficial" market burgeoned in the distribution of commodities by parastatals, while bribes rivaled salaries as important sources of income for individual bureaucrats.

As this class formed within the state apparatus, using the public sector as its economic base and nationalization as the means of its rise, the ideology it produced justified state ownership and state property. Every ruling class seeks to identify its particular interests with the general interests of society. The emerging bureaucratic petty bourgeoisie was no exception: the expansion of the state sector was identified as the building of socialism and the period of its own formation as that of transition to socialism. But in this petty bourgeois conception, socialism was stripped of the class struggle, of its political content, and was set forth as an economic ideology in its statist conception.

While the core of the bureaucratic petty bourgeoisie formed as the economic bureaucracy, its fringe included individuals who also held positions in multinational and Indian enterprises. Between 1967 and 1969, a section of the governing bureaucracy had started private companies which were appointed as the subdistributors of the PMB and the NTC. When these subdistributing agents were reappointed after 1969, they went into partnership with Indian capitalists. Given their weak economic base, however, the partnerships were in fact no more than Indian capitalist enterprises in which individual bureaucrats held nominal but lucrative official positions. As the emerging bureaucratic petty bourgeoisie consolidated its alliance with multinational and Indian capital in 1969 and 1970, this section also multiplied the directorships it held in private companies. The Immigration Act of 1969 required all noncitizens working in the country to apply for "entry permits" before May 1, 1970; those not granted permits were to leave the country. The purpose, according to the Commission for the Africanization of Commerce and Industry, was to effect "a systematic replacement of non-Africans and other noncitizens by Ugandan Africans in the senior executive posts in all commercial and industrial firms operating in Uganda." [113]* The commission gave, at most, five years for the Africanization of all posts held by noncitizens. As befitted an intermediary class, the most important positions within the emerging bureaucratic petty bourgeoisie were both within the state apparatus and within the enterprises of multinational and Indian capital; consequently, lucrative salaries and exorbitant bribes were their sources of income.

In this environment, the forces of the "right," the petty bourgeois guardians of law and order, posed as the guardians of public virtue. None other than Abu Mayanja (a member of the post-coup cabinet) introduced a bill in Parliament requiring the government to conduct an anticorruption commission of inquiry under the aegis of UN experts. He charged that some of the ministers had acquired wealth so rapidly that they were no longer desirable public servants and must resign, and he proposed that all members of the economic bureaucracy be asked to make a public declaration of their wealth. Felix Onama, minister of defense, responded thus: "There is no corruption in public life in Uganda." [115]

But statements cannot negate reality. With almost indecent haste, using the economic bureaucracy as its base, a class of *wabenzi* emerged.† No wonder that when petty bourgeois intellectuals chided the great leader's charter as "documentary radicalism," they found a sympathetic audience that went far beyond their narrow class base.

---

* Commenting on the above report in Parliament, the minister of commerce and industry, Mr. Kalema, stated: "The Government will do everything possible within that Article [20 of the Constitution] to make sure that Africans go to the top of as many companies as possible.

"The Bill to which I am referring [Immigration Control Bill] will introduce a system of work permits, which will be very closely controlled and which will make sure that employers are making provisions for the replacement of the expatriates." [114]

† *Wabenzi* is a Kiswahili term for those who own a Mercedes-Benz, the *wa-benzi*.

4. THE AFRICAN PETTY BOURGEOISIE

At the same time that it consolidated its alliance with multinational and Indian capital, the bureaucratic state moved against the African petty bourgeoisie. The Trade Licensing Act of 1969, although primarily aimed at the Asian petty bourgeoisie, also adversely affected the African petty bourgeoisie, particularly its lower section. The act stipulated an annual license fee of Shs. 500 for an African trader. Even in the established urban trading centers—that is, in areas where premises were relatively costly, minimum stock relatively large and the volume of trade relatively large—available figures show that 36 percent (Greater Kampala), 61 percent (Kawempe), 58.3 percent (Mengo) and 68 percent (Nakawa) of all traders had annual receipts of Shs. 12,000 or less.[116] The vast majority of these must have been Africans. Given that the figure is an average, for the petty trader profits were a much slimmer margin of annual receipts. An annual license fee of Shs. 500 must have been prohibitive for many. As the petty bourgeois parliamentary opposition declared: "You are trying to murder the small man." [117]

Meanwhile, the upper section of the petty bourgeoisie found its economic base disintegrating in the face of a formidable combination: the Indian commercial bourgeoisie and the rising members of the economic bureaucracy, both combining forces as the distributing agents of the PMB and the NTC.

Whereas prior to 1968 the marketing and processing of foodstuffs took place at the local level, in small quantities, at multiple markets and multitudes of factories, now all nationally produced basic commodities were bought by the cooperatives and gathered at national public auction by the PMB.* Bulk sales favored the big over the small trader, the large over the small miller, and the big over the small capitalist. They made possible, under the aegis of the state, further centralization of capital,

---

* In the throes of the 1969 crisis, the state raised the prices offered the grower. Maize went from Shs. 18 to Shs. 24 a bag and millet from Shs. 40 to Shs. 55.[118] The cooperatives, organized in their refusal to buy crops on behalf of the PMB because of the low prices offered the grower, now had no alternative but to resume buying on behalf of the board.

thereby reinforcing the monopoly structures in the underdeveloped economy. The impact of the PMB's monopolized marketing structures was the elimination of the small African miller and the consolidation of the large Asian miller. One of the African millers, a member of Parliament, told the House:

> Mr. Speaker, I happen to own a small maize mill in Hoima and towards the end of the season, that was in May, June, and July, Mr. Speaker, no African with a small maize mill could buy maize from the Board. All the maize was being sold to big Indians in the country who used to buy 10,000 bags of maize at a go. And, Mr. Speaker, the Board was only interested in selling maize—not to a small man but only to the big shots in Kampala and Jinja.[119]

The same trend was also manifest in the transport sector, where the colonial practice of granting monopoly rights to big transporters on all the major routes was faithfully pursued by the bureaucratic state. Out of six companies authorized to run services on the major bus routes, two—UTC, Ltd. (a London Company) and Eastern Province Bus Company (Indian capital) —monopolized the bulk of the traffic.* When asked about state guaranteed monopolies to big business, a cabinet minister explained:

> Licenses are issued in perpetuity, which means that when a firm has been issued with a license, you cannot possibly apply for the same route which is already operated by that firm until the Board is satisfied that the firm has failed to run that route. . . .[121]

To the petty bourgeoisie, history seemed to be repeating itself. The state it faced appeared a reincarnation of the colonial state, its big-capital orientation institutionalized in law, while that same legality was evoked to explain and justify its own perpetuation.

But these were partial measures, and their impact, however

---

* There were five major routes in Uganda with the following licensed carriers:[120] (1) Jinja-Tirinyi-Iganga: Elgon Taxi, Ltd., Eastern Province Bus Co., Ltd., and The Tirinyi United Bus Co.; (2) Jinja-Kampala: UTC, Ltd., East African Road Services, Ltd., and Uganda Land Bus and Touring Co., Ltd.; (3) Kampala-Masaka: UTC, Ltd.; (4) Kampala-Masaka-Mbarara: UTC, Ltd.; (5) Kampala-Jinja-Mbale: The East African Road Services, Ltd., UTC, Ltd., Elgon Taxi, Ltd., and The Eastern Province Bus Co., Ltd.

drastic, was on different sections of the petty bourgeoisie at different times: the traders at one point, small transporters at another, millers at another, and kulaks at yet another. The organizational base of the petty bourgeoisie, the cooperatives, were still relatively independent of state control. While they had been subject to strict managerial and financial supervision under the Cooperative Societies Act of 1946 (amended in 1952), this act had been repealed upon independence and replaced by the Cooperative Societies Act of 1963, which gave them complete financial and managerial autonomy. In 1970, having consolidated its alliance with the Asian commercial bourgeoisie and expanded state control over the economy, the bureaucratic state prepared to undermine the substantial organizational independence of the cooperatives. The 1963 act was replaced by the Cooperative Societies Act of 1970, whose purpose, according to the minister introducing it in Parliament, was

> to give government greater powers for the guidance, direction and control of the Cooperative Societies and unions generally, and on matters of finance and management of their affairs particularly, in order to make the movement a worthy vehicle of the new political culture of Uganda.[122]

Specifically, the act embodied six important measures:

1. A provision to enable the minister to maintain close supervision and control over the funds of societies and unions "to prevent them from being squandered by individual officials, whose main object has been self-enrichment." Clause 21 gave the minister power to appoint auditors and audit accounts "at least once a year."

2. The same clause made it mandatory for every registered society to submit estimates of income and expenditures of both revenue and capital to the minister for approval. The minister was empowered "to state in writing what estimates he approves and such estimates [would] be binding on the society."

3. The minister was given authority to restrict societies from "indiscriminate borrowing."

4. The minister was given the power to decide whether societies should receive deposits and loans from nonmembers and to rule on the conditions under which such deposits or loans should be received.

5. Clause 45 gave the minister the power "to approve whether a registered society may invest or deposit funds in any registered company, statutory corporation, financial institution, or any bank incorporated in Uganda."

6. Clause 76 prohibited societies "from being represented by lawyers before the arbitrators of the Registrar."

In substance, then, the state appropriated to itself control over all expenditures, borrowing, or investment, while giving itself the power to propose and enforce any measure on the cooperatives. Such was the content of bureaucratic hegemony over the petty bourgeoisie. With the Cooperative Societies Act of 1970, the antagonism between the governing bureaucracy and the petty bourgeoisie reached its maturity.

There was, however, an objective limit on this assault. The small traders and the local cooperatives performed an essential function in the social distribution of commodities by collecting exports and distributing imports at their points of origin and destination. It was the recognition of this objective fact that prompted a decisive change in the relation of the state to the Asian petty bourgeoisie.

5. THE ASIAN PETTY BOURGEOISIE

After the 1966 and 1969 crises, state policy was directed against the entire petty bourgeoisie, both African and Asian, a partial reversal of the pre-1966 years when the state had sought to liquidate the Asian petty bourgeoisie in order to consolidate the economic base of the Africans.

We have seen that there were two distinct classes among the Asians in Uganda: the bourgeoisie, small in number but dominant in its appropriation of the social surplus product, and the petty bourgeoisie, made up of small traders (*dukawallahs*) and clerks in the civil service. The state related to each of these classes separately.

The weapon the state used against the Asian petty bourgeoisie was the passport: the "right to trade" increasingly became the "right of a citizen," and an Asian trader without a passport was ultimately without the legal right to trade. Even in 1965, Asian members of Parliament were complaining that applications for Uganda citizenship were not being dealt with and were demanding that the government expedite the issue.[123] By 1967, according to the minister of internal affairs, there were 10,527 Asians who had applied for but not been granted Uganda citizenship.[124] For those sufficiently affluent, the passport had become a purchasable commodity, available for a high enough bribe. By 1970, out of a total of 76,600 Asians resident in Uganda, 30,000 were Uganda citizens,[125] while some 12,000 had applied for citizenship under the 1962 constitution and reapplied under the 1967 constitution, but their applications had not yet been processed.[126] The *Uganda Argus* reported a parliamentary reply by the minister of internal affairs on government policy vis-à-vis Asians who had applied for passports:

> Concerning citizenships, Mr. Bataringaya said that he was under pressure from the House to be very "hard" on the question of citizenships. If he "dished out" citizenships as Mr. Arain appeared to wish, the House would demand his resignation. He cautioned Mr. Arain to be very careful when speaking of people of Asian extraction. He had to be aware that when issuing citizenship the question of loyalty was uppermost, and although he did not wish to imply that all people of Asian extraction were bad, there were however doubts about some of them.[127]

In 1969, the state passed the Trade Licensing Act, which required all noncitizens to possess a valid license from the authorities if they wished to carry on business.* Those busi-

---

* Noncitizen traders were not all Asians, although politically the term "noncitizen trader" was used for an Asian trader. There were many non-Uganda African (particularly Kenyan) traders. A 1969 questionnaire in the trading areas in and around Kampala showed the following results:

Uganda Citizenship by Area and Race
(in percent)

	Asians	Africans	Average
Greater Kampala	(n = 155)	(n = 200)	(n = 355)
Citizen	59.5	79.9	69.9
Noncitizen	40.5	20.1	29.9
Kawempe	(n = 8)	(n = 51)	(n = 59)
Citizen	100.0	92.1	93.2
Noncitizen	0.0	7.8	6.8

nesses not issued government permits were compelled to close. The prerequisite for a permit was capital of Shs. 80,000.[128] In a survey of businessmen in Kawempe, Mengo, and Kampala Central (the three main trading areas in Buganda), it was found that 55 percent of Asian businessmen in Kawempe, 49.9 percent in Mengo, and 16.5 percent in Kampala had *less* than Shs. 60,000 in annual receipts. At the same time, 31.5 percent of the Asian businessmen in Kawempe, 41.8 percent in Mengo, and 30.6 percent in Kampala Central had annual receipts of between Shs. 60,000 and Shs. 240,000. Receipts of Shs. 80,000 represented a third of the annual sales of the most substantial of these enterprises.[129] The point of the Trade Licensing Act was to make a legal distinction between the petty bourgeoisie and the commercial bourgeoisie. It was directed against the former while providing safeguards for the latter.

By 1970, as a result of the Trade Licensing Act, Asian traders had begun a gradual departure from Uganda. At the same time, the antagonism between the African petty bourgeoisie and the bureaucratic state had reached new heights. Yet with a phased departure of the Asian traders, the objective role of the African petty bourgeoisie in the social distribution of commodities was likely to *expand*, not diminish. It was this realization that prompted Obote to announce in late 1970 that he was considering granting rights of citizenship—and therefore the right to trade—to 30,000 Asians.[130] Those among the Asians who desired this right were traders, not those in the civil service or in private companies who were targets of state-directed "Africanization"

	Asians	Africans	Average
Uganda Citizenship by Area and Race *(in percent) (cont.)*			
Mengo	(n = 12)	(n = 103)	(n = 115)
Citizen	83.3	79.6	80.0
Noncitizen	16.7	20.4	20.0
Nakawa	(n = 3)	(n = 67)	(n = 70)
Citizen	66.7	68.8	68.6
Noncitizen	33.3	29.8	30.0

Source: Jack Parsons, "Wholesale and Retail Trade and Traders in Uganda: A Survey Report," p. 17. Survey taken in 1969.

measures and who wanted to depart as soon as possible for greener pastures. Obote's announcement, in other words, was a declaration that the governing bureaucracy preferred an Asian to an African petty bourgeoisie. The latter was a political threat; the former was not.

This was December 1970. Before it had time to implement its declared intention, the bureaucratic state was toppled by a *coup d'état.*

The 1971 Coup

At the same time that it sought to control the cooperatives, the rising bureaucratic petty bourgeoisie attempted to secure monopoly control over *all* national organizations, political or nonpolitical, unions of workers or worshippers. In other words, the bureaucratic state sought hegemony. At the same time, the petty bourgeoisie, its own organizational base threatened, sought an alternative basis for organization, within unions or spiritual organizations, and ultimately within the armed forces. The crisis within the ruling class became the crisis of the social formation, and it was reflected in every single national organization, regardless of its formal nature.

1. TRADE UNIONS

In the ten-year period from independence to the coup, the trade union movement in Uganda was ridden with conflicts among its leadership. Although this factionalism has often been reduced to the level of personal greed and ambition,[131] such an analysis is a classic example of the failure to place working class organization in the context of the larger political economy, and thus to relate it to class struggles at the state level. This factionalism was not rooted in individual conflicts alone but had an objective basis, one that becomes clear if we examine the political alliances of each set of competing leaders.* There were

---

* Although our purpose is not to reduce the working class to its organizational expression, it is clear that working class organization in Uganda from the 1952 Ordinance to the 1971 coup was confined to trade unions, and that the very nature of trade union organization conformed, in the narrowest sense, to the division capital imposed on labor at the level of production. Furthermore, as we show, the leadership of these unions came from within the petty bourgeoisie and

three distinct factions: those without positions in official unions but with an independent base in sections of the working class (the "left"); those official union leaders with direct ties to the UPC and the governing bureaucracy (the "center"); and those official union leaders independent of the governing bureaucracy but with ties to the petty bourgeoisie (the "right"). Of these three, the left faction, which organized the unofficial strikes after independence, was expelled from both the party and the UFL in 1964. While the UFL was dissolved and replaced by the state-controlled FUTU that same year, that segment of the UFL leadership with direct ties to the UPC was given leading positions within the FUTU (Reich as president and Kibuka as secretary-general). In other words, the FUTU was the UFL purged of its left faction.

After 1964, there remained two prominent factions: the center (FUTU), linked to the governing bureaucracy; and the right (TUC), with ties to the petty bourgeoisie. The struggle between the two remarkably paralleled the struggle between the governing bureaucracy and the petty bourgeoisie, as did the fortunes of each faction.

Once the FUTU was under its control, the governing bureaucracy sought to give it de facto recognition as the sole representative of Uganda workers by nominating its delegates to the International Labor Congress (to the exclusion of the TUC leadership). But it was not until the 1966 crisis that the governing bureaucracy sought to ban the TUC (*and* the FUTU), and in their stead establish a single state-appointed union, the Uganda Labour Congress (ULC). And yet the governing bureaucracy, in the throes of a major political crisis, did not feel

---

not the working class. In other words, trade unions, though formally organizations of workers, were in fact organizations for the *control* of workers and for carrying out sectional struggles between ruling class factions. A study of working class politics, then, would have to go beyond the unions to the shop floor and examine the various forms that the struggle of labor against capital took. Such detailed research is not within the scope of this book. Also, inasmuch as this struggle was not about the question of state power, we feel justified in leaving it out in our analysis of the principal contradictions that informed the politics of Uganda up to 1972.

sufficiently confident to appoint the ULC leadership; instead it let the member unions elect their own leadership. Given a choice between a set of leaders directly subservient to the governing bureaucracy (former FUTU leaders) and those independent of it (former TUC leaders), the unions chose the latter. Ironically, then, after 1966 the ULC was the only *national* organization with a leadership that had ties with the petty bourgeois opposition.

Between 1966 and 1968, relations between the ULC leadership and the state took a turn for the worse.[132] In 1968, Kibuka (now a prominent member of the UPC[133]), with the help of the police, staged a "revolution" and established himself as the secretary-general of the ULC.[134] Immediately afterward, the government established a one-man commission of inquiry into trade unions, a "fact-finding commission" that made the following recommendations:

1. That the minister of labour have power to veto any candidate submitted by member unions for election as a ULC officer.

2. That the ULC have more full-time officials and that it should have "full powers to control unions."

3. That unions should contribute 50 percent of their funds to the ULC, and that failure to do this or to collect union dues result in penalties.

4. That the ULC associate with the British TUC and have no other international affiliations.

5. That no trade union official be allowed to be a member of Parliament or hold any other paid office.

6. That a separate department, the Registry of Trade Unions, should administer the law and provide an advisory service for unions.[135]

These recommendations were in fact a detailed strategy for state hegemony over trade union organization. But as the unions became working class organizations in name and not in orientation, as they became organizations of bureaucratic control rather than democratic expression, the interest of the constituency in what was only formally its own organization declined heavily, as the table on the following page shows.

Neither did the material position of labor show any improve-

Trade Unions and Membership, 1954–1966

Year		Number of unions	Number of members
1954		4	680
1956		10	2,530
1958		16	7,370
1960		24	20,970
1962	(Independence)	40	90,000
1964	("left" expelled)	40	96,000
1966		27	65,000

Source: Roger Scott, *The Development of Trade Unions in Uganda*, Table 2.

ment after the independence strikes, in spite of manufacturing investments in the 1960s. Precisely because of the import-substituting character of Ugandan industrialization, although the urban product per person employed shot up at a rate of 12–14 percent a year, the introduction of capital-intensive technology precluded any increase in employment.[136] As early as 1964, those "with jobs were grimly hanging on to them. For manual labor, especially in the lower skill groups, the labor shortage of the fifties was but a dream." [137]

The 1969 crisis resulted in spiraling inflation, which particularly affected the urban workers and the working peasantry. In the face of spreading unrest, the bureaucratic state played its trump card. Just as in 1965 it had attempted to exploit ethnic divisions among workers by barring militant Kenyans from leadership positions,[138] it now proceeded to expel Kenyan workers en masse from Uganda on grounds of improving the conditions of national labor.[139] This was the first mass expulsion in Uganda's history. Those expelled were members of the working class, and no other class so much as whispered opposition; neither was there any international recognition of their plight. At the same time, along with the 1970 May Day nationalizations, the bureaucratic state declared all strikes illegal. Obote argued that since the means of production were nationalized, there was no reason to retain the "archaic principle and practice of strikes." [140] In the name of socialism, the proletariat was deprived of its final weapon of defense against the emerging bureaucratic petty bourgeoisie.

In spite of the expansion of the state sector and the alliance with the Asian bourgeoisie, the revolt of the petty bourgeoisie and the continued balance-of-payments crisis kept the economy from stabilizing. The political crisis was reflected in commodity scarcities and soaring prices. Between the third quarter of 1969 and the fourth quarter of 1970, the cost of living index in Kampala for "high income" groups rose by 6.5 percent, for those with a "middle income" by 9.5 percent, and for the "low income" group by 18.5 percent. Of particular significance was the 22.5 percent rise in food prices for the low-income group, an increase that predated the drought of early 1971.[141]

The workers, without their own political organization—the prerequisite to independent action by any social force—were ready to support any other class or section of society that might lead the opposition to the bureaucratic state.

2. RELIGIOUS INSTITUTIONS

It was not only in the trade unions that the fragmentation within the ruling class gave an objective basis to conflicts within the organization, transforming individual conflicts for position into factional struggles of larger political significance. This process was true of every single nationally organized institution that could potentially be the organizational base of the petty-bourgeois opposition, be these institutions celestial or temporal. The short-run conflict between personalities or internal tendencies became related to and found a base in the long-run contradiction between social forces. All three organized religions in Uganda—Catholicism, Islam, and Anglicanism—became highly politicized in the decade between independence and the coup. Of these, Islam and Anglicanism were torn apart with internal dissension, either promoted or assisted by the bureaucratic state and the petty bourgeoisie.*

---

* Catholicism remained an exception, maintaining its internal unity during the period under consideration. The reason for this, too, is *political*. The politicization of the Catholic Church predated independence. The Catholic hierarchy was denied its share of access to the economic surplus, either through

The crisis in the Church of Uganda (Anglican) came to the fore upon the retirement of Archbishop Brown in 1965. The chairman of the principal diocese of Buganda, the Namirembe Diocese Christian Association, issued a statement that "Buganda Christians had been discriminated against, that the Luganda prayerbooks no longer contained references to the monarchy, and that Baganda bishops were not to be considered in the choice of [Brown's] successor." [142] To resolve the issue, Mr. Wamala suggested the two Buganda dioceses secede and form a distinct office: the demand of the Baganda kulaks had become that of the Buganda church. The governing bureaucracy intervened in the ensuing crisis by giving political and material assistance to the newly elected Archbishop (Eric Sabiti) to help him establish power over the two Buganda dioceses. The factionalism persisted, and at the state-initiated Provincial Assembly, called to resolve the crisis, the Baganda delegates absented themselves while the new Archbishop counseled national unity and viewed "with alarm the growing pressure for each tribe to have its own bishop," a trend "serious not only for the church but also for the Government." [143]

The factionalism persisted until the coup, which resolved the political contradiction between the petty bourgeoisie and the nascent bureaucratic petty bourgeoisie. The crisis of the church was cut down to size. In the face of a warning from Amin[144] about "the consequences of internal divisions," a compromise ensued.

Factionalism within Islam was much more serious. At independence, the prominent Muslim organization in the country was the Uganda Muslim Community (UMC), led by Prince Badru Kakungule, an uncle of the *kabaka* and a prominent member of the petty bourgeoisie. (In fact, most prominent

---

land grants or state positions. The petty bourgeoisie, on the other hand, was predominantly non-Catholic. Catholic chiefs and intelligentsia, with active support from the Church, organized as the DP in opposition not only to the Protestant chiefs and landlords (PP) but to what it considered the non-Catholic petty bourgeoisie (KY and UPC). For the petty bourgeoisie, either in Buganda or outside, there was thus little possibility of gaining a political base within the Catholic Church, and there were therefore no grounds for the bureaucratic state to fear the Church as a potential base for petty bourgeois oppositional politics.

figures in the UMC were from the petty bourgeoisie.) After the collapse of the KY–UPC alliance in 1965, the governing bureaucracy encouraged the formation of a rival organization, the National Association for the Advancement of Muslims (NAAM), led by a cabinet minister (Adoko Nekyon), a member of Parliament (A. Balinda) and the major-general of the army (Idi Amin). Relations between the UMC and NAAM were so strained that physical clashes were common, including one confrontation with the police that cost two lives.[145] By 1968, the UPC and Obote were openly supporting the NAAM and declaring that those failing to do so were "disloyal to the state." [146] After the coup, the NAAM was dissolved and UMC regained its former monopoly position. Significantly, however, just prior to the coup General Amin stopped attending NAAM meetings and started attending UMC meetings, speaking publicly against the intrusion of politics in religion.[147]

3. THE ARMY

Before we can understand the coup, it is important to underline the social position of the armed forces. First, an army is not a social class.* It is neither formed nor reproduces itself at the level of the social process of production. Like bureaucrats, intellectuals, and priests, an army is not directly involved in the social process of production; it appropriates its share of the surplus because of its relation to a particular social class, or classes, that control state power.† In other words, soldiers do not *form* a social class; they *serve* social classes.‡

---

* I am thus in total disagreement with Michael Lofchie[148] and Ali Mazrui,[149] both of whom consider the army a social class—the former on the basis of its high income, the latter because of its distinctive institutional interest.

† Similarly, the social function of intellectuals is to produce ideas, to legitimate or to expose, to mystify or to demystify reality. In understanding the political significance of intellectuals, their class *origin* is not emphasized as much as the class *content* of their ideas: Whose interests do they serve? Intellectuals are thus classified as bourgeois, petty bourgeois, or proletarian depending on the social class whose interests they articulate, *not* depending on their class origin.

‡ It is only by understanding that the army is a social category situated outside the economy that we are able to understand specific historical moments such as the "move to the left," when the governing bureaucracy attempted to transform itself into a class, the bureaucratic petty bourgeoisie. For this to

Second, the army is a part of the state's coercive apparatus. As the bourgeoisie consolidated its rule over the state in the advanced capitalist countries, it also consolidated its hold over the armed forces: the ideology of professionalism and civilian control articulated this ruling class supremacy. In such circumstances, conflicts within the army remain at the level of individual or group conflicts, transitory in their significance: the aim of any particular group is to replace another in a high position, not to challange the power of the state. But the problem in Uganda, as in many neocolonies, was that the ruling class failed to consolidate. The political crisis of underdeveloped capitalism is the *fragmentation* of the ruling class.

This fragmentation is not just a result of its specific historical formation, but also of its dependent character: it cannot establish effective control over the nationally generated surplus, which is primarily appropriated by imperial capital.[150] Such fragmentation gives inordinate strength to the section of the class that directly controls the state apparatus. The political struggles between opposing factions typically center on the method of accumulation: whether it should be through the creation of state property or private property. When a ruling class fails to consolidate even at the level of the economy and there follow acute political struggles between its factions, the governing faction seeks to establish hegemony, just as the opposing faction seeks an alternate basis of organization. In all institutions—be they cooperatives, trade unions, or religious institutions—existing internal conflicts become tied to external political contradictions between factions within the ruling class. The crisis of the ruling class becomes the crisis of the entire social formation.

Under such circumstances, if the opposing faction attempts to make contact with a group of officers in the army, individual or

happen, however, it was necessary that the bureaucracy, hitherto a social category outside the economy, create for itself an independent base within the economy. Thus the "move to the left" and the associated nationalization decrees: the core of the nascent bureaucratic petty bourgeoisie was the economic bureaucracy forming itself within "parastatals," state *economic* organizations. As we shall see, a qualitatively different process would emerge with regard to the soldiers under the postcoup government of Amin.

group conflicts within the army also acquire a political basis, and if any one seeks to intervene in politics, it does so in alliance with a faction in the ruling class. To understand the class basis of a coup, then, it is important to bear two points in mind: first, it is not the army which intervenes in politics, but a particular faction within the army. Second, without a fragmented ruling class, there are no factions within the army (only competing groups and individuals), and no coups. In other words, the factionalism within the army, in its political significance, reflects the fragmentation within the ruling class.

After independence, all three East African armies mutinied, demanding "Africanization"—higher positions and better pay—but only in Uganda were all the major demands granted by the state power, for only in Uganda was there a serious split within the ruling class. By 1967, Uganda soldiers were the highest paid of any in East Africa, as the accompanying table shows.

Annual Salaries of East African Armies, 1967
(pounds)

Ranks	Uganda	Kenya	Malawi	Zambia
Commander	2,900	—	—	—
Brigadier	2,500	2,520	—	3,066
Colonel	2,300	2,175	2,440	2,696
Lieutenant Colonel	1,935	1,935	2,000	2,217
Major	1,690	1,690	1,271	1,779
Captain	1,200	1,200	954	1,368
Lieutenant	905	905	668	1,003
2nd Lieutenant	790	790	615	949
Cadet	516	312	312	638
Warrant Officer I	963	813	455	784
Warrant Officer II	648	525	383	547
Sergeant	510	316	242	370
Corporal	—	194	161	292
Private	285	129	108	180

Source: Michael Lofchie, "The Uganda Coup: Class Action by the Military," p. 21.

The mutiny did not become a coup, however, or even an attempted coup, because the fragmentation within the ruling class was not yet an open political struggle, and there was no attempt by the opposing faction to make any contact with the mutiny. In the absence of political leadership from the outside, the soldiers' action was equivalent to an economic strike for an economic demand. While successful as a mutiny, it was not translated into a political act.

By 1966, however, the political contradictions within the ruling class had matured and burst into the open as an acute political struggle. The KY–UPC alliance was no more. The petty bourgeoisie had organized as the "Ibingira group," the "right" faction of the UPC, and had captured the leadership of the party and consolidated its forces in Parliament. During the 1966 crisis, the Ibingira group in Parliament made "precautionary contacts" with certain army officers plotting to overthrow Obote.[151] The Ibingira faction in the army was led by Brigadier General Shaban Opolot and its core was a group of Sandhurst-trained officers. During the state of emergency in 1966, Opolot was jailed, as was the Ibingira group. The coup was preempted. Opolot was replaced by Amin.

Following the 1967 crisis, the importance of the armed forces increased as the ruling bureaucracy, ideologically and organizationally bereft, increasingly relied on the repressive state apparatus. By 1968, the ministry of defense allocation was 10.2 percent of the national budget (in Kenya, it was 6.9 percent and in Tanzania 3.8 percent) or more than £17 million (equal to the combined military expenditure of Kenya and Tanzania). With the 1969 crisis, the fragmentation within the ruling class was complete. At the conclusion of that year's party conference, there was an assassination attempt on Obote's life and a pro-Obote officer, Brigadier Okoya, second in command of the army, was shot and killed. It appeared that the petty bourgeois opposition had gained allies within the army.

The response of the state was threefold: to weaken the army by strengthening alternative armed organizations and by promoting internal divisions within the army itself; to establish an intelligence apparatus that would watch over the army; and to isolate key officers who were under suspicion.

The counter to the 7,500-man army was the élite 1,000-man

Special Forces, favored in terms of arms, equipment, and budgetary allotment.* The long-run strategy, embodied in the 1970 National Service proposals, called for the establishment of a People's Militia, to be trained in National Service Camps under the direction of a cabinet minister. At the same time, Obote proceeded to manipulate ethnic divisions within the army in order to control it (just as he had promoted ethnic divisions within the working class for the same reason). Acholi and Langi officers were given promotions while other northerners were excluded.† Then a paramilitary organization called the General Service Unit (GSU) was given the task of spying on the entire state apparatus, including the army and the bureaucracy.‡

The key officer Obote tried to isolate was General Amin. He

---

* Although the Special Forces were first established during the last phase of the colonial period, they only assumed significance as an armed force in the last phase of the Obote years.

† The composition of the Uganda army at independence was predominantly northern. Some observers have attempted to see a natural or biological justification for this. Thus Mazrui ascribes the northern dominance in the rank-and-file to the "fact" that the lanky pastoral northerners are a "martial" people.[152] The argument ignores both empirical and historical evidence. The northern predominance in the army was a direct result of the British qualification for entry, a minimum height of 5 feet 8 inches that ruled out the shorter southern peoples.[153] This had not always been the case. We have seen that the army the British used to conquer the north in the early phase of colonialism was a Baganda army, officers and men included. In the following decades, however, as the south became the predominant cash-crop growing area and the physical base of the working class, and the primary function of the army became one of quelling rebellions among the southern kulaks, peasants, and workers, the colonial state introduced technical requirements that made possible the building of a primarily northern army. The ideology that justified this move was that the northerners were a "martial race." Today, however, that same ideology is paraded as "science" by petty bourgeois intellectuals.

‡ A large section (47 percent) of the colonially inherited "higher" bureaucracy was Baganda in origin, although its social origin was primarily from among chiefs and landlords, not kulaks and traders. The *governing* bureaucracy, on the other hand, was northern, as was the economic bureaucracy created in the wake of the "move to the left." As he promoted ethnic divisions within all national organizations—trade unions, churches, the bureaucracy, and the army—Obote began to identify his opposition increasingly as an ethnic one. The purpose of the GSU was to spy on the Baganda members of the "higher" administrative bureaucracy and on army officers.

was sent to Egypt as Uganda's official delegate at President Nasser's funeral. In his absence, the army was "reorganized": every officer was promoted one grade and chiefs of staff were appointed for the army and the air force—previously the chain of command had run directly from Amin to troop unit commanders; now it ran from the new chiefs of staff to the president's office.[154]

Upon his return, Amin shifted his religious affiliation from NAAM to UMC, from the religious congregation of the ruling power to that of the petty bourgeoisie. It was this coalition of the Amin faction in the army and the civilian petty bourgeoisie that was responsible for the coup.

Behind the coup was also an external power, Israel, although its involvement was of secondary significance.* Relations between Israel and Uganda began as early as 1963, when Obote visited Israel. Following his visit, various important Israeli leaders—Golda Meir (foreign minister) in 1963, Levi Eshkol (prime minister) in 1966, and Abba Eban (foreign minister) in 1969—visited Uganda and cemented relations between the two countries. The Israelis did not simply have economic "aid" projects in Uganda; their officers also trained the police, the intelligence, and the army. After 1969, Uganda occupied a central place in Israel's Arab-African policy. Northern Uganda was the base that Israel used to materially assist the southern Sudanese (Anyanya) guerrillas. But events took a decisive turn following the May 25, 1969, coup in Sudan that brought General Nimeri to power. Relations with Uganda improved visibly. Talks began on a formal treaty between the two. The Israeli use of northern Uganda as a base to supply the Anyanya guerrillas was in imminent danger. When, in August 1970, the Israeli chief of the central intelligence organization, General Zamir, sought refueling rights in Uganda for the arms ferry to the Anyanya, Obote refused. At the same time, the cabinet's security committee ruled to terminate Israeli training of the police force.

---

* In 1971, when thrown out of Uganda, the Israelis were unable to topple the Amin government in spite of vigorous efforts. The reason was simple: internal contradictions had not yet matured for an Israeli-supported coup to succeed. At the same time, an Israeli invasion was politically out of the question.

Finally, there was the Steiner affair. A West German mercenary and a former French Foreign Legionnaire who had fought in Biafra and was now with the Anyanya, Rolf Steiner, came out of the Sudan in August 1970 to make contact with an Ugandan army unit. He was arrested by the police and the Ugandan authorities decided to deport him to the Sudan. His diaries record two meetings that had taken place between General Amin, an Israeli military officer, and the Anyanya commander, General Joseph Lagu, in the southern Sudan. Amin was the man the Israelis had worked through before, and he was the one they assisted during the coup.[155]

The outcome of the political crisis in Uganda was a *coup d'état*, in spite of the fact that by 1971 the bureaucratic state had very little support outside of its own ranks precisely because the only classes capable of independent political organization, the petty bourgeoisie and the proletariat, were paralyzed. The proletariat remained a social force only in that it could follow; it was incapable of initiating action. The petty bourgeoisie, on the other hand, possessed an adequate organizational base in the cooperatives, but lacked a class organization strong enough to permit it independent political action. The army possessed precisely what the petty bourgeoisie lacked: arms and disciplined organization. Conscious of its political weakness, the petty bourgeoisie had sought allies within the army since 1966.

Although his class base was the petty bourgeoisie, Amin was no simple "representative" of a class. In fact, he emerged as a strong man, relatively independent of his class base. The strength of Amin's personality, so evident in the months after the coup, was the political expression of the organizational weakness of the petty bourgeoisie.

The coup found immediate political support from the former colonial power, Britain. The source of Britain's contradictions with Uganda lay not in the latter's internal economic policy but in its foreign policy. The only progressive aspect of the bureaucratic state had been its active support for liberation movements, and that extended to breaking relations with Britain over the Rhodesian UDI and an attempt to form a "progressive bloc" at the 1971 Singapore Commonwealth Conference to oppose the sale of British arms to South Africa. When the coup occurred in January 1971, the British government was the first to recognize the new regime.*

And yet, favorable as the external environment was for the coup, the conditions for its realization were internal. The coup represented the failure of the governing bureaucracy to transform itself into a bureaucratic petty bourgeoisie. Without a mass popular base, in the throes of a crisis of accumulation, and faced with the opposition of the petty bourgeoisie—the strongest section of which (the Baganda kulaks) did in fact possess a mass base—the rule of the governing bureaucracy was reduced to the rule of the gun. As political struggle took the form of armed confrontation, the state was reduced to its coercive apparatus. Each time it wielded the army as a weapon, the weapon became sharper and the officer corps increasingly conscious of its critical position. In its struggles against the bureaucratic state, it was to be expected that the petty bourgeoisie would make political overtures to a section of the army. Only when it was jolted awake by the assassination attempt on the president and the successful assassination of Okoya did the bureaucratic petty bourgeoisie attempt to sheath the weapon and put it under lock and key. But by then the weapon had become the arbitrator. Once force met with force and gun was raised against gun, it disintegrated and the castle was reduced to dust. The very rapidity of the disintegration was testimony to the narrow base of the bureaucratic state. Meanwhile, the "common man," in whose name the class had claimed to rule, long accustomed to watching from the grandstands, applauded the change of guard.

Notes

1. James Y. Obol-Ochala, "Customary Land Law and the Economic Development of Uganda," pp. 219–232.

---

* The London *Times* could hardly conceal its delight at the sudden turn of events in Uganda. It wrote: "[Dr. Obote's] regime was no longer worth protecting—hostile to British interests, contemptuous of Europeans, as oppressive as Dr. Nkrumah's, ethnically divisive and patently so unpopular that no British Government would be able to shore it up, let alone wish to be associated with it."

2. UP, *White Paper on Mechanisation*, May 1954, p. 6.
3. UP, *Report of the Agricultural Productivity Committee*, 1955, p. 60.
4. Uganda Parliamentary Debates, *Hansard*, vols. 27–30, July 9, 1964, p. 2373.
5. Horace Campbell, "A Week in the Second Republic of Uganda," p. 8.
6. Ibid., p. 9.
7. E. A. Brett, "Problems of Cooperative Development in Uganda," pp. 6–7.
8. UG, *Report of the Commission of Inquiry into the Cotton Industry*, 1966, pp. 24–25.
9. UG, *Report of a Committee of Inquiry into the Affairs of the Busoga Growers' Cooperative Union, Ltd.*, 1965, p. 22.
10. Brett, p. 30.
11. Ibid., pp. 18–19.
12. UP, *Report of the Commission of Inquiry into the Affairs of the Bugisu Cooperative Union, Ltd.*, Sessional Paper No. 14 of 1958, p. 12.
13. Brett, p. 21.
14. UG, *Report of the Committee of Inquiry into the Affairs of the Busoga Growers' Cooperative Union, Ltd.*, 1965, p. 17.
15. Ibid., p. 22.
16. Ibid., p. 8.
17. UG, *Teso District Annual Report, 1964*, p. 1; quoted in L. Stevens, "Uganda Since the Coup," p. 4.
18. UG, *Teso District Annual Report, 1967*, p. 1; quoted in ibid.
19. *Mengo District Annual Report, 1962*, p. 8; quoted in ibid.
20. Brett, p. 14.
21. George R. Bosa, *The Financing of Small-Scale Enterprises in Uganda*, p. 14.
22. Ibid., p. 15.
23. G. R. Bosa, "African Businessmen in Uganda," p. 19.
24. The information on the operation of ABP, Ltd., is taken from two sources: chapter 4 in Bosa, *The Financing of Small-Scale Enterprises in Uganda*, pp. 45–64, and Jack Parsons, "The Africanization of Trade in Uganda," pp. 12–14.
25. UP, *Report of the Commissioners for Africanization*, part 1, Sessional Paper No. 7 of 1962.
26. Gus Edgren, "Employment in Tropical Africa," p. 18.
27. A. Baryanuha, *Factors Affecting Industrial Employment*.
28. All information of the 1963 strikes from Roger Scott, *The Development of Trade Unions in Uganda*, pp. 80–82, 155; and Scott, "Labour Legislation and the Federal Issue," pp. 26–27. Although all

four leaders of UPC–YL were released by executive order in a week, they were reimprisoned "on a similar charge of intimidation of non-Africans."

29. Akiki B. Mujaju, "The Demise of the UPC–YL and the Rise of NUYO."
30. Ibid.
31. A. G. G. Gingyera-Pincyewa, "Prospects for a One-Party System in Uganda."
32. UG, *Report of the Commission of Inquiry into Relations Between Management and Workers in the Sugar Industry*, August 12, 1964, p. 1.
33. Ibid., pp. 11–12.
34. Emory Bundy, "Uganda's New Constitution," p. 25.
35. Apollo Nsibambia, "Federalism: Its Rise and Fall in Uganda," p. 15.
36. For details, see Bundy, p. 25.
37. Nsibambia, p. 15.
38. Quoted in *Uganda Herald*, April 15, 1948, p. 1.
39. F. L. McDougall, *The Growing Dependence of British Industry upon Empire Markets*, London, HMSO, Empire Marketing Board Publication No. 23, December 1929, pp. 26–27.
40. Ibid., p. 27.
41. Governor to Secretary of State, No. 99 of March 6, 1930, in CO 536/161.
42. Ibid.
43. Memorandum from the Colonial Office to Governor of Uganda, The Colonial Empire and the Economic Crisis, August 6, 1948, in Maini Papers AR MA 5/34, Standing Finance Committee, 1944–49, p. 1.
44. Memorandum from Secretary of State to Officer Administering the Government of Uganda, September 27, 1945, Financial Results of the War in U.K., in Maini Papers, AR MA 5/33, Standing Finance Committee, 1944–47, p. 2.
45. Memorandum from the Colonial Office to Governor of Uganda, The Colonial Empire and the Economic Crisis, August 6, 1948.
46. Circular from Secretary of State to Governor, Uganda; received August 10, 1947, in Maini Papers AR MA 5/29.
47. Combined Raw Material Board to Governor of Uganda, The Natural Rubber Position of the United Nations, February 24, 1944, in Maini Papers AR MA 5/29.
48. *Uganda Herald*, July 27, 1947; October 9 and 23, 1946; January 8, 1947.
49. Memorandum from the Colonial Office to Governor of Uganda, The Colonial Empire and the Economic Crisis, August 6, 1948, p. 2.

50. *Uganda Herald*, April 15, 1948, p. 1.
51. *Uganda Herald*, February 24, 1948, p. 5.
52. *Uganda Herald*, October 14, 1950, p. 1.
53. Read P. Dunn, Jr., *Cotton in East Africa*, p. 43.
54. Note of a meeting held July 21 to discuss Bunyoro Tobacco Marketing Policy. Minute No. 259 of 1946/47, Appendix to Minutes of the 89th Meeting of the Standing Committee on Finance, held in Kampala, August 22, 1947; in Maini Papers AR MA 5/34.
55. *Uganda Herald*, February 24, 1948, p. 1.
56. Colonial Office, *The British Territories in East and Central Africa, 1945–1950*, p. 45.
57. Memorandum from Colonial Office to Governor of Uganda, The Colonial Empire and the Economic Crisis, August 6, 1948, p. 3.
58. *Uganda Herald*, December 9, 1950, p. 4.
59. UP, *Annual Development Report for Period Ending September 1947*, p. 3.
60. Ibid.
61. *Uganda Herald*, April 1, 1952, p. 4.
62. Acting Governor to Secretary of State, September 1, 1932, in CO 536/173 (File No. 22164).
63. Colonial Office to Sir Bernard H. Bourdillon, December 8, 1932, in ibid.
64. H. T. Allen, Colonial Office, to Mr. Overman, October 22, 1932, in ibid.
65. Bottomley, Colonial Office, to Bernard Bourdillon, February 2, 1933, in ibid.
66. Colonial Secretary, quoted in memorandum on Colonial Development and Welfare Bill, by Joint East Africa Board, in Maini Papers AR MA 5/21.
67. *Uganda Herald*, April 24, 1951, p. 1.
68. Ibid.
69. At the end of 1966 these three banks held approximately 79 percent of the total banking assets in the country. The other three expatriate banks in Uganda—the Bank of Baroda (India), the Bank of India, and the Netherlands Bank—accounted for about 10 percent of the total commercial bank assets and were highly specialized in their operations. See I. Gershenberg, "The Impact of Independence on the Role of Commercial Banking in Uganda's Economic Development."
70. Ibid., p. 12.
71. Diana Hunt, "Some Aspects of Agricultural Credit in Uganda," p. 1.

72. In "The Impact of Independence on the Role of Commercial Banking."

73. All details from John Loxley, "The Development of the Monetary and Financial System of the East African Currency Area, 1950–1964," pp. 174–194.

74. Uganda Development Corporation, Ltd., *Annual Report*, 1956.

75. *Uganda Argus*, February 22, 1955, p. 1.

76. See Loxley.

77. See Jack Santongo, "The Outstanding Friend," in Robert Becker and Nitin Jayant Madhvani, eds., *Jayant Madhvani*, p. 36.

78. UG, *Report of the Commission of Inquiry into the Affairs of All Cooperative Unions in Uganda*, 1967.

79. Mr. Nekyon, Parliamentary Debates, February 6, 1968, The Minor Crops Bill, 2nd reading, *Hansard*, vols. 78–81, p. 2695.

80. President's speech, December 1, 1965, Uganda Parliamentary Debates, *Hansard*, vols. 51–54.

81. Mr. Nekyon, Uganda Parliamentary Debates, September 14, 1965, *Hansard*, vols. 51–54, p. 3357.

82. Questions and answers in Parliament, September 22, 1970, *Hansard*, vol. 104, p. 3.

83. Mr. Chowdhry, Uganda Parliamentary Debates, March 8, 1965, *Hansard*, vols, 41–45, p. 1280.

84. The Minor Crops Bill, Uganda Parliamentary Debates, February 6, 1968, *Hansard*, vols. 78–81, p. 2665.

85. NTC files; quoted in Parsons, "The Africanization of Trade in Uganda," p. 15.

86. Ibid., p. 15.

87. Ibid., p. 16.

88. Mr. Mugeni, Uganda Parliamentary Debates, February 6, 1968, *Hansard*, vols. 78–81, p. 2700.

89. Mr. Onama, Uganda Parliamentary Debates, February 6, 1968, *Hansard*, vols. 78–81, p. 2695.

90. Mr. Magara, Uganda Parliamentary Debates, September 30, 1970, *Hansard*, pp. 104–106.

91. Paul G. Clark, *Development Planning in East Africa*, p. 52.

92. The President's Communication from the Chair of the National Assembly on April 20, 1970; in A. M. Obote, *The Common Man's Charter*, p. 26.

93. All figures from *Uganda's Third Five-Year Development Plan, 1971/72–1975/76*, Entebbe: Government Printer, p. 36.

94. Colonial Office, *The British Territories in East and Central Africa, 1945–1950*, p. 41.

95. "Uganda Bank Pleads for Confidence," in *Political Africa* (Ghana), vol. 2, no. 5 (May 1971), p. 16.

96. *Uganda's Third Five-Year Development Plan*, p. 36.

97. Obote, pp. 11–12.

98. UG, Statistics Division, Ministry of Planning and Economic Development, *Background to the Budget, 1970–71*, p. 49.

99. Mr. Kalema, Uganda Parliamentary Debates, October 5, 1970, *Hansard*, vol. 104, p. 186.

100. Yash Tandon, "The Pragmatic Industrialist," in Becker and Madhvani, eds., p. 17.

101. Quoted in ibid.

102. See *Uganda Argus*, May 2, 1970, p. 1.

103. *Uganda Argus*, May 7, 1970, p. 4.

104. "U.K. Companies in Uganda Hopeful Despite Coup," *The Times* (London), January 26, 1971, p. 15.

105. A. M. O'Connor, *Railways and Development in Uganda*, p. 84.

106. *Uganda Argus*, May 7, 1970, p. 4.

107. Mr. Latim, Uganda Parliamentary Debates, February 24, 1969, *Hansard*, vols. 87–89, p. 364.

108. See Issa Shivji, *Class Struggles in Tanzania*.

109. Mr. Latim, Uganda Parliamentary Debates, February 24, 1969, *Hansard*, vols. 87–89, p. 364.

110. *Uganda Argus*, May 2, 1970, p. 1.

111. *Uganda Argus*, May 24, 1970, p. 1.

112. *Uganda Argus*, May 7, 1970, p. 4.

113. Parsons, "Wholesale and Retail Trade and Traders in Uganda," p. 8.

114. In Uganda Parliamentary Debates, October 5, 1970, *Hansard*, vol. 104, p. 186.

115. Quoted in "Thought of the Month: Corruption in East African Public Life," *East Africa Journal*, November 1967, p. 7.

116. Parsons, "Wholesale and Retail Trade and Traders in Uganda," p. 8.

117. Mr. Mugeni, Uganda Parliamentary Debates, March 13, 1969, *Hansard*, vols. 87–89, p. 597.

118. Mr. Magara, Uganda Parliamentary Debates, September 30, 1970, *Hansard*, vol. 104, p. 104–106.

119. Ibid.

120. Uganda Parliamentary Debates, April 24, 1967, *Hansard*, vol. 82, p. 3197.

121. Ibid.

122. Uganda Parliamentary Debates, July 23, 1970, *Hansard*, pp. 198–201.

123. Mr. D. A. Patel, Uganda Parliamentary Debates, June 24, 1965, *Hansard*, vols. 46–50, p. 2348.

124. Mr. Bataringaya, Uganda Parliamentary Debates, April 26, 1967, *Hansard*, vols. 67–70, p. 1871.

125. Figures given by the Indian High Commission in Uganda at a conference in New Delhi, December 22, 1969; quoted in Douglas Tilbe, *East African Asians*, p. 4.

126. *Uganda Argus*, May 7, 1970, p. 4.

127. Ibid.

128. Tilbe, p. 5.

129. Jack Parsons, "Wholesale and Retail Trade and Traders in Uganda," p. 9.

130. *Uganda Argus*, December 14, 1970, p. 1.

131. See Scott, *The Development of Trade Unions in Uganda*.

132. *Uganda Argus*, April 23, 1968, p. 1.

133. *Uganda Argus*, May 18, 1968, p. 1.

134. *Uganda Argus*, April 23, 1968, p. 1.

135. *Uganda Argus*, June 17, 1969, p. 1.

136. Clark, p. 19.

137. E. R. Rado, "Review of Walter Elkan's 'Migrants and Proletarians,' " p. 83.

138. *Uganda Argus*, April 26, 1965, p. 1.

139. *Uganda Argus*, October 6, 1970, p. 1.

140. *Uganda Argus*, April 26, 1965, p. 1.

141. All figures from Michael Tribe, "Uganda 1971: An Economic Background," pp. 19–20.

142. *Uganda Argus*, November 13, 1965; quoted in Akiki B. Mujaju, "The Fusion of the Spiritual and the Temporal." Although a number of empirical facts in this discussion on religious conflict are taken from Mujaju's paper, I am in total disagreement with his thesis. He contends that "the extent to which the Church, as an organization, brings pressure to bear on the political systems on matters internal to the Church itself is largely a function of its internal organizational and authority relationships" (p. 7). Lacking an analysis of the "political system" and the contradictions in it, he is in fact unable to see the relation between the spiritual and the temporal.

143. *Daily Nation*, December 10, 1970, p. 1; quoted in Mujaju, pp. 15–16.

144. Ibid., p. 17.

145. *Uganda Argus*, October 7, 1968, p. 1.

146. Uganda Parliamentary Debates, February 9, 1968, *Hansard*, vols. 78–81, p. 2781.

147. *Uganda Argus*, August 22, 1970, p. 3; quoted in Mujaju, p. 40.
148. Michael Lofchie, "The Uganda Coup: Class Action by the Military," pp. 19–35.
149. Ali A. Mazrui, "Ethnic Stratification and the Military-Agrarian Complex: The Uganda Case."
150. On this point see Samir Amin, *Neo-Colonialism in West Africa* and *Maghreb in the Modern World*, p. 146–147.
151. *Africa Report*, December 1966, p. 37.
152. In "Ethnic Stratification and the Military-Agrarian Complex."
153. *Africa Report*, December 1966, p. 37.
154. *New York Times*, January 27, 1971, p. 3.
155. See David Martin, *General Amin*, pp. 25, 34, 43–44, 158–159; and "Middle East Stakes in the Heart of Africa."

9
After the Coup

The Asian Expulsion

After the coup, the leadership of the bureaucratic petty bourgeoisie took refuge in Dar-es-Salaam. With a core of some 600 soldiers who had escaped at the time of the coup, and another 1,000 or so in the Sudan, training camps were established, awaiting a suitable opportunity to make a bid for a return to power. True to its class character, the only form of armed opposition the bureaucratic petty bourgeoisie could consider was that of an invasion. Its principle was not to unite with the people and bring their interests to the fore, but to champion its own interests and hope the people would remain passive bystanders. It could not champion the interests of the people, for they were objectively antagonistic to its own; neither could it arm the people without fearing the possibility of their independent organizational expression and thus the loss of its own leading role. It should not be the least surprising, then, that in its hour of need it turned, not to the people of Uganda, but to friendly ruling classes elsewhere. Nor should it be surprising that as its instrument it sought to train another professional mercenary armed force and invade.

This fact had a decisive impact on Amin's policy, in both its external and internal dimensions. In his foreign policy, in spite of close relations with Israel, Amin continued the rapprochement Obote had begun with the Sudan. A formal agreement was concluded in 1971. When their supplies from northern Uganda dried up, a section of the ex-Anyanya guerrillas joined Amin's military forces. Amin's reward was the removal of Obote's military base in the Sudan. The effect on Israeli-Ugandan relations was immediate and it formed the backdrop of the expulsion of the Israeli mission from Uganda.

But Obote's armed camps in Tanzania remained. In light of this fact, the existing factionalism within the army assumed primary significance. It was necessary that it be immediately and effectively resolved. Shortly after the coup Amin ordered a major recruitment drive for the armed forces. In three months the army more than doubled as about 10,000 men were recruited. The core of the new recruits were some 4,000 Sudanese ex-Anyanya fighters, along with a sprinkling of former Zairian freedom fighters. The bulk of the remainder came from Amin's own West Nile District; 40 percent of these were Muslims.[1] In sum, the new army was primarily a *mercenary* force. The greatest care was taken to ensure that the condition of their survival was the continuation of Amin's rule.

Amin then set about methodically resolving the factional split within the army through the physical elimination of the opposing faction. Thousands of Acholi and Langi officers were systematically murdered in a wave of massacres. A few escaped to Tanzania to tell the grim details.[2]* The new order had received its birthmark, stamped in cold blood.

In the decade between independence and the coup, the contradiction between the petty bourgeoisie as a whole and Asian capital remained secondary, while the struggle within the petty bourgeoisie was resolved. In fact, the contradiction between the two fractions of the petty bourgeoisie (the governing bureaucracy on the one hand and the kulaks and traders on the other) was brought out precisely by the question of *how* the state was to be used to undermine the base of the Asian

---

* It is extremely difficult to verify the extent of the massacres. One attempt to do so by two American journalists, Nicholas Stroh and Robert Siedle, resulted in their murder at the Mbarara barracks in July 1971. The only sources on these massacres are the few victims who have managed to escape.

commercial bourgeoisie and hence strengthen that of the petty bourgeoisie. The point was that there were two alternate methods of using state power: to create state private property* or to create individual private property. The method adopted would strengthen either the section of the class based within the state apparatus or that located outside of it. Objectively, then, the contradiction within the petty bourgeoisie had to be resolved before the contradiction with the commercial bourgeoisie could be dealt with. Its resolution was the coup. Then, after the state power had consolidated its coercive apparatus, the contradiction between the petty bourgeoisie and Asian capital (both the Asian petty and commercial bourgeoisies) emerged as the principal contradiction. Amin brought the same decisive resolution to this contradiction that he had to factionalism in the army. Just as the Obote faction in the army was physically eliminated, so these two classes were physically expelled.

As we have seen, the Asian expulsion was not the first in Uganda's neocolonial history. It was preceded by that of Kenyan workers during the Obote years. The expulsion of entire classes or sections of classes, nationally based but nonnational in origin, has also been seen in countries other than Uganda. The expulsion of nonnationals, as a political event, has punctuated the period following independence in a number of African countries. Its objective basis, in the context of a dependent capitalist economy, is the failure to expand the productive forces and thus the economic base of the appropriating classes. Given a relatively stagnant economy, with little more than simple reproduction of the productive forces taking place, the secondary contradictions among the propertied classes intensify. For the working class, the crisis of accumulation of the propertied classes appears as an unemployment crisis. To make room at the top or the bottom, where there exist nonnational classes (or sections of classes) like the Kenyan workers or the Indian commercial bourgeoisie in Uganda, expulsion becomes one way of resolving the crisis of the dependent ruling class. The official ideology produced and propagated as an explanation of the

---

* By *private* property is here meant class property, whether the legal form is that of state ownership or individual ownership.

event—be it racial, national chauvinist, or tribal chauvinist—
should not obscure the class content and the objective basis of
the expulsion as a political phenomenon.

But let us follow the events to their conclusion.[3] On June 28,
1971, the general assured the African traders that his government would do everything in its power to place the economy in
their hands. On October 7, a census of the Asian population only
was ordered, and every Asian was required to carry a "green
card." On December 7, following the "Asian census," Amin put a
stamp of finality on the noncitizen status of many Asian traders
by canceling the applications of over 12,000 Asians for Ugandan
citizenship. At the same time, he called together a conference of
"Asian community leaders" and accused them of economic
malpractice, of sabotaging government policies, and of failing to
integrate into the community—by which he meant (of course)
the petty bourgeoisie community. Threats to the commercial
bourgeoisie, articulated in a racial form, continued. On January
5, 1972, Amin warned thirteen representatives of the Asian
community that "Uganda is not an Indian colony." A week later
he said he would like to see Ugandans owning businesses on
Kampala's main street. Meanwhile, the state power attempted
to use its economic apparatus against the commercial bourgeoisie. On May 9, the minister of finance was instructed to tell the
Bank of Uganda to give available money to Africans and not to
Asians. But Uganda was a neocolony. Commercial financing was
controlled, as we shall see, by British banking capital, not by the
Bank of Uganda. The process reached its culminating point on
August 9 when—addressing the Annual Conference of Cooperative Societies in Uganda, a congregation of the petty bourgeoisie—Amin proclaimed that noncitizen Asians would have to
leave Uganda in three months.

In the first few days after the announcement, Amin vacillated
between expelling all Asians or just Asian commercial capital.
Publicly, this was articulated in his indecision over whether or
not to exempt professionals from the expulsion order. Another
issue was legal. An expulsion confined to noncitizens would
leave the bulk of big Asian capital untouched; furthermore, it
might also leave this section of the Asian bourgeoisie in control
of the material assets of the entire class once the process came

to a conclusion. Once this was realized, the class struggle lost its veil of legality. Political actions were shorn of their legal forms and the class content lay bare for all to see. The citizen Asians, asked to queue in order to confirm the validity of their citizenship, found their passports and certificates torn up. Eventually all Asians were expelled. Neither citizen nor professional remained.

The process of expulsion highlighted the social composition of Amin's new army. Apart from the estimated 4,000 ex-Anyanya and other mercenaries, most of the 10,000 new recruits were either from West Nile or were Muslims. The Muslim Nubians in East Africa are predominantly urban; their social origin is from among the urban unemployed, living on the fringes of respectable society, partaking of the social product through either temporary employment or temporary crime. Newly recruited, these soldiers were not yet subject to a disciplined organization. While their social origin did not affect their political behavior, it did determine their social behavior. The expulsion was seized upon as an opportunity for private accumulation. Armed greed led to kidnapping, extortion, theft, and even murder.

The theft of Asian property, even at its most chaotic, followed an established pattern. Everything the Asians had to leave behind was guarded carefully by the army and police officials. Any potential looters were shot dead on sight. Amin's orders were that the Asians' property be guarded as ruthlessly as the Asians themselves were being expelled. The same material interest was at stake in both cases, for once the Asians had departed a large part of their businesses, houses, and cars would be legitimately acquired by the upper sections of the army and of the petty bourgeoisie. It was here that contradictory interests between army officials, potential members of the property-owning petty bourgeoisie, and the rank-and-file became evident. The soldiers realized that when the time came for the legal allocation of Asian property, the sun would shine only on high-ranking officials. If ordinary soldiers were to share in the spoils, their opportunity for doing so was before the Asians' departure, and to do this they had to resort to loot and plunder, unprotected by the halo of bourgeois legality.

It is tempting to see in this process an historical similarity, the reoccurrence of what Marx described as the "primitive accumulation of capital" in England, "a set of events written in the annals of mankind in letters of blood and fire." The difference could be ascribed to an originality of forms: in England, embezzlement of church funds, robbery on the high seas, and the expulsion of peasants from the land; in Uganda, embezzlement of state funds, robbery on the highways, and the expulsion of the Asians.* But the analogy would be highly limited and formal, and thus quite misleading. Its limits are those of the Ugandan petty bourgeoisie, constrained by the historical and international context of its development. The petty bourgeoisie is not an autonomous class with effective control over the use of the nationally generated economic surplus; on the contrary, it is a dependent class, an intermediary in the exploitation of the neocolony by the centers of imperial capitalism. What it amasses is not capital, but wealth; its is not the productive accumulation of an industrialist but the unproductive riches of a merchant. Its riches are not destined to be transformed into means of production, thereby expanding the productive base of the economy; it will merely lubricate the export-import economy, at most permitting the assembly of a few luxury goods internally, thereby facilitating the metropolitan-style consumption of this intermediate class. This is not the bourgeoisie of capitalist development; it is the petty bourgeoisie of capitalist underdevelopment. Its objective constraints, the historically created international links of the neocolony, were brought into the open during the process of expulsion.

In October 1972, when Asian businesses started closing down en masse, the main streets of Kampala were lined with signs saying "Property of Barclays Bank D.C.O." or "Property of Standard Bank." Financial connections usually hidden in small print in the text of a contract or an agreement were now advertised for all to see. The fact was that the Indian commercial bourgeoisie was still a dependent class. Functionally, it lubricated the export-import economy; financially, it was heavily reliant on and subordinate to British banking capital. It was

---

* To other specifically English forms, slavery and colonial plunder, it is difficult to find even *apparent* parallels in Uganda.

clear that unless the state moved against the British banks, the primary beneficiary of the Asian expulsion would be the British big bourgeoisie, not the Ugandan petty bourgeoisie. Thus there began the second phase of the "economic war." Confined to British capital, it focused on banking capital but extended to its weakest section, the plantations.

Whereas the first phase of the economic war nationalized the compradore sector (the commercial sector of the export-import economy), replacing the Asian compradore class with an African one, its second phase abrogated the primary dependence of the economy on a single metropolitan power (Britain) and diversified this dependence. The new international friends of the Amin government were the Soviet Union and France (through Libya), who were the primary suppliers of arms; Saudi Arabia and Libya, which gave small but critical grants at times of crisis, such as the time of the severe foreign-exchange shortage in the months prior to the scheduled OAU conference in Kampala; and increasingly, India and Pakistan. While Pakistani teachers and technicians have provided the necessary personnel to replace those who have departed, Indian capital (specifically, the House of Birla) is expanding its operations in the country's manufacturing sector through both investments (a jute mill) and management contracts (Birla is currently negotiating management contracts on the bulk of what used to be the Madhvani industrial empire).* While the internal expression of the unilateral dependence on British capital was the colonially nurtured Asian bourgeoisie, the expression of multilateralized dependence on international capitalism is the postindependence nationalist petty bourgeoisie, which is fast expanding into a commercial bourgeoisie.

But the rise of the petty bourgeoisie to the position of a commercial bourgeoisie has not been smooth. Its political

---

* Although Amin first attempted to get technical assistance from Germany, and later from Japan, exploratory studies showed that the machinery used in much of the manufacturing industry (such as the sugar factory at Kakira) was so dated that spare parts and technicians could only be found in the Indian subcontinent. The technical structure of Uganda industry was thus one factor compelling Amin to turn to Indian and Pakistani technicians and equipment to avert a serious drop in manufacturing production.

weakness, evident in its inability to come to power through an independent struggle, meant its ascent to power through an armed coup. The expression of this political weakness was the strength of Amin's own individuality. In fact, the weakness of the petty bourgeoisie as a class remains necessary for the survival of Amin's power as the personalization of class rule. Amin's policy has precisely the effect of preventing the consolidation of the petty bourgeoisie, and thus its rise to the stature of a class that governs for itself.

Hence the continuation and even the institutionalization of terror in Uganda since the Asian expulsion. The petty bourgeoisie advances as a class, but not necessarily as individuals. The rule of private property is consolidated with each passing day, but there is not the same security for any particular expression of it. Businessmen survive—in fact, they prosper. But it is not rare for a businessman to be killed or his property to be appropriated.* The result has been a rapid erosion of Amin's own social base. The petty bourgeoisie, ardent supporters of Amin at the time of the 1971 coup and the 1972 expulsion, were delighted with his rule when it brought them the fruit of their wildest dreams, but now they suddenly find the taste turning bitter in their mouths. As its internal social base rapidly disintegrates, the state power has attempted to secure its rule by transforming its military apparatus in to a nonnational mercenary force. While the core of its army is the disciplined ex-Anyanya guerrillas, the provider of arms is imperialism. Today, the Amin dictatorship is simply a dictatorship of arms.

Amin, however, is caught in an insoluble contradiction. While officially encouraged terror prevents the consolidation of a

---

* The terror, of course, is not directed only at the members of the petty bourgeoisie. Its target includes any potential class opposition to the present order, and any particular opposition to the core of the petty bourgeoisie, the Baganda petty bourgeoisie. Individual progressives of any hue (from university-based progressives to liberals like the university vice-chancellor, Mr. Kalimuzo), are killed unless they flee. So are prominent members of the Baganda Catholic hierarchy, those who traditionally opposed the petty bourgeois Lukiko, from Benedicto Kiwanuka (chief justice and leader of the DP) to Father Kiggude (editor of the liberal Catholic paper *Munno*). Thus the ambivalent attitude of the petty bourgeoisie to official violence: the same violence that periodically terrorizes its members also eliminates its historical opposition.

commercial bourgeoisie, it also prevents the stabilization of the economy. Price rises and commodity scarcities become a daily phenomenon. The result, increasingly, is economic retaliation by the cash-crop growing peasantry and a refusal to sell crop surpluses on the market as spiraling inflation renders paper money worthless—Uganda's version of the Soviet scissors crisis of the 1920s. Such an economic crisis could fast turn into a political crisis, for both the state power and the petty bourgeoisie. On the other hand, if the petty bourgeoisie is allowed to consolidate its base in the interests of stabilizing the economy, this will undermine the objective basis of Amin's power. Amin's dominant role is possible precisely because it is necessary—because the petty bourgeoisie is too weak to rule as a class. A consolidated commercial bourgeoisie would mean the substitution of class rule for individual rule. In such circumstances, Amin's role would diminish drastically. Far more likely, rendered unfit precisely because of his present exaggerated stature, Amin would be replaced by another individual situated much more closely within the ruling class.

But the political weakness of the petty bourgeoisie also makes another process possible: the integration of individual members of the army officer corps into the ranks of the petty bourgeoisie as its material base expands. Unlike the precoup governing bureaucracy, the army officers are not transforming themselves into a class by developing an independent economic base. Quite the contrary: members of the officer corps are being integrated into the emerging commercial bourgeoisie, and their individual interests are beginning to coincide with its class interests, even though their recent origin is the armed forces, their ethnic origin the West Nile, and their religious affiliation Islam. Amin, the very leader who made possible their new class position, now appears as the primary obstacle to consolidating this position. Given their origin in the armed forces, the resolution of this contradiction may well be another coup. Numerous attempts to assassinate Amin in the past year would seem to bear out this prediction. And yet, what is striking is the relative stability of state power in the short run. The political contradiction has been late in maturing precisely because the economic crisis has been late in developing. The aftermath of the Asian expulsion was not just a decline in export-crop production by the peasantry; just as important was a far more rapid drop in luxury import consumption. With the expulsion of the Asian commercial bourgeoisie, the primary consumer of conspicuous-consumption goods until late 1972, there was a dramatic change in the structure of consumption in the neocolony. Even though the economic base of the petty bourgeoisie has expanded, the change in its consumption habits has been relatively slow. The fall in export production has been more than matched by that in import consumption. Had it not been for the phenomenal expansion in arms imports, the economic crisis—and with it the political crisis—would have been even further delayed.

But the rule of arms has brought into being a tendency of far greater significance in the longer run. This is the intensified appropriation of the producers in the countryside. The tendency in some western regions has been toward the creation of a landless peasantry: a petty bourgeois or an army officer, with the aid of a group of soldiers, evicts small holders from their plots and encloses their land as private property. Elsewhere, a version of warlordism is becoming evident. The local army commanders, in alliance with the local cooperatives, forcibly appropriate both food and industrial crops from the peasants, consume the former and export the latter to either Kenya or Ruanda, circumventing state export agencies and hence state taxation. Under the protective umbrella of imperialism there emerges both a greedy commercial bourgeoisie with an insatiable appetite, unable to challenge imperialist appropriation but dissatisfied with the crumbs on the table, and a landless peasantry whose wretchedness is a recent historical creation. Its ranks expanding with the passage of time, this appropriated rural mass, a natural ally of the urban proletariat, becomes fertile ground for organization by a revolutionary party. Whatever the form of appropriation of the producers, rural and urban, exploitation no longer wears an alien face and its class character emerges in the open. At the same time, those who organized the workers in the years after independence, along with the exiled intelligentsia, after the failure of instant panaceas and the reckless invasions of the two years after the coup, have begun to recognize the necessity of a prolonged struggle and an organization that can sustain it. The order creates its own gravediggers, and the time of reckoning draws near.

The Neocolonial State

The neocolonial state was not created at independence. It was, in fact, inherited by the petty bourgeoisie from its colonial mentor, the metropolitan bourgeoisie. To understand the nature of the neocolonial state, then, it is necessary to recapitulate our discussion of the colonial state.

The colonial state represented an absentee ruling class, the metropolitan bourgeoisie. As a result, it also performed functions that in an independent country would be the preserve of the ruling class. At the level of the economy, not only did it regulate production, but it determined its very nature, consequently creating the economic structures of the underdeveloped economy and with it the necessary class relations. Thus, the overdevelopment, as Hamza Alavi has observed,[4] of its administrative (the colonial bureaucracy) and coercive (the colonial army and police) apparatus.

It is also critical to grasp the nature of the colonial state at the level of politics.* Although it dominated the economic processes in the colony, there was a marked absence of political process in the colonial state. Since it represented an absentee ruling class, there was no need for political institutions that would mediate and peacefully resolve contradictions between different sections of the ruling class, at the same time making possible a class democracy. Political institutions were thus not an integral part of the colonial state apparatus; they were added at independence. In neocolonial countries, parliament is a constitutional innovation; its structure is the result of constitutional conferences immediately prior to independence. The political apparatus lacked a basis in the history of the neocolony.

---

* It should be clear, as it was earlier, that here we are speaking of nonsettler colonies. Settler colonies (for example, Kenya) did possess a political state apparatus. Kenya is also the only petty-bourgeois state in East Africa that retains some measure of class democracy.

Because of these characteristics, while classes form in the colonial period and a class struggle develops, as Cabral recognized, this struggle is "muted": "In the colonial period, it is the colonial state which commands history." [5] This muted class struggle breaks out into the open only with independence. While the *content* of colonial appropriation persists after independence—the national economy remains integrated with and subordinate to the metropolitan economy—the *form* of this relation changes: the underdeveloped economy is now supervised by an indigenous ruling class.

The ruling class in independent Uganda was the petty bourgeoisie. Because imperialist exploitation of the neocolony remained—unlike in the case of developed capitalism—this ruling class had a weak economic base and was fragmented at the level of politics: the "underdeveloped" petty bourgeoisie is not a consolidated class. It forms a class only inasmuch as its different sections—traders, bureaucrats, and kulaks—unite politically when confronted by a common class opposition. However temporary the unity, a shared class interest begets a common class organization. Such was the case in Uganda when the petty bourgeoisie came together to form a coalition government against the bureaucratic chiefs. The unity of the opposition persisted for a few years after independence because it was faced with yet another opposition: the workers. But once this opposition was crushed, the common organization dissolved and different sections assumed their relative independence, each a social force with a distinct organization and ideology. Their weak economic base exacerbated an already intense struggle between the separate petty bourgeois factions.

The fragmentation of the petty bourgeoisie has an objective basis in its weak economic base. The crisis of accumulation of the underdeveloped economy is at the same time the crisis of accumulation of the petty bourgeois ruling class, emphasizing the critical role of the state in the very process of accumulation. It is the struggle within the petty bourgeoisie that determines the method of accumulation and the manner of appropriation of the surplus. Given that it is located both within the state (state bureaucracy) and outside of it (kulaks, traders), the petty bourgeoisie has two alternative methods of accumulation: to use the state to create public property, which the petty bourgeoisie would then control *indirectly* through its control over the state; or to use the state to expand individual private property, which the petty bourgeoisie would control *directly* through ownership. The former necessitates an ideology that justifies the use of state economic action, of nationalizations. This ideology is socialism stripped of its emphasis on class struggle, robbed of its political (class) content, and put forth as an economic ideology. Such is the birth of petty bourgeois socialism, one version of which was Obote's "Common Man's Charter."

As the fragmentation of the ruling class intensifies, class democracy disintegrates. Parliament is dissolved. The opposition is jailed. Elections are scrapped or reinstituted in a controlled version. Preventive detention becomes law. All those political institutions, the constitutional innovations that were supposed to mediate the struggle between contending factions within the ruling class, are dissolved one after another. Any pretensions of class democracy vanish. Its political apparatus dissolved, the state emerges as a brute coercive force.

It is at this juncture that the neocolonial state most clearly resembles the colonial state. It is through its two arms, the bureaucracy and the army, its inheritance from the metropolitan bourgeoisie, that the state penetrates civil society at every pore. But it is the army, the coercive institution, that becomes almost synonymous with the state. Its technological sophistication and coercive capacity, however, are not an expression of the level of development of the productive forces in the national economy. Quite the contrary. Its means of coercion come as "aid" from its imperial protectors, as does the training of its officers.

Their opposition no longer mediated, the contending factions become locked in combat.* The governing faction, that faction

---

* The case of Kenya would seem to be an exception, for there the fragmentation of the petty bourgeoisie was less important than the integration of its various sections: the bureaucrat acquires the shop of the departing Asian businessman and buys land in the countryside; the son of the kulak becomes a bureaucrat; the African businessman purchases agricultural property. Two factors seem to have made this integration possible. First is the overwhelming presence of multinational capital and its predominant interest in a stable

which immediately occupies the positions of state power, attempts to create its own independent economic base—that is, it attempts to become a class by itself. The struggle has now reached full maturity and becomes one of life and death. As we saw in the case of Uganda, one form of resolution of the fragmentation within the ruling class is the armed coup. A cursory glance at the politics of most African countries shows that it is also the most frequent form of resolution.

It is the economic base of the faction that emerges victorious that defines the political character of the state. In Africa today, the petty bourgeois regimes can be roughly divided into those that use the state to create public private property (the so-called progressive regimes) and those that do so to create individual private property (the "reactionary" regimes). In Uganda, the 1971 coup represented the fall of the "progressive" petty bourgeoisie and the rise of the "reactionary" petty bourgeoisie. This difference in the manner of appropriation of surplus conditions the nature of future class formation. With the creation of state property, the dominant class that emerges is a bureaucratic bourgeoisie; when the emphasis is on the use of the state to create individual private property, the petty bourgeoisie transforms itself into a commercial bourgeoisie. Given the nature of neocolonialism, however, both are *dependent* classes. Neither is able to qualitatively transform the productive forces within the economy, and thereby solve the crisis of underdeveloped capitalism. Whatever its ideology or its foreign policy, neither class can be characterized as progressive in a historical sense.

The Ugandan petty bourgeoisie, for all its similarities to other neocolonial situations, is also a specific case. So far as other East African petty bourgeois classes are concerned, the colonial state was literally handed down to them at independence; this was

---

economy and political order. Second, the Kenyan petty bourgeoisie is the only one in East Africa to have experienced the spectre of an armed organization of the oppressed *independent* of its leadership—the Mau Mau armed resistance of the 1950s in the Kikuyu highlands. While the squatters formed the backbone of the Mau Mau, the petty bourgeoisie joined the "loyalist" Home Guard. Today, the Kenyan petty bourgeoisie, most distrustful of the masses, is even more mindful of the need for class unity.

less the case in Uganda. There, the territory controlled by the petty bourgeois state was demarcated during the colonial period. Here, this process was not completed until after independence. The unified territory of Uganda was not born until after the 1966–1967 crisis. Its birth was the result of intense political struggles: the petty bourgeois state played an important role in its own consolidation. The result is that the Ugandan petty bourgeoisie is politically a little less flabby and a little more decisive than its counterparts in the rest of East Africa. It is this historical circumstance that explains the fact that in Uganda, much more than in Kenya or Tanzania, the class struggles have been fought out to their decisive conclusion. This is so whether one considers the 1966–1967 crisis, the 1970 expulsion of Kenyan workers, the 1971 coup and the following massacres, or the 1972 Asian expulsion. It is in this sense that Amin, a person who possesses moments of decisiveness most uncharacteristic of petty bourgeois leaders, is a product of Uganda's history.*

Today, as the Amin clique loses its social base within the emerging commercial bourgeoisie, it wields power through sheer force of arms. But these sophisticated weapons of destruction are not a testimony to the development of national productive forces; they are a timely loan from its imperial watchdogs. Thus comes to light the international dimension of the class struggle. The struggle against class rule in Uganda is not simply a struggle against the Amin dictatorship; it is principally a struggle against imperialism.

---

* Thus, although his base in the Ugandan petty bourgeoisie has eroded, Amin still captures the imagination of the various petty bourgeois formations on the African continent. In sharp contrast to the empty rhetoric of "African socialism" that has marked the limits of the "progressive" regimes in Africa, Amin's "economic war" possessed content. More than any other event, it was the Asian expulsion that established his reputation as a "man of action." In this too, as we have shown, Amin reflects the historical specificity of the Ugandan petty bourgeoisie.

Notes

1. *The Times* (London), January 27, 1971, p. 2.
2. *The Observer*, December 23, 1972; *The Guardian* (London), January 19, 1973; and Colin Legum, ed., *Africa: Contemporary Record*, p. 3272.
3. This narrative follows L. Stevens, "Uganda Since the Coup," pp. 15–16, and was checked against the relevant issues of *Uganda Argus*. See also *East Africa Journal*, February 1972, pp. 2–5.
4. Hamza Alavi, "The Post-Colonial State."
5. In "Brief Analysis of the Social Structure in Guinea," in Cabral, ed., *Revolution in Guinea*, p. 69.

Bibliography

Unpublished Theses

Akingbade, Peter Idowu. "The History of the Kingdom of Toro from its Foundation to 1928." University of East Africa, M.A., 1967.

Bowles, B. D. "Nationalism in Uganda, 1950–1962." Kampala: Makerere University, Ph.D., 1971.

Carter, Felice. "Education in Uganda, 1894–1945." London: Ph.D., 1967.

DeSouza, F. R. S. "Indian Political Organizations in East Africa." London: London School of Economics, Ph.D., 1959.

Ehrlich, Cyril. "The Marketing of Cotton in Uganda, 1900–1950: A Case Study of Colonial Government Economic Policy." London: Ph.D., 1958.

Evans, Anne F. M. "The Africanization of the Civil Service in Uganda: A Problem of Decolonization." Manchester: University of Manchester, M.A., 1964.

Fowler, A. H. "The Role of International Public Finance in the Economic Development of Uganda." Leeds, England: University of Leeds, Ph.D., 1969.

Hines, H. "The Role of the Foreign Office in the Affairs of East Africa: 1883–1895." London: M.A., 1955.

Hutton, Caroline R. "Unemployment and Labour Migration in Uganda." University of East Africa, Ph.D., 1968.

Loxley, John. "The Development of the Monetary and Financial System of the East African Currency Area, 1950–1964." Leeds, England: University of Leeds, Ph.D., 1966.

McGregor, Gordon Peter. "The History of King's College, Budo,

Uganda, in Relation to the Development of Education in Uganda." University of East Africa, M.A., 1965.

Manners, A. J. "Social Stratification and Political Change in Two East African Kingdoms." London: University of London, M. Phil., 1971.

Motani, N. A. "The Growth of an African Civil Service in Uganda, 1912–1940." London: Ph.D., 1972.

Obol-Ochala, James Y. "Customary Land Law and the Economic Development of Uganda." Dar es Salaam: L.L.M., 1971.

Okereke, O. "The Role of the Cooperative Movement in the Economic Development of Uganda." University of East Africa, M.A., 1968.

Othieno, Titus Maurice. "An Economic Study of Peasant Farming in Two Areas of Bukedi District, Uganda." University of East Africa, M.Sc., 1967.

Sheriff, A. M. H. "The Rise of a Commercial Empire: An Aspect of the Economic History of Zanzibar, 1770–1873." London: Ph.D., 1971.

Ssekamwa, John Crysostom. "The Development of the Buganda Treasury and Its Relationship with the British Protectorate Government, 1900–1955." Kampala: Makerere University, M.A., 1970.

Watson, Tom. "A History of C.M.S. High Schools in Uganda, 1900–1924: The Education of a Protestant Elite." University of East Africa, Ph.D., 1968.

Wood, A. W. "Educational Policy and Social Development in Uganda, 1935–1964." London: M. Phil., 1967.

Unpublished Articles

Beattie, J. H. M., "The Kibanja System of Land Tenure in Bunyoro," East African Institute for Social Research (EAISR) Conference Paper, Kampala: Makerere University (mimeo), February 1953.

Bere, R. M. "Northern Province: Uganda," memorandum for the Royal Commission 1953–55, Kampala: Makerere University Archives (mimeo), February 6, 1953.

Brett, E. A. "Problems of Cooperative Development in Uganda." UN Research Institute for Social Development, Geneva (mimeo), 1970.

Campbell, Horace. "And the Africans Organized to Enter the Marketplace." Kampala: Makerere University (mimeo), 1974.

————. "A Week in the Second Republic of Uganda, February 5–12, 1973: The Rise of the Lumpen Militariat." Kampala (mimeo), 1973.

Ehrlich, Cyril. "The Poverty of Uganda, 1893–1903." Makerere Institute for Social Research (MISR), Kampala (mimeo), n.d.

Gershenberg, I. "The Impact of Independence on the Role of Commercial Banking in Uganda's Economic Development, 1960–1968." MISR, Kampala: EDRP No. 166 (mimeo), n.d.

Gor, Simeon. "Country Study of Uganda." MISR, Kampala (mimeo), n.d.

Hunt, Diana. "Some Aspects of Agricultural Credit in Uganda." MISR, Kampala: EDRP No. 105 (mimeo), August 26, 1966.

Mafeje, Archie. "The Fallacy of Dual Economies Revisited—A Case for East, Central and South Africa." The Hague (mimeo), 1974.

Mazrui, Ali A. "Ethnic Stratification and the Military-Agrarian Complex: The Uganda Case." University Social Science Conference (USSC) Paper, Dar es Salaam (mimeo), 1974.

Mujaju, Akiki B. "The Demise of the UPC–YL and the Rise of NUYO." Kampala: Makerere University, September 9, 1971.

Mujaju, Akiki B. "The Fusion of the Spiritual and the Temporal: The Crisis of Church Institutions in Uganda." Kampala: Makerere University (mimeo), 1972.

Mukwaya, A. B. "The Rise of the Uganda African Farmers' Union in Buganda, 1947–1949." EAISR Conference Paper, Kampala: Makerere University (mimeo), 1957.

Oram, Nigel. "Why Indians Came to East Africa." EAISR, unpublished monograph, Kampala: Makerere University, n.d.

Parsons, Jack. "The Africanization of Trade in Uganda: Background to and Perspectives on Government Policy." Kampala: Makerere University, n.d.

————. "Wholesale and Retail Trade and Traders in Uganda: A Survey Report." Kampala: Makerere University (mimeo), n.d.

Perlman, M. L. "Land Tenure in Toro," EAISR Conference Paper, Kampala: Makerere University (mimeo), January 1962.

Ramchandani, R. R. "Asians' Role in the Cotton Industry of Uganda— A Study in Economic History." MISR, Kampala (mimeo), n.d.

Sakarai, Lawrence J. "Merchant Trade with and Settlement in East Africa." Bombay: University of Bombay (mimeo), n.d.

Scotton, James F. "The Early Uganda Press: From Protest to Nationalism." Paper presented at the 13th Annual Meeting of the African Studies Association, Boston, October 21–24, 1970.

Ssekamwa, John Crysostom. "Submission and Reaction in Buganda, 1926–1945." USSC Paper, Kampala (mimeo), December 1969.

Stevens, L. "Uganda Since the Coup," Kampala (mimeo), 1972.

Thomas, Clive. "Issues of Transition to Socialism in Tanzanian-Type Economies." Dar es Salaam (mimeo), 1972.

Yoshida, M. and Belshaw, D. G. R. "The Introduction of the Trade Licensing System for Primary Products in East Africa, 1900–1939." EAISR Conference Paper (mimeo), 1965.

Zwainenberg, Roger. "An Economic History of East Africa." Dar es Salaam: University of Dar es Salaam, 1974.

Published Articles

Alavi, Hamza. "The Post-Colonial State." In Kathleen Gough and Hari P. Sharma, eds. *Imperialism and Revolution in South Asia.* New York: Monthly Review Press, 1974.

Banaji, J. "The Mode of Production in Indian Agriculture," *Political and Economic Weekly* (Bombay), December 1972.

Bosa, G. R. "African Businessmen in Uganda," *East Africa Journal,* April 1967.

Buell, R. Leslie. "The Destiny of East Africa," *Foreign Affairs,* April 1928.

Bundy, Emory. "Uganda's New Constitution," *East Africa Journal,* July 1966.

Edgren, Gus. "Employment in Tropical Africa," *East Africa Journal,* July 1965.

Ehrlich, Cyril. "Cotton and the Uganda Company, 1903–1909," *Uganda Journal,* September 1957.

Gingyera-Pincyewa, A. G. G. "Prospects for a One-Party System in Uganda," *East Africa Journal,* October 1968.

Goodie, Jack. "Feudalism in Africa?" *Journal of African History,* vol. 4, no. 1 (1963).

Gray, John Milner. "Ahmed Bin Ibrahim—The First Arab to Reach Buganda," *Uganda Journal,* vol. 2, no. 2 (September 1947).

Hazelwood, A. "Trade Balances and Statutory Marketing in Primary Exporting Countries," *The Economic Journal,* March 1957.

Hobsbawm, E. J. "From Social History to the History of Society," *Daedalus* (Winter 1971).

Kajubi, W. Senteza. "Coffee and Prosperity in Buganda: Some Aspects of Economic and Social Change," *Uganda Journal,* vol. 29, no. 2 (1965).

Lofchie, Michael. "The Uganda Coup: Class Action by the Military," *The Journal of Modern African Studies,* vol. 10, no. 1 (1972).

Mackay, A. G. "The Solution to the African Problem," *Church Missionary Intelligencer,* January 1890.

Mangat, J. S. "Was Allidina Visram a Robber Baron or a Skillful and Benevolent Commercial Pioneer?" *East Africa Journal,* February 1968.

Martin, David. "Middle East Stakes in the Heart of Africa," *The Observer* (March 1971).

"Military in Uganda," *Africa Report,* December 1966.

Nsibambia, Apollo. "Federalism: Its Rise and Fall in Uganda," *East Africa Journal,* December 1966.

Nye, E. W. "A Short Account of the History and the Development of

Cotton in Uganda," *The Empire Cotton Growing Review*, vol. 8, no. 4 (October 1931).

Owens, J. W. "Insight into Labour," *East Africa Journal*, November 1966.

Rado, E. R. "Review of Walter Elkan's 'Migrants and Proletarians,'" *East African Economic Review*, new series vol. 1, 1964.

Scott, Roger. "Labour Legislation and the Federal Issue," *East Africa Journal*, November 1966.

Steiger-Hayley, T. T. "Wage Labour and the Desire for Wives Among the Lango," *Uganda Journal*, vol. 8, no. 1 (September 1940).

"Thought of the Month: Corruption in East African Life," *East Africa Journal*, November 1967.

Tribe, Michael. "Uganda 1971: An Economic Background," *Mawazo* (Makerere University), vol. 3, no. 1 (June 1971).

Books on Uganda

Alpers, E. A. *The East African Slave Trade*. Published for the Historical Association of Tanzania, Dar es Salaam, by East Africa Publishing House, Nairobi, 1967.

Apter, David. *Political Kingdom in Uganda*. Princeton, N.J.: Princeton University Press, 1967.

Baryanuha, A. *Factors Affecting Industrial Employment*. EAISR Occasional Paper No. 1, Nairobi: Oxford University Press, 1967.

Beattie, John. *The Nyoro State*. Oxford: Oxford University Press, 1971.

p'Bitek, Okot, trans. *Song of Lowino*. Nairobi: Modern African Library, 1966.

Becker, Robert, and Madhvani, Nitin Jayant, eds. *Jayant Madhvani*. London: privately printed, 1973.

Bosa, George R. *The Financing of Small-Scale Enterprises in Uganda*. MISR Occasional Paper No. 3, Nairobi: Oxford University Press, 1969.

Burke, Fred G. *Local Government and Politics in Uganda*. Syracuse, N.Y.: Syracuse University Press, 1964.

Clark, Paul G. *Development Planning in East Africa*. Nairobi: East Africa Publishing House, 1965.

Coupland, R. *The Exploitation of East Africa, 1856–1890: The Slave Trade and the Scramble*. London: Faber and Faber, 1939.

Delf, George. *Asians in East Africa*. London: Institute of Race Relations, Oxford University Press, 1963.

Dunn, Read P. *Cotton in East Africa*. Memphis, Tenn.: National Cotton Council, 1949.

Ehrlich, Cyril. *The Uganda Co. Ltd.: The First Fifty Years*. Kampala: The Uganda Co. Ltd., 1953.

Elkan, Walter. *Migrants and Proletarians: Urban Labour in the Economic Development of Uganda.* Published on behalf of EAISR by Oxford University Press, London, 1960.

Fallers, L. A. *Bantu Bureaucracy: A Study of Integration and Conflict in the Political Institutions of an East African People.* Published for EAISR by W. Heffer, Cambridge, 1958.

Fallers, L. A., ed. *The King's Men: Leadership and Status in Buganda on the Eve of Independence.* Published for EAISR by Oxford University Press, Nairobi, 1964.

Fleming, J. T. *Recent Developments in Kisoga Land Tenure.* Entebbe: Government Printer, 1961.

Gertzel, Cherry. *The Development of Political Parties in Uganda.* Staff Seminar for Political Science, Kampala: Makerere University, 1966.

————. *Party and Locality in Northern Uganda, 1945–1962.* London: Athelone Press, 1974.

Goldthorpe, E. *An African Elite: Makerere College Students, 1922–1960.* Published on behalf of EAISR by Oxford University Press, Nairobi, 1965.

Good, Charles M. *Rural Markets and Trade in East Africa: A Study of the Function and Development of Exchange Institutions in Ankole, Uganda.* Chicago: University of Chicago Press, 1970.

Gregory, J. W. *The Foundation of British East Africa.* London: Horace Marshall and Son, 1901.

Gregory, Robert G. *India and East Africa.* London: Oxford University Press, 1971.

Gukiina, Peter M. *Uganda: A Case Study in African Political Development.* Notre Dame: University of Notre Dame Press, 1972.

Harlow, V. and Chilver, L., eds. *History of East Africa,* vol. 2. London: Oxford University Press, 1965.

Hattersley, C. W. *Uganda by Pen and Camera.* London: The Religious Tract Society, 1913.

Hollingsworth, L. W. *The Asians of East Africa.* London: Macmillan, 1960.

Ingham, Kenneth. *A History of East Africa.* New York: Praeger, 1965.

Johnston, Harry. *The Uganda Protectorate,* vol. 1. London: Hutchinson and Co., 1902.

Kaggwa, Apollo. *The Customs of the Baganda.* New York: Columbia University Press, 1934.

Karugira, Samwiri Rubaraza. *A History of the Kingdom of Nkore in Western Uganda to 1896.* Oxford: Oxford University Press, 1971.

Legum, Colin, ed. *Africa: Contemporary Record,* vol. 5. New York: Praeger, 1973.

Leys, Colin. *Politicians and Policies: An Essay on Politics in Acholi,*

Uganda, 1962–1965. Nairobi: East Africa Publishing House, 1967.

Low, A. and Pratt, C. *Buganda and British Overrule, 1900–1955*. Published on behalf of EAISR by Oxford University Press, London, 1960.

Low, D. A. *The Mind of Buganda: Documents of the Modern History of an African Kingdom*. London: Heinemann, 1971.

Lugard, Frederick D. *The Rise of Our East African Empire: Early Efforts in Nyasaland and Uganda*. London: Frank Cass and Co., 1968.

McDermott, P. L. *British East Africa or Imperial British East Africa Company: A History of the Formation and Work of the Imperial British East Africa Company* (an official history). London: Chapman and Hall, 1893.

Mair, Lucy P. *An African People in the Twentieth Century*. London: George Routledge, 1934.

Mangat, J. S. *A History of the Asians in East Africa c. 1886 to 1945*. Oxford: Oxford University Press, 1969.

Martin, David. *General Amin*. London: Faber and Faber, 1974.

Masefield, G. B. *Agricultural Change in Uganda, 1945–1960*. Palo Alto, Calif.: Stanford University Press, 1965.

Meister, Albert. *East Africa: The Past in Chains, the Future in Pawn* (P. N. Ott, trans.) New York: Walker, 1968.

Milton Obote Foundation. *Labour Problems in Uganda*. Kampala, 1966.

Morris, H. S. *Indians in Uganda*. Chicago: University of Chicago Press, 1968.

Mulira, E. M. K. *Troubled Uganda*. Fabian Colonial Bureau Pamphlet, Controversy Series No. 6, London: Fabian Publications, 1950.

Mukherjee, Radhakrishna. *Uganda: The Problem of Acculturation*. Berlin: Akademie-Verlag, 1956.

O'Conner, A. M. *Railways and Development in Uganda*. Nairobi: Oxford University Press, 1955.

Obote, A. M. *The Common Man's Charter*. Kampala, typescript.

Ogot, B. A. and Kieran, J. A., eds. *Zamani: A Survey of East African History*. Nairobi: East Africa Publishing House and Longmans, Green, 1968.

Oliver, Roland. *The Missionary Factor in East Africa*. London: Longmans, 1965.

Oliver, R. and Page, J. D. *A Short History of East Africa*. Baltimore: Penguin Books, 1962.

Powesland, A. G. *Economic Policy and Labour: A Study in Uganda's Economic History* (Walter Elkan, ed.). Kampala: EAISR, 1957.

Richards, Audrey, ed. *East African Chiefs: A Study of Political Development in Some Uganda and Tanganyika Tribes*. Published for EAISR by Faber and Faber, London, 1960.

Richards, Audrey. *Economic Development and Tribal Change: A Study of Immigrant Labour in Buganda*. Published for EAISR by W. Heffer and Sons, Kampala, 1952.

Robertson, Douglas W. *The Historical Considerations Contributing to the Soga System of Land Tenure*. Entebbe: Government Printer, 1940.

Roscoe, John. *The Baganda: An Account of their Native Customs and Beliefs*. London: Macmillan, 1911.

————. *The Bagesu and Other Tribes of the Uganda Protectorate*. Cambridge: Cambridge University Press, 1924.

————. *The Banyankole: Report of the Mackie Ethnological Expedition to Central Africa*, part 2. Cambridge: Cambridge University Press, 1923.

————. *The Northern Bantu*. London: Frank Cass and Co., 1966.

————. *Twenty-Five Years in East Africa*. Cambridge: Cambridge University Press, 1921.

Scott, Roger. *The Development of Trade Unions in Uganda*. Nairobi: East Africa Publishing House, 1966.

Stonehouse, John. *Prohibited Immigrant*. London: The Bodley Head, 1960.

Thomas H. B. and Scott, Roger. *Uganda*. Published for the Government of Uganda by Oxford University Press, London, 1935.

Tilbe, Douglas. *East African Asians*. Race Relations Committee, Friends House, London, 1970.

Vere-Hodge, E. R. *Imperial British East Africa Company*. Published in association with East African Literature Bureau by Macmillan, London, 1960.

West, H. M., ed. *The Transformation of Land Tenure in Buganda Since 1896*. African Social Research Documents No. 2. Leiden: Afrika-Studiecentrum, 1970.

West, H. M. *The Mailo System in Buganda*. Entebbe: Government Printer, 1964.

Winter, E. H. *Bwemba Economy: The Development of a Primitive Subsistence Economy in Uganda*. Kampala: EAISR, 1955.

Wrigley, C. C. *Crops and Wealth in Uganda*. Kampala: EAISR Study No. 12, 1959.

Zajadacz, Paul, ed. *Studies in Production and Trade in East Africa*. IFO Institute, Munich: Weltforum Verlag, 1970.

Other Books Cited

Althusser, L. and Balibar, E. *Reading Capital*. London: New Left Books, 1970.

Amin, Samir. *Maghreb in the Modern World*. Baltimore: Penguin Books, 1970.

Amin, Samir. *Neo-Colonialism in West Africa*. New York: Monthly Review Press, 1974.

Baran, Paul. *The Political Economy of Growth*. New York: Monthly Review Press, 1968.

Bloch, Marc. *Feudal Society*. Chicago: University of Chicago Press, 1966.

Cabral, Amilcar. *Revolution in Guinea: Selected Texts*. New York: Monthly Review Press, 1969.

Davidson, Basil. *Black Mother, Africa: The Years of Trial*. London: Victor Gollancz, 1961.

————. *Lost Cities of Africa*. Boston: Little, Brown, 1959.

Emmanuel, Arghiri. *Unequal Exchange*. New York: Monthly Review Press, 1972.

Fitch, Bob and Oppenheimer, Mary. *Ghana: End of an Illusion*. New York: Monthly Review Press, 1966.

M. Fortes and E. E. Evans-Pritchard, eds. *African Political Systems*. London, 1966.

Frank, A. G. *Capitalism and Underdevelopment in Latin America*. New York: Monthly Review Press, 1969.

Geertz, Clifford. *Agricultural Involution*. Berkeley: University of California Press, 1963.

Harris, Joseph. *The African Presence in Asia: Consequences of the East African Slave Trade*. Evanston, Ill.: Northwestern University Press, 1971.

Lenin, V. I. *Selected Works*. Moscow: Progress Publishers.

Mandel, Ernest. *Marxist Economic Theory*. New York: Monthly Review Press, 1968.

Mao Tse-tung. *Selected Works*. Peking: Foreign Languages Publishing House.

Marx, Karl. *Capital*. Moscow: Progress Publishers.

————. *The Eighteenth Brumaire of Louis Bonaparte*. Moscow: Progress Publishers.

————. *The German Ideology*. New York: International Publishers, 1967.

——. *The Poverty of Philosophy*. Moscow: Progress Publishers.

Moraes, Frank. *Sir Purshotamdas Thakordas*. Bombay, 1957.

Oliver, R. and Oliver, C. *Africa in the Days of Exploration*. New York: Prentice-Hall, 1965.

Pim, Alan. *Economic History of Tropical Africa*. Oxford: Clarendon Press, 1940.

Polanyi, Karl. *The Great Transformation*. Boston: Beacon Press, 1944.

Poulantzas, Nicos. *Political Power and Social Classes*. London: New Left Books, 1973.

Shivji, Issa. *Class Struggles in Tanzania*. New York: Monthly Review
  Press, 1976.
Speke, J. H. *Journal of the Discovery of the Source of the Nile*.
  Edinburgh and London: W. Blackwood and Sons, 1863.

Index

AATUF, 239
Abataka Abasogo (Basoga Elders), 207
Acholi district, 52, 154, 167, 194n, 208, 209, 219
Acholi people, 20, 23
Advisory Committee on Native Education in the British Tropical African Dependencies, 106n
African Business Promotions, Ltd. (ABP, Ltd.), 236–37, 246, 261
African Civil Servants' Association, 213
African Loan Fund, 202
African Local Government Ordinance (1949), 194
African Produce Growers, 181
African-American Institute, 267n
Aga Khan, 82–83, 259n
Alavi, Hamza, 312
Alibhoy, Adamjee, 80n
Allen, G., 86n
Alur, 150n, 217
Amalgamated Association of Card and Blowing-Room Operatives, 57n
Amalgamated Association of Operative Cotton Spinners, 57
Ambalal Sarabhai, 93
Amery, Col., 55, 98
Amin, Idi, 286, 287, 288n, 308–10, 316; coup by, 290–93; Indian expulsions and, 302–3, 305

Anglican Church (Church of Uganda), 178, 286
Anglicanism, see Protestants
Ankole, 43n, 45, 50, 52, 106, 128, 130, 131n, 194n, 196, 216, 219
Annual Report of the Protectorate, 1901, 51; 1909–1910, 163n; 1915–1916, 158; 1929, 99
Anstey, Vera, 86n
Anyanya guerrillas, 292, 303, 309
Arain, Shafiq, 235, 279
Arua, 164
Arusha Declaration (1967), 269, 270
Asian Civil Servants' Association, 213
Asians, see Indians
Assam, 50
Associated Match Co., Ltd., 258n
Associated Paper Industries, Ltd., 258n

Baganda, 3n, 17, 29, 32–33, 42–47, 120, 164
Baganda Clerical Workers' Union, 239
Baganda Common People (Bakopi Bazukulu), 179, 206
Baganda Motor Drivers' Association, 177
Bagisu, 22
Balfour Committee on Trade, Final Report of, 249
Balibar, Etienne, quoted, 145
Balinda, A., 287

Bamuta, Yusufu, 127, 172, 177
Bamuta Cotton Company, 177
Bank of England, 180
Bank of Uganda, 266, 305
Banking Act (1969), 266
Baran, Paul, 7n
Barclays Bank D.O.C., 256, 307
Basoga Elders (Abataka Abasogo),
207
Bassude, L. C. B., 203
Bataka Association, 123, 124, 171, 172
Bataka Party, 181
Bataka Union, 179, 206
Bataringaya, Mr. (minister), 279
Batoro, 27
Baumann and Co., 106, 107, 255n,
256n
BCC (British Cotton Corporation), 94,
95, 98
BCGA, see British Cotton Growing
Association
Beattie, John, 23n–24n, 153n
Bell, Governor, quoted, 49
Berlin Act (1885), 94
Binaisa, Godfrey, 244
Bleachers' Association, Ltd., 57n
Bleachers Association of Manchester,
255
Bloch, Marc, 23n–24n
Blue Book, 1907–1908, 50; 1911–1912,
53
Board of Trade, see British Govern-
ment, Board of Trade of
Bombay, 95
Bombay Chamber of Commerce, 88
Bombay-Uganda Company, 93
Bonomo, P., 258n
Borup, K., 45, 86n
Bottomley, Mr. (British Colonial
Office), 99n, 255n
Bourbon, 18
Boustead and Clark (company), 78, 79
Bradford Dyers' Association, Ltd., 57n
Brett, E. A., 233, 234
Brewer, H. A., 159
British Cotton Corporation (BCC), 94,
95, 98

British Cotton Growing Association
(BCGA), 45, 56, 57, 73–75, 86, 87, 90,
93, 103
British East Africa Corporation, 86n,
88, 93, 94
British Government, Board of Trade
of, 98; Colonial Office of, 50, 53n,
58–60, 67, 71, 74, 78, 82, 88–90,
97–100, 102, 126n, 131n, 133, 142,
149, 156, 176n, 190, 197n, 211, 251,
253, 254n–55n, 265n; Foreign Office
of, 50, 210, 211; Treasury of, 60, 156
British Raw Cotton Commission, 252
British Steel Reinforcement, Ltd.,
255n
British-American Tobacco Co., Ltd.,
107
Brookbond-Liebig, 268
Brown, Archbishop, 286
Brussels Act (1890), 94
Buganda, 17n, 51, 55, 75, 79n, 106, 139,
141, 201; British rule of, 40–45;
feudal society in, 23–35; independence and, 228–29; land control in,
120–29; Lukiko, see Lukiko; 1966–
1967 crisis in, 242–46; petty bour-
geoisie in, 148, 151–55, 170–82, 206–
15, 218–20; Treasury of, 125–27
Buganda African Motor Drivers
Union, 151
Buganda Agreement (1900), 41, 43, 51,
72, 120, 121n, 123–24, 128–29, 164,
165, 171
Buganda Bus Service Company, 201
Buganda Chamber of Commerce, 76,
165
Buganda Cooperative Society of Wandegeya, 203
Buganda Growers Association, 197
Buganda Seed Cotton Buying Association, 101
Buganda Taxation Agreement (Devel-
opment Tax) (1922), 122
Bugisu, 47, 52, 194n, 196
Bugisu Growers' Cooperative Union,
231, 232, 233–34
Bukedi, 208

Bukona Estates Ltd., 52n–54n

Bulunge Bua Buganda (Common People of Buganda), 172–73

Bunyoro-Kitare, 43, 49, 128, 152; feudal society in, 23–35; "Lost Counties" issue and, 243–44; petty bourgeoisie in, 171, 194–95, 216, 232; poll tax in, 130, 131n

Bunyoro Growers' Cooperative Union, 232

Burma, 50

Buruli Growers' Cooperative Union, 232

Busoga, 24, 43, 45, 128, 130, 232; petty bourgeoisie in, 153–55, 171, 206–7

Busoga African Motor Drivers' Union, 191

Busoga Farmers' and Traders' Association, 207

Busoga Growers' Cooperative Union, 198, 232, 234

Busoga Seed Cotton Buying Association, 100, 101

Busulu and Nvujjo Law (1928), 124, 134, 148, 152, 166, 172, 219n, 243

Buxton, Sir Thomas Fowell, 85n, 86n

Buxton, Sir Thomas Fowell Victor, 85n

Bwemba, 47, 106

Cabral, Amilcar, 313

Calico Printers' Association, Ltd., 57n, 255, 258

Candole, Mr. (middleman ginner), 90n

Carter, Chief Justice, 91

Carter Commission, *see* Commission of Inquiry into the Cotton Industry (1929)

Catholic Action Movement, 218

Catholics (Catholicism), 43, 159, 216–20, 285

Central Bank of Uganda, 257

Central Council of Indian Associations of Uganda, 82, 105, 213

Central Missionary Fund, 159

Ceylon, 50

Chamberlain, Austen, 250

Chillington Tool Co., Ltd., 256n

Chillington Tool Co. (E. Af.), Ltd., 256n

Chinese laborers, 156

Chowdhry, Mr. (minister), quoted, 262

Church Mission Society, 45, 53, 85n

Church of Uganda (Anglican), 178, 286

Churchill, Sir Winston, 59

Chwa, Daudi, 123

Clove and Copra Ordinance (1934) (Zanzibar), 105n

CMS (missionary society), 162

Coffee Grading Ordinance, 106

Coffee Industry Ordinance, 199

Colonial Development Act (1929), 250, 253

Colonial Development and Welfare Act (1940), 253

Colonial Development Corporation of U.K., 256n

Colonial Office, *see* British Government, Colonial Office of

Commercial and Industrial Policy Committee, 57; 1914 Report, 46n

Commission for the Africanization of Commerce and Industry, 273

Commission of Inquiry into the Cotton Industry (1929) (Carter Commission), 99–101, 103, 104

Commission of Inquiry into the Cotton Industry (1938), 79, 103, 104n

Commission of Inquiry into the Labor Situation in Uganda (1938), 150

Commissioners of Africanization of Commerce and Industry, 1968 Report, 169

"Common Man's Charter," 270, 314

Common People of Buganda (Bulunge Bua Buganda), 172–73

Commonwealth Conference (1971) (Singapore), 293

Communist Manifesto, The (Marx and Engels), 8

Concrete Constructions (Ug.), Ltd., 255n

Conference of the Provincial Commissioners (1922), 129

Congo, 245

Congo Basin Convention, 255n

Congo Basin Treaties (Berlin Act, 1885, and Brussels Act, 1890), 94–95

Cooper, Benjamin, 45

Cooperative Societies Act (1946), 197, 213, 235, 277

Cooperative Societies Act (1963), 235, 277

Cooperative Societies Act (1970), 277–78

Cotton Control Board, 91–92

Cotton Lorry Disarmament Conference (1932), 102

Cotton Ordinance (1926), 92

Cotton Spinners' and Manufacturers' Association, 57n

Cotton Spinners' Provincial Association (Bolton), 57n

Cotton Zone Ordinance (1933), 102

CPP (Ghana party), 219n

Crown Cork Co. (E. Af.), Ltd., 256n

Crown Cork Co. (Ug.), Ltd., 256n

Dalal, C. P., 103, 105

Damondar Jinabhai, 93

Democratic Party (DP), 218–20, 269, 286n

Descendants of Kintu, 173, 175–76, 178, 206

Deutsche Geselschaft (Industrial Development Corp., West Germany), 256n

Development Finance Company of Uganda, 256n, 268n

Devonshire White Paper ("On the Indian Question") (1923), 82

Dini ya Papa (Religion of the Pope), *see* Democratic Party

District Administrations (District Councils) Ordinance (1955), 194

Dobb, Maurice, 24n

Dodd, John, 254n

Duncan, Gilby & Mathieson, Ltd., 256n

Dundas Reforms (1944), 179

East Acholi Cooperative Union, 232

East Africa Ginneries, 93

East Africa Indian Association, 79n

East Africa Indian National Congress, 81–82

East Africa Protectorate, *see* Kenya

East Africa Road Services, Ltd., 276n

East Africa Royal Commission, 1953–1955 Report, 192, 195, 200–1, 230

East Africa Syndicate, 49

East African Batteries (Ug.), Ltd., 268n

East African Currency Board, 257n

East African Distilleries, Ltd., 256n, 268n

East African Standard, 210

East African Tobacco Co., 179n

East African Transport Corps, 151

Eastern Province, 55, 77n, 79n, 100, 121n, 123

Eastern Province Bus Company, 276

Eastern Province Chamber of Commerce, 107n

Easton, David, 2

Eban, Abba, 292

Ehrlich, Cyril, 85n, 86n

Eighteenth Brumaire of Louis Bonaparte, The (Marx), 84, 206

Elgon Taxi, Ltd., 276n

Eliot, Sir Charles, 80–81

Emigration from India to the Crown Colonies and Protectorates, Committee on (1910), 69n

Empire Cotton Growing Committee, 57, 74, 98

Empire Cotton Growing Research Centre, 179

Empire Marketing Board, 247

Engur (founder of UNC), 209

Entebbe, 179

Eshkol, Levi, 292

European Center for Overseas Industrial Equipment and Development, 267n

Export-Import Corporation, 271

Ex-Soldiers League, 59

Fabian Colonial Bureau, 177
Falconbridge Nickel Mines, Ltd., 256n
Fanon, Frantz, 221
Federation of Master Cotton Spinners Association, 57n
Federation of Partnership of Uganda African Farmers, 208, 210
Federation of Uganda Trade Unions (FUTU), 241, 282
Fenton, P. L., 105
Fine Cotton Spinners' & Doublers' Association, Ltd., 57n
"First New Nation, The" (Lipset), 6n
Five-Year Development Plan, 230, 264
Foreign Office, see British Government, Foreign Office of
Fort Portal, 164, 240
Foster Brothers, 93
France, 308
Frank, Andre Gunder, 6
Franklin, Col., 99n
Frobisher, Ltd., 256n

Gayaza High School for Girls, 163n
General Clerical Union, 192
General Service Unit (GSU), 291
Gershenberg, I., 257n
Gertzel, Cherry, 209
Gisu, 217
Gokuldas, Mathurdas, 93
Goldthorpe, E., 163, 217
Goodie, Jack, 23n–24n
Gosho Kabushiki Kaisha Ltd., 93
Governor's Inquiry into the Cotton Industry (1923), 79, 95
Gowers, Governor, quoted, 100, 102
Growers' Cooperative Union, 232
Gulu, 164

Hailey, Lord Malcolm, 173
Hamites, 17
Harris (author), 19n
Hattersley, Bishop, 51, 162
Hausa-Fulanis, 3n
Hima, 27, 33n, 34

Hobsbawm, E. J., 5
House of Birla, 305
Hunt, Diana, quoted, 257n
Hutton, J. R., quoted, 73–74

Ibingira, Grace, 241, 244, 245
ICFTU, 239
ICI (UK), 256n
Iganga, 179n
Immigration Act (1969), 273
Imperial British East Africa Company, 43
Imperial Treasury, see British Government, Treasury of
Imperialism: The Highest Stage of Capitalism (Lenin), 222
Import Duties Act (1931), 250
Indian Association (Dar es Salaam), 82
Indian Association of Kampala and Jinja, 213
Indian Merchants' Chamber, 213
Indians (Asians), 44, 49, 76, 78n–79n, 108, 174, 175; attacks upon, 182–83; as civil servants, 156–57; as dependent capitalists, 80–105; expulsion of, 304–8; as indentured laborers, 67–72; rise of African petty bourgeoisie and, 203, 213–16; Uganda economy and, 141, 144, 165, 180, 258–59, 269–71, 278–81
Industrial Mission of the Church Missionary Society, see Uganda Company
Industrial Promotion Service, Ltd. (IPS), 258, 259n
International Labor Congress, 282
International Monetary Fund, 265
International Ore and Fertilizer Corp., 256n
Iru, 27, 33n, 34
Iserdas Bhogilal, 93
Islam, see Muslims
Ismailia Council (Zanzibar), 83
Ismailia Provincial Council (Uganda), 83
Ismailis, 82–83

Israel, 292, 302
Iteso Cooperative Union, 232, 235

Jaffer, Banadali, 90*n*
Jamal Ramji and Co., 106
Jamal Walji, 93
Japanese Cotton Trading Co., Ltd.
(Nippon Menkwa Kabushiki Kaisha), 94
Jinja, 164, 179*n*
Jinja Cotton Buying and Ginning
Company, 93
Johnston, Sir Harry, 33*n*, 41–42, 51,
110

Kabaka Yekka (KY), 4, 212, 220, 244,
260, 286*n*
Kabale, 64
Kaggwa, Michael Kawalia, 166*n*
Kaggwa, Sir Apollo, 126, 166*n*
Kakonge, John, 241, 245
Kakungule, Prince Badru, 286
Kakunguru, General, 43
Kalema, Mr. (minister), 274
Kalidas, Mr. (middleman ginner), 90*n*
Kalimuzo, Mr. (university vice-chancellor), 309*n*
Kampala, 34, 158*n*, 164, 179, 275, 279*n*,
280, 307
Kampala General Agency, 93
Kamya, Augustine, 214
Karamojong, 20
Karungira, Samwiri Rubaraza, 24*n*–
25*n*, 33*n*
Kawempe, 275, 279*n*, 280
Kayonza, 27
Kenya (East Africa Protectorate),
49*n*, 238, 242, 270, 289, 290, 312*n*,
314*n*–15*n*
Kibuga, 182
Kibuka (UFL leader), 239, 241, 282,
283
Kieran, J. A., 19*n*
Kigezi, 52, 106, 194*n*, 196, 219, 230;
Annual Report, 1930, 65; Annual
Report, 1931, 65

Kiggude, Father, 309
Kikuyu College (Kenya), 163
Kilembe Mines, Ltd., 256*n*
King's College (Budo), 163, 164
Kirk, Sir John, 68–69, 70*n*
Kisubi, 179*n*
Kisubi College, 163
Kivu, James, 177
Kiwanuka, Benedicto, 309
Koja, 179*n*
Kulubya (treasurer), 147–48, 173, 174,
178, 179
Kyebambe, Mukama, III, 29

Lagu, Joseph, 293
Lancashire and Cheshire Coal Owners'
Association, 57*n*
Land Alienation Law, 179
Langi, 20
Lango, 23, 52, 154, 167, 193*n*, 194*n*,
201, 208, 232, 235
Lango Cooperative Union, 232
Lango Shopkeepers' Association, 203,
209
League of Nations, 82, 190*n*; Advisor
on Cooperation, 197
Leggett, Major, 97
Lenin, V. I., 1, 8*n*, 11, 222
Lennox-Boyd, Colonial Secretary, 189
Lever Bros. (London), 106, 107
Libya, 308
Lipset, Seymour Martin, 6*n*
Lira, 164
Liverpool Cotton Association, 57*n*
Liverpool Uganda Company, 198
Livingstone, David, 19*n*
Llewellyn, Mr. (businessman), 94
Lofchie, Michael, 287*n*
Lombard Banking of London, 256*n*
London *Times*, 294*n*
Luande, Humphreys, 239
Lugard, Lord Frederick D., 33, 34, 43,
67–68, 71, 161
Lugbara, 43*n*, 150*n*
Lukiko, 147, 148, 207, 208; attacks
upon landlord control of, 172–75,

178–79; landlord interests and, 121–28; 1966–1967 crisis and, 242–46; petty bourgeois politics and, 193–95, 209–10, 220, 228

Lumu, Dr., 244

Lyttleton, Colonial Secretary, 209

Mabira Forest (Ug.) Rubber Company, Ltd., 58

Madhvani, Muljibhai, 258, 267, 271

Madhvani Group, *see* Muljibhai Madhvani and Company

Mafatlal and C. Parikh, 93

Mafatlal Gaganlel, 93

Magara, Mr. (minister), quoted, 276

Magezi, George, 238

Maini, Sir Amer, 197, 213

Mair, Lucy, 34

Makerere College, 157, 158, 163, 176n, 179, 181, 182, 217

Malawi, 289

Manchester Cotton Association, 57n

Maoli, 194n

Margach and Margdi, 93

Marketing of Native Produce Ordinance (1935) (Kenya), 105

Marubeni-Ida Co., Ltd., 258n

Marx, Karl, 1, 6, 8, 11, 25n, 26, 84, 206, 307

Masaka, 47, 164, 179n, 232

Masaka-Buganda Cooperative Society, 203

Masaka-Bukedi Company, 201

Masaka-Bwavu Federates Cooperative Union, 232

Masinda, 164

Mau Mau movement, 238, 315n

Mauritius, 18

Mayanja, Abu, 212, 274

Mayanja-Nkangi, S. S., 244

Mazrui, Ali, 287n, 291n

Mbale, 164, 179n, 232

Mbaràra, 164, 179n

Mbarara, D. C., 46

Mboya, Tom, 239n

Mechanical Cultivation Office (Busoga), 1967 report, 230–31

Mehta, N. K., 258

Mehta industrial group, 93, 258n

Meir, Golda, 292

Mengo, 34, 232, 235, 275, 280; Battle of (1892), 43

Mengo Day School, 163n

Miester, Robert, 8n

Mill Hill Mission, 162

Miller, Henry Edward, 86n

Mishambi, G. T., 25n

Mitchell Cotts (E. Af.), Ltd., 256n

Morris, H. S., 82, 83

Mubende, 164, 179n, 232

Mubende Cotton Trading Company, 93

Mugeni, Mr. (minister), quoted, 275

Mugwanya, Mr. (politician), 218

Mujaju, Akiki B., 300

Mukasa, Shem Spire, 177

Mukasa, Spartus, 177

Mukherjee, Radhakrishna, 22–23

Mukwaya, A. B., quoted, 183

Mulago Hospital, 177

Muljibahai Madhvani and Company (Madhvani Group), 93, 258n, 259n, 308

Musazi, Ignatius K., 176, 181, 208

Muslims, 43n, 217, 285–87, 303

Mutesa I, 30

Nakasero Trading Company, 93

Nakawa, 275, 280n

Namirembe Diocese Christian Association, 286

Nanji Kalidas Mehta, 93

Narandas Rajaram and Co., Ltd., 87–88, 90, 93, 97

National and Grindleys Bank, The, 256, 268

National Association for the Advancement of Muslims (NAAM), 287, 292

National Bank of India, Ltd., 54n, 87, 96, 97, 108

National Cotton Council, U.S., 252

National Service proposals (1970), 291

National Trading Corporation (NTC), 261–26, 271, 273, 275; report of (1967), 263

National Union of Youth Organizations (NUYO), 241

Native Hellenic Church, 177, 178

Native Produce Marketing Ordinance (1932), 105–7, 165

Native Taxation Law (1927), 125n

Nekyon, Adoko, 240, 287; quoted, 261

Ngongwe Ginnery, 198

Ngwenge (founder of UNC), 209

Nimeri, General, 292

Nippon Menkwa Kabushiki Kaisha (Japanese Cotton Trading Co., Ltd.), 94

Nippon Rayon Co., Ltd., 259n

Nkore, 24, 31, 33n, 34, 43n

Nkrumah, Kwame, 222, 294n

North Mbale Cooperative Union, 232

Northern Counties Amalgamated Association of Weavers, 57n

Northern Province, 100, 153, 154

Nsibirwa, Martin Luther, 127, 147–48, 173, 174, 178, 179

Nubian, 306

Nygnza Textile Industries, Ltd., 254, 255, 258

Obote, Milton, 265, 266n, 280–81; Amin and, 287, 290–92, 294n, 303, 314; quoted, 266

Ogot, B. A., 19n

Okoya, Brigadier, 290, 294

Old East Africa Trading Co., 106

Oldham Chamber of Commerce dinner (1901), 45

Olin Mathieson Chemical Corporation, 256n

Olyech (founder of UNC), 209

Oman, Sultan of, 19

"On the Indian Question" (Devonshire White Paper) (1923), 82

Onama, Felix, 240, 274

Opolot, Shaban, 290

Orde Brown, G. St. J., 190n

Ormsby-Gore Commission, 46, 82, 92

Osaka Shoresen Kaisha, 94

Otim, Ben, 209

Overman, Reid, 254n, 255n

Overseas Motor Transport Co., Ltd., 175n–76n

Owen Falls Dam, 253

Pakistan, 308

Pasha, Emin, 43n

Phelps-Stokes Fund, 160

Piecegoods Buying Pool, 251

Poll Tax Agreement (1909), 121n

Price Assistance Fund, 181

Produce Marketing Board (PMB), 261, 262–64, 271, 273, 275–76

Progressive Party (PP), 218n–19n, 286n

Protectorate Government Financial Rules (1919), 126

Protestants (Anglicanism), 43, 159, 164, 216–17, 218n–19n, 285, 286

Puri, M. G., 80n

Pyaralli Abdulla Ltd. & Family, 259r

Radia, V. V., 258n

Railway African Union, 191, 192, 239

Ramdas Khimji, 93

Registration of Titles Act, 230

Reich (UFL leader), 239, 241, 282

Registrar of Cooperative Societies in Ceylon, 197

Religion of the Pope (*Dini ya Papa*), *see* Democratic Party

Rigby, C. P., 66

Roscoe, John, 29, 31

Rostow, W. W., 5

Royal Institute, 51

Royal Society of the Arts, 73

Ruanda, 65, 149, 154, 155

Sabiti, Eric, 286

Sadler, J. H., 51

St. Germain-en-Laye, Convention of (1922), 95

Salema (residence), 174

Salaries Commission Report, 191

Salisbury, third marquess of, 41

Sandhurst, 242
Saudi Arabia, 308
S. C. Parikh and Company, 93
"Scheme of Development for African Education" (UP), 160
Sempa, A. K., 203
Sheriff, Abdul, 18n, 19n
Siedle, Robert, 303n
Sikh Saw Mills & Ginners, Ltd., 258n
Singo-Central Office, 93
Small Industries Scheme, 202
Societa in Accomandita Luigi Pomini, 258n
Societa per Azioni Fratelli Orsenigo, 258n
Songo Bay Estates, 268n
Soroti, 158n, 164, 240
South Bukedi Cooperative Union, 232
Soviet Union, 308
Special Forces, 291
Speke, J. H., 31
Stafford, D. N., 55
Standard Bank of South Africa, Ltd., 53, 256, 307
Steel Corporation of East Africa, Ltd., 258n
Steiger-Hayley, T. T., 167, 168
Steiner, Rolf, 293
Stevens, L., 235
Stonehouse, John, quoted, 168
Straits Settlement, 50
Stroh, Nicholas, 303n
Sudan, 302, 303; 1969 coup in, 292–93
Sukulu Mines, Ltd., 256n

TANU, 270; Youth League (TYL) of, 242
Tanganyika Cotton Co. (Holding), Ltd., 255n
Tanzania, 270–71, 290, 303
Teso, 194n, 195, 201, 208, 232; Annual Report, 1960, 235
Teso Traders' Association, 203, 209
Thackordas, Sir Purshotamdas, 93
Thomas, Clive, 144
Tobacco Marketing Board, 252

Toro, 24–26, 29, 43n, 128, 129n, 130, 131n, 153, 158n, 171, 216
Tororo Chemical and Fertilizers, 256n
Tororo Exploration Co., Ltd., 256n
Tororo Industrial Chemical Fertilizers, 268n
Toyo Menkwa Kabushiki Kaisha, Ltd., 93
Trade Licensing Act (1901), 164
Trade Licensing Act (1964), 275, 279–80
Trade Union Congress (TUC), 238–39, 282
Trades Dispute (Arbitration and Settlement) Act (1964), 240
Trades Licensing (Amendment) Ordinance (1932) (Tanganyika), 105n
Trades Unions Ordinance (1952), 190–91
Trading Centers Ordinance (1932), 106n
Transport and General Workers Union, 191
Treasury, British, *see* British Government, Treasury of
Turga Chemical Industries, Ltd., 256n

Ugadev Bank, Ltd., 256n, 258
Uganda Action Group, 84
Uganda African Civil Servants Association, 164
Uganda African Farmers' Union (UAFU), 181–82
Uganda African Welfare Association (UAWA), 173
Uganda Argus, 189, 203, 215, 279
Uganda Buying and Ginning Company, 93
Uganda Commercial Bank, 257
Uganda Commercial Company, 93
Uganda Company, Ltd., 45, 53, 85, 88, 93, 182
Uganda Cotton Association, 213
Uganda Cotton Buying and Ginning Co., Ltd., 88
Uganda Cotton Ginners' Association, 90n

Uganda Cotton Rules (1913), 77; (1918), 75, 78; (1922), 78
Uganda Cotton Union, 93
Uganda Credit and Savings Bank, 199*n*, 202
Uganda Development Commission, 55, 57
Uganda Development Corporation (UDC), 202, 253–55, 258
Uganda Farmers' Union, 208
Uganda Federation of Labour (UFL), 238–41, 282
Uganda Fish Marketing Corp., Ltd., 256*n*
Uganda Fishnet Manufacturing, Ltd., 258*n*
Uganda Grain Milling Co., Ltd., 255*n*
Uganda Growers' Cooperative Union, The, 197, 232, 233
Uganda Growers' Cooperative Union, The, Mubende District, 232
Uganda Herald, 53, 101, 183, 201*n*
Uganda (Independence) Order, 243
Uganda Labor Congress (ULC), 282–83
Uganda Land Bus and Touring Co., Ltd., 276*n*
Uganda Lint Marketing Board, 252
Uganda Meat Packing, Ltd., 256*n*, 258
Uganda Motor Drivers' Association, 191
Uganda Muslim Community (UMC), 286–87, 292
Uganda National Congress (UNC), 208–12, 214, 219*n*
Uganda National Movement (UNM), 214–15
Uganda National Traders Association, 236
Uganda Peoples' Congress (UPC), 212, 220, 239–41, 244, 260, 265, 266, 269–70, 282, 286*n*, 287; Youth League of, 240–41
Uganda Peoples' Union (UPU), 212
Uganda Railway, 44, 49, 68, 158*n*, 213

Uganda Solutea, 268*n*
Uganda Teachers' Association, 219*n*
Uganda Traders' Convention (1959), 204
Uganda Transport Co., Ltd. (UTC), 176*n*, 276
Ugationers, Ltd., 268*n*
UGCC (Ghana party), 219*n*
Uketa Development Corporation, 258*n*
Unga, Ltd., 255*n*
United Commercial Agencies, Ltd., 258*n*
United Garment Industries, Ltd., 258*n*
United Nations, 274
United States, 221–22, 247–48
Universal Asbestos Manufacturing Co., Ltd. of Waterford, England, 255*n*
Universal Asbestos Manufacturing Co. (E. Af.), Ltd., 255*n*

Verona Mission, 162
Village Headman Ordinance, 51
Virjee, Nasser, 81
Visram, Allidina, 80–81, 86
Vithaldas Haridas and Company, 93

Wallis Inquiry into Local Government (1953), 194
Wamba, 22, 43*n*
Wamala, Prime Minister, 178–79, 286
Weber, Max, 6
West Acholi Cooperative Union, 232
West Indies, 50
West Nile, 52, 133, 149, 153, 194*n*, 219, 232, 303
West Nile Cooperative Union, 232
Western Kingdoms and Busoga Act (1963), 243
Western Province, 154
White Fathers, 162
"White Paper on Mechanization in Agriculture" (1954), 155*n*
Wiggins and District Cotton Employers' Association, 57*n*

Wilson, Henry Carus, 86*n*
World Bank, 236
Worthington Plan, 253
Wrigley, C. C., 35, 155

Yamato Shirts Co., Ltd., 258*n*
Young Baganda Association (YBA), 164

Young Basoga Association, 100, 207
Young Men of Toro, 171

Zambia, 289
Zamir, General, 292
Zanzibar, 66–67, 71
Zoete and Gordon (financial trust), 94*n*